MW00629183

STORMING
THE NATION

STORMING
THE NATION

THE UNKNOWN CONTRIBUTIONS OF
JOSEPH SMITH'S
POLITICAL MISSIONARIES

DEREK R. SAINSBURY

RSC
BYU

DESERET
BOOK

Library of Congress Cataloging-in-Publication Data

Names: Sainsbury, Derek R, 1972- author.
Title: Storming the nation : the unknown contributions of Joseph Smith's
        political missionaries / Derek R Sainsbury.
Description: Provo : Religious Studies Center, Brigham Young University
        [2020] | Includes bibliographical references and index. | Summary: "This
        volume uncovers the significant but previously unknown contributions of
        the electioneers who advocated for Joseph Smith's 1844 presidential
        campaign. The focus is the cadre of more than six hundred political
        missionaries--who they were before the campaign, their activities and
        experiences as electioneers, and who they became following the
        campaign's untimely collapse" Provided by publisher.
Identifiers: LCCN 2019046471 | ISBN 9781944394929 (hardback)
Subjects: LCSH: Smith, Joseph, Jr., 1805-1844--Political activity. | Church
        of Jesus Christ of Latter-day Saints--Political activity. | Political
        campaigns--United States--History--19th century. | Presidents--United
        States--Election--1844. | Deseret--Politics and government--19th
        century. | Utah Territory--Politics and government--19th century.
Classification: LCC BX8695.S6 S25 2020 | DDC 324.973/058--dc23
LC record available at https://lccn.loc.gov/2019046471

Dedicated to the men and one woman of the cadre for the kingdom of God, including my fourth great-grandfather Nathaniel Ashby. Also, to my wife, Meredith, who has sacrificed the most to allow their stories to come to light.

CONTENTS

ACKNOWLEDGMENTS

I began researching this book in 2003. Sixteen years later, it has transformed from a graduate class project to a dissertation to its present form. I never imagined it would take so long. Many obstacles and providential delays have, however, improved the finished product. I have had much help along the journey. My wife, Meredith, is most responsible for seeing this story published. From day one until its completion, she has won eight battles with cancer and endured other serious health concerns. Yet throughout she has been supportive, too often the widow of a "Joseph Smith for President"–obsessed husband. She also assisted in research trips to the Church History Library of The Church of Jesus Christ of Latter-day Saints to help transcribe and count Nauvoo Temple ordinances. Her suggestions during the different stages of this work have been crucial. My sons, Briant, Nathan, and Joshua, encouraged me to continue when I was most discouraged and, during my writing, supplied Diet Coke.

I thank the staffs at the Church History Library, Utah State Historical Society, and special collections departments of Brigham Young University and the University of Utah for assistance. Special thanks go to Meredith Sainsbury, J. B. Haws, Eric Hinderaker, Scott Esplin, Thomas Wayment, Spencer McBride, Johnathan Moyers, Susan Trump, Benjamin Park, Don

Brugger, and others who read parts of this manuscript in its various forms. Each gave needed corrections and suggestions that have made the book better. I appreciate the work of personnel at Brigham Young University's Religious Studies Center; those not already named include production supervisor Brent Nordgren, graphic designer Emily V. Strong, and student editing interns Julie Newman and Emily Cook. Also, a hearty thank-you to leaders of the Church and the Joseph Smith Papers Project for making available the Council of Fifty minutes that validated and deepened what I had been thinking and writing for years.

I save the biggest nonfamilial thank-you for University of Utah professor Robert "Bob" Goldberg. I went to the University of Utah to work with Latter-day Saint historian Dean May, who tragically died before my first class. Bob took me under his wing, taught me how to be a good historian and how to navigate and balance a doctoral student's life, and served as my dissertation committee chair. His mentorship, friendship, and advocacy of Latter-day Saint studies are valuable to me. In his office one day, I expressed to him my thanks and, correctly, named him the "Thomas Kane of Mormon studies." He gave me his trademark smirk and lifted a framed citation, saying, "Yes, I even have the award to prove it." Indeed, it was a well-deserved award named after Thomas Kane himself. Bob, an eternal thank-you for making me a better historian and a much better writer, and most importantly for inspiring me to be a better, more thoughtful, and more compassionate person.

JOSEPH SMITH RAN FOR PRESIDENT?

As the Lord God lives Joseph shall be President next term.
—Sidney Rigdon

More than six hundred strong and scattered from Maine to Louisiana and from Nauvoo to New York City, they were the largest missionary force Joseph Smith ever dispatched. It would be sixty years before Latter-day Saint missionaries served again in such numbers. These men and one woman were storming the nation as political missionaries advocating the restored gospel and the presidential campaign of the prophet. Facing stiff resistance but also finding surprising success, these electioneers offered their fellow Americans religious and political salvation. But when enemies assassinated Joseph, their campaign collapsed.

Most Americans do not know that Joseph Smith ran for president of the United States. Almost none appreciate that he was the first presidential candidate to be assassinated. Even among members of The Church of Jesus Christ of Latter-day Saints, only a small percentage realize that Joseph campaigned for the White House. Fewer still know that hundreds of electioneer missionaries canvassed the nation for him or make the connection between his campaign and assassination. Only very few of the hundreds of thousands of these electioneers' living descendants know their ancestors were political missionaries.

Many would agree that 27 June 1844 was *the* pivotal day for nineteenth-century Latter-day Saint history. On that day assassins murdered Joseph Smith, president and prophet of the church, and his older brother Hyrum, patriarch of the church. Their deaths at Carthage Jail in western Illinois shocked and splintered the Latter-day Saint community. A plurality would eventually follow Brigham Young, but his ascendancy to the highest rung of church leadership was not the only significant consequence of that fateful day. Equally important in steadying and strengthening the struggling church would be the more than six hundred electioneer missionaries who, at the time of the assassination, had been campaigning for Joseph Smith's presidential run. Their difficult missions at tremendous personal sacrifice had strengthened their commitment to Joseph[1] and his restoration of the "Zion" ideal of a righteous theocratic society—an ideal at odds with pluralistic, individualistic, and democratic nineteenth-century America. This cadre of devoted electioneers would later help Brigham relocate the Saints and create that Zion community in the Great Basin. In this way the ramifications of Joseph's political campaign, together with his assassination, are more telling in shaping the destiny of the church than has been appreciated. Too few know that Joseph's robust campaign, and the doughty missionaries assigned to it, stamped their identity on the church in the West. Ironically, the sizable influence of the campaign, assassination, and cadre of electioneers on the progress of the church was commonplace knowledge from 1844 through the early twentieth century.

However, memory changed. While the last of the electioneers were passing away, Latter-day Saint leaders began making accommodations so the church could become acceptable to the rest of the nation. The original meaning of the campaign, the electioneers, the assassination, and theo-democratic Zion surrendered to a church eager to move past scornful public perceptions of plural marriage and theocratic governance. In 1902 church leaders authorized B. H. Roberts to revise, edit, and add commentary to the previously serialized "History of Joseph Smith." Roberts wrote within the context of the Senate hearings to seat apostle and Senator-elect Reed Smoot, and a mere decade removed from his own disputed congressional election. Those skeptical that the Saints had truly changed scoured every word from Latter-day Saint leaders and publications. When Roberts's work—which became the standard treatment of the church's history for a century—rolled off the presses, Joseph's campaign was no longer remembered as a serious attempt or even a meaningful event. In the toxic national anti-Mormon atmosphere of Roberts's and Smoot's political scandals, Joseph's pursuit of the presidency was forgotten or overlooked, relegated to a historical footnote in the church's official history.[2]

Historians of the 1844 election are utterly silent on Joseph's presidential aspirations, probably because his assassination ended the campaign prematurely. Traditional Latter-day Saint historians, following Roberts's lead, have not considered Joseph's candidacy to have been sincere, but rather have seen it as a symbolic gesture with pragmatic undertones. In their view Joseph sought only to bring national attention to the plight of the Saints, lessen local political tensions, offer a candidate Latter-day Saints could support in good conscience, and create opportunities to spread the gospel. However, "New Mormon" historians in the last third of the twentieth century began to change the narrative. They contended in varying degrees that Joseph's nomination was serious but fatally flawed. Recent scholarship is finally giving Joseph's candidacy the thoughtful treatment it deserves.[3]

The most common question I hear from modern Latter-day Saints on this topic is, "Why did he run?" This is an understandable inquiry in an era when the church has strongly emphasized political neutrality for more than a century. It seems unimaginable that a prophet would seek the presidency *and* request the faithful to politick for him. However, the prophet Joseph's campaign occurred in a different time and setting, both of which must be understood to better comprehend his decisions. Joseph's conclusion to seek the presidency grew from the fusing of unredeemed persecutions, fear of future oppression, and the inspired desire to establish the political kingdom of God as part of Zion.[4] From its founding in upstate New York in 1830, the church and its members endured oppression for their religious, social, economic, and political principles that clashed with pluralistic American social norms. Intolerant fellow citizens drove their Latter-day Saint neighbors from New York, Ohio, and Missouri. The

Missouri expulsion, sanctioned and enforced by the state government, increased Joseph's urgency and determination to protect the church and himself from future abuse.

The situation in Illinois followed the same pattern. The economic success of the Saints, disagreement over doctrine, accusations of polygamy, and expedient bloc-voting for the Saints' allies and against their enemies fostered tension between the church and its new neighbors. In the fall of 1843, finding himself and the church in an increasingly untenable position, Joseph wrote to the likely presidential candidates in the upcoming 1844 election. He asked each what his policy would be toward the Saints if elected. Unsatisfied with the responses, on 29 January 1844 church leaders determined to "have an independent electoral ticket . . . [with] Joseph Smith . . . [as] candidate for the next Presidency; and . . . [to] use all honorable means in our power to secure his election."[5]

The presidential election of 1844 had a significant impact on the church. Its prophet-leader Joseph Smith ran a third-party candidacy emphasizing national unity during a time of intense and often violent sectional and political partisanship. On 11 March 1844 Joseph created the Council of Fifty—an organization formed to establish the political kingdom of God on earth—in preparation for the second coming of Jesus Christ. This council coordinated Joseph's presidential campaign and the search for a western sanctuary. Its members operated under Joseph's vision of "theodemocracy," a system of governance in which "God and the people hold the power to conduct the affairs of men in righteousness . . . for the benefit of ALL."[6] In short, Joseph saw theodemocracy as a government of people who willingly support leaders they believe are divinely called and inspired. Distinct from the church, the political kingdom would protect the rights of all citizens regardless of religious denomination or political affiliation and seek the establishment of virtuous government.

Such a theodemocracy required a faithful aristarchy to govern it. Aristarchy, a political philosophy that Joseph strongly championed, differed from aristocracy. It was governance by upright and inspired men without regard to social rank or wealth. As the prophet declared, "Certainly if any person ought to interfere in political matters, it should be those whose minds and judgments are influenced by correct principles—religious as well as political."[7] The Council of Fifty viewed itself as the aristarchy of the nascent kingdom of God on earth. By late spring, they determined that Joseph's campaign was the best option to protect the church and adjourned to join a cadre of more than six hundred electioneers, mobilizing the electorate. Within the church there was a convinced confidence about the campaign. If victory was not certain, the bargaining power of a strong national showing was. Protection for the Saints seemed within grasp.[8]

Meanwhile, apostates joined with Joseph's political enemies in Illinois and Missouri to publish the *Nauvoo Expositor*, a newspaper hostile to the church. As mayor of Nauvoo, Joseph ordered the press destroyed. This put in motion events that led to his incarceration and subsequent murder. Joseph's campaign died with him, yet his death triggered important changes within the church concerning leadership succession, the western exodus, and future settlement of the Saints.

The campaign missionaries directly experienced these momentous events. Having begun their service in mid-April, they campaigned and preached through mid-July 1844. Their tireless efforts strengthened their loyalty to Joseph, the Quorum of the Twelve (with whom they labored), and one another. The shared trauma provoked by the assassination of their beloved prophet-candidate further molded them into a dedicated cadre committed to Joseph's ideals.[9]

Working alongside the Twelve throughout the campaign, the electioneers began orbits around the men who would be the church's future centers of gravity. Franklin D. Richards best captured the connection between this particular political-missionary service and increased trust and responsibility in the church. During his campaign mission, he privately penned, "I cannot do justice to the feelings of my heart, but acknowledge the tender mercies increasing my lot in company with these brethren of the twelve on my way to perform this important mission, the faithful and acceptable performance of which involves my future prosperity in church life."[10]

I have labeled these men and one woman a "cadre," a French word meaning literally "a frame of a picture." It originates from the Italian *quadro* (Latin *quadrum*), "a square." As used by both cultures, a cadre was "the permanently organized framework of a military unit," that is, the officers. The word was co-opted by Communists in the 1930s to describe

a "group or cell of workers trained to promote the interests of the Party."
Presently the word describes "a group of trained or otherwise qualified
personnel capable of forming, training, or leading an expanded organization, as a religious or political faction."[11] This term is ideal for the electioneer missionaries for two reasons. First, they were the ones chosen and
trained to promote Joseph's candidacy and to marshal the Latter-day Saint
and wider electorate to vote for him. Church leaders carefully instructed
these men regarding the urgency, importance, and divine purpose of their
assignments. Second, and most important, their sacrificial service bonded
them to church leaders, to one another, to Zion, and to the ideals of theodemocracy. Forged and qualified by dedicated service, they capably helped
lead the theodemocratic kingdom of God after Joseph's death. They became the officers of Zion's theodemocratic government. A cadre indeed.

Yet my characterization of these men as a cadre of Latter-day Saint political activists is more an analytical tool to recover their important history
than it is an indicator of the way they thought about themselves. By ret-
rospectively organizing them as a distinct group, we can reconstruct their
history before, during, and after the 1844 election in order to illuminate
their immense contributions. To be sure, they and their church leaders *did
not* view themselves as the "election cadre." By contrast, the men of Zion's
Camp and the Mormon Battalion did perpetuate an enduring collective
identity, even holding regular reunions until the end of their lives. The
men in each of these groups (some would become cadre members) toiled
together as a unit, inspired by a common cause and forging the natural
human bonds and identity so common to proximate, shared struggle. The
electioneers also did so, but in atomized units spread out across the nation.
Their identity and bond were strongly tied to the cause of theodemocratic
Zion, the apostles, and to their immediate cadre colleagues. The premise
of this study is that despite not having a large-group identity or noted historical presence like that of an army or movement, the electioneers had
a surprisingly strong influence on the history of the church. Their signal
contributions have remained hidden in part because they have not been
studied as a collective body through time.[12]

Because a large majority of the electioneer missionaries helped establish the Saints in the West, their understudied (and, sadly, undervalued)

story is a crucial subset of Latter-day Saint and American western history. This book sets forth the multifaceted story of these six hundred–plus political missionaries—who they were before the campaign, their activities and experiences as electioneers, and who they became following the campaign's untimely collapse. It narrates the vital contributions they made in the succession crisis, the exodus from the United States, and the building of Zion in the Great Basin. Importantly, it describes how their campaigning with the Quorum of the Twelve Apostles using theodemocratic themes, coupled with the shock of Joseph's assassination, spurred their development into effective religious, political, social, and economic leaders— leaders who left an indelible imprint on Latter-day Saint history.[13]

NOTES

1. While it is customary in historical writing to refer to persons by their last names, the electioneers did not use distant surnames but rather knew their leaders as "Brother Joseph" and "Brother Brigham." The strong, loyal friendship between these men and Joseph and Brigham is central to this story. The electioneers acted in their assigned labors in large part because of how they felt toward these two leaders. While other historical persons herein are referenced by their last names, for these two prophets I often use their first names only. Furthermore, although Joseph's claims of revelation from God cannot be proved or disproved by historical methodology, I will not hedge by writing about Joseph's revelations in terms of "he claimed" to receive them. As Richard Bushman put it, "The signal feature of [Joseph's] life was his sense of being guided by revelation. . . . To blur the distinction—to insist that [Joseph] Smith devised every revelation himself—obscures the very quality that made the Prophet powerful. To get inside the movement, we have to think of Smith as the early Mormons thought of him—as a revelator." Bushman, *Rough Stone Rolling*, xxi.

2. Forgetting of history was particularly common around the turn of the twentieth century. Southerners' belief in the "Lost Cause" of the Confederacy and the forgetting of early black Latter-day Saints are two examples. See W. Paul Reeve, *Religion of a Different Color*.

3. To my knowledge, only one secular historian of the 1844 election mentions Joseph Smith. Carwardine, *Evangelicals and Politics of Antebellum America*, argues that evangelical Whigs fought against the Saints in western Illinois because of their alleged allegiance to the Democratic Party.

For examples of Joseph's absence from histories treating the 1844 election, see Saffell and Remy, *Encyclopedia of U.S. Presidential Elections*; Byrne and Marx, *Political History of Presidential Elections*; Cornog and Whelan, *Illustrated History of American Presidential Campaigns*; Schlesinger and Israel, *History of Presidential Elections, 1789–1968*; Brock, *Parties and Political Conscience*; Southwick, *Presidential Also-Rans and Running Mates, 1788–1996*; Boller, *Presidential Campaigns*; "Presidential Elections since 1789"; Scott, *Pursuit of the White House*; Havel, *U.S. Presidential Candidates and the Elections*; Shade, Campbell, and Coenen, *American Presidential Campaigns and Elections*; and Watson, *Politics of Jacksonian America*.

Examples of traditional Latter-day Saint interpretations are Durham, *Joseph Smith, Prophet-Statesman*, 145–46; Barrett, *Joseph Smith and the Restoration*, 576–77; Roberts, *Comprehensive History of the Church*, 11:208–9; Roberts, *Rise and Fall of Nauvoo*, 254; Grant, *Kingdom of God Restored*, 300; and Berrett, *Restored Church*, 178–79.

"New Mormon" interpretations began with Andrus, *Joseph Smith and World Government*. Flanders, *Kingdom on the Mississippi*, emphasizes Joseph's campaign as rooted in the political alienation of the Saints and a novel effort to defend the kingdom; Hansen, *Quest for Empire*, saw Joseph's candidacy as a desperate attempt to establish the political kingdom; Hill, *Quest for Refuge*, believes the candidacy was politically unrealistic yet a sincere means of rejecting American pluralism; Remini, *Joseph Smith*, considers Joseph's political actions as pragmatic and designed to defend the Saints, not win an election; Bushman, *Rough Stone Rolling*, interprets the extensive missionary effort as a sign of Joseph's clear goal to restore the ideal of a "patriot king" within a religious context, as the true inheritance of the American Revolution.

Two forthcoming books—Park, *Kingdom of Nauvoo*, and McBride, *When Joseph Smith Ran for President*—will deepen our understanding of the campaign.

4. For a full discussion of the concept of Zion, see chap. 1.

5. Barrett, *Joseph Smith and the Restoration*, 568–69, 571. See also JSJ, 29 January 1844; and JSH, E-1:1869.

6. *Times and Seasons*, 15 April 1844. For instructive discussions of theodemocracy, see Andrus, *Joseph Smith and World Government*, 5–15; and Mason, "Theodemocracy in Nineteenth-Century Mormonism," 349–75.

7. *Times and Seasons*, 15 March 1844.

8. See *Church History in the Fulness of Times*, 270. For contemporary definitions of *aristarchy* and *aristocracy*, see *Webster's 1828 Dictionary*. For Joseph's endorsement of aristarchy, see Durham, *Joseph Smith, Prophet-Statesman*, 51–52. On the political kingdom of God, see Allen and Leonard, *Story of the Latter-*

day Saints, 186–87; Hill, *Quest for Refuge*, 125; Hansen, *Quest for Empire*, chaps. 3–4; and Flanders, *Kingdom on the Mississippi*, 240, 279–81, 292, 302.

9. I exclude the Quorum of the Twelve Apostles from my definition of the cadre of electioneers. In the spring of 1844, members of the Twelve were already elite members in the religious and political arms of Zion. My primary focus is those who volunteered and accepted the Twelve's call to preach and electioneer for Joseph. This is not to imply that the apostles were not part of the electioneering effort. Far from it—they orchestrated and led the campaign. Their efforts and voices are included in this study.

10. Richards, Journal, 24 May 1844.

11. Definitions are from etymonline.com and wordreference.com.

12. In the historiography on Joseph Smith, Margaret Robertson's honors thesis is the only attempt to study the activities of the electioneers. See Robertson, "Campaign and the Kingdom," also published under the same title in *BYU Studies* 39, no. 3 (2000): 147–80. Robertson analyzed the then-known number of missionaries and came to the traditional interpretations. She found no serious intent to elect Joseph or to establish the political kingdom of God. To her mind these missionaries were in no substantial way different from the legions of missionaries who served the church before and after the 1844 election. Robertson's brief work captured only about half of the electioneers this book does. Furthermore, her interpretation mistakes the campaign's consequences as its motivating purposes.

13. The publication of the Council of Fifty minutes by the Joseph Smith Papers Project has only confirmed and deepened my earlier impressions of how seriously Joseph and those around him took the campaign.

CHAPTER 1

SEEKING "POWER TO PROTECT THE INNOCENT"

I am the greatest advocate of the Constitution of the United States there is on the earth. . . . The only fault I find with the Constitution is [that] . . . although it provides that all men shall enjoy religious freedom, yet it does not provide the manner by which that freedom can be preserved.

—Joseph Smith, 15 October 1843[1]

Electioneer Experience: Robert and John Thomas. Robert Thomas was in Mississippi when he first heard that the prophet Joseph Smith was dead. He and his companion-cousin John Thomas, both in their early twenties, had been electioneering in Tennessee and Mississippi for two months. They had joined The Church of Jesus Christ of Latter-day Saints only five months earlier, baptized by fellow electioneer Benjamin L. Clapp. Initially, Robert was wary of Clapp and his companions, believing them to be "deceivers."[2] Yet he read the Book of Mormon and listened to the missionaries. Soon Robert chose baptism, which took place in a partially frozen pond. That cold February night Clapp prayed for Robert to be able to speak in tongues, and he did so at that night's meeting.

Just as Robert began to speak in tongues, two men arrived, intending to disrupt the gathering. Interpreting Robert's words, a church member declared there were men prepared to violently end the meeting. The two visitors sat stunned. One slowly stood and stammered, "We came here tonight intending to break up this meeting." Pointing at Robert, he continued, "Robert, I know him, and he could not talk in a new language if it was not of the gift of God." The two men then requested baptism. Clapp was impressed with Robert and soon took him on a short but successful mission to Alabama. When the two missionaries returned to Mississippi, the Thomas families were preparing to move to Nauvoo, Illinois. They all took their first railroad ride to get to Vicksburg, Mississippi, where they boarded a steamboat, arriving in Nauvoo around mid-April. For four weeks Robert Thomas rented a room in Joseph's Nauvoo Mansion.

Robert spoke daily with the prophet for a month, receiving a crash course on his new faith directly from its founder. Joseph and other leaders took notice of Robert's spiritual and speaking talents. In May apostle Heber C. Kimball approached Robert and John Thomas and announced, "I want you two to go on a Mission." They were directed to the Seventies Hall, where electioneer missionary Joseph Young ordained them seventies, and then Kimball told them to report to Abraham O. Smoot, president of the campaign in Tennessee. They boarded a steamboat headed back down the Mississippi and found Smoot in Dresden, Tennessee. Smoot assigned them to Huntington County, where they began preaching the gospel and electioneering for Joseph Smith. Although mobs threatened them and cold, wet nights without shelter weakened their bodies, they persisted in their difficult mission day after day, week after week.

*   *   *

What drove two young Southern men to preach and electioneer *in the South* for religious government and the abolition of slavery—tenets of Joseph's presidential platform? In a nation founded on freedom of religion, why did these missionaries of an unpopular church advocate their leader and prophet for US president? The answers are not found in the Thomas brothers alone. Scattered across the nation, more than six hundred other electioneer missionaries were zealously promoting Joseph's unique presidential campaign. Why did they choose to do so?

To understand Joseph's presidential aspirations and the devotion of this cadre of electioneers, one must know something of The Church of Jesus Christ of Latter-day Saints, specifically its founding narrative and the actuating doctrine behind its encompassing mission—to restore not only the true church of Jesus Christ but also the Zion kingdom destined to govern the world during the Millennium.

CHURCH OF CHRIST RESTORED

The Latter-day Saint movement began with Joseph Smith Jr., who was born on 23 December 1805, in Sharon, Vermont. His family eventually settled near Palmyra, New York, in the so-called burned-over district during the Second Great Awakening. Intense religious revivals there engulfed every family, including the Smiths.[3] Twelve-year-old Joseph was perplexed about which church to join. After two years of searching, he became convinced that he must ask God directly. The result of his prayer is known as the "first vision." In this vision, Joseph testified, God and Jesus Christ appeared and forbade him to join any of the sects then on the earth. Three years later an angel named Moroni visited Joseph and told him that God had "a work" for him to do and that his "name should be had for good and evil among all nations, kindreds, and tongues." Moroni added that "there was a book deposited, written upon gold plates, giving an account of the former inhabitants of this continent" and containing "the fulness of the everlasting Gospel."[4] Joseph obtained the plates and in March 1830 published a translation of them entitled *The Book of Mormon.*[5]

On 6 April 1830, Joseph organized the Church of Christ in Fayette, New York. He dictated a revelation declaring he was to be "a seer, a translator, a prophet, an apostle of Jesus Christ, an elder of the church through the will of God."[6] Thus the church was born with new, translated, ancient scripture *and* continuing revelation through the prophet. Missionaries with copies of the Book of Mormon began spreading the news of the restoration. Four missionaries journeyed to the western border of Missouri during the winter of 1830–31 and, along the way, converted many of Sidney Rigdon's congregation near Kirtland, Ohio, doubling the church's membership.[7] As part of this mission, they covenanted to place a pillar on the spot for the temple of the "New Jerusalem"—Zion. Although erecting the marker would wait a year, the idea of building a New Jerusalem—a city of Zion—consumed Joseph and the Saints.[8]

LATTER-DAY SAINT DOCTRINAL BASIS OF ZION

Zion is a biblical name for Jerusalem and her righteous inhabitants, and building a city of Zion in America—a "New Jerusalem"—was the primary impulse behind the Latter-day Saint movement. With the Book of Mormon and his own revelations declaring that Zion would be built before the second coming of Jesus Christ,[9] Joseph admonished the Saints to "establish the cause of Zion" and "move the cause of Zion in mighty power for good."[10] He taught that Zion would be located "on the borders by the Lamanites."[11] Zion was to be a refuge as God poured out wars, plagues, and destructions preceding the second coming. The marriage of the cause of Zion to the concept of the New Jerusalem concretized in the Saints' minds. For the early Saints, Zion was not only a location in the western United States that was safe from the world's imminent destruction, but also heaven's great work of preparing the earth for the return of Jesus Christ.[12]

Further clarification came in revelations known as the Book of Moses. The antediluvian prophet Enoch lived in a city known as the city of Zion. Its people were so righteous that "in the process of time, [that holy city was] taken up into heaven." God also "called his people Zion," making Zion not just a place but a people. Further, the revelation explained that Zion encompassed more than contemporary Christianity: "And the Lord called his people Zion, because they were all of one heart and one mind, and dwelt in righteousness; and there was no poor among them."[13] Zion was to have a social component consisting "of one heart," a political or governing component of "one mind," an economic component of "no poor among them," and a religious component of "dwel[ling] in righteousness."

Another revelation required the Saints to gather to Ohio. To emphasize the centrality of unity in creating Zion, it declared, "Be one; and if ye are not one ye are not mine."[14] Regarding this doctrine of gathering, Joseph later instructed, "What was the object of gathering . . . the people of God in any age of the world? . . . The main object was to build unto the Lord a house whereby He could reveal unto His people the ordinances of His house."[15] Thus the temple became the earthly locus of Zion where heaven and earth literally met. Later the Saints learned that the temple was where they would make covenants to individually and collectively create Zion's four components (religious, social, economic, political).

The concept of Zion in the revelations divided the world into two parts. The first was Zion and her grouped congregations called "stakes," where Saints gathered to build up a Zion society.[16] They would receive knowledge and power in Zion's temple and then go into the mission field (the second division of the world) to preach and make proselytes. These converts would, in turn, gather to Zion, help build it, and serve missions themselves. World renewal would come from Zion and her ever-expanding stakes. Thus, less than a year after its founding, the church's primary aim was to gather converts and to become Zion—a people prepared for the second coming. Revelations associated with Zion laid the foundation for a communal economic system called the law of consecration. Joseph also received instructions outlining the familial patriarchal order, including the doctrine of eternal marriage and the principle of plural marriage.[17] Lastly, he received inspiration on establishing the political kingdom of God.

Zion was so central to what Joseph knew the restoration of Christianity to be that when persecution prompted the use of secret names in the original 1835 edition of the Doctrine and Covenants, Joseph chose the name Enoch—the prophet-leader of the original Zion. Of course, Zion with its peculiar social, political, economic, and religious ramifications was antithetical to the beliefs of fellow American citizens. In violent frontier America, this meant conflict almost anywhere the church bloomed. Thus the Saints of Joseph's day, including most of the future electioneers, would flee persecution in Ohio and Missouri and start over again in Illinois.

ZION IN OHIO AND MISSOURI

Electioneer Experience: Lorenzo Snow. Lorenzo Snow's encounters with persecution typified the experiences of many other electioneers during the first decade of the church. Twenty-one-year-old Snow initially scoffed when his older sister Eliza joined with the Saints in nearby Kirtland, Ohio.

In 1836 he left Oberlin College "with disgust" and joined Eliza in Kirtland. Still skeptical about the church, he nevertheless enrolled in its Hebrew class in preparation to continue his education elsewhere. Instead Snow had a spiritual awakening and chose to unite with the Saints. He later penned, "I totally relinquished all my favorite ideas and arrangements of Classical Education [and] I took up my valise and went forth without purse or scrip to preach the Gospel."[18]

Early image of Lorenzo Snow, the first electioneer. Courtesy of Church History Library.

Later, fleeing persecution, Snow departed for Missouri with his father's family. Snow's devotion to the church had grown in two years, owing in part to his having "witnessed very many marvelous scenes of the power of God in the Temple." Now in Missouri he "stood with weapons in hand to defend his father's house" from the gathering mobs. He would never use them; instead he was called on another mission, this time to Kentucky, Illinois, and Ohio. While he preached and for income taught school for a season, tensions in Missouri boiled over and mobs viciously attacked the Saints. Tragically, his adored sister Eliza was gang-raped and his family driven from the state. In a twist of irony, he learned of the expulsion by reading a letter by Eliza in a newspaper. Snow and thousands of other Latter-day Saints, including future cadre members, would be haunted the rest of their lives by the harrowing experiences they endured at the hands of violent mobs.

*   *   *

The church's experience from 1830 to 1837 centered on the towns of Kirtland, Ohio, and Independence, Missouri. Here the Saints received revelations that solidified church governance and learned doctrines that shaped

belief and practice. Jackson County, Missouri, became the revealed location of Zion. Saints flocked there to receive stewardship inheritances and
to build up Zion while seeking to become a Zion people.

BUILDING RELIGIOUS ZION

Latter-day Saints believed the authority to act in God's name was available
to all male congregants and that it derived directly from heavenly messen-
gers. While Joseph and his scribe Oliver Cowdery translated the Book of
Mormon in the summer of 1829, angels visited them. John the Baptist restored the "lesser priesthood" of Aaron. The New Testament apostles Peter,
James, and John restored the "higher priesthood" of Melchizedek, an Old
Testament priest-king. This system of priesthood had clear church-state
undertones, a theme that Joseph fully developed in Nauvoo with temple
ordinances. The Aaronic priesthood was a preparatory priesthood dealing
with temporal matters and the ordinances of baptism and the sacrament
(communion), while the Melchizedek priesthood included the authority
to bestow the gift of the Holy Ghost and to direct the church by revelation.
A revelation in 1830 named Joseph Smith "as first elder of this church"
and Oliver Cowdery as "second elder."[19] Continued church growth led to
additional revelations that created more priesthood offices necessary for
governing the church.[20]

A bishop to manage temporal matters was the first new office.[21] Joseph
soon ordained the first high priests, who were higher in authority than
elders.[22] In 1832 the First Presidency became the highest presiding council
of the church.[23] The first high council was called in 1834, consisting of
twelve high priests.[24] A year later Joseph organized two other quorums of
leadership. First was the Quorum of the Twelve Apostles, modeled after
the apostles of primitive Christianity. They were appointed as "special witnesses of the name of Christ" and served under the direction of the First
Presidency. The other quorum was the Seventy, directed by seven presidents, to act under the direction of the Twelve.[25]

The combination of sacral priesthood and church government,
though foreign to most other contemporary religions, became a pillar of
the church. Ordinary men were considered worthy of power to stand in

Kirtland Temple, ca. 1900. Photo by S. T. Whitaker. Temples and temple ordinances were at the heart of building Zion. Courtesy of Church History Library.

the presence of God and act with the authority of prophets of old. Such power was entrusted without consideration of economic or intellectual capacity. Men qualified for priesthood office because of their righteousness and loyalty. Another strength of the priesthood was its combination of hierarchical and democratic elements. Democratic features included its openness to all men, the naming of leaders as "presidents," and the law of common consent, which required that priesthood officers be approved by church members. These were not elections but opportunities to publicly support the officers. Those selected by revelation were subject to God, not the people.[26]

The centrality of the temple to Latter-day Saint theology is best expressed by the Saints' determination to build temples long before other religious buildings. The dedication of the Kirtland Temple was the pinnacle of religious Zion in Ohio. January–May 1836 was the greatest era of spiritual manifestations in Latter-day Saint history. Church leaders and members saw visions of Christ, angels, and prophets. Joseph presented

the quorums of the priesthood for approval in order of authority, thus ce-
menting church leadership. On Easter, 3 April, Joseph recorded that Jesus
Christ appeared to him and Oliver Cowdery, accepting the temple. Then
Moses, Elias, and Elijah restored priesthood keys to gather and seal God's
children, thereby "turn[ing] the hearts of the fathers to the children, and
the children to the fathers."[27] These priesthood keys were essential to direct
the gathering to temples, the heart of Zion, where the ordinances of salvation could be performed.[28]

BUILDING SOCIAL ZION

By 1831 Joseph had learned that the restoration of Zion would include
the social order of the biblical patriarchs. Adam, Enoch, Noah, and Abraham were all part of this system of organizing and governing families and
nations by the priesthood authority received from sacred covenants with
God. Couples were promised an eternal union and endless posterity, per-
petuating God's covenant. Joseph eventually understood the Saints would
make the same covenants and receive the same blessings. A corollary
to this doctrine was plural marriage, as practiced by some of the patriarchs and prophets. Joseph later recorded a revelation stating that Abraham, Isaac, Jacob, and others took additional wives who "were given unto
[them], and [the patriarchs] abode in my law." Plural marriage would be
part of the "[restoration] of all things."[29]

BUILDING ECONOMIC ZION

In early 1831 Joseph organized Zion economically in Jackson County after
receiving revelations detailing the law of consecration. The bishop received
members' consecrations of property and possessions and then assigned
stewardships for each family or individual. The size of the stewardships
depended on the circumstances, wants, and needs of the families. Relative
economic equality would bring unity, and unity would bring Zion. In 1833
Joseph sent the leaders in Missouri a plat for the city of Zion. At the center of the city was space for "temples."[30] Though other contemporary uto-
pian groups envisioned communitarian towns, Joseph's was unique. There

was no civil government or commerce at Zion's core. It was to be literally a holy city, where every building would display the words "Holiness to the Lord."[31] Although this plat was never implemented in its particulars, Joseph later utilized its principles for laying out settlements in northern Missouri and Illinois.

The Saints' expulsion in the winter of 1833–34 destroyed hopes for consecration in Jackson County. In 1836 in Ohio, Joseph and others created the Kirtland Anti-Banking Safety Society to stimulate commerce. However, persecution, the national economic panic of 1837, and poor management led to its collapse and with it the collapse of the local economy. Many blamed Joseph for their financial problems, accusing him of being a false prophet. Economic Zion had been a disaster in both states.[32]

BUILDING POLITICAL ZION

As early as 1830, Joseph talked about establishing an actual kingdom of God on earth. In fact, the Saints felt more like citizens of Zion than citizens of the United States (although in Ohio and Missouri they, like their fellow Americans, exercised their right to act individually in politics). Complicating matters in Missouri, however, was the fact that most Saints came from the North while most "old settlers" were transplants from the Deep South. The Saints' increasing numbers stirred the fears of the settlers, many of whom saw the Saints as religious fanatics. Aggravating the situation was the Saints' peculiar belief that the neighboring American Indians were among God's covenant people. Some Saints boasted that thousands of converts, including Indians, were coming and that the "Gentiles" (non-Latter-day Saints) would be destroyed when Zion was established.

The brewing conflict erupted over slavery. A misunderstanding convinced the Missourians that the Saints were inviting free blacks into their slave state. Leading citizens organized in July 1833 and signed a manifesto demanding the Saints leave the county. The meeting quickly became a mob that destroyed the Saints' press and tarred and feathered two leaders. The vigilantes forced local church leaders to sign an agreement. To speed the process, they turned to further violence in October. Light casualties occurred on both sides. Local officials called out the militia, giving legal sanction to their deeds. They confiscated the Saints' weapons and forced them out of the county, destroying their homes, farms, possessions, and animals. The refugees fled during the height of winter, crossing the Missouri River into Clay County.

Encouraged by a revelation, Joseph and the Saints turned to the government for redress. It implied that if appeal to government failed, the Saints might have to respond with force.[33] Yet petitions to local government officials and judges were ineffective because most of them were leaders of the mob. Fearing civil war, Missouri's governor refused to help the Saints. When President Andrew Jackson and other federal officials also denied the Saints' petitions, a new revelation authorizing an army was not far behind. In February 1834, the high council sanctioned Joseph's determination to "redeem" Zion and named the prophet "commander-in-chief of the armies of Israel."[34] He was to recruit an army to march to Missouri and return the exiles to their lands. Known as the Camp of Israel, and later Zion's Camp, this group of men had an important impact on the church's future.[35]

The story of Zion's Camp is one of sacrifice, futility, and leadership development. The camp numbered more than two hundred. At the news of their approach, mobs reorganized in Jackson County, burned the remaining Latter-day Saint homes, and prepared for confrontation. Negotiations to restore the refugees to their lands proved fruitless. Surprisingly, Joseph dictated a revelation chastising the Missourians and other Saints for their selfishness and disobedience. It also stated that "mine elders should wait for a little season, for the redemption of Zion."[36] Within days, Joseph disbanded the camp. Although Zion's Camp failed to restore the Saints to their lands, the men's experience with Joseph and one another prepared some for future leadership. Joseph judged the men who had volunteered at the risk of death and remained faithful to have passed a critical test, qualifying them for increased priesthood office. Back in Ohio, eight of the Twelve Apostles and all the Seventy were chosen from Zion's Camp's ranks. A decade later, Joseph's presidential campaign would offer similar opportunities for the electioneer cadre.

The Saints' experience in Ohio ended in religious schism, economic collapse, and refugees retracing the steps of Zion's Camp to Missouri. In

1837 apostates created a separate church. After failed attempts at reconciliation, church leaders excommunicated the dissenters. By the end of
the year, 10 to 15 percent of members had withdrawn from the church.[37]
Lawsuits and mobs hounded Joseph and others in Kirtland, forcing
them to flee to Missouri. The remaining loyal Saints soon followed their
leaders west.[38]

ZION FLEES MISSOURI

Electioneer Experience: Levi Jackman. Cadre member Levi Jackman experienced the crucible of Missouri. His family was baptized in 1831 and
moved to Independence, Missouri, in 1832. Mobs drove them and thousands of others out of the county the following year. But Jackman did not
go quietly, repeatedly firing his rifle to defend his family. In 1834 Joseph
chose Jackman to serve on the newly formed Missouri high council. Eventually, Jackman settled near the town of Far West, becoming a justice of the
peace. However, the Mormon War of 1838 changed everything. His family, again homeless and suffering the bitterness of winter, stumbled across

Missouri to Illinois. The next year, Jackman
and hundreds of others swore affidavits
against Missouri. He reported $1,825 of
lost property and other damages. He would
never receive a penny. Jackman's dream of a
heavenly Zion in Missouri ended in nightmare, one shared by all Missourian Saints.[39]

*   *   *

From 1836 to 1838 the Saints in Missouri
tried to create Zion in newly formed Caldwell and Daviess Counties. Internal and
external threats made the attempt a short,
futile one. Disaffected leaders joined with
external enemies to drive the Saints from
the state. Religious, economic, and politi-

*Before becoming an election-
eer, Levi Jackman experienced
the horror of the Missouri
persecutions. Sutterley Bros.
photo ca. 1865–73 courtesy of
Church History Library.*

cal differences stoked the simmering conflict that saw Saints killed, their women raped, and their property stolen or destroyed. Once again, they limped away as exiles—this time to Illinois.

Many Missouri church leaders became disaffected in 1838. The high council, including Levi Jackman, excommunicated most of them, even assistant president of the church Oliver Cowdery. Cowdery's response captured the intensity with which some Saints struggled to reconcile their beliefs with Zion's social, economic, and political demands: "I will not be influenced, governed, or controlled, in my temporal interests by any ecclesiastical authority or pretended revelation whatever, contrary to my own judgment."[40]

On Independence Day 1838, Sidney Rigdon of the First Presidency delivered an emotional oration warning that the Saints would fight rather than suffer further persecution. "It shall be between us and them a war of extermination," he declared.[41] Some Saints proudly published and foolishly distributed copies of the speech. These harsh words, though spoken in self-defense, were inflammatory and, ironically, foundational to the events that drove the Saints from Missouri. Adding to the tension, 1838 was an election year. When some Saints tried to vote in Gallatin, Daviess County, enemies confronted and blocked them. A brawl ensued with injuries on both sides.[42]

Conflict spread. Missourians laid siege to the Latter-day Saint town of DeWitt, beginning "a war of extermination."[43] Joseph appealed to Governor Lilburn W. Boggs for assistance. When Boggs replied that "the quarrel was between the Mormons and the mob" and that "we might fight it out," the Saints chose evacuation.[44] Now emboldened, hostile forces marched toward Daviess County. Alarmed, the Saints mustered their own militia units. Because the enemy forces were themselves county militia detachments, a kind of militia civil war emerged. Sixteen years before Kansas was bleeding from violent confrontations over slavery, and twenty-three years before the massive bloodletting of the Civil War, Missouri was hemorrhaging.[45]

Two events turned public opinion and the government of Missouri squarely against the Saints. Disaffected former church leaders swore out affidavits that Joseph taught he was above the laws of Missouri and that the

Saints would destroy their enemies. Concurrently, at the Battle of Crooked River, three Saints, including apostle David Patten, were killed and several wounded on both sides. Exaggerated, one-sided reports reached Boggs, who believed them. In response, he issued the infamous extermination order: "The Mormons must be treated as enemies and must be exterminated or driven from the state if necessary for the public good."[46]

Even before word of the order reached Caldwell County, the deadliest event of the Mormon War occurred. At Hawn's Mill, a mob killed seventeen Saints and seriously wounded thirteen others. Their brutality included murdering defenseless men and boys, even a ten-year-old. The massacre became forever burned in the psyche of Latter-day Saints as evidence of bigotry and persecution toward them.[47] A siege of Far West ended with the imprisonment of church leaders and the expulsion of the entire community from the state. Joseph and others, arrested on charges of treason against the state, remained prisoners through the winter of 1838–39. As spring began and the government could not build a solid case against the prisoners, public opinion in Missouri turned against Governor Boggs. While being transferred in April 1839, the prisoners were allowed to escape. They hastily joined the expulsed Saints in Illinois.[48]

NAUVOO: THE NEW ZION

Electioneer Experience: John Tanner. Future electioneer missionary John Tanner followed Joseph Smith from Ohio to Missouri and then to Illinois. Tanner first encountered the church as a wealthy hotelier and landowner in New York. In 1832 two missionary brothers (and future cadre members) challenged Tanner, a devout Baptist, to read the Book of Mormon. Jared and Simeon Carter promised that if he read the book, his leg—long lame and afflicted with sores—would be made whole. Tanner read the book and believed it was true, and Jared Carter took him by the hand and commanded his leg to be healed. Tanner never used crutches again. The next day the Carter brothers baptized Tanner and his family. Tanner sold his vast holdings and moved to Kirtland. He gave Joseph much of his wealth to invest in the community and to build the Kirtland Temple. He marched in Zion's Camp, lost the rest of his fortune in the collapse of the Kirtland Safety Society, and eventually fled to Missouri.

During the siege of Far West, Captain O'Dell of the militia-mob struck Tanner in the head with his gun, cutting a seven-inch gash to the bone. Blood smothered his face in such an awful manner that his captors momentarily felt remorse. They left him with his family, who recognized him only by his voice. Later in the day the militia returned and arrested Tanner and his son-in-law Amasa Lyman (a future electioneer missionary). After being released for lack of evidence, Tanner rejoined his family in Illinois. For the third time in six years, Tanner reestablished himself in a new Zion community and, once again, prospered.[49]

*　　*　　*

Like John Tanner, future electioneer cadre members and other Saints looked for a new beginning in Illinois. Joseph became adamant about creating Zion; he was more motivated and focused than ever, realizing his teachings and actions could lead to his death. He understood that most Saints, let alone other citizens of the United States, were not ready for Zion, including some doctrines he shared only sparingly. "I never have had opportunity to give them [the Saints] the plan that God has revealed to me," Joseph privately lamented.[50] In Nauvoo, he revealed doctrines and practices to trusted associates so that, should he die, they might give them later to the full church. Joseph realized that in order to build Zion within the borders of the United States, they needed government protection. This he vigorously sought from city, state, federal, and even international leaders.[51]

Convinced that goodwill toward the church existed outside Missouri, Joseph petitioned the federal government. When he met with President Martin Van Buren at the White House in late 1839, the president, not wanting to offend his political allies, was ambivalent to Joseph's pleas. "Gentlemen, your cause is just," Van Buren admitted, "but I can do nothing for you—if I do anything, I shall come in contact with the whole State of Missouri."[52] A congressional committee dismissed the Saints' petition for redress, suggesting they seek justice in the courts, an avenue that was already a dead end. Joseph was furious: "Is there no virtue in the body politic?"[53] Van Buren's rebuff pushed the Saints politically into the arms of the Whigs. When Joseph returned to Nauvoo, he wrote to a friend that "the effect has been to turn the entire mass of people, even to an individual, . . . on the other side of the great political question."[54] Though overwhelmingly Democrats, in 1840 the Saints voted as a bloc against Van Buren and for the Whig candidate William Henry Harrison—the eventual winner. As the Saints began to hold the political balance of power in eastern Illinois, both parties took notice.[55]

Joseph secured a charter creating the city of Nauvoo and used it as a wall of defense "to create and protect a city-state."[56] The charter allowed for the concentration of branches of government, creating effective control by elected church leaders. The commissioned militia, the Nauvoo Legion, would serve as a defensive hedge against future mob actions.[57] Joseph saw these as necessary measures to protect the church from a repeat of what happened in Missouri. He stated, "The City Charter of Nauvoo is . . . for the salvation of the church, and on principles so broad that every honest man might dwell secure under its protective influence without distinction of sect or party."[58] Joseph and other church leaders were elected to city offices. The election results showed how entwined church and state were. Half of the candidates received 100 percent of the vote and the others no less than 97 percent.[59]

To Thomas Sharp of nearby Warsaw, the Saints and their religion, charter, and militia seemed sinister. Correctly, he understood that the church was not just another Christian sect. What Latter-day Saints declared as the restored church of Jesus Christ and the establishment of Zion, Sharp viewed as a growing, dangerous, and un-American political empire cloaked in the guise of religion. He began a campaign in his newspaper, the *Warsaw Signal*, against Joseph and the Saints. Sharp was instrumental in forming the Anti-Mormon Party in Hancock County. The initial slate of candidates in that party defeated the Saints in the county elections. However, the continual influx of converts to the area would soon reverse the numbers.[60]

In fact, from 1839 to 1841, missionaries in Great Britain netted thousands of converts. Many immigrated to Nauvoo following the 1841 First Presidency proclamation for all Saints to gather there. The promise was that "by a concentration of action and a unity of effort" they would finally see Zion built.[61] Another revelation, naming Nauvoo as a "cornerstone of Zion," commanded the Saints to construct a temple wherein the Lord promised to reveal necessary ancient ordinances.[62] Further, the church was to send a proclamation to the rulers of the world, giving notice that Zion was on the earth. Nauvoo was to be an "international religious capital."[63]

During this time Joseph introduced ward units—ecclesiastical, geographic subdivisions of a stake that were overseen by a bishop. The bishops primarily governed in temporal matters and did not preside at sacrament meetings, although they occasionally called more traditionally religious meetings. The church's adoption of the word *ward*, a contemporary term denoting a political and geographic subdivision of a city, furthered the idea of Zion as a merger of church and state.[64]

The relative calm in Nauvoo afforded Joseph the opportunity to teach doctrines and practices that he had not widely revealed about the patriarchal order of Zion. This included the principle of plural marriage, which he privately taught to the apostles and a few others. Like Joseph, they were emotionally torn as they attempted to reconcile their cultural monogamy with polygamy. The acceptance and practice of plural marriage became an intense spiritual struggle and, ultimately, a test of loyalty to Joseph.[65]

THEODEMOCRACY AND ARISTARCHY

In the spring of 1842 Joseph began to tie political Zion to theological salvation in what he later termed "theodemocracy, where God and the people hold the power to conduct the affairs of men in righteousness."[66] In April Joseph began receiving revelations outlining the political kingdom of God that would create this theodemocracy.[67] He announced, "I have the whole plan of the kingdom before me, and no other person has."[68] This was to be the government spoken of by the Old Testament prophet Daniel that "the God of heaven [would] set up . . . , which [should] never be destroyed . . . but . . . should consume all . . . kingdoms" and thus govern the earth during the Millennium—when "they [the Saints] shall be priests [and kings] of God and of Christ, and shall reign with him a thousand years."[69] The revealed name for the government was "The Kingdom of God and His Laws, with Keys and power thereof, and judgment in the hands of his servants, Ahman Christ."[70] Joseph's incremental movement toward a presidential campaign and a theodemocratic Council of Fifty emerges when one connects the dots from the spring of 1842 to the spring of 1844, as will be seen.[71]

Some five months before the 1838 Mormon War in Missouri, Joseph issued a motto that crystallized his view of the political kingdom of God. Titled "The Political Motto of the Church of Latter-day Saints," it declared in part, "All good and wholesome laws; and virtue and truth above all things / And Aristarchy live forever!!!"[72] *Aristarchy*—the core characteristic of what might be termed "political Zion"—referred to "a body of good men in power, or government by excellent men."[73] An earlier revelation reminded the Saints, "Nevertheless, when the wicked rule the people mourn. Wherefore, honest men and wise men should be sought for diligently, and good men and wise men ye should observe to uphold."[74] For Joseph the words *good, excellent, honest,* and *wise* were personified in men who had proved their faithfulness to the cause of Zion.

Joseph drew on aristarchic principle in March 1842 when he created the Nauvoo Female Relief Society, an organization that assisted the poor, raised funds for the temple, and watched over the women of the church. Joseph introduced the women to sacred doctrines related to future temple worship, declaring that their society "should move according to the ancient Priesthood."[75] The Relief Society was a microcosm of aristarchic theodemocracy. Revelation designated officers chosen for their goodness or excellence, including loyalty to Joseph and the church. Once nominated, members then voted to sanction the appointments, the already-familiar practice of common consent. Leaders were to continue "so long as they shall continue to fill the office with dignity."[76] In other words, good or excellent leaders were to remain in their offices as long as their righteousness, competence, and loyalty endured. Thus formed, the female presidency of the organization governed by revelation, not by constitution.

In Nauvoo Joseph introduced temple ceremonies over a two-year period. In part, these sacred ordinances prepared church leaders to rule in the coming kingdom of God. While the temple was being built, Joseph introduced the endowment ordinance in his red brick store to several trusted

On the upper floor of his red brick store in Nauvoo, Joseph organized the Relief Society, introduced the endowment, led his presidential campaign, and directed the Council of Fifty. Photo attributed to B. H. Roberts, ca. 1886. Courtesy of Church History Library.

associates in May 1842. Initiates were promised that if they were faithful, they would eventually become "kings [and queens] and priests [and priestesses] unto God."[77] Until his death in June 1844, Joseph administered the endowment to nearly one hundred loyal friends, male and female, calling them the "Anointed Quorum." In May 1843 Joseph began sealing select couples into an eternal marriage covenant. The ultimate purpose of these ordinances was to bind disciples to God, husbands to wives, and children to parents ad infinitum in the patriarchal order of Zion. However, through these ordinances, Joseph also created the groundwork for a theodemocracy governed by an aristarchy.[78]

Joseph took another step toward theodemocracy just weeks after initiating the endowment. At the temple site he "addressed them [citizens of Nauvoo] on the principles of government at considerable length, showing that [he] did not intend to vote the Whig or Democratic ticket as such, but would go for those who would support good order &c." Then the "meeting nominated candidates for Senate, Representatives, and other officers."[79] Here was theodemocracy at work. The prophet, at the Saints' most important religious space, nominated for political office those men he felt were faithful, competent, and loyal. Later, leaders officially announced the nominees and the Saints consented by voting for them.

Not coincidentally, on the afternoon before Independence Day in 1842, Joseph preached to eight thousand Saints on the Book of Daniel, emphasizing the theme "that in the last days the God of heaven would set up a kingdom."[80] A week and a half later the *Times and Seasons*, which Joseph edited, continued the theme in the article "The Government of God." Whether written by the prophet or simply approved by him, the thoughts were certainly his. Summarizing the distresses of world history, the article asked, "Where is there a man that can step forth and alter the destiny of nations and promote the happiness of the world?" The answer was the government of God: "It has been the design of Jehovah, from the commencement of the world, and is his purpose now, to regulate the affairs of the world in his own time; to stand as head of the universe, and take the reins of government into his own hand." God's government had existed with the patriarchs. "Their government was a theocracy," the article stated; "*they had God to make their laws, and men chosen by him to administer them* . . . in both civil and ecclesiastical affairs; they were both one . . . ; so will it be when the purposes of God shall be accomplished." The article then placed this government within the context of building Zion and the restoration of the church. Speaking of this theocracy, the article definitively proclaimed, "This is the only thing that can bring about the 'restitution of all things, spoken of by all the holy prophets since the world was.'" God's government was essential to fulfilling the destiny of Zion and, ultimately, the millennial reign of Christ.[81]

Joseph further developed the principles of theodemocracy and the kingdom of God throughout 1843. He declared: "[It is] our duty to concentrate all our influence to make popular that which is sound and good, and unpopular that which is unsound. 'Tis right politically for a man who has influence to use it."[82] Theodemocracy allowed for the concentration of Joseph's influence to advance Zion. In May Joseph addressed the members of the Nauvoo Legion, reminding them that those holding national power had ignored the Saints' petition for protection and redress. "When they give me power to protect the innocent," he declared, "I will never say I can do nothing for their good; I will exercise that power so help me God."[83] Interestingly, Joseph asserted "when," not "if," he held national power.

POLITICAL PRESSURE AND PERSECUTION

The Saints' political power was the central issue of the 1842 Illinois gubernatorial election. Their support of Democrat candidate Thomas Ford— the lesser of two evils in their eyes—was vital to his election. The Whigs, whom the Saints had supported the past two years, were incredulous. While Whiggery was more opposed to Latter-day Saint interests than the Democrats were, both parties became convinced that the political future of Illinois lay in the staggering Latter-day Saint immigration. Immigrants became voting citizens in only six months and, under the Nauvoo Charter, in only sixty days for city elections. This increased the power of the Saints' voting bloc, yet their support was fickle. They no longer fit either party's calculus for political success but rather loomed as an unpredictable and unmanageable obstacle.[84]

Joseph could not evade the political realities and consequences of his situation and choices. His adversaries were strong, and not all came from outside the church. For example, future electioneer missionary Benjamin L. Clapp accused Joseph and Hyrum Smith of attempting "to take away the rights of the citizens" during the 1843 Nauvoo City Council election. Religion's claim on political choice denied deep-seated feelings of political freedom in the young republic, even among some Saints. Early church leader Oliver Cowdery became disaffected in part for this very reason. William Law, a member of the First Presidency, was just months away from a similar decision to part ways with the church.

During the August 1843 congressional elections, Law accused Joseph and Hyrum of political manipulation. Joseph had pledged his vote to Whig Cyrus Walker in a desperate exchange for legal help. Walker believed that if Joseph voted for him, so would all his followers, the pattern of the past three years. Walker and his Democrat rival Joseph Hoge campaigned strenuously in Nauvoo the week of the election, knowing that the Saints were the key to victory. Two days before the election, Hyrum addressed the Saints, declaring that the best interest of the people was to vote for Hoge. Law, himself a Whig, strongly objected, stating that he knew Joseph preferred Walker. Hyrum retook the stand and, with both hands holding up the Democrat ballot, shouted, "Thus sayeth the Lord" to a resounding cheer. The next morning on his way to protest at the Sunday worship meeting, Law confronted Joseph and Hyrum, whereupon Hyrum maintained that he had in fact received a revelation.

Joseph announced at the meeting, "I have not come to tell you to vote this way, that way, or the other." He went on: "The Lord has not given me Revelation concerning politics. I have not asked the Lord for it. I am a third party [and] stand independent and alone." Joseph said he intended to honor his commitment to vote for Walker but that the Whig had withdrawn "all claim to your [the Saints'] vote . . . if it will be detrimental to your interest as a people." Then Joseph addressed Hyrum's earlier declaration. "Brother Hyrum tells me . . . that he has had a testimony that it will be better for this people to vote for Hoge, and I never knew Hyrum [to] say he ever had a revelation and it failed. (Let God speak and all men hold their peace.)"[85] The reference to all men included Law. "I never authorized Brother Law to tell my private feelings," Joseph thundered. "I utterly forbid these political demagogues from using my name henceforth and forever."[86] Law was furious. The next day the Saints voted for Democrat Hoge, who won the election. Already disaffected with Joseph regarding Nauvoo's economics and unsure of the plural marriage revelation, Law now became politically estranged.[87]

However, unlike Oliver Cowdery and William Law, most Saints stayed politically loyal to their prophet. After talking with Joseph, the aforementioned Benjamin L. Clapp made a public apology, and the nomination meeting was "settled and mutual good feelings restored to all parties."[88] In the city election, Joseph was unanimously reelected mayor of Nauvoo along with his slate of candidates. In the Saints' view the right people were nominated to office because of their competence and loyalty and then were elected by church members in obedience to men whom they viewed as living prophets.

In September 1843 Joseph introduced the final priesthood ordinance. It also reflected elements of theodemocracy and aristarchy. He called it "the fullness of the priesthood," but it became commonly known as the "second anointing." This ordinance was a "promise of kingly powers and of endless lives. It was a *confirmation* of promises that worthy men could become kings and priests and that women could become queens and priestesses in the eternal worlds."[89] Joseph administered the ordinance to chosen members, making them kings and priests "in and over" the church.[90] Such "anointed ones" were necessary to rule the kingdom of God. Those receiving this ordinance were kings and priests endowed with the fullness of priesthood power, "given . . . all that could be given to men on the earth" and thus had the power of legitimate heavenly governance. According to Joseph, government had apostatized, just as religion had. Thus, with proper authority in ordained kings and priests, or "God's Anointed Ones," as they were referred to, the kingdom of God could be restored.[91]

On 28 September 1843, Joseph began administering second anointings. In time he conferred the ordinance on twenty men and their spouses.[92] At the same meeting Joseph created a "special council." It was no coincidence that this occurred in conjunction with the second anointings. An appendage of the Anointed Quorum, this was a protocouncil of the future Council of Fifty. It consisted of twelve church leaders who chose Joseph as president of the council by common consent. The prophet led the group in prayer, which included a petition "that his days might be prolonged until his mission on the earth is accomplished."[93]

*   *   *

As October 1843 approached, Joseph Smith could look back with admiration on the thirteen years of the church's beginnings. The fledgling church had blossomed into a community of more than twenty thousand on two continents. He had revealed doctrines to create a Zion society to prepare the world for the second coming of Jesus Christ. Yet this Zion had religious, economic, political, and social features that inflamed neighbors. New scripture, revelations, and doctrines, coupled with gathering converts under priesthood authority, seemed blasphemous and despotic to many Americans. Economic cooperation challenged free market capitalism. Continued rumors of polygamy denied traditional social values. Collective political power in the name of religion, unfettered to political party, was anathema in an age of powerful party politics. Consequently, the Saints were driven by force from New York, Ohio, and Missouri. Now Joseph's attempt to create Zion in Nauvoo, Illinois, was threatened. Sensing the coming conflict, the prophet and his new "kings and priests" sought a solution to maintain peace and secure Zion. By 1844 Joseph would decide to protect Zion by running for president of the United States.

NOTES

1. JSH, E-1:1754 (15 October 1843). Spelling and punctuation have been modernized for all historical quotations herein unless otherwise noted.
2. This and other quotations in this section are from Thomas, "Historical Sketch and Genealogy," 8–13.
3. See Cross, *Burned-Over District*; Hatch, *Democratization of American Christianity*; Abzug, *Cosmos Crumbling*; Kling, *Field of Divine Wonders*; and Quinn, "Joseph Smith's Experience."
4. JSH, A-1:5.
5. Book of Mormon title page.
6. Doctrine and Covenants 21:1.
7. See *Church History in the Fulness of Times*, 82; Van Wagoner, *Sidney Rigdon*; and Harper and Harper, "Van Wagoner's *Sidney Rigdon*," 261–74.
8. See Bushman, *Rough Stone Rolling*, 122.
9. See 3 Nephi 21:1, 23–24; 20:22; 22; Ether 13:3–6, 10; and Doctrine and Covenants 45:66–67.
10. Doctrine and Covenants 6:6; 11:6; 12:6; 21:7. See Isaiah 33:20; 52:1 for an Old Testament prophecy of the return of Zion.
11. Doctrine and Covenants 28:9.
12. See Doctrine and Covenants 97:19–21, 25. On the similarities and differences of Latter-day Saint millenarian thought with its contemporaries, see Cohn, *Pursuit of the Millennium*, 13; Bushman, *Rough Stone Rolling*, 166; and Underwood, *Millenarian World*, 30–41.
13. Moses 7:18–20. The Book of Moses came forth as a result of Joseph Smith's inspired revision of the Bible. See Matthews, *"Plainer Translation,"* 25–26.
14. See Doctrine and Covenants 38:27, 31–32.
15. JSH, D-1:1572 (11 June 1843).

16. The term *stake* is from Isaiah 54:2, describing the expansion of Zion: "Enlarge the place of thy tent, and let them stretch forth the curtains of thine habitations; spare not, lengthen thy cords, and strengthen thy stakes." Zion was to expand like a great tent, extending more curtains secured by stakes. See Bushman, *Rough Stone Rolling*, 176, 220.

17. See Doctrine and Covenants 42; 132.

18. Lorenzo Snow, Journal, 33.

19. Doctrine and Covenants 20:2–3.

20. For priesthood development, see Prince, *Power from on High*; Quinn, *Mormon Hierarchy: Origins*, Bushman, *Rough Stone Rolling*; and Doctrine and Covenants 13. For arguments on the date of the restoration of the Melchizedek Priesthood, see the works in this footnote and Lawson, "History of the Office of High Priest." For the official position of the church, see *Church History in the Fulness of Times*, 56; Porter, "Restoration of the Aaronic and Melchizedek Priesthoods," 33; and Doctrine and Covenants 107:1–5.

21. Edward Partridge was called by revelation as the first bishop in the church on 4 February 1831. See Doctrine and Covenants 41:9–10; see also 42:31, 34; 68:14. See also McKiernan and Launius, *Book of John Whitmer*, 66.

22. See JSH, A-1:118 (6 June 1831).

23. See Doctrine and Covenants 81:1–2.

24. See Doctrine and Covenants 102.

25. See Doctrine and Covenants 107:23–38.

26. See Bushman, *Rough Stone Rolling*, 160, 175, 203, 263, 265, 267.

27. See Doctrine and Covenants 110:11–16.

28. See Bushman, *Rough Stone Rolling*, 313–16; and *Church History in the Fulness of Times*, 166–67.

29. Doctrine and Covenants 132:37, 45. This revelation was recorded in 1843, but historical evidence shows that Joseph understood the doctrines and principles as early as 1831.

30. The description specified public buildings such as "houses of worship, schools, etc." Quoted in Bushman, *Rough Stone Rolling*, 220.

31. Bushman, *Rough Stone Rolling*, 220.

32. Section 42 of the Doctrine and Covenants was known as the "law of the Lord" and contained the divine laws required to build up Zion. On the law of consecration, see *Church History in the Fulness of Times*, 96–97, 99; Bushman, *Rough Stone Rolling*, 154–55; Parkin, "Joseph Smith and the United Firm," 4–66; and Doctrine and Covenants 72:9–15. On the Kirtland Safety

Society, see *Church History in the Fulness of Times*, 171–72; Bushman, *Rough Stone Rolling*, 331–32; Backman, *Heavens Resound*, 315–23; Shipps, "Mormons in Politics," 48; and Backman, "Kirtland Temple," 221.

33. See Doctrine and Covenants 101:76–89.

34. Minute Book 1, p. 42.

35. See Doctrine and Covenants 101:55–58.

36. See Doctrine and Covenants 105:2–13.

37. See *Church History in the Fulness of Times*, 177.

38. See Bushman, *Rough Stone Rolling*, 339; and Backman, *Heavens Resound*, 328.

39. See Jackman, "Short Sketch," 14:2–7; and Johnson, *Mormon Redress Petitions*, 246.

40. Oliver Cowdery to the high council at Far West, Missouri, 12 April 1838, in Minute Book 2, p. 120.

41. Rigdon, *Oration*, 12. See *Church History in the Fulness of Times*, 192.

42. See *Church History in the Fulness of Times*, 194; and Bushman, *Rough Stone Rolling*, 356–67.

43. Gentry, "Latter-Day Saints in Northern Missouri," 201. See *Church History in the Fulness of Times*, 197.

44. "Extract, from the Private Journal of Joseph Smith Jr.," 3. See *Church History in the Fulness of Times*, 197.

45. See *Church History in the Fulness of Times*, 195–96, 198.

46. Lilburn W. Boggs to John B. Clark, 27 October 1838, 61.

47. See Bushman, *Rough Stone Rolling*, 365; and *Church History in the Fulness of Times*, 204.

48. See Bushman, *Rough Stone Rolling*, 375–76; and *Church History in the Fulness of Times*, 202–8.

49. See Tanner, *John Tanner and His Family*, 92–94.

50. Joseph Smith, letter to Presendia Huntington Buell, 15 March 1839, in JSH, C-1:898[a].

51. See Esplin, "Significance of Nauvoo," 19–38. Lyman Wight claimed after Joseph's death that the prophet had said he did not expect to live to be forty; see *Wilford Woodruff's Journal*, 2:432.

52. JSH, C-1:1016; and Joseph Smith to Hyrum Smith and the Nauvoo High Council, 5 December 1839, in Smith, "Letterbook 2," 85–88. What exactly Joseph wanted the president to do is unclear. Perhaps he hoped that Van

Buren would mention the Saints in his written address to Congress. See *JSP*, D7:xxv–xxvi.

53. Smith, "Extract, from the Private Journal of Joseph Smith Jr.," 9.

54. Joseph Smith to Robert D. Foster, 11 March 1840, in *JSP*, D7:227.

55. Van Buren was the architect of the Jacksonian Democratic Party and was elected president in 1836, following two terms of orchestrating the election of Andrew Jackson. Van Buren's rejection of the Saints was particularly galling since many of them had campaigned for him. See Quinn, *Mormon Hierarchy: Origins*, 182. The Saints voted for all of Harrison's electors except Abraham Lincoln, whose name they replaced to include one Democrat.

56. Quinn, *Mormon Hierarchy: Origins*, 106.

57. See Kimball, "Nauvoo Charter," 40–47. Joseph was commissioned a lieutenant general, the only such rank for the period between George Washington and Ulysses S. Grant.

58. JSH, C-1:1131 (16 December 1840); and Kimball, "Nauvoo Charter," 40–47.

59. See Quinn, *Mormon Hierarchy: Origins*, 107. Shipps, in "Mormons in Politics," 56–57, observes: "Perhaps [in Liberty Jail] he realized that building Zion inside the boundaries of the United States required something more. . . . When the Mormons began at the beginning once again, Smith turned to politics in an effort to surround Zion with constitutional sanction." See also *Church History in the Fulness of Times*, 243.

60. See *Church History in the Fulness of Times*, 265. Most of the new arrivals were from the British Isles. The term *Anti-Mormon* as used here refers specifically to the political party. As Nauvoo grew, so did ties between the church and government. When the apostles returned in 1841, six of the seven were elected to the now-expanded city council. In 1842 Joseph received all but three votes for the new office of vice-mayor, and his brother William was elected to the state legislature. See Quinn, *Mormon Hierarchy: Origins*, 108–9.

61. See JSH, C-1:1147 (15 January 1841); and Bushman, *Rough Stone Rolling*, 413; and Smith, "Proclamation, 15 January 1841," *Times and Seasons*, 15 January 1841, 276.

62. Doctrine and Covenants 124:2.

63. Bushman, *Rough Stone Rolling*, 405; and Flanders, *Kingdom on the Mississippi*, 68.

64. See JSH, D-1:1424 (4 December 1842); and Leonard, *Nauvoo*, 204 and endnote 10. It was not until the Saints were settled in Utah that bishops became the presiding officers spiritually and temporally in wards.

65. See Jenson, *Historical Record*, 233; Compton, *In Sacred Loneliness*; and Bushman, *Rough Stone Rolling*, 437–46, 490–99.

66. Joseph Smith, "The Globe," *Times and Seasons*, 15 April 1844, 510. For a discussion of theodemocracy, see Hartshorn, Wright, and Ostler, *Book of Answers*, 7.

67. Joseph most likely began receiving revelations regarding the political kingdom of God on 7 April 1842. See Council of Fifty, Minutes, 10 April 1880.

68. JSH, D-1:1389 (29 August 1842).

69. Daniel 2:44; and Revelation 20:6.

70. Council of Fifty, Minutes, 10 April 1880.

71. See Quinn, "Council of Fifty," 1.

72. Smith, "Motto, circa 16 or 17 March 1838," in JSJ, 16 or 17 March 1838. See "History and Genealogy of John Chapman Duncan," 447 (the only reference I could find of the motto's use during the campaign).

73. Noah Webster, ed., *An American Dictionary of the English Language* (New York: S. Converse, 1828), s.v. "aristarchy."

74. Doctrine and Covenants 98:9–10.

75. Cleveland, "Female Relief Society of Nauvoo," 30 March 1842, 21.

76. Cleveland, "Female Relief Society of Nauvoo," 17 March 1842, 7.

77. Revelation 1:6.

78. See Joseph Smith's sermon known as the "King Follet discourse," delivered on 7 April 1844 and recorded in *Wilford Woodruff's Journal*, 2:384, especially the statement "And you have got to learn how to make yourselves God, king and priest, by going from a small Capacity to a great capacity to the resurrection of the dead to dwelling in everlasting burnings" (original spelling and punctuation preserved).

79. JSH, C-1:1338 (26 May 1842).

80. Smith, "Letter to the Citizens of Hancock County," *The Wasp*, 2 July 1842, 2.

81. "The Government of God," *Times and Seasons*, 15 July 1842, 856–57; emphasis added.

82. Smith, "Discourse, 21 February 1843," as reported by Willard Richards in JSJ under that date.

83. JSH, D1:1547 (6 May 1843).

84. See Hampshire, "Nauvoo Politics," 3:1000; and Nauvoo Charter, section 7.

85. JSJ, 6 August 1843.

86. JSH, E-1 (6 August 1843).

87. For more on the exchanges of these two days, see Cook, "William Law, Nauvoo Dissenter," 47–72; Wicks and Foister, *Junius and Joseph*, 45–46; and W. Wyl, "Interview with William Law in Shullsburg, Wisconsin, 30 Mar 1887," *Salt Lake Daily Tribune*, 31 July 1887, 6.

88. JSJ, 4 February 1843.

89. Leonard, *Nauvoo*, 260–61; emphasis added. See also JSH, E-1 (6 August 1843).

90. Ehat, "Joseph Smith's Introduction of Temple Ordinances," 74–75.

91. Heber C. Kimball, in journal kept by William Clayton, 26 December 1845, as quoted in Ehat, "Heaven Began on Earth," 3–4.

92. See Ehat, "Heaven Began on Earth," 3 and note 16. Four were future electioneer missionaries: Reynolds Cahoon, Alpheus Cutler, Levi Richards, and William W. Phelps.

93. JSH, E1:1738 (28 September 1843). The members of the protocouncil were Joseph Smith, Hyrum Smith, John Smith, Newel K. Whitney, George Miller, Willard Richards, John Taylor, Amasa Lyman, John M. Bernhisel, Lucien Woodworth, William Law, and William Marks.

CHAPTER 2

QUEST FOR THE PRESIDENCY—AND A KINGDOM IN THE WEST

You have seen it announced that Joseph Smith is a candidate
for the Presidency of the United States. Many think this is a hoax—
not so with Joe and the Mormons. . . . Joe is really in earnest.

—Correspondent of the *Missouri Republican*, 25 April 1844[1]

On 29 January 1844 church leaders nominated Joseph Smith for president of the United States. Joseph formulated his political views in a pamphlet titled *General Joseph Smith's Views of the Powers and Policies of the Government of the United States.* He had it distributed throughout the country, and many local, regional, and national newspapers commented on it. In the ensuing months, church leaders organized a systematic campaign to elect Joseph. On 9 April, the final day of the church's annual conference, they gave political instruction to more than a thousand men and asked for volunteers to become electioneer missionaries. Two hundred and forty-four responded immediately. Eventually more than six hundred were engaged in this new cause. Joseph's campaign was unlike any other in the history of the nation: the prophet-leader of a new faith pursuing the presidency with a cadre of supporters canvassing the nation for him. In the backdrop of the campaign was Joseph's evolving vision of theodemocracy, aristarchy, and the establishment of the kingdom of God.

"WHO SHOULD BE OUR NEXT PRESIDENT?"

On 1 October 1843, just three days after Joseph created his "special council" of trusted associates mentioned earlier, apostle John Taylor, a council member and editor of the Nauvoo newspaper *Times and Seasons*, asked in print, "Who Shall Be Our Next President?" The editorial was undoubtedly a distillation of the council's meeting. The election was "a question of no small importance to the Latter-day Saints," declared Taylor. He rehearsed the injustices of Missouri and the Saints' inability to receive redress from any level or branch of government. The special council had decided to enter national politics. "We make these remarks for the purpose of drawing the attention of our brethren to this subject, both at home and abroad," Taylor wrote. Church leadership was ready to decide "upon the man who will be the most likely to render us assistance in obtaining redress for our grievances—*and not only give our own votes, but use our influence to obtain others.*" Taylor concluded, "We shall fix upon the man of our choice, and notify our friends duly."[2]

Two nights later, Joseph and Emma Smith held a dinner party for more than one hundred couples, including those of the special council. As the evening ended, the attendees approved a list of resolutions. The contents of the resolutions delineated a discernible focus on a political Zion, with Nauvoo as its "emporium," the Nauvoo Charter as its standard for "protection of the innocent," the Nauvoo Legion as a "faithful band of invincibles" to defend it, and Joseph Smith—whether prophet, general, or mayor—the epitome of leadership.[3] Two weeks later, Joseph's preaching became decidedly more political. "I am the greatest advocate of the Constitution of the United States there is on the earth. . . . The only fault I find with the Constitution is it is not broad enough to cover the whole ground," he declared. The later manuscript history added, "In my feelings I am always ready to die for the protection of the weak and the oppressed in their just rights."[4]

Taylor's article produced a response within a month. In early November Joseph huddled with members of the special council to discuss a letter from John L. Heywood, a Latter-day Saint and future electioneer missionary. A Colonel Frierson had offered Heywood his Democratic political connections to persuade Senator John Calhoun and Congressman Robert Barnwell Rhett, both of South Carolina, to present a Latter-day Saint memorial to Congress. In return, Democrats expected support for Calhoun's expected run for the presidency.

Instead, Joseph wrote to each of the five likely candidates: Senator John C. Calhoun, General Lewis Cass, former vice president Richard M. Johnson, Senator Henry Clay, and former president Martin Van Buren. He asked, "What will be your rule of action relative to us as a people, should fortune favor your ascension to the chief magistracy?"[5] Joseph was looking for someone to rally the Saints to for quid pro quo protection. At this point, he was not committed to entering national politics himself. For example, in November Joseph received correspondence from newly baptized James Arlington Bennet, an influential easterner. Bennet offered to protect the Saints if the prophet helped him become governor of Illinois. Still dealing with accusations of political manipulation in the August election, Joseph forcefully declined: "Shall I, who have witnessed the visions of eternity, . . . shall I turn to be a Judas? . . . Shall I, who hold the keys of the last kingdom, . . . stoop from the sublime authority of Almighty God to be handled as a Monkey's cat's paw, and pettify myself into a clown to act the farce of political demagoguery? No, verily no!"[6]

In late December, letters from Cass, Clay, and Calhoun reached Nauvoo. Lewis Cass wrote, "I do not see what power the President of the United States can have over the matter, or how he can interfere in it." Clay's response also offered no assistance: "Should I be a candidate," the senator penned, "I can enter into no engagements, make no promises, give no pledges to any particular portion of the people of the United States." Calhoun opined, "According to my views, the case does not come within the Jurisdiction of the Federal Government, which is one of limited and specific powers."[7] The other candidates never replied.

That same month Missourians brazenly kidnapped and tortured a Latter-day Saint and his son. This exponentially increased Joseph's desire to protect himself and all Latter-day Saints.[8] He held a special council meeting, where it was decided to petition the federal government "to receive the city of Nauvoo under the protection of the United States Government."[9] "I prophesy, by virtue of the holy Priesthood vested in me, in the name of Jesus Christ," Joseph declared, "that if Congress will not hear our petition and grant us protection, they shall be broken up as a government."[10] A city ordinance created a police force to protect Nauvoo and the prophet. As anti-Latter-day Saint forces and threats grew, Joseph publicly lamented, "Is liberty only a name? Is protection of person and property fled from free America?"[11] One peril came from First Presidency member William Law. He accused Joseph of forming the police to intimidate him and others. Already economically and politically alienated, Law and his wife stopped attending Anointed Quorum meetings and protested plural marriage. Joseph dropped Law from the First Presidency, and estrangement over Zion between the two was complete. In a few months church leaders would excommunicate Law, who would respond by launching an opposition movement.[12]

As 1844 dawned, Joseph and the Saints were increasingly isolated politically.[13] On 2 January 1844, Joseph replied to Calhoun in the Nauvoo papers, and his caustic response was reprinted in newspapers nationwide. Whig papers delighted in Joseph's castigation of Calhoun. "All men who say that Congress has no power to restore and defend the rights of her citizens," he declared, "have not the love of the truth abiding in them."[14] On 19 January, Joseph expounded on the Constitution and the candidates for president. He entertained some guests on 28 January and "lectured to them on politics, religion, &c."[15] Politics—particularly national politics—was now on Joseph's mind daily.

GENERAL JOSEPH SMITH FOR PRESIDENT

The question posed in the *Times and Seasons* in October 1843—"Who shall be our next president?"—was answered by church leaders on 29 January 1844. Joseph met with the "Twelve Apostles, together with . . . Brother Hyrum and J[ohn] P. Greene . . . to take into consideration the proper course for this people to pursue in relation to the coming Presidential Election." This group was fundamentally the protocouncil of "priests and kings" formed in the autumn. They decided it was "morally impossible for this people . . . to vote for the reelection of President Van Buren." Nor could they vote for Henry Clay, whose counsel to them was to move to Oregon.[16] At this point Willard Richards moved "that we have independent electors and that Joseph Smith be a candidate for the next presidency and that we use all honorable means to secure his election."[17] The council unanimously agreed. Joseph responded confidently:

> If you attempt to accomplish this *you must send every man in the city who is able to speak in public throughout the land to electioneer and make stump speeches, advocate the Mormon religion, purity of election, and call upon the people to stand by the law and put down mobocracy.* David Yearsly must go. Parley P. Pratt to New York, Erastus Snow to Vermont, and Sidney Rigdon to Pennsylvania. After the April Conference we will have general Conferences all over the nation, and I will attend as many as convenient. *Tell the people we have had Whig and democratic Presidents long enough: we want a President of the United States. If I ever get into the presidential chair, I will protect the people in their rights and liberties.* I will not electioneer for myself. Hyrum, Brigham, Parley, and Taylor must go. . . . *There is oratory enough in the church to carry me into the presidential chair the first slide.*[18]

Joseph intended to send hundreds of men throughout the nation preaching *and* electioneering. He was already contemplating specific geographical assignments for the missionaries. His platform would be one of unity and universal protection of civil liberties. The April conference would launch a national campaign mobilizing Latter-day Saints to influence the electorate to vote for the prophet.

This was not a mere public relations campaign. The nomination called for independent electors eligible to represent Joseph in the electoral college, creating the necessary campaign infrastructure to have him elected.[19] To emphasize the blessing of heaven on the decision of that day, Joseph recorded what occurred that morning: "Captain White of Quincy . . . drank a toast, 'May Nauvoo become the empire seat of government!'"[20] Before retiring that night, Joseph began dictating to William W. Phelps his *Views* pamphlet.[21]

Views called for unity and lamented how the Constitution's promise of equal rights had been trampled by devious and immoral men: "*Unity is power*, and when I reflect on the importance of it to the stability of all governments, I am astounded at the silly moves of persons and parties to foment discord in order to ride into power on the current of popular excitement." Joseph praised the wisdom of the early presidents, a quality he believed had been lost. "Now, oh people! people!" he pleaded. "Turn unto the Lord and live, and reform this nation. Frustrate the designs of wicked men."[22]

He proposed reducing the membership and pay of Congress. Prison reform, stemming from his legal experiences in four states, was another tenet. Joseph also addressed the nation's biggest obstacle—slavery. Through financial redemption, he proposed abolishing it by 1850. The sale of federal land would "pay every man a reasonable price for his slaves" and thus "break off the shackles from the poor black man, and hire him to labor like other human beings." Joseph advocated a new national bank with branches in every state and territory. He also addressed the divided sovereignty of federalism and states' rights, which had hampered the Saints' efforts to obtain redress. More than any proposal, Joseph's determination to give the federal government more power grew from the unredeemed sufferings of the Saints.[23] "Give every man his constitutional freedom and the president full power to send an army to suppress mobs. . . . The governor himself may be a mobber; and instead of being punished, as he should be for murder or treason, he may destroy the very lives, rights, and property he should protect." The prophet supported Manifest Destiny—the doctrine that the United States was destined to stretch from the Atlantic to the Pacific Ocean. He believed Oregon "belongs to this government honorably" and called on the Union "to spread from east to the west sea." Joseph envisioned annexing not just Oregon but also, if they were willing, Texas, Mexico, and Canada.[24] He implored the people of the nation to "arise, phoenix-like," and "cheerfully help to [restore]" America's greatness. He then added, similar to what he had declared on 29 January 1844 after his council unanimously agreed to his candidacy, "We have had Democratic

GENERAL SMITH'S

VIEWS

OF THE POWERS AND POLICY OF THE

GOVERNMENT

OF THE

UNITED STATES.

NAUVOO, ILLINOIS:

PRINTED BY JOHN TAYLOR:

1844.

Joseph's electioneers distributed copies of this pamphlet throughout the nation. Photo by author. Document courtesy of Church History Library.

presidents, Whig presidents, a pseudo-Democratic-Whig president, and now it is time to have *a president of the United States.*"[25]

Joseph saw his candidacy simultaneously as unifying, restorative, and inspired. By deploring factionalism while advocating policies each party cared about, he appealed to voters across the political spectrum. Unsurprisingly, his central theme was unity—the underlining principle of Zion. Whereas political parties fragmented and disenfranchised, he would unite. His campaign was also restorative. God had sanctioned the American nation and her Constitution prepared by "wise men . . . raised up unto this very purpose."[26] Yet for Joseph, the nation and its leaders had become corrupted. "But . . . [it is] my determination to arrest the progress of that tendency . . . and restore the government to its pristine health and vigor."[27] Finally, Joseph understood his campaign as part of a divine plan. "I would, as the universal friend of man, open the prisons, open the eyes, open the ears, and open the hearts of all people, to behold and enjoy freedom— unadulterated freedom; and God . . . *should be supplicated by me for the good of all people.*"[28] Heaven and earth combined as Joseph chose words he also used to describe the kingdom of God: "Make HONOR the standard with all men; . . . and the whole nation, *like a kingdom of kings and priests, will rise up with righteousness, and be respected as wise and worthy on earth, and as just and holy for heaven.*"[29]

On 6 February 1844 John Taylor held a dinner party for the First Presidency, the ten apostles currently in Nauvoo, and their wives. With the group enthusiastic about Joseph's candidacy, the evening turned to "the propriety of establishing a moot congress for the purpose of investigating and informing ourselves on the rules of national intercourse, domestic policy, and political economy."[30] Willard Richards sketched out a hypothetical federal government. Brigham Young was president, with John Taylor as vice president and Richards as the secretary of state. Other apostles and Sidney Rigdon found themselves in cabinet positions or in the senate. Richards listed other names for "members of the house," representing each state and territory.[31]

The names read like a who's who of future Council of Fifty members and other electioneer missionaries. Of the forty-two nonapostolic names, only five would not serve as campaign missionaries. Most would labor in the same state on the list. Church leaders were already discussing not only who their electioneers would be but also where they would campaign. At some point that night, Joseph advised against creating this "moot organization and congress" for fear of "excit[ing] the jealousy of our enemies."[32] A month later Joseph changed his mind and created more than a moot congress—he organized the Council of Fifty, the genesis of the kingdom of God on earth.[33]

The men reconvened the evening of February 7 at Joseph's office to discuss "means to promote" the coming campaign and finishing *Views*. The next day, 8 February, they held a public political nomination meeting in the assembly room above Joseph's red brick store. William W. Phelps read *Views*, its first public reading. Joseph then declared, "I would not have suffered my name to have been used by my friends on anywise as president of the United States . . . if I and my friends could have had the privilege of enjoying our religious and civil rights as American citizens, even those rights which the Constitution guarantees unto all her citizens alike." Since no governmental hand had assisted the Saints, Joseph decided "to obtain what influence and power I can, lawfully, in the United States for the protection of injured innocence." He was willing to die to defend his people's liberties: "If I lose my life in a good cause I am willing to be sacrificed on the altar of virtue, righteousness, and truth in maintaining the laws and Constitution of the United States, if need be, for the general good of mankind."[34]

Some have used the statement "I would not have suffered my name to be used" out of context to argue that Joseph was not serious about his campaign. However, such language was common in contemporary politics where ambition for the presidency was a public faux pas. Furthermore, his words give the reasons for his campaign and reveal the ultimate price he was willing to pay—his own life.[35] His campaign was deadly serious. The apostles called for a vote in support of Joseph's candidacy and platform. It was affirmatively unanimous. The next night a similar session was held for others who could not fit in the room the day before. A third meeting occurred the following week. An editorial in the *Times and Seasons* declared, "There is perhaps no body of people in the United States who are at the present more interested about the issue of the presidential contest than are the Latter-day Saints." "Our course is marked out," it continued, "and our motto from henceforth will be General Joseph Smith."[36]

News of Joseph's campaign disturbed many non–Latter-day Saint residents of Hancock County. The Anti-Mormon Party held a county convention and publicized a "wolf hunt" around Nauvoo on 9 March—a direct threat to Joseph. With the scarring scenes of Missouri in his mind, the prophet immediately countered. Assembling the apostles, he raised the subject of fleeing the country entirely. Joseph instructed them to send a company to California and Oregon to find a location "where [they could] remove to after the temple [was] completed, and where [they could] build a city in a day, and have a government of [their] own."[37] This was a drastically different option than gaining protective political power through election. Joseph pragmatically began preparing the Saints' withdrawal from the United States so they could establish their own government—the theo-democratic kingdom of God.

The Twelve selected men for the exploring company. "Jonathan Dunham, Phineas H. Young, David D. Yearsley, and David Fullmer volunteered to go; and Alphonzo Young, James Emmett, George D. Watt, and Daniel Spencer were requested to go."[38] Ironically, except for Dunham, everyone in this original group instead became electioneer missionaries. Two days later Joseph instructed the Twelve to select others and stipulated that those selected must each must be a "king and priest" so that among the "savage nations" they would "have power to govern"—a direct allusion to second anointings. Joseph added, "If we don't get volunteers, wait till after the election."[39] Within a week twenty-four men enlisted to join the Western Exploring Expedition, as they named it. Thus Joseph simultaneously prepared to rally his followers and other voters to elect him president of the United States *and* to seek refuge in the West.[40]

Either option, the presidency or autonomy in the West, would provide the desired result—protection for Zion and her priesthood ordinances. On 25 February Joseph attended a meeting of the Anointed Quorum. They prayed that his *Views* "might be spread far and wide and be the means of opening the hearts of the people." He then prophesied "that within five years we should be out of the power of our old enemies, whether they were apostates or of the world; and told the brethren to record it, that when it comes to pass they need not say they had forgotten the saying."[41] He proved correct. In 1849 the Saints were safely creating Zion in the Great Basin. Joseph himself lay buried—a victim of assassination, largely because of his candidacy.

Church leaders mailed fifteen hundred copies of *Views* to the "president and cabinet, supreme judges, senators, representatives, principal newspapers in the United States, . . . and many postmasters and individuals."[42] The *Nauvoo Neighbor* for 28 February carried the headline "Joseph Smith for President." An article called for united campaigning: "It becomes us, as Latter-day Saints, to be prudent and energetic in the cause that we pursue, and not let any secondary influences control our minds or govern our proceedings." Electing the prophet was now "an imperative duty," requiring the Saints "to use all [their] influence at home and abroad for the accomplishment of this object." They would succeed "by lecturing, by publishing, and circulating his works, his political views, his honor, integrity and virtue . . . and present him before the public in his own colors, that he may be known, respected, and supported."[43] The cry "General Joseph Smith for President!" now became the primary mission of the church, its leaders, and its members.

A meeting of church leaders on 4 March 1844 nominated James Arlington Bennet as Joseph's vice-presidential running mate. As a national author, previous regional newspaper editor, and noted philanthropist, Bennet had the gravitas Joseph sought. Four months earlier Joseph had vehemently declined Bennet's political support. Then Joseph was dealing with the backlash of supporting his brother Hyrum's revelation in the congressional elections. At the time the prophet wanted his name out of politics. Further, Joseph was most likely suspicious of Bennet and his motives. But in March everything was different: no national candidate was coming to rescue the Saints, Joseph was leading a serious campaign for the presidency, and he and his associates were looking everywhere for political allies. Bennet now seemed more than palatable.

Writing to Bennet on the council's behalf, Willard Richards revealed the thoughts of Joseph's inner circle. He reported enthusiastic astonishment "at the flood of influence that is rolling through the Western States in his [Joseph's] favor, and in many instances where we might have least expected it." Joseph's candidacy seemed only logical given his role as God's prophet. "General Smith is the greatest statesman of the 19th century. Then why should not the nation secure to themselves his superior talents, that they may rise higher . . . and exalt themselves through his wisdom?" Bennet's earlier desire to have Joseph help him become governor of Illinois was "mere sport, child's sport." "For who would stoop to the play of a single State," Richards continued, "when the whole nation was on the board?"

While all nascent campaigns speak in confident tones, there was something different here—something divinely confident. Richards instructed Bennet: "If glory, honor, force, and power in righteous principles are desired by you, now is your time. You are safe in following the counsel of that man who holds communion with heaven; and I assure you, if you act well your part, victory's the prize." Success would occur as they "go to it with the rush of a whirlwind, so peaceful, so gentle, that it will not be felt by the nation till the battle is won." Richards gave Bennet his campaign role. "Get up an electoral ticket—New York, New Jersey, Pennsylvania, and any other state within your reach. Open your mouth wide, and God shall fill it. Cut your quill, and the ink shall flow freely." A special conference would convene on 6 April in Nauvoo, and then "our Elders will go forth by hundreds or thousands and search the land, preaching religion and politics; and if God goes with them, who can withstand their influence?" Two days later, the *Nauvoo Neighbor* added Bennet's name under Joseph's on its front-page banner.[44]

In Nauvoo, conversation everywhere centered on politics, even at religious meetings. On 7 March 1844, Joseph, William W. Phelps (his chief political adviser), and apostle John Taylor (his campaign manager) addressed an audience of eight thousand at the temple site. Joseph announced, "We are Republicans and wish to have the people rule, but they must rule in righteousness. Some would complain with what God Himself would do." The key for good rule was the righteousness of the people and the leaders—something the restored gospel produced. Phelps then read *Views*. The thousands assembled voted to support Joseph for the presidency "with one exception."[45] Joseph famously declared: "As to politics, I care but little about the presidential chair. I would not give half as much for the office of president of the United States as I would for the one I now hold as lieutenant-general of the Nauvoo Legion. . . . We have as good a right to make a political party to gain power to defend ourselves," he declared, "as for demagogues to make use of our religion to get power to destroy us. . . . As the world has used the power of government to oppress and persecute us," he continued, "it is right for us to use it for the protection of our rights." Joseph stated, "We will whip the mob by getting up a candidate for president." He overflowed with confidence. "When I get hold of the Eastern papers, and see how popular I am, I am afraid myself that I shall be elected," he proclaimed.[46]

The next day, church leaders received information that James Arlington Bennet was an immigrant from Ireland, making him constitutionally ineligible for the vice presidency.[47] Seeking a new candidate, they decided to write to Colonel Solomon Copeland, who had befriended the missionaries, including Wilford Woodruff, in Tennessee in the mid-1830s. The council instructed Woodruff to write a letter extending the invitation. Woodruff penned the document a week later. He outlined the Saints' suffering in Missouri and their inability to get any redress. "We deem it no longer necessary," he continued, "to use our influence promoting men to the highest offices of this government who will not act for the good of the people but for their own aggrandizement and party purposes." Instead, Woodruff wrote, they would have their own candidate, "and that candidate is General Joseph Smith." "And sir," Woodruff continued, "the request I wish to make of you is to know if you are willing to permit us to use your name as a candidate for vice president at the next Election." Woodruff included a copy of *Views* and invited Copeland to come visit Nauvoo. Copeland never responded.[48]

THE COUNCIL OF FIFTY:
THE CAMPAIGN AND THE KINGDOM OF GOD

On 9 March 1844, Joseph spent most of the frustrating day in his role as mayor. In a rarity, the city council voted against Joseph on an issue. Toward the end of the debate, Joseph stated: "It was the principles of democracy that the people's voice should be heard when the voice was just, but when it was not just it was no longer democratic, but if the minority views are more just, then aristarchy should be the governing principle; i.e., the wisest and best laws should be made."[49] Rule by aristarchy was more sensible than government by the popular or mistaken. Joseph's comments show he had decided the time had come to implement the revelation of almost two years earlier regarding the kingdom of God.

The next day, Sunday, 10 March, he preached on the need to obtain "endowments of the fulness of the Melchizedek Priesthood and of the kingdom of God," a theodemocratic theme. Late that afternoon Joseph gathered the apostles and other members of the protocouncil at the Nauvoo Mansion. They read two letters from apostle Lyman Wight and Bishop George Miller, leaders of the small colony in Wisconsin that provided lumber for the temple. A federal Indian agent had blocked proselytizing and lumber procurement. From Wight and Miller's viewpoint, the government was not only failing to protect Zion, now it was actively impeding it. They proposed increasing their colony and moving to the independent Republic of Texas. Joseph was intrigued. He asked the men around him, "Can this council keep what I say, not make it public?" They all assented. The time had come to begin organizing the kingdom of God. The group met again that night at the red brick store.[50]

The next day, 11 March, Joseph officially organized the kingdom of God in Henry Miller's home. Twenty-three men were present, including eleven future cadre members. The council had three immediate purposes: to discuss the idea of colonizing within the Republic of Texas, to seek "the best policy . . . to obtain their rights from the nation and ensure protection for themselves and [their] children," and to "secure a resting place in the mountains . . . where [they could] enjoy the liberty of conscience guaranteed to us by the Constitution."[51] "All seemed agreed," the minutes record, "to look to some place where we can go and establish a theocracy either in Texas or Oregon or somewhere in California."[52] The council was informally called the Council of Fifty, but the official, revealed name was "The Kingdom of God and his Laws, with the keys and power thereof, and judgement in the hands of his servants. Ahman Christ."[53] They admitted more members over the following days.

Every male to whom Joseph had given the second anointing and was thus a legitimate king and priest was placed in the Council of Fifty.[54] The theological underpinnings of temple ordinances were foundational to the council for at least two reasons. Anointed Quorum members had already made covenants not to discuss their endowments and so theoretically could be trusted. Also, members of the Council of Fifty needed the legitimate, governing authority of heaven that came from the temple ordinances. As the first meeting finished, the men of the council were elated. "The most perfect harmony prevailed during the whole of this council," the minutes state. "Many great and glorious ideas were advanced," William Clayton wrote in his journal, with the minutes agreeing that "the brethren all feel as though the day of our deliverance was at hand."[55]

In the view of the early Latter-day Saints, while the establishment of the United States and its Constitution were inspired, their roles were merely preparatory to the kingdom of God. Orson Pratt later explained, "A republic was organized upon this continent to prepare the way for a kingdom which shall have dominion over all the earth to the ends thereof."[56] On 12 May 1844 Joseph preached, "I calculate to be one of the instruments of setting up the kingdom of Daniel by the word of the Lord, and I intend to lay a foundation that will revolutionize the whole world."[57] While most modern Saints interpret this verse to mean the church, that is not what Joseph was declaring. The context clarifies that he was referring to an actual kingdom, the one he established two months before. Joseph would make this distinction clear to the Council of Fifty: "The kingdom . . . is an entire, distinct, and separate government," he taught. It "was not a spiritual kingdom, but was designed to be got up for the safety and salvation of the saints by protecting them in their religious rights and worship."[58] The expectation was that eventually the kingdom of God would spread theodemocracy to every nation and bring order to a chaotic world before and in the aftermath of the second coming.

The kingdom of God as Joseph envisioned it would tolerate and defend the religious freedom of the religions and societies that would persist in the first part of the Millennium.[59] Under this system of theocratic governance in a pluralistic society, people outside the church would "be admitted to the right of representation . . . and have full and free opportunity of presenting their views, interests and principles, and enjoying all the freedom and rights of the Council."[60] To this end, Joseph included three "gentiles" in the council: Uriah Brown, Edward Bonney, and Merius G. Eaton. Three of fifty members certainly did not fully represent pluralistic participation, yet the token accommodation was made in good faith.[61] Joseph was adamant about securing religious freedom for all. He expressed hope that every man in the council would, when aged, be able to say in retrospect that "the principles of intolerance and bigotry never had a place in this kingdom, nor in my breast" and would be "ready to die rather than yield to such things. . . . Only think! When a man can enjoy his liberties and has the power of civil officers to protect him, how happy he is." Joseph was so animated as he finished his discourse that the two-foot ruler he was "pretty freely" using "broke . . . in two in the middle."[62]

The Council of Fifty met once or more a week for the next two months. New members were added until their number reached fifty. The council sent ambassadors to Washington, DC, with petitions. They also sent Amos Fielding to England with unspecified overtures and Lucien Woodworth to Texas to negotiate establishing a Latter-day Saint colony in the Texas Republic. Reflecting the Council of Fifty's belief that they were more than a body to protect the church within the United States, Orson Hyde referred to the council members as "stand[ing] on the summit of all earthly power," and Parley P. Pratt referred to them as "the most exalted council with which our earth is at present dignified."[63] They were "not tied to any country"[64] because the prophet was "already president pro tem of the world"[65]—"God's messenger to execute justice and judgment in the earth."[66]

During his sermon on 24 March 1844, Joseph announced that he had uncovered a conspiracy to kill him, his family, and other church leaders. He named William Law and others as conspirators. The enmity between Law and Joseph was now public. At some point in the council's 26 March meeting, Joseph's mood turned sober. Several of the apostles recorded two months after his death what they remembered of the prophet's words:

> Brethren, the Lord bids me hasten the work. . . . Some important scene is near to take place. It may be that my enemies will kill me, and in case they should, and the keys and power which rest on me not be imparted to you, they will be lost from the earth; but if I can only succeed in placing them upon your heads . . . I can go with all pleasure

and satisfaction, knowing that my work is done, and the foundation laid. . . . Upon the shoulders of the Twelve must the responsibility of leading this church henceforth rest.

The record then states that Joseph and Hyrum Smith placed all the keys of authority on the Twelve. Joseph then continued: "I roll the burden and responsibility of leading this church off from my shoulders onto yours. Now, round up your shoulders and stand under it like men; for the Lord is going to let me rest awhile."[67]

In retrospect, Joseph's apparently self-evident declarations that "some important scene is near to take place" and "it *may* be that my enemies will kill me" were prescient.[68] The apostles may have remembered only the parts of his speech alluding to his possible death because it *had* in fact happened. No contemporary journals or other writings of that day, including the Council of Fifty minutes, attribute such sentiments to Joseph or mention any forebodings of approaching catastrophe. There did not seem to be serious concern about the prophet being killed. In fact, the events of the next three weeks would show the council members full of confidence in their plans to see him elected president. That the "important scene" would be Joseph's death was only one possibility among many. And the statement that the Lord was going to let Joseph "rest awhile" could mean he would have some greater responsibility outside the church, such as his current position as chairman of the Council of Fifty, or even president of the United States.[69]

As April conference approached, Joseph and the Council of Fifty were excitedly engaged—far from the melancholy of impending doom. They coordinated Joseph's presidential campaign, prepared for possible resettlement of Zion in the West, negotiated with other countries through ambassadors, and learned the ways of the kingdom of God so that they might become effective "kings and priests." All of this created an electric atmosphere as the long-awaited April conference drew near. On the eve of the conference, Joseph held Council of Fifty meetings on 4–5 April, and some of the ideas discussed would exuberantly flow into the discourses of the conference.[70] Lurking in the background were enemies, political and otherwise, plotting the destruction of Joseph and his Zion.

APRIL CONFERENCE 1844

The much-anticipated conference opened on 6 April 1844, the fourteenth anniversary of the church. Nauvoo swelled to almost twenty thousand Saints. Sidney Rigdon spoke first and, unsurprisingly, made union of church and state his theme:

> I recollect in the year 1830 I met the whole Church of Christ in a little old log house, . . . and we began to talk about the kingdom of God as if we had the world at our command. . . . The time has now come to tell you why we had secret meetings. We were maturing plans fourteen years ago which we can now tell. . . . When God sets up a system of salvation, he sets up a system of government. When I speak of government, I mean what I say. I mean a government that shall rule over temporal and spiritual affairs.[71]

Rigdon was straightforward: church and state were to become one. It was a topic that absorbed him. Not only had he addressed it in the Council of Fifty in a "spirited and animated manner,"[72] but he would return to it twice more in the April 1844 conference.

Next, apostle John Taylor spoke. He declared that the Founding Fathers and others created "kingdoms and empires that were destined to dissolution and decay." In comparison, the Saints were "laying the foundation of a kingdom that [should] last forever—that [should] bloom in time and blossom in eternity." To ensure his audience understood the gravity of the moment, he declared, "We are engaged in a greater work than ever occupied the attention of mortals."[73] While some preaching took place throughout the day, there was no doubt what was on the minds of the leaders of the church—the theology and politics of governance.

The next morning, Sunday, 7 April, Hyrum Smith addressed the congregation. "We are now the most noble people on the face of the globe, and we have no occasion to fear," he asserted. The reason for his exuberance, he declared, was that he had a "big soul." The Saints all had big souls. "As soon as the gospel catches hold of a noble soul, it brings them all right up to Zion." The prophet then stood. The congregation, amazed by what they had heard thus far, were about to be theologically stunned by the doctrinal crown of Joseph's teachings. What began as a funeral sermon for the recently deceased King Follett became an astonishing announcement: "God himself was once as we are now, and is an exalted man, and sits enthroned in yonder heavens! . . . And you have got to learn how to be gods yourselves, and to be *kings and priests* to God, the same as all gods have done before you, namely, by going from one small degree to another, and from a small capacity to a great one; from grace to grace, from exaltation to exaltation."[74]

The following day Joseph announced, "The whole of America is Zion, from north to south."[75] The temple was to be completed so that "men may receive their endowments and be made kings and priests unto the Most High God."[76] Zion was to grow throughout the Americas as endowed kings and priests built up branches and sent converts to Nauvoo for their endowments. This dovetailed with Joseph's campaign platform to annex Oregon, Mexico, and Canada.

As these three days ended, Latter-day Saints understood that they had "big" and "noble souls"—big enough to one day become gods. Meanwhile,

Engraving depicting the 6 April 1844 conference in Nauvoo, during which electioneer missionaries were called. Engraving ca. 1845 by Lloyd George (b. 1817) courtesy of Church History Library.

they were to become "kings and priests" through temple ordinances and to seek to convert the entire Americas. Furthermore, as the church grew, it was destined to govern not just spiritually but temporally. Church leaders would channel the feelings of exuberant eagerness at the conference into a determined, vibrant campaign for Joseph.

On the last day of the conference, 9 April, church leaders held the special meeting for the elders that the Nauvoo papers had announced for two months. Brigham addressed the congregation of more than eleven hundred. He challenged the elders to zealously build up the church and establish Joseph's political views. "We are acquainted with the views of Gen. Smith, the Democrats and Whigs, and all factions. It is now time to have a president of the United States. Elders will be sent to preach the gospel and electioneer. The government belongs to God. No man can draw the dividing line between the government of God and the government of the children of men."[77] Brigham roared, "This is a fire that cannot be put out. . . . We will turn the world upside down."[78]

The previous evening Hyrum had announced that the church leaders "calculate to send out about 1000 of you. Put 1000 el[ders] together and you can raise a hell on earth. You will have a great deal of knowledge. We want you to be successful."[79] Now Hyrum charged the potential missionaries to "[not] fear man or devil; electioneer with all people, male and female, and exhort them to do the thing that is right. We want a president of the U.S., not a party president, but a president of the whole people, . . . a president who will maintain every man in his rights."

Hyrum's call to action was buttressed by the desire to create both religious and political union. "I wish all of you to do all the good you can," he declared. "We will try and convert the nations into one solid union." He "despise[d] the principle that divides the nation into party and faction." Hyrum charged the electioneer missionaries, in words reminiscent of his candidate brother two months earlier, "Lift up your voices like thunder; there is power and influence enough among us to put in a president." Success would follow. "I don't wonder," Hyrum confidently finished, "at the old Carthaginian lawyer being afraid of Joseph Smith being elected."[80]

Brigham again stood. He "requested all who were in favor of electing Joseph to the presidency to raise both hands." All but one raised their hands. The audience spontaneously began "clapping their hands and gave many loud cheers" that echoed across the hilltop.[81] Never had there been more excitement in the leadership and ranks of the church than at this moment. The minutes record, "The dearest and biggest vote and the most unanimous vote that ever passed in the world went for Joseph to be president."[82] When the audience settled, Heber C. Kimball announced that conferences would be set up in each of the states to campaign for Joseph and to select delegates for a national convention. Whereas leaders had earlier counseled missionaries to not depart until their domestic situations were settled, the urgency of the campaign changed everything. "A great many of the elders will necessarily have to leave their families," Kimball said, "and the mothers will have to assume the responsibility of governing and taking care of the children to a much greater extent."[83] Amasa Lyman (a future cadre member) echoed the same sentiments two days later in a council meeting. He did "not think any sacrifice too great to make for the glories of this kingdom, even if it requires us to leave father, mother, wives, and children."[84]

Brigham then called for volunteers to preach and electioneer. "A great company moved out and returned to the right of the stand and were numbered."[85] It took an hour and a half for the clerks to process their names and information. In the end they recorded 271 names, covering three pages of minutes. Names of those who would serve for twelve months were written first, followed by those volunteering for six months, and then those serving three months. The leaders then adjourned the conference for an hour. When it reconvened, the names "were read and corrected" and "places [were] assigned for their missions."[86]

*   *   *

The nucleus of Joseph's electioneer missionaries was now prepared, called, and assigned. However, the cadre was smaller than expected. Church leaders had hoped for closer to one thousand. Only a quarter of the elders in the meeting had stepped forward. If the numbers greatly disappointed them, however, they did not express it at the time. In fact, Joseph recorded that the April conference had "been the greatest, best, and most glorious five consecutive days ever enjoyed by this generation."[87] The time had come for the electioneer missionaries to "turn the world upside down."[88]

NOTES

1. Correspondent of the *Missouri Republican* from Nauvoo, Illinois, 25 April 1844, as quoted in Baker, *Murder of the Mormon Prophet*, 190. This was reprinted in newspapers across the nation.

2. JSH, E-1:1771 (emphasis added); also *Times and Seasons*, 1 October 1843, 343–44.

3. JSH, E-1:1744 (3 October 1843).

4. JSJ, 15 October 1843; and JSH, E-1:1754 (15 October 1843).

5. Joseph Smith, "Letter to Presidential Candidates," 4 November 1843.

6. JSH, E-1:1778 (13 November 1843); also Joseph Smith to James Arlington Bennet, 13 November 1843.

7. For Cass's response, see Lewis Cass to Joseph Smith, 9 December 1843. For Clay's response, see JSH, F-1:28 (15 November 1843). Clay's letter was not made public until after his nomination as the Whig candidate in May 1844. For Calhoun's response, see JSH, E-1:1845–46 (2 January 1844).

8. On the kidnapping, see JSJ, 6 December 1843.

9. JSH, E-1:1798 (8 December 1843).

10. JSJ, 16 December 1843.

11. JSH, E-1:1804 (14 December 1843).

12. See Bitton, *Martyrdom Remembered*, 1; and JSH, E-1:1857 (8 January 1844).

13. For Joseph's desire to reach out to the non–Latter-day Saint community, see Bushman, *Rough Stone Rolling*, 227–30.

14. See JSH, E-1:1849.

15. JSJ, 26 January 1844.

16. See JSH, E-1:1869.

17. JSJ, 29 January 1844.

18. JSH, E-1:1868–70; emphasis added. There are a few details in this account that are not in Joseph's journal of the same date. For clarity of language and the fact that those who filled in the gaps were present that day, I have used this manuscript source.

19. The Joseph Smith Papers' historian Spencer McBride has recently come to the same conclusion. See McBride, "Joseph Smith's Presidential Ambitions," 21–30.

20. JSJ, 27 January 1844.

21. The pamphlet was Joseph's, but it was primarily written by W. W. Phelps. Joseph asked Phelps three days earlier to write a response to President Tyler's recent annual address to Congress. Undoubtedly, Phelps had been thinking or writing about many of the items that would eventually be in the pamphlet. See Tyler, "Message of the President of the United States," 1–4; and *Nauvoo Neighbor*, 27 December 1843, 1–2. John M. Bernhisel also seems to have contributed to the pamphlet. See JSH, E-1:1895 (20 February 1844).

22. Smith, *Views*, 4, 8; emphasis added.

23. Smith, *Views*, 8 passim.

24. Smith, *Views*, 10.

25. Smith, *Views*, 10, 11; emphasis in original.

26. Doctrine and Covenants 101:80.

27. Smith, *Views*, 8.

28. Smith, *Views*, 12; emphasis added. Joseph told a group of people when asked who he was that "Noah came before the flood, I have come before the fire." As reported by Abraham H. Cannon in Cannon, Diaries, 16:30.

29. Smith, *Views*, 9; emphasis added and original capitalization preserved.

30. *Manuscript History of Brigham Young*, 159.

31. See Richards, Proposed Plan for a Moot Organization and Congress.

32. *Manuscript History of Brigham Young*, 159–60.

33. See Council of Fifty, Minutes, 11 March 1844, in *JSP*, CFM:40.

34. JSH, E-1:1886 (8 February 1844). In a touch of irony, on this day when *Views* was first publicly read, Joseph's journal records, "Held Mayor's court, and tried two negroes for attempting to marry white women; fined one $25 and the other $5." JSJ, 8 February 1844.

35. See JSH, E-1:1886 (9 February 1844); and Taylor, "Who Shall Be Our Next President?," *Times and Seasons*, 15 February 1844, 439. Church historian B. H. Roberts argued that Joseph's candidacy was not serious; see Roberts, *Comprehensive History of the Church*, 2:209. His conclusions are now seen as outdated.

36. *Times and Seasons*, 15 February 1844, 440, 441.

37. JSJ, 20 February 1844.

38. JSH, E-1:1896–97 (21 February 1844).

39. JSJ, 23 February 1844.

40. Seventeen of the twenty-four would serve as electioneer missionaries. Most had not been anointed "kings and priests." Joseph may have been planning to give them the second anointing.

41. JSH, E-1:1898 (28 February 1844).

42. JSH, E-1:1898 (27 February 1844).

43. JSH, E-1:1900 (1 March 1844). The 1 March 1844 edition of the *Times and Seasons* also carried the banner "Joseph Smith for President."

44. Willard Richards to James Arlington Bennet, 4 March 1844, as found in JSH, E-1:1904 (4 March 1844). Bennet is not to be confused with James Gordon Bennett, the famous contemporary editor of the *New York Herald*.

45. JSH, E-1:1908 (7 March 1844).

46. JSH, E-1:1912 (7 March 1844).

47. This information about Bennet's immigrant status proved to be false. The son of Irish immigrants, he was born in New York. See Wilford Woodruff to Solomon Copeland, 9 March 1844.

48. There is no evidence that Solomon Copeland and his wife were ever baptized. Two of their slaves, Lewis and Robert Copeland, did join the church in 1836. See "Academy Tennessee Branch," *Amateur Mormon Historian* (blog). Some have assumed Solomon was a Latter-day Saint; see Winkler, "Mormon in Tennessee," 48.

49. Nauvoo Stake High Council Minutes, 9 March 1844.

50. JSJ, 10 March 1844.

51. JSH, E1:1928 (10 March 1844). Original members were as follows. Nonelectioneers: Joseph Smith, Hyrum Smith, Brigham Young, Heber C. Kimball, Willard Richards, Parley P. Pratt, Orson Pratt, John Taylor, George A. Smith, Levi Richards, Newel K. Whitney, and William Clayton. Electioneers: William W. Phelps, John M. Bernhisel, Lucien Woodworth, George Miller, Alexander Badlam, Peter Haws, Erastus Snow, Reynolds Cahoon, Amos Fielding, Alpheus Cutler, and Lorenzo D. Wasson.

52. *JSP*, CFM:40.

53. *JSP*, CFM:48 (14 March 1844). See Clayton, journal, 1 January 1845, as quoted in Ehat, "Heaven Began on Earth," 2; Andrus, *Joseph Smith and World Government*, 4; and Minutes of Council of Fifty, Saturday, 10 April 1880. The council was also referred to by other names, including "Special Council," "General Council," "Grand Council of the Kingdom of God," and "The Fifties." However, it was generally known as the Council of Fifty.

54. The lone exception, Isaac Morley, entered the council the next year.

55. *JSP*, CFM:44–45 (11 March 1844); and *Nauvoo Diaries of William Clayton*, 11 March 1844.

56. Orson Pratt, "The Kingdom of God," in *JD*, 3:73 (8 July 1855).

57. JSH, F-1:18 (12 May 1844).

58. *JSP*, CFM:128 (18 April 1844); and Brigham Young, "The Kingdom of God," in *JD*, 2:309–10 (8 July 1855).

59. See *JSP*, CFM:128 (18 April 1844).

60. Taylor, Revelations, 1882–1883, MSS 1266, 17 June 1882.

61. See Ehat, "Heaven Began on Earth," 4.

62. *JSP*, CFM:100, 101 (11 April 1844).

63. Orson Hyde to Joseph Smith, 9 June 1844, p. 1; and Parley P. Pratt to Joseph Smith and Quorum of the Twelve, 19 April 1844, p. 2.

64. George A. Smith, *JSP*, CFM:116 (18 April 1844).

65. Lyman Wight and Heber C. Kimball to Joseph Smith, 19 June 1844.

66. Orson Hyde to Joseph Smith, 9 June 1844.

67. See Hyde, "Statement about Quorum of the Twelve," ca. 8 September 1844 and March 1845.

68. Emphasis added.

69. Some assert that this 26 March 1844 meeting was actually a 22 or 23 March meeting of the Anointed Quorum. However, no evidence points to women in attendance, which would have been the case with a meeting of the Anointed Quorum. Furthermore, in the meeting Joseph declared that several attendees needed the endowment before the temple's completion, which would make no sense if this were an Anointed Quorum meeting, as by definition its members had already received their endowments (whereas 25 percent of the Council of Fifty were not endowed). Circumstantial evidence also points to this being a Council of Fifty meeting. During the succession crisis, some members of the Council of Fifty argued that the keys rested with them as well as with the Twelve.

70. See Van Orden, "William W. Phelps's Service in Nauvoo." The multiple options being considered by Joseph fit his pattern of seeking revelation to guide the church by first following the counsel to "study it out in your mind" (Doctrine and Covenants 9:8). See also Andrus, *Joseph Smith and World Government*, 45–46.

71. "Conference Minutes," *Times and Seasons*, 1 May 1844, 522–24.

72. *JSP*, CFM:73 (26 March 1844).

73. "Conference Minutes," *Times and Seasons*, 15 July 1844, 578. In a Council of Fifty meeting the following week, Hyrum Smith would say, "We have greater power and are called to a greater work" than even that of Moses and Enoch. *JSP*, CFM:93 (11 April 1844).

74. JSH, E-1:1957–58, 70–71 (7 April 1844); emphasis added.

75. JSH, E-1:1982 (8 April 1844).

76. JSH, E-1:1982 (8 April 1844).

77. JSH, E-1:1993 (9 April 1844).

78. General Church Minutes, 9 April 1844, 35.

79. General Church Minutes, 8 April 1844, 32.

80. JSH, E-1:1995–96 (9 April 1844).

81. JSJ, 9 April 1844.

82. General Church Minutes, 9 April 1844, 36.

83. JSH, E-1:1998 (9 April 1844).

84. *JSP*, CFM:103 (11 April 1844).

85. Roberts, *History of the Church*, 6:325. See also *Manuscript History of Brigham Young*, 165.

86. JSJ, 9 April 1844. The minutes record the name of each volunteer and the state he was to labor in. Some names are underlined to indicate that they have not been assigned. Several assignments are crossed out and new ones recorded, corroborating that the names were read and corrected. The change in assignments was most likely from the church leaders. Joseph's journal says 244 volunteered. However, in Thomas Bullock's minutes, there are 277 names. Six are either crossed out or are repeats, leaving the number at 271. See "Minutes and Discourses, 6–9 April 1844," pp. 37–39, https://www.joseph smithpapers.org/paper-summary/minutes-and-discourses-6-9-april-1844 -as-reported-by-thomas-bullock/40.

87. JSH, E-1:2000 (9 April 1844).

88. General Church Minutes, 9 April 1844, 35.

CHAPTER 3

CALLED AND SENT FORTH: ELECTIONEER PROFILES

I cannot do justice to the feelings of my heart, but acknowledge the tender mercies increasing my lot in company with these brethren . . . on my way to perform this important mission [to campaign for Joseph Smith], the faithful and acceptable performance of which involves my future prosperity in church life.

—Franklin D. Richards, 27 May 1844[1]

Electioneer Experience: Franklin D. Richards. At the April 1844 conference, twenty-three-year-old Franklin D. Richards and his brother Samuel, age nineteen, received assignments to electioneer with Amasa Lyman, copresident of the Indiana campaign. A month later, their uncle, apostle Willard Richards, insinuated that their campaigning missions would extend to England. The next day, 4 May, their twenty-five-year-old cousin Ed Pierson arrived in Nauvoo from Massachusetts. Accompanying him were missionary companions Elijah F. Sheets and Joseph A. Stratton, who had just completed an assignment back East in which they baptized more than one hundred converts. On 5 May Brigham Young formally extended the Franklin brothers' mission to England, to be undertaken after the campaign. With the poor timing of a young husband, Franklin "revealed the fact of [his mission] appointment to the family" at a wedding celebration.

The news shocked his young bride of less than two years, causing her "considerable sorrow of heart" to the point of "weep[ing] openly for a day or two." On 13 May, Franklin, excited about his upcoming mission, went to hear "Elder Taylor lecture on Politics." At the 17 May state convention for Joseph, Brigham ordained Franklin and Stratton high priests and gave them "letters of introduction and licenses." Four days later at six o'clock in the morning, Franklin and fifty to sixty other electioneers boarded the steamboat *Osprey* to head to their various assignments in the East. The group included his brother Samuel, Stratton, Sheets, and Pierson, as well as apostles Brigham Young, Heber C. Kimball, and Lyman Wight.[2]

Franklin D. Richards was one of more than six hundred electioneers who campaigned for Joseph. Daguerreotype ca. 1850–60 by Marsena Cannon. Courtesy of Church History Library.

*   *   *

The departure of this early group of electioneer missionaries illustrates church leaders' efficiency in calling and assigning them, as well as the faithful responsiveness of those called. Franklin and Samuel Richards were among the original campaigners, yet their major change in assignment was met with excitement and firm resolve. Sheets, Stratton, and Pierson arrived in Nauvoo in early May expecting to spend the summer there, yet in less than three weeks they were headed back East as electioneers—Stratton to Delaware, Sheets to Maryland, and Pierson back to Massachusetts. Sheets wrote, "[The call] came rather unexpected to us, but we took courage."[3] At St. Louis the group, having swelled to nearly one hundred, split in different directions. Their arrival was published in the *St. Louis Era* on 31 May. Newspapers from Maine to Louisiana and in the political centers of New York City, Philadelphia, and Washington, DC, reprinted the news that the electioneer missionaries were coming. The Richards brothers, Stratton, Sheets, Pierson, and others took the steamer *Louise Phillipe*, destined for Pittsburgh, while the rest continued south.

Over the next several weeks, the Richards group crisscrossed the eastern states to their different assignments, working together, separately, or with new recruits. The latter included such men as Samuel H. Rogers and James H. Flanigan, who had already been proselytizing and had switched their efforts to campaigning. Occasionally they interacted with "field" electioneer missionaries like Thomas King and James Greig. These were Saints who joined the campaign effort in towns and cities across the nation, bringing with them their diverse abilities and local knowledge. Whether they were called in the April 1844 church conference, dispatched later from Nauvoo, transferred from proselytizing missions to campaigning, or recruited in the field, members of the growing cadre for the kingdom of God all shared a passionate desire to establish Zion and elect Joseph Smith as president of the United States.

THE CALL TO SERVE

Between the request for volunteers on 9 April 1844 and the publishing of names in the Nauvoo newspapers a week later, the number of electioneer missionaries grew from 271 to 336.[4] Church leaders, looking for more, continued to recruit in Nauvoo and the surrounding communities. The search for help extended across the nation as scheduled conferences of the church netted recruits. In all, at least 621 electioneer missionaries campaigned in all twenty-six states and the territories of Wisconsin and Iowa.

In deciding whom to count as an electioneer missionary, it is helpful to turn to a statement by campaign manager and apostle John Taylor. In the 28 February 1844 edition of the *Nauvoo Neighbor*, he urged the Latter-day Saints "to use all [their] influence at home and abroad for the accomplishment of [electing Joseph] . . . by lecturing, by publishing, and circulating his works, his political views, . . . and present[ing] him before the public in his own colors, that he may be known, respected, and supported."[5] Obviously this appeal applied to those who would volunteer to be electioneer missionaries as well as to those who circulated Joseph's political platform via church newspapers. It also applied to the chosen electors and delegates in states that held their conventions before the campaign ended. Naturally there are overlaps in these categories, but the vast majority of electioneer missionaries were the volunteers and those formally called as such. In any event, Taylor's words clearly encapsulate the defining work of the electioneers.

The call to serve as an electioneer came in four distinct ways. The majority, 336 or 54 percent, volunteered or were selected during or just after the April conference. The Twelve asked the initial 271 to indicate which state they wished to labor in. Most chose their birth state; others chose a different state or expressed no preference. As a result of up-the-line review, a few had their initial choice crossed out and a different state written in. When the *Times and Seasons* list of 15 April appeared, most of the electioneers retained their requested assignments. The Twelve appointed one or two missionaries as presidents for each state. These men were responsible for publishing Joseph's *Views* and holding periodic conferences to organize missionary work, assign individual electioneering tasks, and prepare state conventions in which electors would be chosen to represent Joseph in the electoral college.

English convert Alfred Cordon was among this first group of electioneer missionaries. On 9 April he recorded, "The conference was . . . then delivered into the hands of the Twelve and after a few remarks, they called upon all the brethren that could go and leave their families to go on a mission, some for 3, 6, or 12 months. I had a strong desire to go out in the vineyard and labor, but I had no means of leaving my family, no, not for one month." The next week on 15 April, Cordon went down to the docks to greet arriving English converts. There apostle Heber C. Kimball approached him "and told [him] that the Twelve had set [him] apart to go to the state of Vermont." Surprised, Cordon replied he would go if that was their will. Arriving at home, he presented the matter to his wife, who faithfully replied, "Go and fulfill the work you are called unto." Less than three weeks later, Cordon's little family hunched over their table to eat the last of their food, unable to collect debts owed to Cordon. "I laid my hands on my wife and children and blessed them," Cordon recorded, "[and] committed them to the keeping of the Eternal God, and on the fourth of May I started on my mission."[6]

The second set of missionaries volunteered or received their calls in or near Nauvoo after the selection of the initial group. This second group consisted of 145 men, representing 23 percent of the total, including those working in and around Nauvoo in official campaign roles. Norton Jacob, David Fullmer, and Moses Smith were three such missionaries. They departed for Michigan on 14 May 1844 in a carriage with Charles C. Rich, president of the Michigan campaign. Curiously, like Rich, all three men had no previous connections to Michigan. However, they were all neighbors in northeast Nauvoo. Most likely, Rich, a member of the Council of Fifty, recruited them to serve with him. Jacob's journal records that "at the spring conference 1844 Br. Joseph directed [that] all the elders of Israel should go into the vineyard. [Joseph] had previously been nominated for president of the United States, and part of the business of the elders would be to set forth his claims to the people."[7] Charles Rich and David Fullmer had worked together on two high councils, and Moses Smith and Norton Jacob were close neighbors who spent their entire mission as companions.[8]

Those of the third group of electioneer missionaries were already serving missions away from Nauvoo and shifted their efforts to Joseph's campaign. There were at least twenty-three such missionaries, representing 4 percent of the cadre. One was Crandell Dunn, who was serving in Michigan at the time he met up with cadre members Ezekiel Lee, Ira S. Miles, Samuel Bent, and Graham Coltrin in Kalamazoo, Michigan, on 28 May. Three days later apostles George A. Smith and Wilford Woodruff arrived and privately met with Dunn, giving him "instructions about Joseph Smith, [the] presidency, and his claims." The next day Dunn was electioneering.[9] On 22 May, David S. Hollister, a member of the campaign's central committee, found Irish convert and missionary James H. Flanigan in Wilmington, New Jersey. That night they gave a lecture on religion and politics. Thereafter Flanigan continued preaching politics throughout the mid-Atlantic states.[10]

Samuel H. Rogers, Flanigan's original missionary companion, had prepared him for such a transition. Having left Nauvoo together in April 1843, a year later they were working in different parts of the mid-Atlantic.

On 21 April 1844, Rogers wrote to Flanigan to encourage his former companion: "Let us fight manfully for King Immanuel. Let all that we do be for the establishment of Zion." Rogers then turned to his new focus of Joseph's campaign. "[Let] us use our endeavors at the ensuing election to get General Joseph Smith the presidential chair of this nation," wrote Rogers, "for he will fill the office as the chief magistrate with dignity and with greatness [and] honor to the nation [better] than any other man in the union. . . . Hereafter our motto is General Joseph Smith for president." Flanigan wrote back, "Be faithful. The cause is good. . . . Vote for Joseph Smith as president."[11]

The final subset of electioneer missionaries consisted of Saints from throughout the nation who either volunteered or were called by members of the cadre. One hundred and fifteen, or 19 percent, of the electioneer missionaries were part of this group. Most often, cadre leaders found or called these men at the conferences held in the states. On 2 July 1844 in Boston, James H. Glines attended a "meeting of the priesthood by invitation," where "much instructions and council was given, and the spirit of the Lord was made manifest." Apostles Heber C. Kimball and Orson Hyde ordained Glines an elder. Then Brigham appointed him to a mission in his native New Hampshire "to preach the gospel and electioneer for Joseph Smith to be the president of the United States." Glines headed for Haverhill, New Hampshire, and made appointments to "speak in favor of the election of the Prophet and of the powers and policy of the government of the United States."[12] Milton Holmes and his father, the branch president of the Georgetown Massachusetts Branch, had for several years chosen not to gather to Nauvoo, much to the chagrin of church leaders. Yet in June 1844 Milton campaigned in Maine with former missionary companion apostle Wilford Woodruff. They had not seen each other for five years. Woodruff recorded, "It was quite a treat to enjoy his company once more."[13]

Regardless of how they were called, many of the electioneer missionaries served with companions they knew. One hundred and thirteen, or 18 percent, worked with family members. Others companioned with close friends from Nauvoo or even former missionary companions. Erastus Snow even took his mother to visit family in Rhode Island on the way to his assignment in Vermont.[14]

A SEASON OF FAREWELL

From 10 April 1844 (when Lorenzo Snow departed for Ohio) until mid-June, hundreds of electioneer missionaries left Nauvoo. Many, like Jacob Hamblin, recorded a sense of excitement. A lowly miner, Hamblin embraced the church in 1842 and became an elder. Hamblin wrote that during the April 1844 conference, "the Quorum of the Twelve Apostles called on the seventies that could leave their families and go on a mission to different parts of the United States to hold forth the prophet Joseph Smith as candidate for the president of the United States." He remembered, "I felt anxious to go on such a mission." Lyman Stoddard, who taught and baptized Hamblin, recommended him. Apostles George A. Smith and Amasa Lyman consequently ordained Hamblin a seventy. They "appointed [Hamblin] to the state of Maryland with Elder Stoddard." Before leaving, Hamblin journeyed "to Wisconsin to see if [he] could convince [his] father's folks of the gospel." To his surprise they had moved to a farm in Iowa, just thirty miles northwest from Nauvoo. Unsuccessful in his attempt to bring them into the church, he returned to Nauvoo. "After a few days [he] started on [his] mission in company with John Myers, as Elder Stoddard had been sent to another source."[15]

Levi Jackman remembered that "Joseph wanted a large number of elders to go out on missions, and I concluded to go."[16] He left 5 June 1844 with Enoch Burns. Norton Jacob, writing eight years later, noted, "Br. Joseph [Smith] directed that all the elders of Israel should go into the vineyard. He had previously been nominated for president of the United States, and part of the business of the elders would be to set forth his claims to the people."[17] James W. Phippin recorded a decade later that "at the April conference 1844 a call was made for volunteers to go into every state of the union to preach and spread abroad the views of Joseph Smith relative to the policy of the government."[18] He departed for New York with Samuel P. Bacon on 18 April. Ira N. Spaulding remembered, "I was counseled to go into the state of Ohio, into Lucas and Richland Counties, amongst my friends to gain an influence among them in favor of President Joseph Smith being elected president of the United States."[19]

Most electioneer missionaries left behind families, often at great sacrifice. Heber C. Kimball made it clear in the April conference that poverty or family concerns were not to hinder men from campaigning. James C. Snow and Alfred Cordon left their wives and children without even a pound of flour. They departed only after their wives insisted that God would provide for them.[20] Some electioneer missionaries sold family heirlooms or other valuables to finance their missions.[21] Before leaving, John Tanner handed Joseph the two-thousand-dollar note still owed him from Kirtland, saying, "Brother Joseph, you are welcome to it." Joseph responded, "God bless you, Father Tanner; your children shall never want bread."[22] Several missionaries were widowers who entrusted their children to the care of neighbors or friends, or simply left them on their own. John Blanchard left behind nine of his eleven children, aged three to twenty, in order to fulfill his mission. A widower for the second time just two months previous, Jacob Morris left his two children behind. More than a dozen of the missionaries were newlyweds, including some who married just weeks and even days before departing. More than seventy electioneers left wives who either were pregnant or had newborn children.[23]

Thirteen cadre members took their wives with them, and at least four of the wives gave birth during their husbands' missions.[24] Jacob Gates, Lewis Robbins, and Crandell Dunn had their wives accompany them on their earlier preaching missions that were now focused on campaigning for Joseph Smith.[25] David L. Savage took his young wife Mary to help her deal with the recent loss of their first child.[26] The most intriguing couple to go was Moses and Nancy Tracy, who took with them their four children, ages two through ten. When Moses received his call, Nancy desired to accompany him and let her parents and in-laws meet their grandchildren for the first, and possibly only, time. Moses counseled with Joseph, who not only sanctioned Nancy's going but also told Moses she would "prove a blessing to him" during his mission. Joseph was correct. Nancy, an educated schoolteacher and naturally more extroverted than her husband, helped teach the gospel and campaign for Joseph's candidacy in New York.[27]

Missionaries expressed mixed emotions at saying goodbye to family and friends to head into an uncertain future. Several mentioned tender farewells at the waterfront of the Mississippi as they boarded steamboats.[28] John D. Lee perhaps best penned their feelings: "I took leave of our beautiful city on board of the steamer Osprey. . . . The importance of my mission came rushing into my mind, banishing grief and anguish!! . . . I lifted up my voice in supplication to the author of all good, demanding protection at his hand in behalf of myself and family. . . . I touched forth into the wide field of our labor perfectly calm and tranquil following my chief leader (Christ) and fearing no danger."[29]

Only a handful of missionaries that were assigned to serve away from eastern Illinois never left Nauvoo.[30] William L. Watkins's unnamed companion would not join him, so Watkins stayed in Nauvoo. Joseph L. Robinson, assigned to his native New York, was preparing to leave in early June when the Saints destroyed the press of the *Nauvoo Expositor*, a newspaper hostile to the church. Because of the tumult that followed, on 9 June during Sunday services "patriarch Hyrum Smith came upon the stand and said he did not want any more elders to go out upon this electioneering mission, as there was a storm brewing and he wanted all that was here to stay at home." Robinson remained in Nauvoo, though he reported, "There were two brethren . . . who went to Brother Hyrum and begged to go as they were preparing to take their wives with them to New York and were anxious to go. He told them to go if they wanted to, so they went but never came back again."[31]

Four electioneer missionaries assigned to Illinois returned to Nauvoo after the *Expositor* affair but before Joseph's assassination: Daniel Allen, David Lewis, Stephen Markham, and Elijah Swackhammer. A few even returned from other states before Joseph's murder. George W. Langley left sometime in May for his native Tennessee and, after baptizing a convert, returned to Nauvoo—all in two weeks. Jacob Gates and Robert T. Burton, serving missions before Joseph's campaign, both returned before Joseph's death—Gates in late May and Burton in early June. Council of Fifty member Jedediah M. Grant returned early from Michigan.

ELECTIONEER MISSIONARY PROFILE

The average electioneer missionary was thirty-five years old, three years younger than Joseph. The oldest, sixty-six-year-old Samuel Bent, was born just two years after the signing of the Declaration of Independence. The youngest was sixteen-year-old Charles H. Basset, who died in 1907. The last to pass away was Harley Mowrey (Morey) in late 1920 at the age of ninety-eight. Seventy-five percent of the electioneers were married. The average length of the electioneers' church membership in 1844 was six years. The average field missionary, however, had been a member of the church only half that time. John W. Roberts and Ezra Thayre of Nauvoo were baptized within six months of the church's organization. Field missionary Breed Searle chose baptism on 3 May 1844, in the middle of the campaign. He hosted a campaign conference a month later.[32]

Eighty-eight percent of the electioneers were born citizens of the United States. Two-thirds were born in the New England states, New York, Pennsylvania, or Ohio (not surprising since early missionary work centered in these states). Twelve percent consisted of immigrants, slightly higher than the contemporary national figure of 9.7 percent.[33] Missionary successes in Canada and Great Britain, coupled with the call for converts to gather to Nauvoo, explain the higher percentage. Of the immigrant electioneers, nineteen were born in Canada, fifteen in Great Britain, five in Ireland, and four in Germany. One-third of the electioneer cadre served in their birth states; others served in states where they had lived for a period of time. Wisely, campaign leaders assigned missionaries where they would have the most influence.

Surprisingly, only 36 percent of the campaigners had served a previous mission for the church. Yet Amasa Lyman and Erastus Snow had already served eight missions each. Those from the Nauvoo area had previous missionary service at a ratio of two to one compared to field missionaries.[34] Those that served previously had preached in neighboring towns and in distant states of the Union, in Canada, and even in Great Britain. Some, such as Benjamin Winchester in Pennsylvania and William I. Appleby in the mid-Atlantic states, were fortunate to see converts baptized by the hundreds. Others, such as Joseph Curtis, struggled to spread the gospel. As he stumbled through his first sermon, the listeners coldly told him to stop preaching and go home. Many cadre members' earlier missions resulted in the conversion of men who would become electioneer missionaries themselves. At least seventy men joined the church through the efforts of their future cadre colleagues, and some of these close relationships continued in the form of electioneer companionships.

Some electioneers experienced persecution in their previous missions. A mob beat Benjamin Brown and Jesse W. Crosby, leaving them for
dead. Simeon A. Dunn also narrowly escaped death at the hands of a mob.
Joel H. Johnson's companion Joseph Brackenbury died from poisoning by
enemies in 1832—the first Latter-day Saint missionary to die while serving. Johnson defended his dead companion's body when members of the
mob offered a reward for digging up and mutilating the corpse. Alfred D.
Young's life was spared when Davy Crockett's nephew's gun, pointed at his
face, did not discharge.

Members of the electioneer cadre had diverse experiences and backgrounds. Daniel Allen was a descendant of Revolutionary War hero Ethan
Allen. In fact, many electioneers had fathers and grandfathers who had
fought in the Revolutionary War or the War of 1812. Ezekiel Lee and
Reynolds Cahoon had served in the latter conflict. William G. Goforth's
father was a nationally renowned physician, Julius Guinard was the
grandson of the president of the College of New Orleans, and the father
of William R. R. Stowell was an eminent lawyer who argued before the
Supreme Court. Others came from humbler backgrounds. Enoch Burns
and John D. Lee suffered abuse and were deserted as children. William L.
Watkins, who was seventeen at the time of the campaign, had suffered an
accident fifteen years earlier that left him with a crippled leg. After his father died while immigrating to the United States, George D. Watt suffered
from depression, experiencing regular suicidal thoughts.

These dissimilar upbringings merge in the stories of Elijah F. Sheets and
Edward Hunter. A wealthy Quaker who lived in Pennsylvania, Hunter built
what he named the West Nantmeal Seminary. It was a finely constructed
building open to preaching for all denominations. To help work his five-
hundred-acre farm, Hunter took in eight-year-old Sheets, an orphan from
the age of six. Sheets lived with and worked for Hunter nine years before
apprenticing to a local blacksmith in 1840. That same year both Hunter
and Sheets joined the church. They began supporting its missionary work
immediately, Sheets as a missionary and Hunter with his wealth.

Though diverse, the electioneer cadre constituted a unified group of
mature, mostly married men trusted to serve because of their loyalty to
Joseph and the church. A third of them had already proved faithful and

diligent in missionary work. Church leaders specifically selected the electioneer missionaries to serve in areas of the nation they were familiar with so they could have increased influence among the people. In this way Joseph and the other leaders maximized the potential of the cadre to influence Latter-day Saints and the general electorate to embrace his platform and help propel him into the presidency. Joseph, confident of divine intervention to aid the cause, was in this election to win. He believed his cadre of electioneer missionaries would be the vanguard of that intervention.

RELIGIOUS BACKGROUNDS

The electioneer missionaries came from varied religious backgrounds (see table 3.1). Several had been ministers in other faiths, and a significant minority had been Methodists, the denomination Joseph favored before his first vision. Coincidentally, several electioneers had spiritual struggles similar to Joseph's while deciding which denomination to join, only to have a certain experience convince them to become Latter-day Saints.

Table 3.1. Electioneers' Previous Religious Affiliation*

Methodist	28%	Anglican	5%
Baptist	17%	Presbyterian	5%
Nondenominational	15%	Congregationalist	3%
Quaker	9%	Restorationist	3%
Radical Sects	6%	United Brethren	3%
Campbellite	5%	Universalist	2%

* Documentation for previous religious affiliation exists for only 65 electioneers, or 11% of the total.

Several electioneer missionaries converted to the church after experiencing visions or dreams or hearing spiritual voices. After reading the Book of Mormon for the first time, Samuel Bent saw a vision that showed him that the fulness of the gospel would be revealed in conjunction with the Book of Mormon and that he would be an instrument in proclaiming that message.[35] In a dream, Jonathan O. Duke witnessed his wife accepting the restoration of primitive Christianity, which he had denied. Startled by the vision, Duke immediately embraced the church.[36] On his way to South America in search of better health, Chapman Duncan heard a voice telling him to go no farther south than St. Louis or "you shall die." Turning and seeing no one, Duncan continued his journey. At St. Louis, he heard the voice instruct him to "go to the place of gathering of my people [and] thou shalt live." Confused and stranded on the wharf, Duncan introduced himself to a fellow passenger. The man, Philo Dibble, announced he was a Latter-day Saint and was traveling to Independence, Missouri, to gather with God's people. Amazed, Duncan followed and was soon baptized.[37] Lorenzo Snow, a college-educated schoolteacher, struggled with his decision of whether to join the church and went into a grove of trees to pray. He recorded, "I had no sooner opened my lips in an effort to pray than I heard a sound just above my head like the rushing of silken robes; and immediately the Spirit of God descended upon me, completely enveloping my whole person, filling me from the crown of my head to the soles of my feet, and oh, the joyful happiness I felt!"[38]

Others experienced miraculous healing before or during baptism. Jedediah M. Grant joined the church after two elders healed his mother of rheumatism. An invalid for eight years, the mother of cadre brothers William, Joseph, and Thomas Woodbury was cured during their family's baptism. Stephen H. Perry's baptism healed him of thirty years of epilepsy. Joseph Shamp, a doctor, was unable to save his dying daughter. After a prayer by two missionaries, Shamp's daughter regained health and survived. He demanded immediate baptism.

Cadre members embraced the concept of Zion and were fiercely loyal to its founder.[39] Israel Barlow rode two hundred miles to meet Joseph and was convinced he was a prophet. John S. Fullmer and Haden Church made similar journeys, coming to the same conclusion. Working as one of Joseph's clerks, Howard Coray recorded, "I had many very precious opportunities" to view Joseph interacting with others. He believed Joseph "was equal to every occasion, that he had a ready answer for all questions."[40] Personal contact was not necessary to fuel such devotion. Alfred Cordon, a convert in England, wrote Joseph in 1842, opening his letter: "Dear Brother, whom, having not seen, I love."[41] The first English convert, George D. Watt, wrote that he believed in Joseph when his pastor spoke of him a year before missionaries appeared. When they did arrive, he outran other potential converts to the water to be the first baptized. John Tanner named his newborn son Joseph Smith Tanner without ever having met the prophet.

Despite a poor first impression, others also became loyal followers of Joseph. Edward Hunter was not impressed with Joseph when he heard him preach in the winter of 1839. Soon, however, he was taken with the devotion of Joseph and his missionaries. On a carriage ride he told the prophet, "How is it that I am attracted to those backwoods boys [missionaries]? I believe I would risk my life for them." Within days he joined the faith.[42] After hearing Joseph preach, George C. Riser took his sick son to Joseph, who healed the boy. Afterward, Riser overheard the prophet joke with apostle Orson Hyde. Initially bothered by Joseph's joviality, Riser wrote, "Upon reflection I could not think of anything they had said but what was innocent, and I felt that a prophet had a right to enjoy himself innocently as well as any other person."[43] Convinced Joseph was God's messenger, Riser received baptism in the frigid December waters of the Mississippi.

Before their missions, the electioneers each held a priesthood office in their newfound faith (see table 3.2). Every male deemed worthy through obedience and loyalty to the church, its leaders, and teachings received a priesthood office. More than 70 percent held at least the office of elder or seventy. Predictably, missionaries from Nauvoo, where many priesthood opportunities existed, held positions in the higher offices in larger numbers than was possible elsewhere. Conversely, field missionaries were overwhelmingly elders and priests. While priesthood offices were open to all worthy men, leadership positions were finite (see table 3.3). The vast majority of electioneer missionaries did not hold leadership positions before the campaign. Those who did were overwhelmingly leaders at the local level. Twenty-two percent of field missionaries were also local presiding elders. This is an indicator that Joseph's campaign was successful in engaging the participation of local leaders and their congregations. Importantly, these were the men who knew conditions on the ground and were most likely to forge personal bonds with voters.

Table 3.2. Electioneers' Priesthood Office, Pre-1844 Campaign*

Priesthood Level	Priesthood Office	Number of Holders and Percentage
Elite	Apostle	1 (0.3%)
Upper	First Council of Seventy	5 (1.7%)
	Patriarch	1 (0.3%)
	Bishop	5 (1.7%)
Lower Upper	High Priest	56 (18.8%)
Middle	Seventy	61 (20.5%)
	Elder	152 (51.0%)
Lower	Priest	11 (3.7%)
	Teacher	3 (1.0%)
	Deacon	3 (1.0%)

* Total electioneers = 298.

Some electioneers were not always steadfast in their loyalty to Joseph and the church. At least thirty received some type of discipline before the campaign. For example, Ezra Thayre was disfellowshipped for disobeying the law of consecration in 1831, excommunicated for apostasy in 1835, and considered "spiritually dead" in 1843.[44] Following the difficult times at Kirtland in 1837, James M. Emmett and others were disfellowshipped or excommunicated. After signing an affidavit for the state of Missouri against Joseph in 1838, William W. Phelps was excommunicated. Lyman O. Little-field and Darwin Chase were brought before the Nauvoo high council for adultery. On 13 April 1844, just days after Jacob Shoemaker's selection as an electioneer missionary in Pennsylvania, the Nauvoo high council disfellowshipped him for stealing George Morris's axe and then beating him "violently." The high council withdrew fellowship "until he [could] make good."[45] All these men reconciled themselves to Joseph and the church in time to campaign. They had regained their places among the faithful and were considered safe in the cause. Expediency may also have figured into their calls since Joseph would need as many supporters as possible if his candidacy was to attract the attention of the masses.

Table 3.3. Electioneers' Priesthood Leadership Positions, Pre-1844 Campaign*

Leadership Level	Leadership Position	Number of Holders and Percentage
General Authority	First Presidency	1 (0.3%)
	Quorum of Twelve	0
	First Council of Seventy	5 (1.7%)
	Presiding Bishopric	0
Regional	Stake President	3 (1.0%)
	Conference/ Mission President	2 (0.7%)
	High Council	17 (5.7%)
Local	Bishop	6 (2.0%)
	Branch President	29 (9.7%)

* Total electioneers = 298. Those holding no leadership position = 235 (78.9%).

ECONOMIC AND OCCUPATIONAL BACKGROUNDS

Joseph's vision of Zion included a society with "no poor among them" (Moses 7:18). The prophet and other leaders struggled from 1831 to 1834 to establish the law of consecration. Among the wealthier electioneer missionaries, several followed this law to the fullest. Daniel Allen, upon joining the church in 1834, sold his farm in Huntsburg, New York, and gathered to Kirtland. There he gave the church the full six hundred dollars from the sale. John Tanner owned twenty-two hundred acres of farmland and a hotel in New York. Following his baptism, he sold everything, moved to Kirtland, and began living the law of consecration. He loaned what was left to Joseph, who never would be able to repay. Many of the less economically fortunate felt the same yearning for Zion. Joseph B. Bosworth preached about Zion, declaring that "he had no property, but if necessary for her [Zion's] deliverance he would sell his clothes at auction, if he might have left him as good a garment as the Savior had in the manger."[46] Enoch Burns gave his last five dollars after his baptism. Dozens of the electioneer cadre lost everything when their stock in Kirtland's Anti-Banking Safety Society became worthless. Despite many who strove to live the law of consecration, it failed. By revelation in 1838, Joseph replaced consecration with tithing.

However, many cadre members yearning for Zion continued to live consecration's principles. After being baptized in 1841, David D. Yearsley sold all his possessions and moved to Nauvoo. There he built the only three-story brick house in town and donated the rest of his money by purchasing stock in church projects. That same year Edward Hunter moved from Pennsylvania to Nauvoo. He invested heavily in Nauvoo real estate and gave Joseph twenty-seven thousand dollars. In the spring of 1844, the prophet was financially strapped and facing numerous lawsuits. Stephen Markham sold his newly finished home, gave Joseph the twelve hundred dollars he received for it, and moved his family into a tent until he could build a cabin.

Cadre members came from diverse occupational backgrounds (see table 3.4). The largest occupational group among them was "business-professional." One hundred and fifty landed farmers dominated this level, with most owning more than fifty acres of land. Some, like Samuel Bent and Increase Van Deuzen, counted their property in the hundreds or thousands of acres. Others had different business occupations. David D. Yearsley owned two general stores and extensive farmland. Eighteen were thriving merchants. Ebenezer Robinson owned several rental properties and managed the Mansion House in Nauvoo. Isaac Chase operated one of the larger sawmills in Nauvoo, and George B. Wallace ran an extensive lumber and contracting business in Boston. Dan Jones owned a steamboat on the Mississippi, and Selah Lane owned a clipper that plied the Atlantic. Lucius N. Scovil operated Nauvoo's largest bakery and confectionary. Several schools sprung up in Nauvoo owing to its burgeoning population, and fourteen electioneers were educators, with eleven of them living in or around Nauvoo. John M. Bernhisel and Levi Richards, personal physicians of Joseph, led a group of a dozen doctors, eight of them living in or near

Nauvoo. John S. Reid and Lemuel Willard were the only lawyers among the electioneers. Henry Sherwood was Nauvoo's marshal, and Jedediah M. Grant was the group's only stockman.

Table 3.4. Electioneers' Occupations, 1844*

Occupation	Electioneers	Jacksonville
Business-Professional	45% (222)	24%
Skilled, Proprietor	18% (90)	18%
Skilled, Nonproprietor	13% (63)	36%
Unskilled	23% (114)	22%

* Total electioneers = 498. Occupational categories are adapted from Doyle, *Social Order of a Frontier Community*, 261. The business-professional category includes property-owning farmers and stock raisers; hotel, grocery, and mill proprietors (excluding clerks); those in legal, medical, clerical, and academic professions; and those in semiprofessional occupations (teacher, journalist, government official, etc.). The skilled-labor category includes those with specialized skills in building (using metal, wood, leather, etc.), mechanics, apprentices, and clerks. *Proprietor* designates skilled laborers earning more than $500 a year. *Unskilled* refers to general laborers.

With Nauvoo quickly emerging as Illinois's second largest city, there was an urgent need for skilled craftsmen. Members of the electioneer cadre who owned their own shops and tools prospered. Howard Egan was Nauvoo's premier rope maker. Daniel Allen ran a tannery and shoe store. Other cobblers with shops included Nathaniel Ashby and Henry Herriman. Jonathan Browning, a nationally recognized gunsmith, produced rifles carrying the inscription "Holiness to the Lord." Dominicus Carter and Osmon Duel were among those with blacksmith shops. The constant construction was a boon to a small army of proprietor carpenters. The temple and finer homes provided work for the cadre's stonemasons and brickmasons, such as Stephen H. Perry and Jonathan O. Duke. Coopers included Henry H. Dean and James C. Snow. James H. Glines and three others owned tailor shops. Other proprietor craftsmen included Levi W. Hancock (cabinetmaker), Elam Luddington (shipbuilder), Joseph L. Robinson (chair maker), Amasa Lyman (cutler), and Charles Warner (auctioneer).

Sixty-three cadre members were craftsmen without the capital to own shops or businesses. Frederick Ott and John B. Walker used their cabinetry skills in the employ of others. Samuel W. Richards worked as a carpenter for his older brother Franklin. Elijah Swackhammer, George T. Leach, and Garrett T. Newell worked in printshops. Samuel Shaw was a steamboat engineer on Lake Michigan. Jesse W. Johnstun worked for a blacksmith in Quincy, Illinois, earning money to attend medical school. Other cadre members included James W. Phippin (harness maker), Stephen Post (blacksmith), Moses Tracy (merchant apprentice), and Stephen Willard (mason). Some of the cadre's immigrants fell into this category. English converts James Burgess and Alfred Cordon worked as a carpenter and potter, respectively. German convert George C. Riser was a shoemaker.

The final group, unskilled laborers, made up almost a quarter of the electioneers. William L. Watkins, a seventeen-year-old, crippled immigrant from England, remembered that upon his arrival in 1843, "Nauvoo was flourishing, although the [immigrant] saints were generally poor."[47] Most unskilled laborers, while poor, found jobs working on the temple site and were paid meager wages from tithing dollars. Nauvoo could absorb the high level of unskilled labor because of the temple project, but the consistent lack of capital created an economic system based primarily on land wealth and limited opportunities for social mobility.

It is instructive to compare this occupational distribution with that of the nearby town of Jacksonville, Illinois. The primary disparity between the two towns is that Nauvoo had a higher percentage of "business-professionals," while Jacksonville had a higher percentage of nonproprietor skilled workers. The reason for the difference was the communitarian values of Zion in Nauvoo, where land distribution and ownership was seen as the right of all who gathered there. Joseph and other church leaders facilitated this as much as possible by offering generous credit terms to members. As a result, almost half of the electioneer missionaries were landed farmers. In contrast, in Jacksonville, as was typical in frontier communities, wealth tended to remain with an early, smaller group of large landowners who persisted over time. Transient skilled and unskilled labor, representing almost half of Jacksonville's population, typified frontier towns where young men were on the move, looking for their next opportunity.

Latter-day Saint field missionaries were an exception with 64 percent in the business-professional category, a significantly greater percentage than in Nauvoo and Jacksonville. This discrepancy is explained by the nature of the men whom leaders recruited in the mission field to campaign for Joseph. Many were local presiding officers of the church who were often called to these positions because of their wealth and local status—attributes that enabled them to influence the church's local growth and to succor poorer members and traveling missionaries.

PARTICIPATION IN PRIVILEGED TEMPLE AND MARRIAGE PRACTICES

Before his death in June 1844, Joseph shared the temple endowment, the sealing ordinance, and the practice of plural marriage sparingly and only among those in his inner circle. Thus it is not surprising that the overall participation of electioneer missionaries in newly introduced temple ordinances and practices in Nauvoo was minimal. Just seven of them—John Bernhisel, Reynolds Cahoon, Amasa M. Lyman, George Miller, William W. Phelps, Joseph Young, and Levi Richards—received the endowment before the campaign. Cahoon and Phelps were the only electioneer missionaries sealed to their wives. However, of the thirty men known to practice plural marriage before June 1844, eleven belonged to the cadre of electioneers. They thus represented a majority of those who practiced plural marriage who were not general church authorities. These were the men Joseph trusted, and they were intensely loyal to him and his vision of Zion.[48]

TRIED IN THE CRUCIBLE OF PERSECUTION

Most of the electioneer missionaries had experienced persecution and suffering in Missouri. Like Joseph, they looked to the federal government for redress for the property, liberty, and lives that had been lost. More than three hundred of them sent affidavits that Joseph took to Washington, DC, in 1839 along with his formal petition for redress of grievances. After the Saints' surrender at Far West, dozens were physically beaten or arrested and saw family members succumb to exposure or suffer abuse, rape, or even murder. The mob whipped and arrested Samuel Bent, whose wife perished from exposure. Hiram Dayton, Jonathan Hampton, and Melvin Wilbur lost children. Missourians gang-raped Eliza Snow, Lorenzo Snow's sister and future plural wife of Joseph. A mob split open John Tanner's head, leaving him for dead. Others of the electioneer cadre were present at the Hawn's Mill massacre. Ellis Eames narrowly escaped while friends were gunned down around him. David Lewis saw his brother wounded and then executed. Franklin D. and Samuel Richards also lost a brother in the massacre. David Evans, Jacob Myers, and Joseph Young gathered up the dead bodies and hastily buried them in the community well.

Wise and politically connected, Dr. John M. Bernhisel was one of few political veterans available to assist with Joseph's presidential campaign. Photograph by George Q. Cannon and Sons (ca. 1890) of an undated engraved portrait by E. G. Williams and Bros. Courtesy of Church History Library.

The suffering in Missouri cast a shadow on the church, including hundreds of the electioneer missionaries. John Loveless recalled, "In this, I was an eyewitness to scenes that, until this day, make my blood run cold and would almost make me fight a legion; women ravished, men murdered, houses burned, property destroyed, the prophet and patriarch, with many others, taken and cast into prison."[49] Jesse Johnstun recorded, "I would have willingly fought until the last drop of my blood had been spilt."[50] Just like their prophet, cadre members never forgot the sufferings and injustices of Missouri. These sons, grandsons, and great-grandsons of the American Revolution grew frustrated at the trampling of their constitutional rights. As no redress or aid materialized, they become more disillusioned with government in all branches and at all levels. Zion was what they longed for, and government and politics seemed increasingly hostile to its fulfillment. These men were battle-tested and ready to contend for political change even before Joseph's campaign called them to action.

POLITICAL INVOLVEMENT

Despite their political focus, few of the electioneers had been directly involved in politics or held office before the campaign (see table 3.5). In fact, 85 percent had never served in any political capacity. Although 11 percent had filled minor positions in government, fewer than 5 percent of them had city, county, state, or territorial experience—and even fewer had previous experience campaigning. This was common for the times, the 1840 election being historically the first in the nation with candidates and their supporters actively campaigning in large numbers.[51] However, the few electioneers who had previously campaigned had intense partisan convictions. For example, like most early Saints, Edward Hunter and Jonathan L. Heywood were staunch Jacksonian Democrats. When Hunter's father, an influential Federalist in the Pennsylvania legislature, died, Hunter was offered his candidacy and could count on a sure election win. Yet he declined because of his Democratic loyalties and opted to run for county commissioner instead. He handily won the office every time he ran. During Joseph's campaign, Hunter represented Pennsylvania in the Illinois convention.

Table 3.5. Electioneers' Government Positions, Pre-1844 Campaign*

Jurisdiction	Position	Number of Electioneers and Percentage
State/Territorial	Legislature	1 (0.2%)
	State Office	1 (0.2%)
County	Probate Judge	0
	County Office	6 (1.1%)
City	Mayor	0
	Justice of the Peace	10 (1.8%)
	Alderman/Council	7 (1.2%)

Minor	Postmaster	3 (0.5%)
	Other**	60 (10.6%)
None	n/a	480 (84.5%)

* Total electioneers = 568.
** Includes paymaster, assessor, militia leader, policeman, Indian agent, and other minor government positions.

Heywood was a well-connected Democrat in Quincy, Illinois. After the election of the first Whig president in 1840, Heywood prepared to return Illinois and the nation to Democracy in 1844. Still a year from his baptism, Heywood wrote his nephew in 1841 about the next national election: "The <u>result</u> may be doubtful, yet I still hope freedom will triumph over unlimited, irresponsible power."[52] In the fall of 1843, Heywood used his Democratic connections to offer Joseph Smith a quid pro quo arrangement with South Carolina senator John C. Calhoun and others. During the campaign, Heywood campaigned in Massachusetts with Brigham Young, Heber C. Kimball, and other influential members of the electioneer cadre.

On the opposite end of Quincy politics was Jonathan Browning, a famous gunsmith and an ardent Whig who was elected several times as justice of the peace. He and his cousin Orville H. Browning were associates of young Abraham Lincoln and worked to elect him to Congress. They had also supported Henry Clay in his presidential aspirations. Jonathan's conversion to the church was so unpopular among Quincy citizens that he moved his family and business to Nauvoo. Like Edward Hunter, Jonathan Browning worked as a delegate at Joseph's Illinois convention.

John M. Bernhisel and William I. Appleby were also Whig activists. Bernhisel was an honors graduate of the University of Pennsylvania and an accomplished doctor when he embraced the church in the late 1830s. He served as a bishop in New York City before moving to Nauvoo and becoming Joseph's personal physician and confidant. Bernhisel was a strident Whig, campaigning for William Henry Harrison in 1840. He was also friends with influential Pennsylvanian politician and judge John K. Kane (father of Latter-day Saint sympathizer Thomas Kane) and national Whig and future Republican leader Thaddeus Stevens. When his loyalties shifted to Zion, Bernhisel acted as an adviser during Joseph's campaign and helped to edit the prophet's *Views*. At the Illinois convention Bernhisel was a New York delegate and also served on the Central Committee of Correspondence for the campaign.

William I. Appleby grew up in New Jersey and became a respected schoolteacher. He spearheaded the county's Whig campaign for William Henry Harrison. "I was active in the strife," Appleby recorded, "using my influence and endeavors in behalf of Harrison's election, attending political meetings, caucuses, &c." In August 1840 an encounter with Latter-day Saint Alfred Wilson, who had just married Appleby's niece, arrested his politics. "While in the height of my political zenith," wrote Appleby, "[Wilson] remarked to me, 'If you was only as zealous in the cause of God as you are in politics, you would make a first-rate preacher.'" Wilson's words stung Appleby, a devout Methodist. After he was baptized by future electioneer colleague Erastus Snow, Appleby recorded the following in his journal: "My politics I laid by, and endeavored to seek after that which would be of more benefit."

William G. Goforth was not a Latter-day Saint, yet his fame, political acumen, and newspaper left their mark on Joseph's campaign. Potrait ca. 1840 by J. W. Taylor courtesy of Becky Pope.

As for the national election, to which he had previously devoted all his energies, Appleby observed: "I attended to my requisite duties, made out the returns &c., but took no part in politics, scarcely inquiring who was elected or who was not." When Joseph's campaign began, Appleby was already serving a mission in the mid-Atlantic states. As Wilson had predicted, Appleby was a successful missionary and preacher. Traveling between Pennsylvania, Maryland, and Delaware, Appleby left dozens of converts in his wake. On 5 May 1844 he met up with electioneer missionary John Wakefield. On hearing of Joseph's candidacy, Appleby enthusiastically mixed his passions—religion and politics. That night he and Wakefield "both lectured on the powers and policy of the government &c."[53]

Joseph's cadre of electioneers also had three former political newspaper editors who helped spread his campaign message. William G. Goforth was a noted doctor from Belleville, Illinois, who had edited a small newspaper titled *The Politician*. In 1840 he led the Whig effort in Illinois to elect William Henry Harrison president. A prominent Freemason, Goforth spoke at the dedication of the Nauvoo Masonic Temple on 5 April 1844. Staying to attend the Saints' conference, Goforth listened with interest at the call for electioneers. Owing to his experience in the previous presidential election and budding friendship with Joseph, Goforth was invited to participate in the prophet's Illinois convention a month later. He became a delegate representing Illinois. During the campaign he split time between Nauvoo and Belleville in support of Joseph.[54]

Samuel Brannan spent a considerable part of his early adulthood in political newspapers. Born in Maine, he moved to Painesville, Ohio, in 1833 with his sister and her husband. They were baptized there, and Brannan apprenticed as a printer. When he received his inheritance, he ambitiously bought out his apprenticeship and invested in land. The financial crisis later known as the Panic of 1837 wiped out both his investments and his faith in the church. Eighteen and restless, Brannan went to New York City and sailed to New Orleans, where his brother lived. The two started a paper that failed after Brannan's brother died of yellow fever. He next worked for, and briefly owned, the antislavery newspaper *Indianapolis Gazette*. Eventually returning to Painesville, he moved back in with his sister, retook his old job, and rejoined his former faith. While he was briefly serving as a missionary in Ohio,

As editor of The Prophet newspaper in New York City, Samuel Brannan advocated fiercely for Joseph's candidacy. Courtesy of the Bancroft Library, University of California, Berkeley.

*William W. Phelps, Joseph's prime
veteran political confidant, helped
write* Views *and other political
literature and letters for the campaign. Daguerreotype ca. 1850–60
by Marsena Cannon courtesy of
Church History Library.*

Brannan contracted malaria and almost died. At the time of Joseph's campaign, Brannan was convalescing in New York City. He enthusiastically took an active role in helping to publish and edit the church's newspaper in New York, *The Prophet*. By the fall of 1844 he was its owner and operator.[55]

The last, and most important, of the three editors was William W. Phelps. A founding member of the Anti-Masonic political party in 1827, Phelps edited two of the new party's New York papers. After reading the Book of Mormon in 1831, he chose to walk away from politics and join the faith. Phelps moved to Missouri and by revelation started a newspaper. At a hearing in November 1838 after the Mormon Missouri War, he testi-

fied against Joseph and other leaders, prompting his excommunication in March 1839. Repentant, he rejoined the Saints in Nauvoo and became a trusted adviser again to the prophet. Phelps wrote most of Joseph's politi-cal correspondence and edited Joseph's *Views* pamphlet. His influence on *Views* was unmistakable and reflected his Anti-Masonry and Whiggish political ideas, "including anti-slavery views, prison reform, anti-elitism, more federal power to protect minorities, promotion of trade and cur-rency, and fiercely anti-Van Buren."[56] One of the Council of Fifty, Phelps was prominent at the Illinois convention and a member of the campaign's Central Correspondence Committee.

*   *   *

Despite their varied backgrounds, the electioneer missionaries who cam-paigned for Joseph in 1844 coalesced around him and his Zion ideal and sacrificed to begin creating it. They gave all they had to their leaders even as their precious property and settlements were stolen, burned, or abandoned. Like other Saints at that time, most had not received temple ordinances or practiced plural marriage. However, of those privileged to do so in 1844, a significant number belonged to the electioneer cadre. While a majority had no experience governing or campaigning, the few who did brought significant experience to Joseph's campaign.

In many ways, the electioneers represented a good cross section of 1844 Latter-day Saint men in Nauvoo and in the scattered branches of the church throughout the nation. So what makes them noteworthy? Unlike their fellow Saints, they chose to be electioneer missionaries, and they were committed not only to Zion but also to the uncertain consequences of seeking to establish a theodemocratic government in a democratic society. They had no qualms about preaching and politicking, which was perhaps a step too far for other Saints. Although they came from different religious, economic, and political backgrounds, the men who campaigned for Joseph in 1844 had two things in common—a desire to build Zion and to see the prophet elected president. At what was often tremendous sacrifice, they tirelessly walked, preached, campaigned, and suffered for those causes. Their diligence began to generate a national interest in Joseph's campaign. More importantly, their experiences molded them into a formidable group of capable men determined to bring about their prophet's cherished religious, economic, social, and political Zion.

NOTES

1. Franklin D. Richards, Journal No. 2, 27 May 1844.

2. The foregoing account is assembled from Franklin D. Richards, Journal nos. 1 and 2, under the respective dates.

3. Sheets, Journal, 6.

4. See "Special Conference," *Times and Seasons*, 15 April 1844, 504–6. Margaret C. Robertson found fifty additional missionaries in her research, bringing the number to 386. See Robertson, "Campaign and the Kingdom," 166n2. I found 235 more, bringing the total to 621.

5. Taylor, "For President, Joseph Smith," *Nauvoo Neighbor*, 28 February 1844, 2.

6. Cordon, Journal and Travels, 3:178–79.

7. Jacob, Reminiscence and Journal, 5.

8. See Rich, Journal, 14 May 1844.

9. Dunn, "History and Travels," 1:41.

10. See Flanigan, Diaries, 108–9.

11. Samuel Hollister Rogers to Daniel Page, 24 April 1844.

12. Glines, Reminiscences and Diary, 39–40.

13. *Wilford Woodruff's Journal*, 2:416.

14. Erastus Snow, Journal, 49.

15. Hamblin, Record of the Life of Jacob Hamblin, 103.

16. Jackman, "Short Sketch," 21.

17. Jacob, Reminiscence and journal, 5.

18. Phippen, Autobiography, 5–6.

19. Spaulding, Autobiography, 199.

20. See Jenson, *Latter-day Saint Biographical Encyclopedia*, 1:794; and Cordon, Journal and Travels, 3:183.

21. See, for example, Terry, Journal, 6 May 1844.

22. Tanner, *John Tanner and His Family*, 3.

23. The information on Blanchard and Morris, as well as for other people in this chapter whose experiences are not keyed to sources in the notes, comes from my own genealogical research. I created a database of the 621 missionaries from an amalgamation of records from Susan Easton Black's fifty-volume *Membership of The Church of Jesus Christ of Latter-Day Saints, 1830–1848* (Provo, UT: Religious Studies Center, Brigham Young University, 1989), Ancestry.com, Personal Ancestral File, censuses, and other genealogical and family websites.

24. The four wives were married to Lebbeus T. Coons, John Cooper, Uriel Nickerson, and Stephen Post.

25. See Dunn, "History and Travels," 1:22. Gates and Robbins took their entire families; see Robbins, Autobiography, 21–23.

26. See Sudweeks, "Biography of David and Mary Savage," 4.

27. Tracy, Reminiscences and Diary, 27–29. I count Nancy among the electioneer missionaries because Joseph specifically directed her to accompany her husband on his mission and is the only wife on record to have campaigned for the prophet.

28. For example, see Lee, Journal, 1; Smoot, Day Book, 1; and Erastus Snow, Journals, 47.

29. Lee, Journal, 1.

30. Four men listed in the 9 April 1844 minutes do not appear in the list printed in the *Times and Seasons* the following week: Jonas (Jonah) Killmer, Harrison Sagers, John C. Annis, and Moses Martin. I found no evidence that they left Nauvoo to campaign. In the minutes, Martin's name appears without an assignment. Annis and Sagers had been involved in unauthorized plural marriages, bringing negative attention to the church in the previous months. While ultimately forgiven by the Nauvoo high council, they were not allowed to campaign—their names were simply crossed out. Another man, named Charles White, and Killmer had the word *ordination* written next to their names in the minutes. Although White did serve an electioneer mission to Massachusetts, there is no evidence that Killmer, who also was from Massachusetts, served.

31. Quoted in Faulring, *American Prophet's Record*, 489; see also Robinson, "History," 93–95. At least ten men did not go to their fields of assignment: Joseph L. Robinson (New York), Amos Davis (Tennessee), David Evans (Virginia), John S. Fullmer (Tennessee), Jonathan Hale (Maine), Levi W. Hancock (Vermont), Jesse Walker Johnstun (Ohio), William W. Phelps (Maryland National Convention), David H. Redfield (New York), and Cyrus H. Wheelock (New York).

32. See "Conference Minutes," *Times and Seasons*, 15 July 1844, 580.

33. See Anderson, *Encyclopedia of the US Census*, 228.

34. A mission here is defined as a period of one month or more preaching away from one's hometown.

35. See Jenson, *Latter-day Saint Biographical Encyclopedia*, 1:368, s.v. "Bent, Samuel."

36. See Duke, Reminiscences and Diary, 1.

37. See Duncan, "Biography," 2–3.

38. Jenson, *Latter-day Saint Biographical Encyclopedia*, 3:786–87, s.v. "Snow, Lorenzo."

39. See Bushman, *Rough Stone Rolling*, 190.

40. Coray, Autobiographical Sketches, 2.

41. "Letter from Alfred Cordon," *Times and Seasons*, 16 May 1842, 795.

42. *Our Pioneer Heritage*, 6:319.

43. Riser, Reminiscences, 6–7.

44. Jesse Wentworth Crosby, Autobiography, 23–24.

45. Nauvoo Stake High Council Minutes, 13 April 1844.

46. JSH, A-1:464 (21 April 1834).

47. Watkins, "Brief History," 1.

48. See Buerger, "Second Anointing," 23, where the eleven men are identified as John D. Lee, Joseph N. Bates Jr., Edwin Dilworth Woolley, Ezra T. Benson, Reynolds Cahoon, Dominicus Carter, Thomas S. Edwards, William Felshaw, Amasa Lyman, Erastus Fairbanks Snow, and Lorenzo D. Young. See also Smith, "Nauvoo Roots of Mormon Polygamy"; and Bergera, "Identifying the Earliest Mormon Polygamists."

49. Loveless, Autobiography, 2.

50. Johnstun, Reminiscences, 2.

51. See Shafer, *Carnival Campaign*, vii, 149–54.

52. Joseph Leland Heywood to his nephew, 28 July 1841.

53. Appleby, Autobiography and Journal, 34–35, 117, 120.

54. See Ford and Ford, *History of Cincinnati, Ohio*, 60; and Mulder and Mortensen, *Among the Mormons*, 14.

55. See Roberts, *Comprehensive History of the Church*, 3:71.

56. Van Orden, "William W. Phelps's Service in Nauvoo," 89–90.

CHAPTER 4

A CAMPAIGN TO
"REVOLUTIONIZE THE WORLD"

We mean to elect him, and nothing shall be wanting on our part to
accomplish it; and why? Because we are . . . fully satisfied that this is the best
or only method of saving our free institutions from a total overthrow.

—Willard Richards to James A. Bennet, 20 June 1844

In June of 1842 *New York Herald* subscribers read a shocking statement. "The Mormon Empire" was rising on the nation's frontier under "Joe Smith," the "modern Mahomet." "It is very evident," the paper's correspondent declared, "that the Mormons exhibit a remarkable degree of tact, skill, shrewdness, energy, and enthusiasm." Their strength was their unity: "In all matters of public concernment, they act as one man, with one soul, one mind, and one purpose." Such was evident in Illinois, where the reporter noted, "They [the Latter-day Saints] have already shown how to acquire power and influence by holding the balance of power between both parties. *They can already dictate to the State of Illinois, and if they pursue the same policy in other states, will they not soon dictate to Congress and decide the presidency?*"[1] The statements echoed one from the *Herald*'s owner and editor a year earlier—James Gordon Bennett, who wrote he would not be "surprised if Joe Smith were made governor of a new religious territory in the west." "One day," Bennett later opined, Joseph could "control the whole valley of the Mississippi, from the peaks of the Alleghenies to the pinnacles of the Rocky Mountains."[2]

An even more startling declaration appeared in correspondence from an army officer: "The Mormons number in Europe and America about one hundred and fifty thousand, and are constantly pouring into Nauvoo," which he estimated to contain thirty thousand "warlike fanatics."[3] Despite there being fewer than ten thousand Latter-day Saints in Nauvoo that year (and certainly fewer than twenty thousand worldwide), it was perception that mattered. Such material was reprinted throughout the country. To most Americans the threat of the growing "Mormon Empire" on their western border was an exotic curiosity, if not a cause for concern. In fact, reports of the movements of Joseph Smith and his followers regularly appeared in newspapers throughout the nation, as did articles reprinted from the Nauvoo papers and from the adversarial *Warsaw Signal*. Even before he announced his candidacy, Joseph was a national celebrity, albeit a largely unpopular one.

Naturally then, when Joseph announced his campaign in late January of 1844, newspapers across the nation weighed in. Church leaders mailed copies of *Views* to hundreds of newspapers, many of which reprinted some or all of the pamphlet. Editors opined on Joseph's platform and chance of success. A few nonpartisan papers gave items of the prophet's platform high marks and predicted the campaign would have an effect in Illinois and perhaps the nation. However, almost all newspapers of the time were partisan—Democratic or Whig—and their political editors frequently mocked both Joseph and his odds of winning, often comparing him to the unpopular, and now partyless, incumbent John Tyler.

However, continued news out of Nauvoo coupled with the arrival of Latter-day Saint electioneer missionaries throughout the country began to turn heads. In an article in the *Daily Missouri Republican* that was reprinted around the country, a correspondent wrote:

> You have seen it announced that Joseph Smith is a candidate for the presidency of the United States. Many think this is a hoax—not so with Joe and the Mormons. It is the design of these people to have candidates for electors in every state of the Union; a convention is to

be held in Baltimore, probably next month. The leaders here are busy in organizing their plans—over a hundred persons leave in a few days for different states, to carry them out as far as possible. I mention these facts only to show that Joe is really in earnest.[4]

As it became clearer that Joseph was serious about seeking the presidency, many papers turned to mocking and deriding him. Almost always these papers tried to connect Joseph and his *Views* to their political rivals. The two great parties were at parity in national politics and were headed for one of the closest presidential elections in history—and they knew it. Their vitriol for the prophet's campaign was calculated to siphon off rival voters and to protect themselves from defections. Sometimes Joseph would enter the fray, just as he had done in responding to John Calhoun and Henry Clay. The Nauvoo papers printed his retorts, which often were reprinted around the country. Importantly, newspapers from Maine to Mississippi reprinted a small article from the *Nauvoo Neighbor* of 24 April 1844, wherein the Saints boasted they could "bring, independent of any party, from two to five hundred thousand voters into the field."[5] As quixotically unrealistic as they were, such numbers created a dangerous perception in Illinois and national politics. More editors began to judge that Joseph's campaign would decide who would win the Prairie State and that it could even influence the national race—a fact church leaders already believed.

JOSEPH SMITH AS KING AND THE NATION'S BEST HOPE

The nine days following the April 1844 conference were filled with activities of such importance to the political kingdom and Joseph's candidacy that Council of Fifty clerk William Clayton wrote in his journal, "Much precious instructions were given, and it seems like heaven began on earth and the power of God is with us."[6] Continuing to meet and plan for several days, the Twelve finalized the list of missionaries, their assignments, and the scheduled conferences. The spiritual climax of the Council of Fifty meetings in Joseph's lifetime occurred on 11 April 1844. The prophet's record of the day cryptically says, "In general council in Masonic Hall, morning and afternoon. Had a very interesting time. The Spirit of the Lord was with us, and we closed the council with loud shouts of Hosanna!" What was so "interesting" that it evoked "loud shouts of Hosanna"? William Clayton's journal clarifies: "We had a glorious interview. Pres. J.[oseph Smith] was voted our P.[rophet] P.[riest] and K.[ing] with loud Hosannas." Erastus Snow, who made the motion for such an anointing, said it was "the happiest moment he ever enjoyed."[7] Though the office of king was an extension of the theological promises of the first and second anointings, it had overt political implications. Joseph was to be the "king and ruler *over* Israel," not just *in* Israel. Joseph's coronation did not give him more power—he remained the chairman of the Council of Fifty, whose decisions had to be unanimous—but it did demonstrate his frame of mind.

The idea of a king in a country founded on a revolt against monarchy was openly championed within the council's deliberations. In the same meeting that Joseph received this kingship, Sidney Rigdon declared, "God designed that we should give our assent to the appointment of a King in the last days; and our religious, civil, and political salvation depends on that thing."[8] The minutes record that another member said "he would like to have a king to reign in righteousness, and inasmuch as our president is proclaimed prophet, priest, and king, he is ready when the time comes to go tell the news to 10,000 people."[9] But that time had not yet come. A week later Joseph warned, "It is not wisdom to use the term 'king' all the while." Instead, Joseph told them to reference him as the "'proper source' instead of 'king.'" The council members would understand what was meant, and any others would not have the opportunity to accuse Joseph and the council of treason.[10] Anxious not to have the council's workings discovered, Joseph later stated, "We must suspend our meetings for the time being and keep silence on the subject, lest by our continual coming together we raise an excitement."[11]

Yet the Council of Fifty met again on 25 April. New members grew the council to fifty-two men. The council established parliamentary procedures, including the need for unanimity regarding their decisions. The committee chosen to write the constitution of the kingdom of God had failed miserably. As reported in the minutes, Brigham questioned "the necessity to get up a constitution to govern us when we have all the revelations and laws to govern us. . . . He would rather have the revelations to form a constitution from than anything else we can get."[12] Eleven days later, Joseph advised the council to "let the constitution alone," for he had received it by revelation. He nonchalantly scribbled it down on a scrap of paper—"Verily thus saith the Lord, ye are my constitution, and I am your God, and ye are my spokesmen. From henceforth do as I shall command you. Saith the Lord."[13]

John Taylor later explained the importance of being a part of such a "living constitution." "It is expected of us that [we] can act right— . . . not acting for ourselves, but we are the spokesmen of God selected for that purpose in the interest of God and to bless and exalt all humanity."[14] God chose his spokesmen, they received revelation on how to govern (aristarchy), and the people assented to their instructions (theodemocracy). As Brigham put it, "Let our president [Joseph] be elected, and let the people say amen to it."[15]

Friends of Joseph had no qualms about his having such power, considering him the best hope for the nation. Eliza Snow, a plural wife of Joseph and older sister of future church president Lorenzo Snow, wrote:

> Those who best knew him [Joseph]—those who comprehended the depth of his understanding, the greatness of his soul, the superhuman wisdom with which he was endowed, the magnitude of his calling as the leader of the dispensation of the fulness of times, and the mouthpiece of God to this generation, considered it a marked condescension for him to be willing to accept the position of President of the United States. . . .
>
> [Yet] his friends were in earnest. They knew that through the revelations of God he was in possession of higher intelligence and more correct understanding of national policies, and particularly the needs of our own government as a republic, than any other man living.[16]

Ironically, Joseph set up the Council of Fifty with its emphasis on virtuous leadership at the very time that presidents of the United States had shed similar governance in favor of catering to the interests of partisan political parties. The latter would have deadly consequences for Joseph.

In an unusual move, the Council of Fifty, while technically not a priesthood quorum, excommunicated dissenters William and Wilson Law and

Lt. General Joseph Smith in Nauvoo Legion Uniform. 1842 painting by Sutcliffe Maudsley (1809–1881). Those advocating Joseph for president believed he alone could save the republic. Courtesy of Church History Museum.

Robert D. Foster. Now apostates, these men would start their own church and print the *Nauvoo Expositor* in an effort to destroy Joseph's reputation and his campaign. But before that occurred, the hundreds of electioneer missionaries just called would spread throughout the United States. These loyal missionaries took with them the confidence and enthusiasm of their leaders, believing that Joseph as president was the best chance for Zion and the last chance for the United States to avoid disaster.

TWO CAMPAIGN CENTERS

Joseph's campaign had two national headquarters—Nauvoo in the West and New York City in the East. Each center had apostolic leaders who edited newspapers advocating Joseph's nomination. Apostle and campaign manager John Taylor edited the *Times and Seasons* and *Nauvoo Neighbor*. In New York City, William Smith, apostle and younger brother of Joseph, became the editor of *The Prophet*. Through these newspapers, church leaders promoted Joseph's candidacy and directed the campaign. They were key factors in a communication network that not only provided vital information but also bolstered morale.

NAUVOO

Once John Taylor published the names and assignments of the electioneers in the *Times and Seasons* on 15 April 1844, Nauvoo became a beehive of political activity. For two months, the electioneers departed almost daily. Joseph and the Council of Fifty continued to orchestrate the campaign as well as consider possible resettlement in Texas, California, or Oregon. More and more it seemed that Joseph's election was the best option to protect Zion, so members of the Twelve continued recruiting more electioneers. Wilford Woodruff and Brigham Young recruited twenty-six volunteers in the nearby town of Lima, while Heber C. Kimball and George A. Smith journeyed to nearby Ramus and netted six more.

Church leaders' actions within and without the Council of Fifty through April and May showed a deliberate and optimistic approach to the campaign. During the 11 April Council of Fifty meeting, Orson

RHODE ISLAND.	
William Seabury 1st	Thomas McTaggart
Melvin Wilbur	

CONEECTICUT.	
E. H. Davis 1st	Q. S. Sparks

VERMONT.	
Erastus Snow 1st	Warren Snow
William Ide	Dominicus Carter
Denman Cornish	Levi Hancock
Jeremiah Hatch	Alfred Cordon
Martin Titus	Charles Snow
William Haight	James Snow
John D Chase	A. M. Harding
Josiah H Perry	Isaac Houston
Amos Hodges	

NEW YORK.	
Charles Wandell 1st	Wm. Newland
Marcellus Bates 2d	Allen Wait
Truman Gillett	Wm. H Parshall
A. A. Farnham	C H Wheelock
Edmund Ellsworth	Timothy B Foot
Gregory Bentley	George W Fowler
Homer C Hoit	Henery L Cook
Isaac Chase	Wm. W Dryer
Simeon A Dunn	Elijah Reed
Daniel Shearer	Solon Foster
James W Phippin	Hiram Bennett
James H Van Natta	Chandler Holbrook
Samuel P Bacon	Lyman Hall
Bradford Elliott	Wm. Felshaw
J R G Phelps	Daniel Fisher
Joseph B Noble	D H Redfield
John Tanner	Martin H Tanner
Thomas E Fuller	Gilbert D Goldsmith
O M Duel	Charles Thompson
Samuel White	B C Ellsworth
Wm. R R Stowell	Archibald Bates
Wm. D Pratt	David Pettegrew
Marcellus McKown	Ellis Eames
Horace S Eldridge	

NEW JERSEY.	
Ezra T Benson 1st	John Pack

PENNSYLVANIA.	
David Yearsley 1st	Wm. P McIntire
Edson Whipple 2nd	Jacob Zundall
John Duncan	Orin D Farlin
Stephen Post	Henry Mower
G W Crouse	George Chamberlain
Jacob Shoemaker	Thomas Hess
Stephen Winchester	A J Glaefke
Hyrum Nyman	Henry Deane
J M Cole	James Downing
Charles Warner	

DELAWARE.	
John Jones	Warren Snow
Jonathan O Duke	Justus Morse

MARYLAND.	
Jacob Hamblin	Lyman Stoddard
Patrick Norris	

VIRGINIA.	
Benj. Winchester 1st	James Park
Seabert C Shelton 2nd	A W Whitney
George D Watt 3rd	Pleasant Ewell
Chapman Duncan	W E Higginbottom
Joseph King	John F Petts
Peter Fife	Alfred B Lambson
Robert Hamilton	David Evans

NORTH CAROLINA.	
A. McRae 1st	John Holt
Aaron Razer 2nd	John Houston
Thomas Guymon	James Sanderson
George Watt	

SOUTH CAROLINA.	
Alonzo LeBaron 1st	John M Emell
Wm D Lyman	Ekells Truly
Wm Smith	

GEORGIA.	
Morgan L Gardner	Isaac Beebee
Miles Anderson	S E Carpenter

KENTUCKY.	
John D Lee 1st	D D Hunt
D H Rogers	M B Welton
Samuel B Frost	Horace B Owens
John O Angus	Joseph Holbrook
Charles Spry	Hiram W Mikesell
John H Reid	Garrett W Mikesell
Wm Watkins	

TENNESSEE.	
A O Smoot 1st	Alfred Bell
Alphonzo Young 2nd	Armstead Moffit
W W Riley	David P Rainey
Amos Davis	James Holt
Libeus T Coons	Warren Smith
Jackson Smith	John J Sasnett
Wm P Vance	Joseph Younger
H D Buys	George W Langley
Alfred D Young	George Penn
J J Caststeel	Henry B Jacobs
Joseph A Kelting	John L Fullmer
Jonathan Hampton	Joseph Monut

ALABAMA	
Benjamin Clapp 1st	George W Brandon
Lorenzo D Butler	Thomas J Brandon

MISSISSIPPI.	
John B Walker	Ethan Barrows
Daniel Tyler	

LOUISIANA.	
J B Bosworth 1st	John Kelly
Wm Nelson	George Pew
Henry H Wilson	Lorenzo Moore

ARKANSAS.	
Andrew A Timmons	Darwin Chase
John A McIntosh	Nathaniel Levett

OHIO	
Lorenzo Snow 1st	L O Littlefield
Lester Brooks 2nd	John M Powers
Alfred Brown	Milo Andrus
John J Riser	John Lovelace
James Carroll	Wm H Folsom

Page from the 15 April 1844 Times and Seasons listing electioneer assignments. Courtesy of Church History Library.

Spencer was "certain of success" in the campaign because of "the union which exists in our midst."[17] "Unity is power," Joseph had written in *Views*. Spencer believed it and was not alone. David D. Yearsley became more outspoken during the meetings on 11 and 18 April. "He wished the day would soon come when he could have the privilege of proclaiming to the heads at Washington that the kingdom of God was set up."[18] He believed the kingdom should be publicly set up in Nauvoo right then. Appointed a campaign president for Pennsylvania, he believed that as king, Joseph already had all the necessary power and authority. "How can a man be elected president when he is already proclaimed king?" he asked his colleagues. Yet Yearsley was eager for his electioneer mission. The campaign to him was a "scarecrow" to "blind the . . . people" into electing Joseph, who was already king. Then the government of God could be "upheld" in Nauvoo as the prophet announced the kingdom of God with himself as its mortal king until Christ returned.[19] Others like Lorenzo D. Wasson also advocated the idea of moving the government to Nauvoo once the election was secured. We are not "playing child's play," he declared. "Our president don't care to go to Washington," Wasson continued. The men they were sending out would bring the needed success. "Our elders," he proclaimed, "are considered as the most ignorant men in the world, but when they open their mouths, they silence the multitudes." The cadre of electioneers would help "revolutionize the world by intelligence."[20]

Joseph agreed with the need to have an independent government. "We [the Council of Fifty] consider ourselves the head, and Washington the tail," Joseph asserted. Wherever they found independence, the laws of the political kingdom of God would be perceived as merely "part of our religion . . . until we get strong enough to protect ourselves." Then Joseph brought the conversation back to why they were running the campaign in the first place. "We want to alter it [the Constitution] so as to make it imperative on the officers to enforce the protection of all men in their rights."[21]

Church leaders held a public meeting in Nauvoo on 23 April 1844 "for the purpose of consulting upon measures for the furtherance of our designs in the next presidential election." Several men addressed the gathering "in a very spirited manner." It was in this meeting that they determined that Joseph's campaign could, as mentioned earlier, "bring, independent of any party, from two to five hundred thousand voters into the field."[22] Although in retrospect such numbers seem overly optimistic, church leaders were not alone in making such forecasts. Important newspapers around the country printed similar statistics.

Joseph was playing a wider hand than just pushing forward his own political campaign. The meeting on 23 April assigned electioneer and Council of Fifty member David S. Hollister "to attend to the Baltimore Convention [of the Democratic Party], to make overtures to that body."[23] Just what specific "overtures" Hollister was to present are unknown, but later national speculation included arrangements to exchange the Latter-day Saint vote for protection, redress, or even the vice presidency for Joseph. Such supposition combined with exaggerated numbers of Latter-day Saint and allied voters received attention nationwide. The perception that the Saints' vote would be important in the upcoming election was gaining momentum nationally and within both political parties.[24] As the public meeting of church leaders concluded, "it was resolved that a state convention be held in the City of Nauvoo on the second day of May next" (later changed to 17 May).[25] Hollister left immediately for the Democratic National Convention.

At the 25 April meeting, buoyed by the success of the public meeting two days earlier, Council of Fifty members decided to put their full weight behind the campaign. Joseph proposed that "those of this council who could, should go forth immediately to electioneer." He had decided that "the easiest and best way to accomplish the object in view [was] to make an effort to secure the election at this contest." Joseph instructed, "Let us have delegates in all the electoral districts and hold a national convention at Baltimore." Other members concurred with this "wise movement," confident that the "work [would] be accomplished."

Willard Richards reminded the council that "since conference the Twelve [had] been using their endeavors to send the elders abroad and give them the necessary instruction." He proposed instructing the electioneers still in Nauvoo "relative to the object of the mission." Joseph agreed. He had complete confidence in the electioneer cadre and wanted the Twelve at the coming meeting to instill that same surety in them. "Let every man [electioneer] assume an authoritative station," Joseph instructed, "as though he were somebody."[26] Thus the electioneers were key to the campaign's success and needed to understand that while on their missions.

Members of the Council of Fifty were not finished finding ways to ensure the prophet's election. They voted "to establish a weekly periodical . . . in all . . . principal cities in the East, West, North, South and every other place practicable." These newspapers would "advocate the claims of . . . Joseph Smith for the presidential chair under the title of Jeffersonian Democracy."[27] Advocates for Joseph used the term *Jeffersonian Democracy* throughout the campaign. Jeffersonian ideals of Republicanism dominated American politics until the rise of Andrew Jackson and the new "Democracy." The associated values included representative democracy to prevent the tyranny of the majority, "natural aristocracy" of virtue and talent, yeoman farming, and the belief that government should not violate individuals' rights of property or person. Many of these themes dovetailed nicely with Joseph's aristarchic theodemocracy: "I go emphatically, virtuously, and humanely for a THEODEMOCRACY, where God and the people hold the power to conduct the affairs of men in righteousness. And where liberty, free trade, and sailors' rights, and the protection of life and property shall be maintained inviolate, for the benefit of ALL."[28]

With the rise of the Jacksonian Democrats and Whigs, Latter-day Saints were similar to other Americans who believed the new politics had corrupted true Republicanism. Thus, in looking for a way to best translate theodemocracy for a gentile audience, church leaders saw in Jeffersonian Democracy what seemed both a good fit and possible enticement for likeminded, disillusioned citizens. With their plans seemingly complete, the council adjourned *sine die*. Two days later, on 27 April 1844, church leaders held a public assembly in which Sidney Rigdon and William Smith instructed the electioneers who had not yet departed on the expectations of their assignments. If they had not caught on yet, the electioneer missionaries now knew that their leaders were both serious and confident about Joseph's election campaign.

On 3 May Joseph once again called on council members and potential recruits to "go into all the states and preach and electioneer for him to be president. And when he is president we can send out ministers plenipotentiary, who will secure to themselves such influence that when their office shall cease they may be received into everlasting habitations."[29] There is much to unpack in that last sentence from the minutes. First, Joseph, basking in the unity of the Council of Fifty in supporting his candidacy, seemed confident he would win the election. Furthermore, he was already thinking of the roles of the council members and electioneers following the election as "plenipotentiary" ministers. A plenipotentiary, as defined by a contemporary dictionary, was "a person invested with full power to transact any business; usually, an embassador [*sic*] or envoy to a foreign court, furnished with full power to negotiate a treaty or to transact other business."[30]

Joseph envisioned that after securing the presidency he would use council members and former electioneers acting in their name as influential ministers of theodemocratic government. In their individual governing offices, this virtuous aristarchy of the incipient political kingdom of God would represent and rule until their death, at which point they would be gloriously "received into everlasting habitations." This plan was the natural conclusion of aristarchic theodemocracy, which these men had been instructed in and had sacrificed to bring about. Their appointment to official government offices would reward their loyalty and sacrifice. "Joseph's measures" would not be lost on Brigham Young and the other apostles present.[31] When it became their turn to lead the church, they would use electioneer cadre members to represent them as the regional and local leaders of the kingdom of God.

Three days later, on 6 May 1844, the council reconvened. Once again Joseph stressed that "all who could, should go electioneering," although some council members would need to "tarry . . . until they be endued with power."[32] Indeed, a handful of the men added to the council had not yet received their temple endowment, and they needed the power in the promises of being future kings and priests. Thus, before they left to electioneer, council members Sidney Rigdon, John P. Greene, William Smith, Almon Babbitt, and Lyman Wight were endowed. The date for the campaign's Illinois State Convention was finalized as 17 May. During that event, the prophet's national convention would be planned. In the 6 May meeting Joseph encouraged those present (and, through them, the electioneers already out in the field) to "work by faith and revolutionize the world, not by power, nor by might, but by pure intelligence." Continuing, he "prophesied in the name of the Lord" that "the elders should have more power and more might and more means than they ever had before," even "one hundredfold."[33] Those present seemed confident that a special power, influence, and intelligence would accompany the electioneer missionaries in their work of convincing the electorate that Joseph should be president.

Still without a formal vice-presidential nominee, Joseph declared he wanted Sidney Rigdon "to go to Pennsylvania and run for vice president." Rigdon would need to establish residency in Pennsylvania in order to abide by the Constitution's provision that the president and vice president be from different states. Rigdon enthusiastically accepted. Lyman Wight reminded the council of a prophecy in which God promised to "vex the nations," particularly the United States.[34] "The nation could not be vexed worse than for Joseph to be president and brother Rigdon vice president," Wight stated. In Joseph Smith's and Sidney Rigdon's minds, their electoral ticket was prophecy being fulfilled. Rigdon "referred to a former prophecy and said I am satisfied God intends to just what we are doing." Joseph "confirmed it."[35]

Candidates for president at the time were pledging to serve only one term as a means of preventing corruption. With this in mind, Rigdon requested a privilege—that after Joseph had been president for four years, Sidney could be president the next term. The council granted the request and Rigdon proclaimed, "As the Lord God lives, Joseph shall be president next term and I will follow him."[36]

On 13 May, four days before the Illinois State Convention, the council met to discuss a letter from Orson Hyde. He reported that their petitions were at a dead end in the capitol. Furious at Congress for once again denying the Saints, the council wrote that "all representatives and senators who do not use their influence as is their duty to do to pass the memorials unaltered shall be politically damned." It was time for "Congress to awake" to the sovereignty of the people and, as their servants, obey. The council also believed *they* were the representatives of *the* Sovereign and would not "stop to inquire of Congress what is popular or unpopular." Rather, they wrote, "We will tell them what is right and what is wrong; and if they will not make right popular, we will turn them out, and put men there who will."[37] Ultimately Hyde would write in June that both houses of Congress and President Tyler refused to move on the petitions. During the meeting, John Taylor, Edward Hunter, and Reynolds Cahoon "were appointed a committee of arrangements for the state convention" that was just days away.[38]

Meanwhile, Joseph's enemies plotted his downfall. Having obtained a printing press from a Whig operative, William and Wilson Law, Robert B. Foster (each of them Whigs), and other apostates printed a prospectus on 10 May for a weekly paper named the *Nauvoo Expositor*. True to its name, the leaflet claimed the forthcoming paper would expose Joseph as a fallen prophet and corrupt leader. The following Sunday, Joseph responded from the pulpit that he was still a prophet and that his enemies were the deceivers. Tension between the two sides mounted with rumors, threats, and counterthreats. In its early May meetings, the Council of Fifty closely followed the actions of the apostates, eventually deciding to hand the Laws, the Fosters, and Chauncey L. and Francis M. Higbee "over to the buffetings of Satan."[39]

Two days before the convention, three influential politicians visited Nauvoo and the prophet. The first, William G. Goforth, was known by Joseph and the Saints and was arriving for the state convention at their invitation. While traveling on a steamboat, Goforth struck up a conversation with fellow passengers Charles Francis Adams and Josiah Quincy. Adams was the son of former president John Quincy Adams and would soon be a political heavyweight in the Whig and Free-Soil parties. Josiah Quincy would become mayor of Boston the next year. Goforth convinced his fellow Whig politicians to stop in Nauvoo to meet the prophet. Goforth informed them that he was attending the Saints' political convention to persuade them to vote for Henry Clay. The three Whigs spent the next day touring Nauvoo with Joseph. The city and the sheer number of Joseph's followers there on the edge of civilization impressed them.

Toward the end of the day the discussion inevitably turned to politics. Adams and Quincy, both abolitionists, applauded the prophet's dedication to end slavery. Quincy, decades later, would write that Joseph had been a true statesman for publishing a plan to end slavery that might have avoided the "terrible cost of the fratricidal [civil] war." The conversation shifted to Henry Clay's recent nomination by the Whig Party. Joseph railed against Clay's ambivalence toward the Saints. Pointing to Goforth, Joseph declared, "He might have spared himself the trouble of coming to Nauvoo to electioneer for [Clay, who] . . . was not brave enough to protect the Saints in their rights as American citizens." Joseph then discussed his *Views* with the visitors and at parting mentioned "that he might one day so hold the balance between parties as to render his election to that office by no means unlikely."[40]

Apparently, Joseph shared such sentiments not only with famous or influential visitors but also with everyday boarders in the Mansion House. A young teacher named Ephraim Ingals spent two weeks visiting Nauvoo during this time. He remembered sitting "at the same table" with Joseph and "saw a good amount of him," often conversing with him. He recalled that Joseph often talked about his candidacy for the presidency, expressing "his belief that he would be elected." The boarders who were not from Nauvoo told him that they believed no one outside the city would vote for him. When asked about the source of his optimism, Joseph simply replied, "The Lord will turn the hearts of the people."[41]

Meanwhile, John Taylor drummed up support in the *Nauvoo Neighbor* for the upcoming convention: "Rally around the standard of freedom which Gen. Smith has raised, battle for liberty side by side with this patriot; enter the political campaign, determined, by all honorable means, to throw off the great burden of corruption under which our beloved country groans, and victory will be the reward of our exertions." Taylor exuded urgency: "Every friend to the triumph of Gen. Smith should be vigilant . . . and use every exertion to secure his success." He declared, "Delay not a moment—the time is short—what remains to be done must be done quickly." According to Taylor, only Joseph's election could save the republic. "Look to him, ye virtuous and patriotic; rally around his standard as the best standard of liberty; fight under his banner, for the salvation of a country whose freedom is jeopardized and whose liberty is endangered," he implored.[42]

When the state convention convened on 17 May 1844, it appointed electioneer cadre member Uriah Brown as its president. Although not a Latter-day Saint, Brown was a senior member of the Council of Fifty.

Brown introduced William G. Goforth and other prominent visitors. Next William W. Phelps read Henry Clay's letter to the prophet. When Phelps read aloud Joseph's rejoinder castigating Clay, the convention audience applauded with three cheers—a clear sign to Goforth that the Saints were not going to vote for Clay. Then the convention created a committee of five to draft resolutions. The committee was composed of electioneers Dr. William G. Goforth (a non–Latter-day Saint), William W. Phelps, Lucian R. Foster, and apostles John Taylor and William Smith. Next the convention assigned apostle Willard Richards and electioneer colleagues Dr. John M. Bernhisel, William W. Phelps, and Lucian R. Foster as the Central Committee of Correspondence. They were some of the few political veterans available to help Joseph. A final committee to appoint electors for Illinois included electioneer comrades Dr. William G. Goforth, Lloyd Robinson, Lucius N. Scovil, Peter Hawes, and John S. Reid. Reid, who was not a member of the church, had been Joseph's attorney in New York in 1830 and happened to be in Nauvoo during the convention.

Seventy delegates, representing each of the states and almost every county of Illinois, voted that "General Joseph Smith, of Illinois, be the choice of this convention for President of the United States." Members of the Committee on Resolutions then presented their work using words rich with the prophet's concepts of Zion, aristarchy, theodemocracy, and the kingdom of God. They declared it was "highly necessary that a virtuous people should arise" and "with one heart and one mind" correct government by "electing wise and honorable men to fill the various offices of government." The electioneers who had already left were "to take charge of [Zion's] political interests, [and] . . . use every exertion to appoint electors in the several electoral districts of the states which they represent." The electors were to give "stump speeches" in their districts and then attend Joseph's national convention in Baltimore on 13 July.[43]

Sidney Rigdon then addressed the meeting, needling both Henry Clay and Martin Van Buren for political dishonesty. Joseph, according to the official report, "spoke with much talent and ability, and displayed a great knowledge of the political history of this nation, of the cause of the evils under which our nation groans, and also the remedy." When influential Whig Goforth arose, instead of outwardly advocating for Clay, he declared he felt "the spirit of obedience that was required of one of old, when he was bade to take off his shoes, for he was walking on holy ground, and that this was a holy cause. . . . The Jeffersonian doctrines have been forsaken," Goforth stated; "merit and qualification have been abandoned." He chose to attack the Democrats, and particularly Van Buren, for abuses against the Saints.

To finish, Goforth announced, "May we now say that in 1844 Joseph Smith, the proclaimer of Jefferson democracy, of free trade and sailors' rights and protection of person and property, with us stands first to the [Democratic National Convention at Baltimore]." Goforth added parenthetically that if Joseph's nomination met with no tangible success at the convention, the gathered delegates should be instructed to support Henry Clay.[44] Goforth felt he had cleverly left the door open to Latter-day Saint support for Clay. John S. Reid spoke of his friendship with Joseph ever since he defended him fourteen years earlier in New York. Appalled both then and since at the treatment of the prophet and his followers, Reid pledged to support their cause. At this point Uriah Brown, an electioneer who was not a Latter-day Saint, adjourned the convention. Joseph and the Council of Fifty had gone out of their way to prominently include as many non–Latter-day Saints friendly to their cause as possible to demonstrate that Joseph could relate to and be elected by those outside the church.

Exhausted, Joseph went home to care for his Emma, who was ill. Even a late afternoon of heavy rain could not extinguish the excitement in Nauvoo about his formal candidacy. Later that evening "the band assembled . . . and several national airs were played, [and] a song prepared for the occasion was sung by Mr. Levi Hancock, and speeches delivered by a number of gentlemen." Joseph, hearing the commotion, stepped outside and saw the large assembly gathered up the street. The celebrants were burning a barrel of tar and toasting the prophet's nomination. When the crowd realized his presence, they carried him on their shoulders twice around the barrel. "The names of Gen. Smith and Sidney Rigdon . . . and Jeffersonian democracy were repeated with universal acclamation until the sound reverberated from hilltop to hilltop." The assembly and band escorted Joseph back to the Mansion House, and "three cheers were given at the 'Mansion' for the General and Sidney Rigdon, which closed the proceedings of the day." Excitement pervaded the city.[45]

The following week, on 25 May, the Council of Fifty held its second-to-last meeting of 1844. It was the last meeting that would discuss the campaign. The council read another letter from Orson Hyde about his interactions with congressmen regarding the church's petitions for redress of grievances. Frustrated, Hyde saw fit to leave the details of the ongoing negotiations to Orson Pratt and was going to start electioneering the following day. The letter contains a phrase that best exemplifies the determination and loyalty of the council and the electioneer cadre to Joseph. Hyde wrote, "Whatever course you [Joseph] shall determine to steer . . . I am with you, heart, hand, property, life, and honor."[46] The council instructed Willard Richards to write their response. The letter, using a play on words, told Hyde that "success at present depends on our faith in the doctrine of election" and that "our faith must be made manifest by our works, and every honorable exertion made to elect Gen. Smith."[47] Furthermore, council and cadre members were with Joseph "heart, hand, property, life, and honor." The foremost doctrine of the Council of Fifty, the electioneer missionaries, and the church itself was to work together for the election of Joseph Smith to the presidency of the United States.

On 29 May John Taylor declared in the *Nauvoo Neighbor*, "Every individual desirous to secure the election of Gen. Smith should use every effort in his power to procure as great a number of subscribers to the *Neighbor* as possible." Taylor declared, "We have a great and mighty object before us; and union, energy, and untiring industry of all will effect its glorious consummation."[48] In a separate article, Taylor praised the "I WILL DO IT!" spirit of the Latter-day Saints and declared, "Huzza for Joseph Smith for the next president, and let all the people say 'amen!'" Taylor declared that the Philadelphia Bible Riots, which targeted Catholic immigrants, proved the nation was descending into chaos. The country needed Joseph Smith:

> So ye wise men, who've nothing else to do,
> Help save the land from wo;
> And rise in your might, like freemen ever true,
> And elect our *Gen'ral Joe!*[49]

The confident and celebratory mood in Nauvoo as June began was captured in a contemporary letter from apostles Brigham Young and Willard Richards to church leader Reuben Hedlock in England: "All things are going on gloriously at Nauvoo. We shall make a great wake in the nation. Joseph for President. . . . We have already received several hundred volunteers to go out electioneering and preaching and more offering. We go for storming the nation."[50]

NEW YORK CITY

Latter-day Saint electioneers stormed New York more than any other state. One hundred and thirty-three missionaries, 21 percent of the total, labored in the Empire State (see table 4.1). Illinois, the second state with the highest percentage of electioneers, received only half as many. New York, the birthplace of the church, became the key state in the election of 1844 for Latter-day Saints and other Americans alike. On 2 April 1844 apostle William Smith and printer George T. Leach created a political association—the Society for the Diffusion of Truth—in New York City to promote Joseph's candidacy. Soon after its organization, Smith assigned Leach to raise funds and publish a newspaper and then left for Nauvoo. Leach acquired a press and a shop in the famous Park Row of lower Manhattan. Within a few blocks' radius, almost a dozen partisan printing houses competed to disseminate their views, the *New York Herald* being the only supposedly neutral exception. The area's ambience, however, was definitively Democratic. The Saints' printshop was contiguous to Democrat headquarters Tammany Hall and just down the street from the Democratic-dominated city hall.

Table 4.1. Electioneers' Missionary Assignments by State*

New York	133	21.4%	Louisiana	8	1.3%
Illinois	70	11.3%	North Carolina	8	1.3%
Ohio	60	9.8%	Alabama	7	1.1%
Michigan	48	7.7%	Georgia	7	1.1%

Indiana	36	5.8%	Arkansas	6	1.0%
Tennessee	33	5.3%	South Carolina	6	1.0%
Pennsylvania	29	4.7%	Connecticut	6	1.0%
Massachusetts	25	4.0%	Mississippi	5	0.8%
Kentucky	20	3.2%	Rhode Island	4	0.6%
Vermont	19	3.1%	Free (Roaming)	4	0.6%
Virginia	18	2.9%	Iowa Territory	2	0.3%
New Hampshire	17	2.7%	Upper Canada	2	0.3%
New Jersey	11	1.8%	Dist. Columbia	1	0.2%
Maine	9	1.5%	Wisconsin Terr.	1	0.2%
Maryland	9	1.5%			
Missouri	9	1.5%			
Delaware	8	1.3%			

* Total electioneers = 621.

The first issue of the society's weekly, named *The Prophet*, was printed on 18 May. Leach edited the paper with Samuel Brannan until William Smith returned in June.[51] The first issue sounded the same theodemocratic themes advocated in Nauvoo: "God does nothing except he revealeth his secrets unto his servants the prophets; therefore it ceases to be a wonder that we should feel anxious to hold him up before the people as a candidate for the next Presidency, for the glory and safety of our nation, for this very reason, that God shall govern and control all your proceedings through his servant Joseph Smith. And we wish the brethren and all those who would wish to see righteousness prevail over wickedness to be unanimous in their choice and use all the influence they can to secure his election."

The first issue of *The Prophet* also reprinted the 15 April 1844 *Times and Seasons* list of electioneers and the instructions given to them under the headline "For President GEN. JOSEPH SMITH of Nauvoo, Illinois 'A Western man with American principles.'" Leach advertised for "a few intelligent active men [who] wanted to canvass for the *Prophet*" and help increase the paper's circulation.

The main editorial of the issue announced, "We this week have hoisted the banner and placed before the world as a candidate for the Chief Magistracy of this Republic the Prophet of the last days, General Joseph Smith of Nauvoo, Ill, and pledge ourselves to use our utmost endeavor to assure his election, being satisfied that he will administer the laws of his country without reference to party, sect, or local prejudice." Leach reported, "We would say to our friends that our prospects are encouraging." His office had received "communications from various parts of the country, hail-

THE PROPHET.
SATURDAY MORNING, JUNE 22, 1844

SUPER HANC PETRAM ÆDIFICABO.

FOR PRESIDENT,
GEN. JOSEPH SMITH,
OF NAUVOO, ILLINOIS.
FOR VICE PRESIDENT,
SIDNEY RIGDON,
OF PENNSYLVANIA.

Page from The Prophet newspaper printed in New York City declaring Joseph's candidacy. Courtesy of Church History Library.

ing [Joseph's] nomination with joy, and we feel confident that if the intelligence of the American people prevail over their prejudice, he will be elected by a large majority."[52]

In a time and location of intense partisanship, Leach pleaded for the "friends of Justice, of Truth, Humanity, and of God to examine [Joseph's] views and let the love of country predominate over the love of party, and through the ballot box we will strike a blow at oppression, hypocrisy, injustice, and treachery." He declared, "We have counted the cost of 'opposing the popular errors of the day,' and can say with continued patronage of the liberal and philanthropic portion of our community that we will . . . eventually . . . make way for the glorious reign of [the] Son of Peace."

Having received both compromise overtures and threats from other polit-
icos in Park Row, Leach responded, "We are not to be bought by promise
or intimidated by threat, but our course will be directed by an eye single to
the glory of God and the good of mankind at large."[53]

A week later Leach printed, "Let the friends of Gen. Joseph Smith
organize immediately in every state, in every town and village, throughout the wide extent of our Republic, and let no stone be unturned that
will tend to secure his election, [for] . . . we know our rights as American
citizens, that we are both willing and able to defend them, through the
medium allotted by our Constitution, viz. the ballot box." Leach sought
to rally those who might be reluctant to publicly support Joseph Smith:
"Let the movement not slack by your negligence of duty, for it is a sacred
duty you owe to your God, and the cause of truth and humanity, to sustain
the effort now made by the free and independent of all parties and of all
sects to place at the head of our once happy country a man of God, an
honest, independent man, influenced by the spirit of the Living God, the
spirit that actuated a Washington, [an] Adams, a Jefferson, a Hancock, and
a Franklin of the times that 'tried men's souls.'" *The Prophet* consciously
sought to tie Joseph to the Founding Fathers.[54]

Leach and Brannan railed against party politics again on 8 June 1844.
After reprinting Joseph's *Views*, their editorial declared, "We contend for
principles unbiased by party, sect, or local prejudices." They understood
that some "looked upon [them] as ridiculous . . . because [they had] the
moral courage to step out of the beaten track of party hacks and sectarian
demagogues and think for [themselves], . . . [for they were] not as mere
machines . . . to be used as tools by men whose only aim is self-exaltation."
Yet this is exactly how many saw both the Saints and Joseph's campaign.
For many gentiles the only difference was that the Saints' political party
was religious and controlled by a "prophet" who was often characterized
as another controlling pope or "modern Mohamet." A religious leader as
a presidential candidate was even more contentious in a nation defiant
of ecclesiastical control over politics, as was being witnessed in the Philadelphia Bible Riots. While many Latter-day Saints may not have sensed
their political campaign was a threat to other Americans, it was seen that
way. To be sure, most people outside the church misunderstood the deep

sincerity of the Zion principle of unity that motivated the Saints. When Leach and Brannan wrote in their 8 June editorial, "Would to God that our citizens, one and all, would take the same stand, and we would then select officers for the good of the country, and not for the especial advancement of faction," they believed that everyone could choose to believe the same and unite with them.

Yet most Americans looked at party politics as the way to advance their self-interests in a pluralistic society. In a nation with no state religion, politics, as French observer Alexis de Tocqueville noted, *was* the state religion. Where the Old World held elaborate state-run religious celebrations, Americans religiously politicked. Latter-day Saints, however, did not see the American republic as a triumphant end or great experiment in democracy, but rather as the preparatory means for establishing the kingdom of God on earth. On that view, government need not depend on the competition of parties within a pluralistic framework but can be the natural, peaceful, virtuous outgrowth of a people united by the desire to please heaven. "What true lover of his country can look at the two great political parties without shedding a tear for the tarnished honor of his beloved country?" questioned Leach and Brannan.

*   *   *

Before returning to New York to assume editorship of *The Prophet*, apostle William Smith was initiated into the Council of Fifty and attended the Illinois State Convention. Undoubtedly influenced by the public teachings of Joseph and the private teachings within the Council of Fifty, the editors in Nauvoo and New York ably amplified Joseph's ideas of establishing theodemocracy, aristarchy, and the kingdom of God. As William Smith left Nauvoo in late May, however, he was only one of hundreds who fanned out to preach the restored gospel and campaign for Joseph. Collectively they became the most unique campaigners in American political history as well as the most unique missionary force The Church of Jesus Christ of Latter-day Saints would ever field.

NOTES

1. "Highly Important from the Mormon Empire," *New York Herald*, 17 June 1842, 2; emphasis in original.

2. "Highly Important from the Far West," *New York Herald*, 3 July 1841, 1; and "Highly Important from the Mormon Country on the Mississippi," *New York Herald*, 15 January 1842, 1.

3. Correspondence, *New York Herald*, 17 June 1842, 2.

4. Correspondence of the *Daily Missouri Republican*, June[?] 1844. The letter to the editors, under the title "Life in Nauvoo," was sent from Nauvoo and dated 25 April 1844. Viewable at http://www.sidneyrigdon.com/dbroadhu/MO/Misr1843.htm#042244.

5. John Taylor and William Clayton, "Public Meeting," *Nauvoo Neighbor*, 24 April 1844, 2.

6. Journal of William Clayton, 18 April 1844, as quoted in Ehat, "Heaven Began on Earth," 13.

7. Council of Fifty, Minutes, 11 April 1844, in *JSP*, CFM:95; original capitalization preserved.

8. *JSP*, CFM:104 (11 April 1844); original capitalization preserved. Much of this paragraph relies heavily on Bushman, *Rough Stone Rolling*, 522–23.

9. G. J. Adams, *JSP*, CFM:105.

10. *JSP*, CFM:128 (18 April 1844).

11. *JSP*, CFM:133 (25 April 1844).

12. *JSP*, CFM:120 (18 April 1844).

13. *JSP*, CFM:130, 135–37 (25 April 1844).

14. Minutes, 3 February 1849, Council of Fifty, Papers, 1844–1885, CHL; and Nuttall, Notebook, 8 April 1881.

15. *JSP*, CFM:121 (18 April 1844).

16. Eliza Snow, *Biography and Family Record*, 75.

17. *JSP*, CFM:105.

18. *JSP*, CFM:106.

19. *JSP*, CFM:125.

20. *JSP*, CFM:127.

21. *JSP*, CFM:128, 129.

22. John Taylor and William Clayton, "Public Meeting," *Nauvoo Neighbor*, 24 April 1844, 2.

23. Taylor and Clayton, "Public Meeting," *Nauvoo Neighbor*, 24 April 1844, 2.

24. See Baker, *Murder of the Mormon Prophet*, 247–48. Baker lists numerous newspaper articles showing that Joseph's campaign and potential negotiations with Democrats were widespread.

25. Taylor and Clayton, "Public Meeting," 2.

26. *JSP*, CFM:133–35.

27. *JSP*, CFM:135.

28. *Times and Seasons*, 15 April 1844, 510; original capitalization preserved.

29. *JSP*, CFM:139.

30. Webster, *American Dictionary of the English Language* (1828), s.v. "plenipotentiary."

31. "Conference Minutes," *Times and Seasons*, 1 November 1844, 694.

32. *JSP*, CFM:157.

33. *JSP*, CFM:157.

34. The Doctrine and Covenants foretells God's vexing the nations in three passages: "vex the Gentiles" (87:5), "vex all people" (97:23), and "vex the nation [the United States]" (101:89). The last is likely the one Wight had in mind since it states the vexing would come if the president of the United States rejected the Saints' petitions.

35. *JSP*, CFM:157, 158.

36. *JSP*, CFM:158.

37. *JSP*, CFM:164.

38. *JSP*, CFM:163.

39. *JSP*, CFM:154–55 (6 May 1844).

40. Mulder and Mortensen, *Among the Mormons*, 141.

41. Ephraim Ingals, "Autobiography of Dr. Ephraim Ingals," 279–308.

42. "The State Convention," *Nauvoo Neighbor*, 15 May 1844, 2.

43. "State Convention," *Nauvoo Neighbor*, 22 May 1844, 2.

44. "State Convention," *Nauvoo Neighbor*, 22 May 1844, 2.

45. "State Convention," *Nauvoo Neighbor*, 22 May 1844, 2. See JSJ, 17 May 1844.

46. Hyde, letter, 30 April 1844.

47. Richards to Orson Hyde, 25 May 1844.

48. John Taylor, "For President, Gen. Joseph Smith," *Nauvoo Neighbor*, 29 May 1844, 2.

49. John Taylor, "Do It," *Nauvoo Neighbor*, 29 May 1844, 2; emphasis in original.

50. Young and Richards to Reuben Hedlock, 3 May 1844.

51. The press also printed a forty-one-page "pamphlet, featuring four works that would have been useful for electioneering missionaries, . . . published as *Americans, Read!!! Gen. Joseph Smith's Views of the Powers and Policy of the Government of the United States. An Appeal to the Green Mountain Boys. Correspondence with the Hon. John C Calhoun. Also a Copy of a Memorial to the Legislature of Missouri* (New York: E. J. Bevin, 1844)." Crawley, *Descriptive Bibliography of the Mormon Church*, 1:258.

52. *The Prophet*, 18 May 1844, 2; original capitalization and emphasis retained.

53. "For President, Gen. Joseph Smith of Nauvoo, Illinois," *The Prophet*, 25 May 1844, 2.

54. "For President, Gen. Joseph Smith of Nauvoo, Illinois," 2.

CHAPTER 5

PERSONAL STORIES OF "STORMING THE NATION"

All things are going on gloriously at Nauvoo. We shall make
a great wake in the nation. Joseph for President. . . . We have already
received several hundred volunteers to go out electioneering and
preaching and more offering. We go for storming the nation.

—Letter, Brigham Young and Willard Richards to Reuben Hedlock, 3 May 1844

As the electioneers began arriving in cities and towns around the nation, newspapers took notice. The *Pittsburgh Morning Post* reported, "We understand that Jo Smith has sent recently fifty-one missionaries into the different states to preach Mormonism and electioneer for the prophet as a candidate for the presidency."[1] Articles reprinted from Nauvoo newspapers put the number of electioneers in the hundreds. The major Boston and New York City papers had correspondents attending and reporting on the electioneer conventions in those cities, and their columns were reprinted by other presses. Thus readers throughout the nation knew that Joseph was running for president, electioneers were canvassing in the states, their own political parties were responding, and the Latter-day Saints' influence on the coming election could have important effects. After Joseph was assassinated, the *Niles' National Register* summed up what some Americans felt about Joseph's campaign:

> Joseph unquestionably indulged some faint hope of extending his rapidly accumulated power from Nauvoo to the extremities of the Union, and dreamed even of expanding those limits far beyond what they now are circumscribed to. His exposé of what he would do if elected president of the United States, his letters to the several candidates, and his nominations by conventions at Boston and elsewhere evince that he was determined to make a demonstration for the capitol and dictatorship.[2]

Joseph and his cadre of electioneer missionaries were determined. Excited with dreams of Zion and theodemocracy, these men were "storming the nation" in hopes of making American and even world history. Little did they know how soon and how abruptly the campaign would end and their efforts would be forgotten.

As the electioneer missionaries departed Nauvoo in the spring and summer of 1844, there was an unusual sense of optimism, enthusiasm, and hope—a palpable excitement. Electioneer George Miller later recorded, "At no period since the organization of the church had there been half so many elders in the vineyard, in proportion to the number of members in the church."[3] Miller never knew how correct he was. The Church of Jesus Christ of Latter-day Saints would not have another missionary force of more than six hundred until the twentieth century and would never have one as proportionately large as the 1844 electioneer cadre.

On 10 April, the day following the organizing meeting, Lorenzo Snow departed by riverboat for Ohio as the first electioneer missionary. Over the next three months hundreds left Nauvoo. The campaign grew in crescendo as electioneers advocated for the prophet in every state of the Union, generating public support and opposition. The electioneers stumped for an independent candidate in what was perhaps the most partisan political environment in American history. Additionally, they fully advocated the third rail of American politics—religion. In the end this mixture of church and state, coupled with the missionaries' sacrifices, would forge a unique bond among electioneer missionaries, their prophet, their apostles, and the cause of Zion.

THE CHARGE TO PREACH

The electioneers preached the gospel of Jesus Christ as restored, primitive Christianity. They usually made appointments to publicly preach at a schoolhouse, courthouse, or home of a friend or family member. Sometimes they preached to individuals and families. Several sermonized at large meetings. For example, Samuel H. Rogers, U. Clark, William A. Moore, James H. Flanigan, and William I. Appleby held a two-day camp meeting, "preaching and testifying" to hundreds.[4] On the other hand, Amasa Lyman disappointedly recorded that one of his gatherings was attended "to my surprise [by] no ladies and some half dozen men and two pigs."[5] The missionaries preached the basic principles of the Restoration: the Book of Mormon, restored priesthood authority, faith in Jesus Christ, repentance, baptism, and reception of the Holy Ghost. In fact, the Twelve Apostles, while attending the different state conferences, "strictly charged [the missionaries] to keep within the limits of the first principles of the gospel and let mysteries alone."[6]

The missionaries saw great success in baptizing converts and strengthening members in the outlying branches of the church. Dozens of journals, other documents, and newspapers record hundreds of baptisms. Often they occurred during the prearranged one- or two-day conferences held throughout the states, where members and interested observers gathered to be instructed in the gospel and to hear Joseph's political platform and the missionaries and local leaders often met to conduct church business. One or more members of the Twelve attended most of the conferences. The 24–25 May conference in Jefferson County, New York, alone counted 150 recent baptisms.[7] One newspaper documented the stunning success of the electioneers: "The Mormons are making converts even in old Connecticut, the land of orthodoxy and steady habits."[8] David Savage recorded that he "baptized a number upon this mission, the Lord working some mighty cures under [his] hands."[9]

Though many electioneers traveled by steamboat on the Mississippi and Ohio Rivers, almost every journal mentioned the exhaustion of what seemed endless (though numbered in many journals) miles of walking, often in extreme weather.[10] Traveling without purse or scrip, they were often denied sustenance and shelter, regularly sleeping outdoors. Henry G. Boyle penned, "We lay out under a pine tree because no one would keep us overnight."[11] Though determined to fulfill their missions, the electioneers were often lonely and missed their families, homes, and even native countries. Franklin D. Richards wrote his wife an eloquent love poem asking "God [to] extend thine arms of love around the partner of my heart, since thou hast spoken from above and called me with my all to part."[12] As he walked through upstate New York, James Burgess longingly reminisced about his native England.[13]

For most electioneers, this was their first time serving as missionaries. Such was the case with twenty-year-old Henry G. Boyle, a Latter-day Saint for only five months. Boyle initially worked with Seabert Shelton, one of the electioneer presidents for Virginia. When the two gave out an appointment to preach, more than five hundred attended. With Shelton delayed, Boyle was asked if he was going to preach or not. "I said I did not know, that I had never attempted to speak in public in all my life," Boyle later penned. "I knew I could not preach without the Spirit of God to dictate [to] me. I felt a great burden resting down upon [me] and great embarrassment at the idea of trying to preach, and yet felt it would be my duty to try. Therefore I made up my mind I would get up and open my mouth and whatever the Lord wished me to say to that people, he would give it to me." Shelton did arrive but asked Boyle to preach. Boyle later wrote, "I never had such a flow of the Spirit of the Lord before that time and but seldom since."[14]

Many electioneer missionaries labored in their home states and while there visited family members, some of whom they baptized. James Holt and his companion Jackson Smith arrived at Holt's father's residence in Wilson County, Tennessee. Holt introduced Smith to his father, "but he [Holt's father] refused to shake hands with him." Even though Jackson Smith was not a relative of Joseph Smith, Holt's father "said he had heard enough about the Smiths, and he did not want to see any of them." Holt retorted that "if he could not entertain [his] fellow-traveler and treat him as a gentleman" they would seek accommodations elsewhere. Holt recorded his father's response: "This cut my father to the quick, and with tears in his eyes, he said, 'James, take your friend in and make yourselves welcome.'" Holt enjoyed the time with his family, spending several days visiting with them and "teaching them the principles of the gospel when they gave [him] an opportunity."[15] His older brother, a Baptist minister, allowed them to preach in his church.

Daniel D. Hunt and his companion Lindsey A. Brady visited Hunt's family in Kentucky. While preaching there, the people paid "good attention" and nineteen were baptized, including twelve members of Hunt's extended family.[16] Guy M. Keyser visited and baptized his mother in upstate New York. David Pettegrew mentioned preaching "the truth to thousands of people" and visiting his "relations in Vermont and New Hampshire."[17] William R. R. Stowell arrived in New York to find many of his relatives receptive to baptism. Stowell's companion William K. Parshall stayed with him after their missions, and the two led a group of converts to Nauvoo in 1845.[18] Edson Whipple visited and baptized family members in Pennsylvania and New York.[19] Moses and Nancy Tracy took their little family to visit relatives in New York. Nancy recorded, "We ended our visit for this time with my relatives, not forgetting to preach to them the gospel and give them Joseph's views on the policy of the government."[20] None joined.

During their preaching, the electioneers sometimes debated with ministers of other faiths, often priding themselves on their performances. Edson Barney noted that his debate in Chicago with a Presbyterian minister went "in my favor."[21] Levi Jackman's audience listened to him intently during a debate, leaving when the opposing minister spoke and returning when Jackman recommenced.[22] William Hyde converted and baptized a minister, as did several other electioneers.[23]

Church leaders ordained at least forty electioneers to higher priesthood offices, either in preparation for or because of added responsibilities while on their missions. Most were made seventies during or immediately following the April conference. A handful were ordained high priests.[24] James H. Glines, a recent convert and a deacon, attended a conference in Boston and was ordained an elder.

The electioneer cadre understood that preaching the restored gospel was a vital part of their assignment. Their efforts produced converts and strengthened local branches. The constant preaching also solidified their own faith. As they sacrificed for Zion, their desire to establish it deepened. Friendships and even marriages were formed. The opportunity of working with and hearing the teachings and testimonies of the Twelve Apostles bolstered their loyalty to these leaders—a foundation that would become immensely important when Joseph's death led to diverse succession claims.

THE CHARGE TO ELECTIONEER

The electioneers undertook their campaign duties with fervor. They understood their call was to preach politics as well as religion. Joseph Holbrook sounded forth the merits of Joseph's *Views* "almost daily."[25] In Delaware Jonathan O. Duke steadily promoted "Joseph Smith's nomination for President of the United States."[26] David Fullmer repeatedly addressed large assemblies in Michigan on what he termed "politicks."[27] In upstate New York on 18 June 1844, Franklin D. Richards gave, in his words, "the first political speech I ever delivered." The next morning "I called the elders together and told them what I had learned during the night upon the subject relative to the course to be pursued in lecturing from Gen. Smith's views on politics."[28] David Savage's wife Mary, who accompanied him on his mission, recorded that he politicked "with great zeal."[29] German-immigrant brothers George C. and John J. Riser returned to the German-speaking areas of Ohio they knew as youths to preach and campaign. They used their father's house as their headquarters, distributing political and religious pamphlets throughout the region.[30] Crandell Dunn's day-to-day account of his work in Michigan is replete with references to preaching and politics.[31] Often companions team taught, the first preaching the gospel and the second lecturing on politics.[32]

The travels and activities of Alfred Cordon and fellow English convert James Burgess reveal the dual nature of the electioneers' assignment. They began their journey in several days of torrential rain with little shelter. They were often "tormented with mosquitos," illness, and fatigue. Walking an average of twenty miles a day, the elders stopped to preach and campaign to anyone who would listen. As they worked through Illinois they met with sharp resistance. They often heard people denounce "Joe Smith" as a "false prophet" and threaten them or Joseph with personal harm.

Impoverished British converts Alfred Cordon (left) and James Burgess (right) traversed 1,100 miles on foot to Burlington, Vermont, in two months, preaching and electioneering all along the way. Courtesy of Alfred Cordon Family Association and Joyce Richmond (Burgess).

Arriving in Chicago, Cordon and Burgess were unable to find work to pay for steamboat passage to Buffalo. After attending a church conference there, they continued their journey to Vermont, walking through Indiana, Michigan, and New York. As they traveled, they stayed with families and "converse[d] with them on the subject of religion [and] explained to them the principles of the doctrine of Christ . . . [and then] read to them General Smith's views on the power and policy of the government of the United States." On 27 June 1844, the day of Joseph's assassination, Cordon and Burgess reached Niagara Falls amid a downpour. They stopped at the Hill Cumorah a few days later, where the prophet had retrieved the gold plates. They continued to Syracuse, New York, preaching and campaigning there several days. The two companions finally reached Vermont on 20 July and remained there preaching until the spring of 1845, finishing their one-year mission. Burgess married a local Latter-day Saint, and the three returned to Nauvoo.[33]

SECTIONAL ELECTIONEERING

Those appointed to be presidents of the electioneers in the different states concentrated their work, and that of their men, on Joseph's campaign. Their journals, and those of their fellow electioneers, describe organized, deliberate, and focused electioneering.

ILLINOIS

On 21 May 1844, four days after the state convention in Nauvoo, approximately one hundred missionaries left Nauvoo on the steamboat *Osprey*—the largest such cohort to leave in one day. The topic of conversation among the passengers turned to Joseph's candidacy. The passengers who were not Latter-day Saints held a mock vote with encouraging results: Joseph Smith, 64; Henry Clay, 46; and Martin Van Buren, 24.[34] Moreover, some people in eastern Illinois, upon hearing Joseph's political ideas, declared they were "the best [they] ever heard."[35] On 17 June at the Ottawa, Illinois, conference, apostle George A. Smith and some electioneers addressed a meeting of five hundred using Joseph's *Views*. Smith recorded that the people "applauded the sentiment very highly and seemed much pleased."[36]

In Chicago, electioneer leaders held a meeting to rally support for the campaign. James Burgess and Alfred Cordon "placarded the city with written handbills" in order to invite all to attend and hear Joseph's views on government. About a dozen electioneers, members of the Chicago branch, and several dozen interested people gathered and elected Cordon president of the proceedings.[37] Electioneers reported, "Joseph's views and measures are liked very much, though many are opposed to the man."[38] Jacob E. Terry subsequently placed an order in Chicago for one thousand copies of *Views*. Trying to sell them on the streets and house to house, Terry had little success interacting with "all manner of men" and was constantly "ordered away from people's doors." For the next two weeks, he alternately worked for money, purchased more copies of *Views*, and attempted to sell them. Often he just gave them away. Leaving Chicago on 14 June, Terry continued to distribute *Views* daily at homes, religious camp meetings, and public debates throughout Illinois and Indiana.[39]

THE MIDWEST

Amasa Lyman and George P. Dykes led Joseph's election efforts in Indiana as campaign presidents. However, they did not leave Nauvoo until 4 June 1844, two days after electioneers held the first conference in Indiana.[40] Soon separated, the two presidents did not completely organize the work before the campaign collapsed as a result of Joseph's death. Yet up until

then, and in addition to the planned conferences there, electioneers labored diligently throughout Indiana. William R.
R. Stowell and his companion William
H. Parshall had breakfast at the home
of a family member when Stowell
began reading *Views* to the elderly
grandfather of the home. "The gentleman seemed very much interested and
inquired earnestly, 'Who is this Joseph
Smith?,'" wrote Stowell. After explaining that Joseph "was the prophet and
the leader of the Mormon Church,
and that the pamphlet he was reading
contained his views on the principles
of government, the gentleman said he
had served under Washington in the
Revolutionary War and that what he
had heard sounded very much like
Washington's views."⁴¹

Council of Fifty member Amasa Lyman led the electioneering effort in Indiana with George P. Dykes. Engraved sketch from 1855 by Frederick Piercy courtesy of Church History Library.

In neighboring Ohio, Lorenzo Snow and Lester Brooks were the campaign's presidents. Brooks was already living in Kirtland, serving as the
stake president. Snow closed his school in Nauvoo when he was called "by
the Twelve on a political mission to Ohio . . . to form a political organization throughout the state . . . for the promotion of Joseph for the presidency." Snow left on 10 April, the day after the conference meeting in Nauvoo was held to recruit and organize the electioneer missionaries. He gave
"on the steamer Osprey the first political lecture that was ever delivered to
the world in favor of Joseph for the presidency."⁴² On 7 June near Kirtland,
Ohio, "lawyers and doctors . . . called to talk of and obtain Gen. Smith's
views" from apostle Brigham Young and Franklin D. Richards, who were
on their way to New York.⁴³

Snow and Brooks presided over a "large convention in the temple in
Kirtland" on 23 June 1844. For a candidacy that was unapologetically blur-
ring the lines between church and state, the temple was a perfect venue

for the convention. Snow and Brooks assigned their missionaries to each of Ohio's
congressional districts. In the following
days they printed more than a thousand copies of Joseph's *Views*. Snow
wrote, "I then procured a horse and
buggy and traveled through the most
populous portions of the country, lecturing, canvassing, and distributing
pamphlets." He "had a very interesting
time—had many curious interviews,
and experienced many singular circumstances, on this my first and last
electioneering tour." Snow remembered, "Many people, both Saints and
gentiles, thought this a bold stroke of
policy, [and] our own people generally, whom I met, were quite willing
to use their influence and devote their
time and energies to the promotion
of the object in view." Reaction to Joseph's campaign was mixed: "To many
persons who knew nothing of Joseph
but through the ludicrous reports in
circulation, the movement seemed a
species of insanity, while others, with
no less astonishment, hailed it as a
beacon of prosperity to our national
destiny."[44]

*Charles C. Rich (above)
and Harvey Green (below)
built an impressive political
machine for Joseph in Michigan.
Courtesy of Church History
Library and Glen Parker.*

Presidents Charles C. Rich and
Harvey Green built a strong political
machine in Michigan. Rich, a member
of the Council of Fifty, departed Nauvoo on 15 May in company with David Fullmer, Norton Jacob, and Moses

Smith. On their way to Michigan they delivered "political lecture[s]" in private homes and public forums. Within days Rich was traveling and campaigning with apostles and fellow Council of Fifty members Wilford Woodruff and George A. Smith. In Kalamazoo, Michigan, on 30 May, the trio spoke at a "political meeting." They then convened a two-day conference at nearby Comstock in the spacious barn of local branch president Ezekiel Lee: "A large and respected audience was assembled . . . composed of many of the most respectable citizens of the county." Apostles Wilford Woodruff and George A. Smith, along with Zebedee Coltrin, David Fullmer, Samuel Bent, and Charles C. Rich, spoke to an "audience who sat in silence manifest[ing] great interest and attention." At the close of the meeting, "that warmth of friendship and feeling of kindness that marks the noble and generous good was manifested by many of the assembly, among whom was Gen. [Horace H.] Comstock and Dr. Hoods."[45] Comstock was the town's namesake and a current state senator. The large congregation of Saints and gentiles accepted Joseph's *Views* with "good satisfaction."[46] On the second day, Rich and Green assigned electioneers to campaign in the different counties of Michigan.[47]

The two presidents then returned to Kalamazoo to preside over "a political meeting in the courthouse." Over the next fortnight, Rich and Green, accompanied at times by other electioneers, preached and politicked throughout Michigan. After a political meeting in Troy Grove, where Rich, David Fullmer, and Norton Jacob read *Views* and gave lectures on politics, "the people appeared well satisfied."[48] On 14 June they held another political rally in Franklin, ahead of the scheduled two-day conference there. The day following that conference, Rich and Green held a public "political discussion" before moving on to Detroit. Returning to Franklin, Rich delivered another "political lecture." On 2 July he and Green returned to Pontiac and took delivery of their order for five thousand copies of Joseph's *Views*. They proceeded to Jackson, where on 6 July they held the state convention in the city courthouse.[49] The convention nominated electors to represent Michigan at the national convention, and the electioneers returned to their assigned counties to politick and distribute *Views*.

Jeffersonian Democracy pamphlet containing the Michigan electors for Joseph's campaign. Courtesy of Church History Library.

THE SOUTH

John D. Lee, electioneer president for Kentucky, presided over a conference on 13 June 1844 in Lebanon County to "organize the efforts" of the
missionaries.[50] Later, Lee would remember, "I felt highly honored to electioneer for a Prophet of God."[51] One of his fellow missionaries was George
Miller, a Council of Fifty member who "preached and electioneered alternately." While attending a large political barbeque, he stood "on the out-
skirts of the immense crowd reading to a few of [his] old acquaintances
Joseph Smith's views of the powers and policy of government." In time
the crowd listening to Miller numbered more than those listening to the
candidate who was speaking. Miller later recorded: "I got on a large stump
and commenced reading aloud Joseph's views on the powers and policy
of government, and backed it up with a short speech, at the end of which
I was loudly and repeatedly cheered; and a crowd bore me off about two
miles to a Mr. Smith's tavern, where they had a late dinner prepared for my
benefit, all declaring that I should not partake of the barbecue prepared

for the candidate who addressed the log cabin meeting, that I was worthy of better respect."[52]

William L. Watkins found a good reception for Joseph's *Views* even in the slave state of Kentucky. He wrote, "I found my friends willing to listen and conversed on the political situation although I was in a slave state. The question of slavery as advocated in the views of the document I carried found great favor."[53] Joseph Holbrook and John Outhouse "continued to preach and put forth Joseph Smith's views, which the people generally liked well," although they did not approve of a "Mormon prophet for president of the United States."[54] For many, the political ideas were acceptable, sometimes even preferred, but the candidate was not.

In neighboring Tennessee, Abraham O. Smoot and Alphonso Young managed Joseph's campaign. They led a conference at Dresden in the Weakley County courthouse on 25–26 May 1844 to organize the campaign and make assignments. They met with stiff resistance on the first day that ended in a chaotic, bloody affair. Held in a private home the next day, the conference arranged geographic campaign assignments and duties to print and distribute Joseph's *Views*. Smoot and Young presided over a second conference in Eagle Creek, Benton County, in early June.[55] From 9 to 11 June, Young, along with several electioneer missionaries, preached and politicked at the conference in Dyer County. Young "called their attention to the murders and robberies committed on [their] people, in this once happy land, merely on account of the religion." Warning them "against tolerating such cruel deeds," Young laid "General Smith's claims before them." Moved by Young's words, six people were baptized and many more committed to Joseph's campaign.[56] One of Young's men, William W. Riley, wrote in his journal that he "delivered a political address to the entire satisfaction of the hearers."[57]

Following the first conference, Smoot contracted in nearby Paris, Tennessee, for the printing of three thousand copies of *Views*. When he returned to retrieve the copies, a lawyer named Fitzgerald intercepted him. He threatened to prosecute Smoot for allegedly violating an 1835 Tennessee law that forbade "any publications to be made in this state or circulated therein that [were] calculated to excite discontent, insurrection, or rebellion amongst the slaves or free persons of color." Though confident he was not violating the statute, Smoot chose to desist from printing until he could "get word from headquarters." Meanwhile, he and his men attended another conference in Benton County with a large and attentive audience without incident. Smoot later returned and paid the printer in Paris for the three thousand copies of *Views*, which he never received.[58]

Seabert Shelton was one of three presidents for Virginia, having received his appointment very early since he was already organizing the work there in April 1844.[59] Yet in the Deep South there was little evidence of campaign success. Several factors may account for this. First, church leaders assigned very few electioneers to Arkansas, Louisiana, Alabama, Mississippi, Georgia, and the Carolinas. Second, Joseph's proposal that the federal government purchase freedom for slaves would not likely have been embraced in slavery's stronghold. Third, because none of the electioneers assigned to the Deep South kept a journal of their missions, all evidence of Latter-day Saint political activity there comes from second-hand sources or inference. It does seem that the electioneers had limited religious success in Mississippi and Alabama. Examples are cousins John and Robert Thomas, who were originally assigned to Kentucky but carried their work to Mississippi to little avail.[60]

NEW ENGLAND

Although Josiah Butterfield and Elbridge Tufts were made responsible for Maine, Butterfield was delayed and never left Nauvoo. Maine was the farthest electioneering locale from Illinois, and the campaign there did not start until a week after Joseph's death (that devastating news would travel slowly). Sylvester B. Stoddard was the first missionary to reach Maine, in late June. He busily prepared for the Scarborough conference, which was to be held on 6–7 July. Apostle Wilford Woodruff and Milton Holmes arrived on 3 July after attending the Boston conference and convention. Tufts arrived two nights later, and the next morning the four electioneers were joined by Samuel Parker at the conference held in a Presbyterian meetinghouse. They took turns speaking to a disappointingly sparse crowd, but the next day saw four hundred people show up and an additional two hundred in the afternoon. The missionaries "had the spirit of speaking," and the now-packed congregation gave the "best of attention." News of Joseph's death arrived two days later, on 9 July, destroying the momentum.⁶¹

Erastus Snow preached and campaigned in Woodstock, Vermont, where he also was to preside over the conferences, organize the work in the state, and perform "those duties that had been particularly imposed upon [him]."⁶² On 11 June he and other electioneers held what was termed a "Jeffersonian Meeting" in the Masonic Hall of Petersborough, New Hampshire. A "mass meeting of the citizens . . . without distinction of sect or party assembled . . . to express their views and feelings touching the political condition of the nation." A "free expression of feelings" from speakers of various views unfolded, with Erastus Snow, Jonas Livingston, and J. C. Little drafting "resolutions expressive of the views of the meeting." The next day the assembly met at the "Town House" to hear the resolutions, which included using "all lawful ways and means to endeavor to reform the abuses of trust and power in . . . government" by selecting "independent candidates." Furthermore, it was resolved that Joseph Smith's *Views* rendered "him worthy [of] the suffrages of all free and enlightened people." After two evenings of "spirited and interesting discussion," all but five attending the meeting agreed to the resolutions.⁶³

Daniel Spencer, whom Joseph called the "wisest man in Nauvoo," was president of the electioneers in his native Massachusetts.⁶⁴ He and several other electioneers participated in the scheduled Boston conference of 29–30 June in Franklin Hall. Overseen by Brigham Young and four other apostles, the two days were a mix of religion and politics. The apostles and certain electioneers "gave instruction to the church on religion [and] the policy of government."⁶⁵ On 1 July a massive crowd

Known as the "wisest man in Nauvoo," Daniel Spencer led an effective campaign in Massachusetts. Image of undated engraved portrait courtesy of Church History Library.

packed the famed Melodeon to participate in the state convention. Various speeches excited the multitude until a riot broke out in the evening. Despite the presence of apostles, Daniel Spencer chaired the convention's second day, this time back at Franklin Hall. During the meeting, Spencer and the others planned smaller conferences in each of the state's ten congressional districts.[66] After the political speeches at the Boston conference and convention, James H. Glines stated, "considerable excitement prevailed throughout the city; very many people were favorably inclined to vote for our candidate for president."[67] The "good feelings" toward the electioneers' message continued in the scheduled conference at Salem on 8–9 July.[68]

MID-ATLANTIC

In Pennsylvania David D. Yearsley and Edson Whipple led the campaign. They left Nauvoo together and "canvass[ed] that state and present[ed] to the people Joseph Smith's views on government, and also . . . advocate[d] his candidacy for the presidency of the United States."[69] Edward

In 1844 the West Nantmeal Seminary in "Mormon Hollow," Pennsylvania, owned by Latter-day Saint convert Edward Hunter, was the informal headquarters of electioneers in the mid-Atlantic states. 2016 photograph by Nora Moulder.

Hunter's Nantmeal Seminary in "Mormon Hollow," north of Philadelphia, became a headquarters for electioneers. Ezra T. Benson, campaign president for New Jersey, left Nauvoo with John Pack. Along the way and throughout New Jersey, they "preach[ed] the gospel and present[ed] Bro. Joseph [Smith] as being the most suitable man for president." On 18 June in Salem County, New Jersey, Benson held "a meeting of the friends of Gen. Smith of Nauvoo, Ill., as a candidate for president." "The friends of Gen. Smith [were] requested to organize in every part of the state immediately and send delegates to the convention at Trenton." Benson concluded the conference with a "very spirited address."[70]

David S. Hollister preached and politicked on the steamboat *Valley Forge* as he made his way to Baltimore to attend the Democrat National Convention and prepare for Joseph's convention. He found the passengers very interested in "national matters," and together they spent much of the journey reading and discussing Joseph's *Views.* Hollister became "a lion among the passengers" and, upon disembarking, received several offers of a coach ride to Baltimore. Arriving between the Whig and Democratic conventions, Hollister, a founding member of the American Anti-Slavery Society, electioneered to all he could "for the promotion of the good cause."[71]

New Jersey campaign president Ezra T. Benson (top) and John Pack (below) held dozens of meetings and distributed thousands of copies of Joseph's Views. Images are a daguerreotype ca. 1850–60 by Marsena Cannon and an engraved portrait ca. 1890, respectively. Both images courtesy of Church History Library.

As a campaign president, Charles W. Wandell feverishly crisscrossed New York state attending and speaking at electioneer conferences. Courtesy of the Community of Christ.

Charles W. Wandell was the senior campaign president of New York. Records from other missionaries and *The Prophet* describe Wandell as busily traversing the state, attending conferences, and organizing the work. Initially arriving in New York City, he lectured on 26 May at the Marion Temperance Hall. Two weeks later he attended a "Jeffersonian Meeting . . . of the friends of General Joseph Smith [that] convened in the Military Hall [on] June 11, 1844." They resolved to have a conference in "Utica, Oneida County, N.Y., on the 23rd of August." Wandell instructed "all the friends of GEN. SMITH . . . to organize in every part of the state immediately and send delegates to the convention in Utica."[72] "Electors favorable to the election of Gen. Smith to the presidency [were to] be selected by his friends in each electoral district of the state and [their names] submit[ted] . . . to the Utica Convention."[73]

In an open letter in *The Prophet*, Wandell wrote that he and Marcellus Bates had arrived to preside, and he instructed missionaries to report their work through the newspaper. Wandell, Bates, and others attended another "Jeffersonian Democracy" meeting in New York City on 17 June. Apostle William Smith was back in town and chaired the meeting, which was "large and enthusiastic." "In a forcible manner" Smith "show[ed] the necessity" of the campaign, deriding the "two great political parties" to "deafening applause." Apostle Orson Hyde and then Wandell Wallace both gave strong defenses of Joseph's campaign, to much acclamation. William H. Miles and David Rogers were chosen as delegates to attend the Baltimore Convention on 13 July. The meeting closed to "nine cheers for Gen. Smith and Sidney Rigdon."[74] The next week Smith would give another forceful speech in favor of his brother at the well-attended Marion Temperance

Hall. Curiously, the papers did not dispatch reporters to these later, larger meetings. Wandell and Bates crisscrossed the state, attending conferences in Cambria on 28–29 June, Genessee on 6 July, and Portage on 14–15 July. At each, Wandell lectured "on the degraded state of [the] country and the importance of the Saints making every effort to usher in the reign of righteousness" with the election of Joseph.[75] The electioneers clearly understood theodemocracy and why their leaders were seeking the prophet's election.

A closer look at the 11 June 1844 meeting, which journalists did attend, reveals bold and determined electioneer missionaries. Held at Military Hall in lower Manhattan, the "Jeffersonian Meeting" included apostles, local Saints, and other New Yorkers. George T. Leach, coeditor of *The Prophet*, was chair. Although the meeting began with only thirty-four participants, by the time it ended, the building was full. Apostolic brothers Parley and Orson Pratt, along with electioneer J. B. Meynell, forcefully decried Martin Van Buren and Henry Clay while setting forth Joseph's *Views* to thunderous applause "mingled with hisses and cries of 'shut up.'"[76]

Parley P. Pratt delivered the most stinging, and subsequently reported, talk of the evening.

MILITARY HALL
193 Bowery, New York, 1868

For some years past we have had no government . . . [because] white men have been shot and hung, and negroes burned without trial, judge, or jury; abolitionists have been mobbed and shot; Catholic churches, dwellings, and convents burned, and fifteen thousand American citizens [Latter-day Saints] robbed of millions and driven from a state, and many of them murdered, and this by executive and legislative authority, without shadow of law or justice, and still there is no redress or protection, though years have

The Military Hall in lower Manhattan served as the meeting place for many campaign meetings in New York City. Courtesy of the Benevolent and Protective Order of Elks of the United States.

passed since the perpetration of these horrid crimes: who then shall dare to say there is a government?

Pratt declared the time had come for drastic change. "Except this nation speedily reform and hurl down such men, and put in men who will execute the laws for the just and equal protection of all, [the nation will be destroyed]." As a persecuted minority, the Saints had "no fault to find with the laws or the Constitution of the country." Rather, their complaint was that they could not "enjoy the benefit of them." The time had come to stand up for the equal rights of all citizens, for "the Catholics may be the sufferers today, the Mormons tomorrow, the Abolitionists next day, and next the Methodists and Presbyterians. Where is safety if a popular mob must rule and the unpopular must suffer?" For Pratt, American liberty was dying and drastic action was needed: "We must—we will—revolutionize this corrupt and degraded country so as to restore the laws and rights of its citizens, or we must and will perish in the attempt. And it matters not whether with many or with few, had I but ten patriots to associate with me I would either restore the country to its rights or leave it and live with the heathens, or sleep with the dead." He touted the prophet as "an independent man with American principles, and he has both [the] knowledge and disposition to govern for the benefit and protection of ALL. . . . HE DARE DO IT, EVEN IN THIS AGE." Pratt's forceful words, though derided in the newspapers, were a clear signal to the gathered audience—Joseph's candidacy was serious. The gloves were off.[77]

TARGETS OF PERSECUTION

Despite the electioneers' passionate politicking and encouraging successes, some Americans vigorously opposed Joseph's *Views*, his candidacy, and his electioneers. Toward the end of the 11 June 1844 Military Hall meeting, "some evil disposed loafer began to play tricks on the gas pipe leading to the room," resulting in the meeting being "broke[n] up in a very unceremonious manner."[78] Many accused the electioneers of being beggars and deceivers.[79] Kentuckians told John D. Lee he was not even human but a "different being, . . . one of the fish kind."[80] People denied shelter to electioneer missionaries simply because they advocated the prophet. Alfred Cordon recorded a typical response by a tavern keeper to a plea for a bed: "The answer was No, No, Joe Smith is a Devil!"[81] Lorenzo H. Hatch was one of several who became seriously ill from constant nocturnal exposure.[82] Jacob Hamblin was so desperate to sleep indoors he even offered what little extra clothing he had for payment, to no avail.[83]

Animosity toward Joseph was strongest in western Illinois, where his influence was the greatest. One man told James Burgess and Alfred Cordon that "if he had power in the country he would not let Smith have one vote and further said if Joe Smith should get elected president, he would go to Africa." One declared that if "Joe Smith got elected he knew a man that would shoot him . . . , [and] it would be doing good to shoot him, for he was a d--n rascal." Other harsh remarks proved prescient. In stating that "he would not mind shooting Joe Smith," one man added that "if there was any chance of him being elected that there was a mob far off that would shoot him."[84] William L. Watkins took a wagon ride near Warsaw with a man who flatly stated, "Joe Smith will never occupy the presidential seat; before he gains the election he will be killed."[85]

But political animosity toward Joseph was not just local, and it could even pit Latter-day Saints against their distant families. Dwight Harding is one example. After being baptized by his childhood friend Joseph Holbrook in 1833, Harding joined with the Saints in Kirtland, Far West, and later Nauvoo to the dismay of his family. Technically not an electioneer, he wrote his father in the early summer of 1844 to urge him and other family members and acquaintances to convert to the church and vote for Joseph. He enclosed a copy of *Views*. His father, Ralph Harding, responded with a stinging rebuke. As for the gift of *Views*, "Dwight, I don't thank you for that," Ralph penned. "The people here aren't such fools as to vote for Jo Smith for president of these United States." Then he expressed what others around the nation felt. "I see what you are after," Ralph accused; "it is for the Mormon[s] to get the power into their own hands for to rule this nation." He lamented, "I hope that time will never come, but if it should I believe that will be awful work." In a later letter Ralph further chastised his son: "I must tell you, Dwight, that you have brought much trouble and disgrace to me in my old age."[86] Throughout Illinois and the nation, many citizens feared Joseph's gaining political power outside Nauvoo, and some even determined he must die.

For some electioneers, reactions to their message often turned dangerous. A group of men tarred and feathered Eli McGinn.[87] A drunken crowd stoned and injured Levi Jackman and Enoch Burns.[88] Another mob beat Benjamin Brown and his companion Jesse W. Crosby. Brown remembered, "Some of them held me while the rest beat me about the head with their fists; but not being able to bruise me sufficiently in this manner, one of them took off one of my boots, and belabored me about the head with the heel of it, until I was covered with blood." They then jumped on him with their knees breaking several of his ribs. Brown feigned death. His attackers then scampered away. After Brown found Crosby, the missionaries escaped to a nearby house, only to be attacked again. The mob threatened to "get possession of both of us, after which they purposed to cut off Elder Crosby's ears, tar and feather us, carry us out into the middle of [the] river, and, after tying stones to our feet, sink us both." Three times that night Brown and Crosby held the door against the mob.[89]

While electioneering in Marion County, Illinois, David Lewis came face-to-face with a member of the mob that had executed his brother and attempted to kill him at Hawn's Mill. Lewis recorded that the former Missourian boasted of his participation at the massacre and "seemed for awhile to think as I was alone that he would frighten me." He "talked very saucy about his being wounded," to which Lewis responded that "[he] wished it was his neck instead of his leg." With thoughts of his murdered brother and his own narrow escape, Lewis wrote, "[I] forg[o]t that I was a preacher, for I felt more like fighting than preaching." However, a crowd had now assembled to hear Lewis. Obviously the "subject of our persecution was uppermost in my mind," Lewis wrote. "I spoke largely on this subject and pointed my finger at . . . [the Missourian] and said, 'There is one of the actors in this cruelty, persecution, and murder.' Every eye was turned to him with scorn, and he arose from the congregation and left the room."[90]

While Joseph Young was preaching in Ohio, a man yelled, "If I hear one say '[the] Prophet Joseph Smith,' damn the Mormon elders," and threatened to "stain his hands with their blood." Young pragmatically recorded, "This gave me the understanding that I must be cautious."[91] Another antagonist threatened George Miller in Kentucky: "If you do not leave this country and put a stop to preaching your religious views and political Mormonism, the negroes are employed to hang you to an apple tree."[92] A Missourian accosted David S. Hollister on a steamboat when he discovered Hollister was a Latter-day Saint electioneer. The man drew a Bowie knife, and a struggle ensued until passengers broke up the fight.[93] Jacob E. Terry and his companion Theophilus Nixon electioneered on the wharf in Chicago, handing out copies of Joseph's *Views*. Terry wrote that a mob led by a former mayor of Chicago "abased us shamefully [and] throw[e]d old tobacco chews and other filth in our faces [and] railed out against the Mormons and against Joseph Smith." The horde taunted Terry to read Joseph's *Views*. As Terry "commenced reading they tore the document to pieces." Terry called for the city marshal only to receive "more abuse" from him.[94]

Abraham O. Smoot, president of the work in Tennessee, quickly learned his men would encounter serious opposition. On 18 May he

Electioneer David S. Hollister's letter describes his being attacked on a steamboat by a "Missourian" with a "Bowie Knife" for advocating "Jo Smith." David Hollister to Joseph Smith, 9 May 1844. © IRI. Used by permission.

preached at the courthouse in Dresden. Soon after he began, someone fired a pistol at him through one window and "brickbats" crashed through another. Frightened, much of the congregation exited while Smoot assured them that if they stayed they would be protected. He continued to preach while electioneer colleague and local member William Camp guarded the door with a shotgun. Smoot wrote that many stayed while he "dispensed the words of eternal life unto them, which [he] did in as plain and conspicuous a manner as possible for the space of one hour."[95]

A week later Smoot and twelve other electioneers held a campaign convention in the packed courthouse. This time they came prepared with hickory sticks to defend themselves. Again their enemies interrupted the meeting. A lawyer sat at the front of the congregation and heaped abuse, continually interrupting the proceedings. As the convention ended, around 150 men forced their way into the courthouse and blocked the exits. The leader of the mob, county sheriff M. D. Caldwell, then stood on a bench and exclaimed, "Fellow citizens, you see that these men [electioneers] are come amongst us to raise insurrection and [are] passing [abolition] principles amongst our slaves."[96] Smoot asked Caldwell what he wanted, to which the sheriff responded, "Blood, [for] you have come here to incite the slaves to kill [their] masters." When some of the mob moved to attack Smoot, the six-foot-tall, two-hundred-pound wife of William Camp stepped forward, pulled up her sleeves, and roared, "Mr. Caldwell, you dare to touch one of them elders and I will see your heart blood." One of the mob yelled to "knock her down," to which the suddenly reticent sheriff responded, "No, Mrs. Camp, they shan't hurt you." With Mrs. Camp in the lead, the missionaries exited the building single file, each with a heavy hickory walking stick in his hand.[97] Not to be outdone by his wife, Mr. Camp then knocked the vexatious lawyer to the ground and "kick[ed] him around the courthouse yard."[98] After the electioneers left, the throng turned on the sheriff, who fled. Caldwell sent a communication the next day to Smoot saying that he could hold meetings in the courthouse again. However, Smoot chose to hold the second day of the convention at a local home to avoid more conflict.[99]

On 1 July 1844, following a two-day church conference, a state convention for Joseph Smith's "Jeffersonian Democracy" began in Boston. Held in the famous Melodeon concert hall, the convention nominated "General Joseph Smith for President [and] Sidney Rigdon for Vice President." Seven of the Twelve Apostles were present. Throughout the day the convention, packed to overflowing, "was addressed with much animation and zeal." During the evening session around 9:30 p.m., feminist-abolitionist Abby Folsom rose and interrupted Brigham Young mid-speech. "The Flea of the Conventions," as she was derisively known, was becoming infamous in New England for derailing large meetings and protesting for women's right to be heard. Loudly demanding two minutes, "rowdies" in the gallery chanted, "Hear her, hear her." The meeting quickly devolved into a cacophony of shouting and yelling. Folsom left, but "a large number of rowdies . . . felt disposed to make [a] disturbance." It started when one young man stood "and commenced a series of rowdy remarks, [being] encouraged by some mob companions until confusion became general in the gallery." The police were called, and while trying to arrest the troublemakers, "they were assaulted and beaten badly by a set of young desperadoes." One received disfiguring cuts to his face. After a prolonged fight, the police cleared the gallery, but the meeting broke up in confusion.[100]

A convention attendee submitted a detailed account to *The Prophet.* The instigators were "'Whig young gentlemen' of this pious, puritanical city," he wrote. "The well-dressed rowdies of Boston assembled en masse to 'rout the Mormon humbugs'" out of "nativist" feelings. By this time a rising number of Protestant nativists centered in large northeastern and mid-Atlantic cities were associated with the Whig Party. Conversely, Latter-day Saints and Catholics, both immigrant laden, generally joined with Democrats. Whig influence and nativism were common threads in the Philadelphia Bible Riots, the Melodeon riot, and the forthcoming assassination of the prophet (all in the summer of 1844). The author demanded: "Must we forever have to hold up the damning effects of bygone persecutions, Roman Catholic persecutions . . . ? Must we rake up the ashes of the convent [burned a month before in Philadelphia] to shake on the heads of the 'Natives' . . . [or remember the] Mormons who have been robbed, whipped, tarred and feathered, hunted, and shot down like mad dogs for daring to worship God after the dictates of their conscience in this enlightened age, in this land of Liberty?" He declared, "There is not on God's footstool a set of whelps more contemptible than our Boston, . . . well-dressed rowdies, vain, empty, brainless, shameless monkeys."[101] To avoid another fracas, the conference moved to Franklin Hall for its second day.

In the face of persecution, the electioneers' unstinting efforts garnered national attention. Partisan presses blistered the campaign and its electioneers, trying to pin the Saints on the other political party. Even so, the campaign was beginning to create interest, and by the end of June it was building momentum. The electioneers were having surprising success in some sectors and awakening strong opposition in others. The Whigs had selected Henry Clay as their candidate, while the Democrats nominated dark horse candidate James Polk. Like the nascent anti-slavery Liberty Party, Joseph Smith's "Jeffersonian Democracy" was gaining support at the fringes—and that support was growing. Church leaders and electioneers alike confidently worked at an exhausting pace, expecting further help from heaven.

If Joseph was not elected directly, they believed, at the least they could control enough votes for one of the parties, probably the Democrats, to offer a deal of protection—similar to how the Catholics were ensconced within the Democratic Party. What the Saints did not yet know was that their envoy to the Democratic National Convention, David S. Hollister, had met with "little success." On 26 June 1844, Hollister reported that his negotiations had been "a series of disappointments" and that he had turned to preparing for the Saints' own national convention. Such disappointments were but the slightest foretaste of utter devastation to come.

*   *   *

Electioneer Experience: John Horner. Three years after nineteen-year-old John Horner was baptized by Erastus Snow in 1840, the young farmer moved to Nauvoo, where he soon met Joseph. At the 9 April 1844 special conference meeting, Horner was "appointed to electioneer . . . [and] endeavor to elect the prophet president." Before leaving for his assignment in his home state of New Jersey, he ordered a thousand copies of *Views* to distribute. One night in early July, "while speaking to a full house of attentive listeners," he ended his political lecture by inviting "all to speak who wished to." Horner most likely expected some positive comments from the enthusiastic following. What he heard instead shocked him and stunned the audience. A gentleman arose and, turning to Horner, declared, "I have one reason to give why Joseph Smith can never be president of the United States; my paper, which I received from Philadelphia this afternoon, says that he was murdered in Carthage Jail, on June 27th." Immediate sober silence "reigned" in the house. Slowly "the gathering quietly dispersed," but not Horner. The news had shaken him to his core. "The grief and sadness" of his heart, he wrote, "was beyond the power of man to estimate."[102]

NOTES

1. "Increase of Mormonism," *Pittsburgh Morning Post*, 8 June 1844, 1.

2. "Mormon Tragedy: Death of Joe and Hyrum Smith," *Niles' National Register*, 13 July 1844, 1.

3. George Miller, "Correspondence," *Northern Islander*, 6 September 1855, 3.

4. Rogers, Reminiscences and Diary, 22–23 June 1844, 49.

5. Lyman, Journal, 25 June 1844, 6:8–9.

6. G. A. Smith, "History," 5.

7. See Jesse Wentworth Crosby, Autobiography, 12; and Crosby, History and Journal, 25–26 May 1844.

8. "Daily Mercantile Courier," *Buffalo Courier*, 2 May 1844, 2.

9. Sudweeks, "Biography of David and Mary Savage," 4.

10. The spring and summer season of 1844 was known as the "Great Flood" in the Midwest. It remains the largest recorded flood of the upper Mississippi and Missouri Rivers. Beginning in late April, rain fell for six consecutive weeks. Several journals note the incredible amount of rain that fell. Some examples are James Burgess, Journal, 6–8, 10, and 13 May; Jackman, "Short Sketch," 24; and Watkins, "Brief History," 2.

11. Boyle, Autobiography and Diary, 10.

12. Franklin D. Richards, Journal No. 2, 1 June 1844, 4.

13. See Burgess, Journal, 30 May 1844.

14. Boyle, Autobiography and Diary, 6.

15. Holt, "Autobiographical Sketch," 5.

16. Hunt, Diary, 1–5.

17. Pettegrew, "History of David Pettegrew," 190.

18. See Little, "Biography of William Rufus Rogers Stowell," 22–23.

19. See Whipple, Record Books, 1:2.

20. Tracy, Reminiscences and Diary, 27.

21. Barney, Autobiography, 2.

22. See Jackman, "Short Sketch," 23.

23. See William Hyde, Journal, 29–30 June 1844.

24. They were Pleasant Ewell, George P. Dykes, Franklin D. Richards, Crandell Dunn, Joseph A. Stratton, and George Wallace.

25. Holbrook, "Life of Joseph Holbrook," 60.

26. Duke, Reminiscences and Diary, 2.

27. Duke, Reminiscences and Diary, 45.

28. Franklin D. Richards, Journal No. 2, 8.

29. Sudweeks, "David and Mary Savage," 4.

30. See Riser, "Unfinished Life Story," 7; Riser, Reminiscences and Diary, 9–10; and Watkins, "Brief History," 1.

31. See Dunn, "History and Travels," 1:41–46.

32. See Jacob, *Record of Norton Jacob*, 5.

33. Cordon, Journal and Travels, 4:4 (27 June 1844); and Burgess, Journal, 5 May–27 June 1844.

34. See Lee, Journal, 2.

35. Burgess, Journal, 7 May 1844. See Cordon, Journal and Travels, 3:183 (7 May 1844).

36. George A. Smith, "History," 2.

37. Cordon, Journal and Travels, 3:200 (26 May 1844); and Burgess, Journal, 25–26 May 1844.

38. "Chicago, Ill., May 27, 1844," *Times and Seasons*, 1 August 1844, 606.

39. Terry, Journal, 29 May–13 June 1844.

40. See Lyman, Journal, 1–11.

41. Little, "Biography of William Rufus Rogers Stowell," 22.

42. Snow, Journal, 48–49.

43. Franklin D. Richards, Journal No. 2, p. 5.

44. Snow, Journal, 48–50.

45. George A. Smith, "History," 8.

46. Duke, Reminiscences and Diary, 42.

47. The assignments are recorded in the back of Rich, Journal, 14, 16.

48. Jacob, Reminiscence and Journal, 6.

49. See Rich, Journal, 14 June and 2, 3, 6 July 1844 (pp. 7, 9–10).

50. Lee, Journal, 13.

51. Lee, *Mormonism Unveiled*, 149; original capitalization preserved.

52. George Miller, "Correspondence," *Northern Islander*, 6 September 1855, 4.

53. Watkins, "Brief History," 2.

54. Holbrook, Life of Joseph Holbrook, 60.

55. Smoot, "Day Book," 2–3.

56. Alphonso Young, letter to the editor, *Times and* Seasons, 1 December 1844, 733.

57. Riley, Diary, 22 June 1844.

58. Smoot, "Day Book," 2–5. See Thomas, "Historical Sketch," 31–32. The transcript of Smoot's journal entry reads "$1000"—which is clearly erroneous—whereas the journal entry itself reads "$10^{00}" (perhaps representing an installment payment since the expected cost for the entire print run would be from $30 to $100).

59. See Boyle, Autobiography and Diary, 6–7.

60. See Thomas, "Sketch and Genealogy of the Thomas' Families," 30–38.

61. Woodruff, *Wilford Woodruff's Journal*, 2:416–20.

62. Erastus Snow, Journals, 48–49.

63. "Jefferson Meeting at Petersborough, N. H.," *The Prophet*, 29 June 1844, 2.

64. Stewart, Histories of Daniel Spencer, 3.

65. Kimball, *Diaries of Heber C. Kimball*, 3:70.

66. See "At a Special Conference of Elders Held at Franklin Hall, Boston July 2nd, 1844," *The Prophet*, 6 July 1844, 3.

67. Glines, Reminiscences and Diary, 39.

68. Kimball, *Diaries of Heber C. Kimball*, 3:71.

69. Whipple, Diary, 1.

70. Benson, "Ezra Taft Benson, I: An Autobiography," 214; and "Jeffersonian Meeting at Salem, N. J.," *The Prophet*, 29 June 1844, 2.

71. David Sprague Hollister to Joseph Smith, 9 May 1844.

72. "A Meeting of the Friends of General Joseph Smith of Nauvoo, Ill," *The Prophet*, 1 June 1844, 2.

73. "Jeffersonian Meeting at Salem, N. J.," *The Prophet*, 29 June 1844, 2.

74. William Smith and William H. Miles, "Great Jeffersonian Meeting," *The Prophet*, 22 June 1844, 2–3.

75. *The Prophet*, 1 June 1844, 1, 4; 20 July 1844, 2–3; and 3 August 1844, 3. The quotation is from the 20 July issue.

76. "Great Mass Meeting," *New York Herald*, 12 June 1844, 4.

77. "Jeffersonian Meeting," *The Prophet*, 15 June 1844, 3; all-caps style preserved.

78. "Great Mass Meeting," *New York Herald*, 12 June 1844, 4.

79. See Little, *Jacob Hamblin*, 17.

80. Lee, Journal, 12.

81. Cordon, Journal and Travels, 3:207 (30 May 1844); capitalization preserved.

82. See Hatch, *Biography of Lorenzo Hill Hatch*, 57–58.

83. See Hamblin, Record of the Life of Jacob Hamblin, 103.

84. Burgess, Journal, 7 May 1844.

85. Watkins, "Brief History," 1.

86. Ralph Harding to Dwight Harding, 22 August 1844 and 3 March 1846. Thanks to Benjamin Park for pointing me to the 22 August letter in 2016.

87. See Cordon, Journal and Travels, 4:3 (17 June 1844).

88. See Jackman, "Short Sketch," 21.

89. Brown, *Testimonies for the Truth*, 22–23.

90. Lewis, Autobiography, 30.

91. Joseph Young, Diaries, 4–5.

92. Miller, *Correspondence of Bishop George Miller*, 20–21.

93. See David Sprague Hollister to Joseph Smith, 9 May 1844.

94. Terry, Journal, 26 May 1844.

95. Smoot, "Day Book," 18 May 1844. See Smoot, "Early Experience," 22–23.

96. Smoot, "Day Book," 25 May 1844.

97. Thomas, "Sketch and Genealogy of the Thomas' Families," 32–33.

98. Smoot, "Early Experience," 23.

99. Smoot, "Day Book," 25 May 1844.

100. Woodruff, *Wilford Woodruff, Fourth President of the Church*, 1 July 1844, 2:415. See *Boston Mail*, 2 July 1844, for another report of the incident.

101. "Whigs of Boston," *The Prophet*, 13 July 1844, 2.

102. Horner, "Adventures of a Pioneer," 214–15.

CHAPTER 6

THE ASSASSINATION AND AFTERMATH

Instead of electing your leader the chief magistrate
of this nation, they have martyred him.

—An angel to John D. Lee, 8 July 1844

Electioneer Experience: William I. Appleby. On 5 May 1844, after preaching in the East for a year, William Appleby encountered electioneer John Wakefield, who gave him a copy of *Views* to acquaint him with Joseph's political platform. The two men discussed the campaign plan of "hundreds of elders . . . abroad in the states, delivering lectures regarding [*Views*] . . . and holding up Joseph as [a] fit candidate for the office [of presidency]. Accordingly, in the evening, we both lectured on the powers and policy of the government." Appleby electioneered across Pennsylvania while en route to Philadelphia, arriving on 13 May. He toured the neighborhood where the Bible Riots had erupted the previous week. "Viewed some of the burning ruins of St. Augustine's Church," he penned, "[and] the bullet holes in houses . . . &c, occasioned by a riotous mob a few days before, in the which several were killed and wounded." The escalating tensions "between the native Americans [i.e., native-born citizens, or "nativists"] and the [immigrant] Catholics," initially a disagreement over which version

After adding his political talent to Joseph's campaign, William I. Appleby calmed the congregations in the East following Joseph's murder. Courtesy of Vicki Jo Hays.

of the Bible should be used in public schools, ignited several days of riots. Appleby saw firsthand the grim result of the deadly violence that Protestants (principally Whigs and more particularly nativists) were willing to inflict on the Catholic minority of mostly immigrants. What he did not know was that enemies would resort to similar violence a month later against the man he was canvassing for—Joseph Smith.[1]

On that fateful day, Appleby was in Georgetown, Delaware, with his companion U. Clark.[2] Clark headed to a nearby town while Appleby spent the evening politicking for the prophet. At that exact time, a thousand miles to the west, a mob assassinated Joseph in Carthage, Illinois. It was not until 10 July that Appleby heard an initial report that the prophet was dead. "I could not credit the report . . . at first," he wrote; "indeed I did not want to believe it, and almost hoped against hope." After a night of troubling thoughts, Appleby found apostles Heber C. Kimball and Lyman Wight, along with other electioneers, in Wilmington, Delaware.

The apostles, on their way to Baltimore, told Appleby and his new companion, Joseph A. Stratton, that they had heard similar news. They all huddled at the home of local electioneer Ellis M. Sanders. Wight's powerful sermon that night gave those gathered "some hopes that our brethren [were] yet alive." Wight, Kimball, Appleby, and Stratton, in company with other electioneers as well as delegates, traveled from Pennsylvania, Maryland, and Delaware to Baltimore the following morning to hold the scheduled national convention. The morning papers printed a copy of a letter from Illinois governor Thomas Ford that "[convinced them] all that the prophet and patriarch [were] <u>dead</u>." Stunned, the group "sat down and wept like children."[3]

Appleby and Stratton separated themselves from the others, "feeling oppressed and mourning the loss of Joseph and Hyrum." As Appleby later contemplated Zion, his thoughts rallied somewhat. He wrote, "[I have] a desire to humble myself, more than ever, with renewed zeal and determination to advance the work, or my diligence, before the Lord, and also to renew my covenant." They rebaptized each other in the Atlantic Ocean and reconfirmed each other on the beach as a sign of their renewed dedication in the face of Joseph's assassination. The next day the entire forlorn band returned to Wilmington. One more day saw Appleby at home in Recklesstown, New Jersey. Conflicted feelings still tearing at him, he penned: "Shedding tears of heartfelt grief and sorrow, before my Father in Heaven, for the loss of my beloved brethren, Joseph and Hyrum. . . . Indeed it was a blow, a loss, that all the church felt and lamented and mourned before heaven. . . . But if they have killed the prophet and patriarch, they cannot kill Mormonism or the church. Its course is onward."

*   *   *

Electioneers throughout the nation likewise reacted with shock, anger, and sadness at the news that their revered prophet and presidential candidate had been assassinated. When the vast majority of electioneers eventually returned to Nauvoo or their hometowns, they were "determined by the aid of heaven's king to preserve and sound the gospel drum, and if possible, with more energy." Church leaders ordained Appleby a high priest for his tireless efforts during the campaign, assigning him to preside over the large Philadelphia Branch. Like Appleby, many church members came to see Joseph's assassination as a religious rejection of the restored gospel and a political refutation of the prophet. As they judged it, the nation had rejected God's will and had blood on its hands. Yet even with the demise of Joseph and the campaign, the hope of Zion and theodemocracy burned in the hearts of the electioneer cadre.[4]

DESTRUCTION OF THE *NAUVOO EXPOSITOR* PRESS

Prominent in the lead-up to Joseph's assassination were the malicious actions of three sets of brothers: William and Wilson Law, Robert and Charles Foster, and Chauncey and Francis Higbee. All six had been Latter-day Saints and friends of Joseph. Plural marriage, economic competition, political differences, and reciprocal charges of sexual immorality and murder plots now divided them from Joseph, and they conspired to destroy him. William Law purchased a printing press from Whig politician Abraham Jonas. Jonas was just one of several such men whose involvement suggests a conspiracy wider than a local mob. On 10 May 1844 the dissenters published the prospectus of their aptly named *Nauvoo Expositor*.

The first and only issue of the *Expositor* ran on 7 June. The dissenters proclaimed Joseph a fallen prophet laden with moral, economic, and political corruption and a "specimen . . . of the most pernicious and diabolical character that ever stained the pages of the historian."[5] Knowing the principles behind Joseph's religious, economic, social, and political Zion, they objected to them and caricatured them. They painted Joseph as a "hellish fiend" who had to be put down.[6] The conspirators created a dangerous environment to ensure the prophet's downfall—a perfect trap. If Joseph did nothing in response, the lies and distortions would incite the mobs that were already mustering, intent on destroying Nauvoo. The accusations would also tarnish Joseph's campaign with damning publicity. If Joseph chose to hinder or destroy the press, the dissidents would have a legal pretext to have him arrested and taken from the safety of Nauvoo. In fact, conspirator Thomas Sharp, head of the Anti-Mormon Party and editor of the *Warsaw Signal*, wrote two weeks *before* the *Expositor*'s only run that "Joe Smith is not safe out of Nauvoo, and we would not be surprised to hear of his death by violent means in a short time."[7]

In the end Joseph chose to destroy the *Nauvoo Expositor* press, unwittingly entering the conspiratorial trap. Members of the Nauvoo City Council had passed a libel law granting them authority to raze the press for being a "public nuisance." Thus legally empowered, Joseph and his associates acted swiftly to prevent a repeat of the Missouri atrocities. They believed they had judicial precedent on their side, and they felt justified, having not exercised prior restraint against the *Expositor*'s first printing.

Still, what was so dangerous about the *Expositor*'s claims that invited such quick and decisive action? Accusations of promiscuous polygamy, economic autocracy, political control—such claims had dogged the church for a decade. This time the *Expositor*'s language made it clear that someone in the Council of Fifty was divulging its decisions to the dissidents, who in turn were publishing dangerous, distorted versions of them. According to Joseph's revelation, the Council of Fifty was to protect Zion and prepare men to rule in the kingdom of God *following* the collapse of the world's governments. As part of its establishment, the council confidentially made Joseph prophet, priest, and king over the house of Israel—not over the United States.

Contrarily, the *Expositor* declared the council a "secret society" formed for the purpose of exerting "political power and influence" and headed by Joseph "as king [and] law-giver,"[8] intent on seizing the US presidency in order to "distribute among his faithful supporters the office of governor in all the different states for the purpose, we presume, of more effectually consolidating the government."[9] Joseph's "Political Revelations" from his position of "self-constituted Monarch" created a "Union of Church and State" to "put down" "all governments."[10] Such distorted declarations were a public relations nightmare for Joseph's campaign. They described him as a conspiratorial, traitorous, egomaniacal, monarchal leader bent on usurping the government. With his most important council compromised, there seemed to be no end to the distortions and lies that could destroy Joseph, his campaign, his Zion, and ultimately his people.[11] A few electioneers were directly involved in the *Expositor* crisis. William W. Phelps, Stephen H. Perry, and Levi Richards were added to the city council to fill vacancies created by departed electioneers, and they voted for destroying the press. Stephen Markham, in his role as policeman, accompanied the city marshal to the *Expositor* office and assisted in the destruction of the press.

The dissenters filed a grievance at Carthage, the county seat. A constable arrested Joseph and members of the Nauvoo City Council on the charge of riot for having destroyed the printing press. Naturally, Nauvoo's Municipal Court released the accused, and a friendly non–Latter-day Saint justice of the peace found them not guilty. These legal moves only served to fan the flames of hostility against the Saints. Thomas Sharp's call to action was a flashpoint: "Citizens ARISE, ONE and ALL!!!—Can you stand by, and suffer such INFERNAL DEVILS!! to ROB men of their property and RIGHTS, without avenging them. We have no time for comment, every man will make his own. LET IT BE MADE WITH POWDER AND BALL!!!"[12]

The next day, committees of angry settlers throughout the county mobilized to drive the Saints from outlying areas into Nauvoo and cut off communication with the rest of the county, state, and nation. John Taylor remembered that "it was with the greatest difficulty that we could get our papers circulated; they were destroyed by postmasters and others, and scarcely ever arrived at the place of their destination." Ironically, the very men who expressed outrage at the destruction of the *Expositor* now practiced their own form of suppression.[13] As a result of the deteriorating situation, Mayor Joseph Smith declared martial law in Nauvoo.

THE ELECTIONEER CADRE
AND JOSEPH'S FINAL DAYS

When Governor Ford arrived in Carthage, Illinois, on 21 June 1844, he demanded that Joseph face trial there. "We dare not come," Joseph wrote Ford, "though your Excellency promises protection." John C. Calhoun Jr., coincidentally in Nauvoo that day, had persuaded Joseph to go to Washington, DC, "to lay the facts before the general government."[14] Under cover of darkness, Joseph, his brother Hyrum, and two trusted associates rowed across the Mississippi River to Iowa. Electioneer John M. Bernhisel, Joseph's personal physician and political adviser, soon joined them. The next day three Nauvoo leaders, including electioneer Reynolds Cahoon of the Council of Fifty, brought a message from Emma to not flee. After consulting with Hyrum, Joseph reluctantly agreed to answer the charges in Carthage. Electioneer Jedediah M. Grant was dispatched to deliver the message to Governor Ford. "We shall be butchered," Joseph flatly told the group. He bade farewell to friends and family in Nauvoo. Nine-year-old Charlotte Leabo, daughter of electioneer Peter Haws of the Council of Fifty, remembered that Joseph stopped at her house on the way to Carthage. He "kissed each of the children and bade them good-bye, telling them to be good, and that they would see him no more."[15]

Joseph and the other defendants (several were electioneers) and their escort arrived around midnight at Carthage's Hamilton Hotel, where the dissidents and other conspirators were lodging. The next day the defendants were released on bail, secured by bonds from electioneers Dan Jones, Edward Hunter, and John S. Fullmer. Before they could depart, Joseph and Hyrum were rearrested on a legally dubious charge of treason for placing Nauvoo under martial law. Clearly the conspirators were determined to keep the brothers in Carthage, on one pretense or another, to murder them. Members of the electioneer cadre remained involved in the developing situation until the last hours of Joseph and Hyrum Smith's final two days. On 26 June, Stephen Markham and Dan Jones, who used hickory "rascal beaters" to defend their brethren from rouge militiamen the day before, tried to fix the broken latch on the jail's bedroom door. John S. Reid filed several legal complaints, and John S. Fullmer smuggled his "single-barrel pocket pistol" into the jail, giving it to Joseph. The electioneers were doing all they could to protect the prophet.[16]

That evening, the Anti-Mormon Carthage Central Committee convened in the hotel. Visitors to the meeting included Governor Ford, Illinois Whig Central Committee member George T. M. Davis, and nearly two dozen men representing almost every state in the nation. Allegedly they had responded to a "secret national call" to join forces against the Saints. This star-chamber council met to decide the fates of the Smith brothers. "Delegates from the eastern states" explained that Joseph's *Views*, proclaimed by the electioneers, was "widely circulated and took like wildfire." They determined that if Joseph "did not get into the presidential chair this election, he would be sure to next." Whether this was hyperbole to solidify support for their assassination plans or an accurate reflection of deeply held conspiratorial fears, the council acted. They would wait for the governor to leave for Nauvoo the next day, and then they would summarily execute the Smiths.[17]

When Markham unintentionally approached the meeting, an alarm was sounded and in the scramble Dr. Wall Southwick, a mysterious land dealer from Texas, grabbed the minutes. Southwick showed Markham the notebook, revealed the meeting's purpose, and promised to give him a copy of the proceedings. Meanwhile, Davis, who attended the meeting, directed a letter to his editor titled "June 26, 1844, 8 p.m., Carthage," thereby beginning a propaganda campaign to justify the Smiths' murders. Davis reported that "before they [the militias] disband, a desperate effort will made to visit summary punishment upon the two Smiths." "You need not be surprised," he continued, "to hear, at any time, of the destruction of the two Smiths by the populace."[18] After hearing Southwick's report, Markham informed Joseph of the plot. "Be not afraid" was the prophet's only response.[19] That night a gunshot awakened the prisoners. Joseph paced the floor before lying back down. Turning to electioneer Dan Jones, he whispered, "Are you afraid to die?" Jones replied, "Has that time come, think you? Engaged in such a cause I do not think that death would have many terrors."[20] Joseph replied that Jones would yet see his native Wales as a missionary.

On the morning of 27 July, Governor Ford broke his promise to take Joseph with him to Nauvoo but kept his promise to demobilize the troops

Electioneers John S. Fullmer and Cyrus H. Wheelock smuggled these pistols into Carthage Jail. Joseph used the "pepperbox" (bottom) in defense during the assassination. Courtesy of Church History Museum. © IRI. Used by permission.

at Carthage. One company remained to "guard" the jail. Some of the disbanded troops, however, went only a short distance out of town before returning to "kill old Joe and Hyrum."[21] Cyrus H. Wheelock, overhearing their communications, visited the jail and smuggled in a six-shooter pepperbox pistol. "Would any of you like to have this?" he asked. Joseph took it. Then the prophet gave John S. Fullmer's pistol to Hyrum, saying, "You may have use for this." "I hate to use such things, or to see them used," Hyrum replied. "So do I," remarked Joseph, "but we may have to, to defend ourselves." Hyrum took the pistol.[22]

With Joseph trapped in jail and his enemies openly plotting his murder, the election campaign would soon be a historical footnote. As for the Council of Fifty, now exposed and caricatured, its members believed they were ready to perform their roles in establishing the political kingdom of God. However, this was not the season they had hopefully supposed. Joseph lamented, "We have the revelation of Jesus, and the knowledge within us is sufficient to organize a righteous government upon the earth, and to give universal peace to all mankind if they would receive it; but we lack the physical strength, as did our Savior when a child, to defend our principles." Wheelock and Fullmer then left with "heavy heart[s]" for Nauvoo around 11:00 a.m. The guards later refused Dan Jones reentry to the jail.[23]

Stephen Markham, the last electioneer to be with the prisoners, sat next to Joseph. "I wish you would tell me how this fuss is going to come out as you have at other times beforehand," he implored. "Bro[ther] Markham," Joseph replied, "the Lord placed me to govern this kingdom on the earth, but the people [have] taken away from me the [reins] of government."[24] In Joseph's mind the campaign was over. He had believed that with divine help he would be elected. But now it was clear that the United States had fully rejected him and in so doing rejected God *and* political salvation.

While returning from an errand, Markham was intercepted by militiamen and forced back to Nauvoo. The occupants of the jail now numbered only four. As the afternoon progressed, they became anxious. Hyrum read to pass the time and Willard Richards penned correspondence. John Taylor, an accomplished tenor, sang Joseph's new favorite hymn, "A Poor Wayfaring Man of Grief." Around 4:00 p.m. the guards were changed.

An hour later the prisoners heard a cry of "Surrender!" and what turned out to be the prearranged firing of blank musket charges by the guards. Richards glanced out the open window and noticed some one hundred men, their faces blackened with wet gunpowder. Assailants rushed up the stairs. The first met Joseph's fist. The small landing leading to the bedroom quickly became crowded. The other prisoners shed their coats and entered the fray. Gunfire erupted from inside and outside the jail. The prisoners pushed desperately on the door to keep the mob out. Hyrum reached for his pistol. A shot pierced the door and struck him just left of the nose. Falling to the ground, he exclaimed, "I am a dead man!" Rushing to his fallen brother, Joseph exclaimed, "Oh my dear brother Hyrum!"

There was no time for mourning. Joseph could hear the door giving way. Soon gunfire flashes and smoke filled the room. Joseph turned, approached the partly open door, and fired the six-shot pepperbox. Three rounds misfired. Three struck, wounding separate men. The mob momentarily paused but then renewed the assault. Richards and Taylor parried the muskets sticking through the crack of the door. "That's right, Brother Taylor, parry them off as well as you can" were the last words Taylor heard Joseph speak. The force of the gunmen sprang the door open. Three-hundred-pound Richards became trapped behind it. Taylor ran to escape through the window, but a ball fired from outside knocked him back into the room. His impact on the windowsill crushed his pocket watch, forever recording the time of the murders—5:16 p.m. and 26 seconds. He rolled under the room's bed. Three more balls struck him. Passing in and out of consciousness, Taylor would nonetheless survive.

More muskets fired into the room. Joseph ran to the window and hung awkwardly on the ledge. With uplifted hands he cried, "Oh Lord my God!" Falling, or perhaps leaping, he landed heavily on his side on the ground fifteen feet below.[25] When someone shouted, "He's jumped the window!" the murderers stampeded down the stairs. Outside, someone dragged the semiconscious Joseph up against a well curb.[26] Levi Williams, the leader of the assault, ordered, "Shoot the God damn scoundrel!"[27] Four riflemen fired. Each ball found its mark. Joseph Smith, prophet and presidential candidate, was dead.[28] The assailants dispersed quickly. Willard Richards and others cared for the wounded John Taylor and prepared crude coffins

Joseph's assassination marked him as the first presidential candidate in US history to be assassinated. Artist unknown. Courtesy of Church History Library.

for the corpses. Richards penned a quick note to Nauvoo in the middle of the night, confirming the deaths and counseling the Saints not to retaliate.

ELECTIONEER REACTIONS TO THE ASSASSINATION

Some electioneers were working in and around Nauvoo on the day of Joseph's assassination. Edward Hunter had gone to Springfield to intercept Governor Ford and "allay the excitement and hostility . . . in the direction of Nauvoo and the 'Mormons.'" Hunter discovered that the governor was already in Carthage. As he returned to Nauvoo, "the whole country was in an uproar," and he and his traveling companions heard constant threats "that the 'Mormon' leaders would never get away alive." Hunter reached Nauvoo in the late afternoon of 27 June, the same time as the murders.

The next day, the Smith brothers' bodies were returned to a grief-stricken Nauvoo. Hunter recorded, "A massive crowd of mourners [was] there, lamenting the great loss of our prophet and patriarch." He recalled,

Edward Hunter saw the dead bodies of Joseph and Hyrum in Nauvoo—a "scene . . . enough to almost melt the soul of man." 1867 photo by Edward Martin courtesy of Church History Library.

"The scene was enough to almost melt the soul of man." Hunter helped carry Joseph's body into the Mansion House, "where thousands of people, bathed in tears, passed in procession, two abreast, to view their mangled remains."[29] Lyman O. Littlefield recorded that he and his wife "had the mournful privilege of looking one sad and brief adieu upon the noble forms of those men of God." He later wrote: "Although forty-four years have since passed away, the powers of memory seldom go back and review the scene—though in gleams of momentary fleetness—without sensations of pain."[30]

Levi W. Hancock took his ten-year-old son Mosiah to the Mansion House and told him "to place one hand on Joseph's breast and to raise [his] other arm and swear with hand uplifted that [he] would never make a compromise with any of the sons of hell." Mosiah recorded that he "took [the vow] with a determination to fulfill to the very letter."[31] Christiana Riser, the wife of George C. Riser, who was electioneering in Ohio, "looked upon the faces of Joseph and Hyrum in death [and] . . . vowed that if she had another son she would name him after the prophet and his brother." Two years later she gave birth to Joseph Hyrum Riser, one of more than two hundred children of electioneers named for Joseph or Hyrum.[32]

The next day William W. Phelps, Joseph's longtime friend, Council of Fifty member, and electioneer gave the funeral sermon. Addressing ten thousand Saints, he proclaimed, "Two of the greatest and best men who have lived on the earth since . . . the Savior have fallen victims to the popular will of mobocracy in this boasted 'Asylum of the oppressed.'" Although the prophet was dead, the priesthood restored through him "remain[ed] unharmed" and other leaders would step into the "'shoes' of the 'prophet, priest and king' of Israel . . . with the same power, the same God, and the same spirit that caused Joseph to move the cause of Zion with mighty power." Hunter remembered, "Their death was hard to bear. Our hope was almost gone."[33]

A few days later Jedediah M. Grant married his sweetheart Caroline Van Dyke. That evening he left on a mission to call the apostles and his fellow electioneers home to Nauvoo. He would accomplish this primarily by dispersing correspondence from Philadelphia (where he was to once again preside over the branch) and giving direction to the eastern Saints.

Milo Andrus and John Loveless were the only missionaries serving away from Nauvoo who returned in time to attend the funeral. They were electioneering nearby when, as Loveless recorded, "we heard of the assassination of the Prophet Joseph and his brother Hyrum . . . [and] went home . . . quickly."[34] Andrus also visited Carthage Jail "and saw the floor stained with the best blood of the present generation."[35] Having returned to Nauvoo, several other electioneers made the pilgrimage to Carthage to pay homage. Joseph Curtis recorded his solemn feelings at seeing blood stains on the walls.[36] Charles C. Rich "visited the jail at Carthage to see . . . where the prophet and patriarch [were] mart[y]red." A mixture of anger, reverence, and determination left with him.[37]

Some distant electioneers who heard of Joseph's assassination in newspaper accounts initially discounted them. In an age of horse and buggy, confirmation of this devastating news through trusted channels could take weeks, leaving the electioneers in growing emotional turmoil as the days passed. Norton Jacob and most of the Michigan electioneers were "attend[ing] a state convention . . . for the purpose of nominating presidential electors." On 5 July 1844 newspapers reporting Joseph's death appeared. "We did not believe the story," Jacob recorded in his journal, "and proceeded to nominate our electors." But while heading to his next assignment with Zebedee Coltrin, Jacob received a letter from Charles C. Rich confirming the assassination. Jacob soon met Moses Smith, who was "completely discomfited by the news of the prophet's death and . . . would preach very little afterwards."[38]

Joseph Stratton learned of Joseph's death on 7 July at the train station in Wilmington, Delaware. "I did not credit the report," he wrote, "although it created a very singular sensation; it seemed to run through me like an electric shock." The next day he read about the assassination in the Philadelphia papers. When he encountered Elijah F. Sheets and three other electioneers on 10 June, the meeting was "quite refreshing to both in this time of excitement." As they discussed the news, "some believed the report was true; others did not." Stratton journeyed to Philadelphia the next week, where Jedediah M. Grant gave the gathered Saints "all the particulars" about the assassination.[39]

Abraham O. Smoot first heard reports of the murders on 8 July. He and his colleagues had "heavy burthens of mind from the alarming story." Smoot wrote, "Awful forebodings seared my mind which I labored to conceal from my brethren and friends . . . by alleging that I had no right to believe the reports, as many such reports had proved too false in days past concerning him." Two days later his "mind [was] still like the troubled sea that casteth up mire and dirt from the whisperings of the Spirit of the probability of the death of Joseph and Hyrum." On 12 July he received the *Nauvoo Neighbor*, which was "dressed in deep mourning," and learned that the "awful tragedy had [in fact] been committed." Shaken, Smoot penned, "Great God, endow me with Christian fortitude, for all my forebodings and fears are more than realized."[40]

En route to their assignment in Vermont, James Burgess and Alfred Cordon read in the Syracuse, New York, papers that Joseph and Hyrum had been killed. In Dover, Vermont, nine days later, they continued preaching and electioneering, believing the reports inaccurate. On 26 July they received a copy of the *Nauvoo Neighbor* that "gave an account of them bringing their dead bodies into the City of Nauvoo and the scene which took place, which would be melting for the heart of any human being having read it," recorded Burgess. "There must be some truth in the matter. It weighed our spirits down with grief to think that two men of God . . . [should] so soon fall by the hands of wicked men; we little thought of it when we left Nauvoo." The idea that the Smiths were dead "pained our very souls," Burgess added.[41]

A small number of electioneers received comfort in what they described as revelatory visions or dreams. George Miller recorded a dream from the morning of June 28, just twelve hours after the assassination. He later remembered that as he lay in bed, "suddenly Joseph Smith appeared to me, saying, 'God bless you, Brother Miller.'" Joseph told Miller that he and his brother Hyrum had been killed by a mob at Carthage after being "delivered up by the brethren as a lamb for the slaughter." "You ought not to have left me," Joseph declared. "If you had stayed with me I should not have been given up." Miller countered, "But you sent me." The prophet replied, "I know I did, but you ought not to have gone," and then approaching Miller as if to embrace him, Joseph said, "God bless you forever and ever." As the dream ended, Miller found himself standing in the middle of the room, arms extended as if returning an embrace. Miller's companion, Thomas Edwards, now awakened, called out, "What is the matter?" Miller said nothing.

During their morning walk, Miller told Edwards of his vision, declaring he was sure it was true and he would be returning to Nauvoo. Edwards responded that Miller "preached too much and [his] mind was somewhat deranged" and that they should fulfill their appointments. Miller agreed, but after their last engagement they headed home. Passing a tavern, they read of the Smiths' deaths. "Brother Edwards, being an excitable man, was wholly unmanned," Miller wrote, "and insisted on an immediate separation, as traveling together might endanger our lives, and broke off from me . . . , and I did not see . . . him until I saw him in Nauvoo, four weeks afterwards."[42]

John D. Lee in Kentucky learned of Joseph's death from newspaper accounts on 5 July. A few days later he recorded a dream-vision. A heavenly messenger appeared to him and showed him "the martyrdom of the prophet and patriarch" and "bid [Lee's] fears depart," for his "labors [were] accepted." The angel explained that Christ's original Twelve and Seventy had felt all was lost when he was "taken and crucified instead of being crown[ed] king (temporal) of that nation, as they fondly expected." "Just so it is with you," the messenger explained. "Instead of electing your leader the chief magistrate of this nation, they have martyred him in prison, which has hasten[ed] his exaltation to the executive chair over this generation."

The angel instructed Lee to "return home in peace and there [a]wait [his] endowment from on high, as did the disciples at Jerusalem."[43]

William R. R. Stowell documented a dream just days after returning to Nauvoo. In it he walked into Joseph's mansion and found him lying in a bed. They greeted each other and then traveled to Stowell's home. After some conversation the prophet wished to go home, but Stowell pleaded for a blessing first. Joseph laid his hands on Stowell and "pronounced many choice blessings . . . [and] declared that the blessings of God should be upon [his] efforts in rolling the latter-day work on." The blessing ended with an emphatic "and you shall be blessed." For Stowell, the dream swept away "the darkness and despondency that had brooded over him," and with "his mind . . . at rest . . . his usual courage and energy returned."[44]

William I. Appleby experienced a vision of Joseph more than a year after the martyrdom. Joseph took Appleby into another room and the two sat in chairs face-to-face. "He commenced instructing and counseling me, with tears rolling down his cheeks, in things appertaining to the cause I am engaged in," wrote Appleby, "which if I hearken to will be to my eternal welfare." He remembered that Joseph "counseled me 'to never find fault or lift my hand against the servants of God.'"[45]

Perhaps most amazing was the experience of James Holt. He and companion Jackson Smith preached and politicked around Holt's family home in Wilson County, Tennessee. They signed a contract in the nearby town of Lebanon for the printing of five hundred copies of *Views*, to be ready, ironically, on 27 June. When Holt returned on that day, his order was not ready. The editor apologized, explaining that "so many people had borrowed the copy to read it that he had lost track of it." When it was discovered that the owner of the pamphlet was in town, some of the townspeople asked

At the exact time of Joseph's assassination, James Holt received a revelation of the deed while preaching a sermon five hundred miles away. Image courtesy of Linda Holt.

Holt to preach and politic. They procured him the courthouse, rang the town bell, and soon the building was overflowing with people eager to hear the "Mormon" who had grown up nearby.

Holt began his sermon two hours before sunset, around 5:15 p.m.—the exact time of the attack on Carthage Jail, five hundred miles to the northwest. Holt later wrote that "the Spirit of the Lord was on [him]" as he taught the first principles of the restored gospel and the persecution of the Saints in a so-called Christian and free land. He preached for two hours, much longer than he had anticipated. He recorded, "In the winding up of my sermon, I had the spirit of revelation come upon me, and I told them that the enemies of the church had taken the prophet of God this day and put him to death, as they had all the prophets of God in all dispensations of the world." "Now," he concluded, "you may have this as a testimony of the gospel, for that is true Mormonism." Stunned at his own words, Holt looked out over the crowd: "No one had anything to say, but all seemed struck with amazement and their eyes filled with tears."

Holt returned to his father's house. He shared his experience with his companion Jackson Smith and also with his father. Neither believed him. Holt responded, "The Spirit of God [can] reveal anything to man that [is] going on in any part of the world," adding, "I kn[o]w that God . . . revealed the truth to me and that I should start for home right away." Skeptical, Smith refused to return to Nauvoo with him.

On his way home, Holt felt drawn to a man on a porch reading a paper. He approached and asked for water as an excuse to talk. After a few swallows, Holt said, "You seem to be quite interested in what you are reading. Is it anything very special?" The man said it "concern[ed] the death of the Mormon prophets." Holt coyly asked where those prophets lived. The man replied, "Nauvoo, and [they] were taken to Carthage and killed." He remarked that the article carried the signature of Governor Ford, so it must be true. Holt thanked the man for the water and continued his journey, the stranger never knowing he had entertained one of Joseph's electioneers. Holt remembered, "This confirmed my impression of the expression I had by the Spirit at Lebanon, for I now had no cause to doubt if I had felt so inspired, but I had not doubted since it was first revealed to me."

The series of events, "instead of . . . weakening my faith, . . . strengthened it," Holt penned, "for I knew that Joseph Smith was a prophet of God."[46]

However, most of the electioneer cadre had no premonition of Joseph's death. The sudden news of his assassination shocked and dismayed these men who had sacrificed to strike out across the nation in his name. Alfred B. Lambson and John Jones Jr. had the martyrs' deaths confirmed upon meeting apostle George A. Smith and other electioneers in Elkhart, Indiana, on 14 July. After hearing David Fullmer preach, the two men "were filled with grief and [they] . . . spent the day in mourning." Indeed, "deep sorrow filled all the Saints' hearts, and many gave themselves up to weeping," recorded George A. Smith. "We all felt much the worse for want of sleep."[47] Crandell Dunn wrote, "The Spirit of God seemed to carry the testimony to all hearts, which caused the silent tear to trickle down the cheeks of [the] brethren."[48]

A twenty-one-year-old Virginian and recent convert, Henry G. Boyle had never met Joseph. On 16 July, while traveling to a conference in Tazewell County, Virginia, he heard the news of Joseph's murder. "I felt depressed in my feeling," Boyle remembered. "I was but a boy and had but little experience. I asked the Lord to strengthen me with his Spirit and enable me to do honor to his cause; my prayer was answered, for I had put my whole trust in him."[49] Nancy and Moses Tracy were returning to Ellisburg, New York, from preaching and electioneering to Nancy's family when they "received the heartrending news that [their] prophet was slain in Carthage jail." "We were horror stricken," Nancy recalled. "My husband sobbed aloud, 'Is it true? Can it be true, when so short a time ago he set us apart to fill this mission and was all right?'"[50]

Irish convert James H. Flanigan, after receiving the news of "the death of our beloved prophet and patriarch, Joseph and Hyrum Smith," recorded that it "shocked the Saints, shocked this realm, and shocked the world."[51] On 14 July Jacob Hamblin felt "very melancholy and [his] spirit [was] depressed" when he received a letter with the dreadful news. "My feelings I will not attempt to describe," he penned. "For a moment, all was lost." While walking to his next appointment, he sensed he could not preach and "felt under no obligation as they had killed the men God had sent to restore all things." Hamblin "could not refrain from weeping, and turned aside to give vent to [his] feelings." As he did so, he encountered a group of men who ridiculed him saying, "I wonder what will become of Elder Hamblin's Mormon president?" Upon hearing this, Hamblin recorded, "I felt that if I could be annihilated it would be [a] blessing to me." The thought that Joseph was dead was more than he could endure. "It appeared to be the weight of a mountain upon me," he remarked. "I thought it would crush me to death."[52]

Those with the gift of language expressed themselves through poems. Joel H. Johnson dedicated a poem to Joseph. The final stanza defiantly declared:

> Thy holy cause I will defend,
> And all thy sorrows, joys and care,
> Shall be my own, till life shall end,
> With thee eternal lives to share.[53]

William I. Appleby's poem praised Joseph's devotion to the cause of Zion in his roles as priest and king:

> And for these truths thy blood was shed, and laid thy body down;
> But thou wilt rule a mighty host, and wear a martyr's crown.
> Millions shall know thou art a king, thy power they shall dread;
> For by [thy] priesthood, thou was't crown'd before thy blood was shed;
> Thou'rt only pass'd behind the veil, to plead the cause above,
> Of mourning, bleeding Zion, which was, thy daily love.[54]

William W. Phelps wrote a poem later set to Scottish folk music. The new song became one of the church's most enduring and endearing hymns. As placed in the 1845 hymnal, two verses capture the post-assassination feelings of the electioneers:

> Praise to his mem'ry, he died as a martyr;
> Honor'd and blest is his ever great name;
> Long shall his blood, which was shed by assassins,
> Stain Illinois,[55] while the earth lauds his fame.

Sacrifice brings forth the blessings of heaven;
Earth must atone for the blood of that man!
Wake up the world for the conflict of justice,
Millions shall know "brother Joseph" again.[56]

Perhaps John D. Lee best captured the poignant feelings of the election-eer cadre regarding the loss of Joseph: "A friend more dear to us than all the riches and honors that could be conferred on us by a thousand such worlds as we now inhabit."[57]

Many electioneers responded to the loss of Joseph and Hyrum with an increased desire to vigorously advance the work of Zion. William Stowell recorded, "While I felt to mourn deeply the loss of our noble leader, my faith was not in the least shaken in the doctrines and principles that the prophet had planted in the earth." He continued, "The spirit of gathering with the Saints and sharing their fortunes, whatever they might be, was still upon me as I continued to labor diligently in preparing for the journey to Nauvoo."[58] Stowell led a small group of Saints across the country in a wagon that defiantly advertised "Nauvoo" on its canvas cover.

Other electioneers responded to Joseph's assassination with unmiti-gated fury. John Loveless was returning to Nauvoo on 28 June when he learned of Joseph's death and had to endure the galling celebratory mood of church enemies.

About one hundred fifty miles below [Nauvoo], we met a boat com-ing down that gave us the news of the prophet's death; a perfect shout was set up by the devils incarnate on our boat, who were on their way up to Nauvoo to fight the Mormons. Had I possessed the strength of Sampson, I would, like him, [have] sunk the whole mass in one gulf of oblivion and sent them to their congenial spirits, the howling devils of the infernal regions.[59]

Most electioneers, immediately and over time, saw the assassination as the rejection of Joseph and the restored gospel by a wicked nation. Amasa Lyman observed a Fourth of July celebration in Cincinnati, just a day after hearing of the murders. He wrote that the people made a "great preparation . . . to celebrate [the] birth of American liberty, which might better have been turned into its funeral."⁶⁰ On 11 July in Rochester, New York, Franklin D. Richards wrote, "While the world exults in the supposed death of the prophet, they might better bemoan their own pending fate and that of our own happy country, in fulfillment of his predictions."⁶¹ William Hyde was furious that the nation had denied Joseph: "They have stained the earth with the blood of the man, or men, through whom God has organized his kingdom on the earth, which kingdom he has decreed shall stand forever. . . . And for that blood the nation will be obliged to atone."⁶²

The electioneers suspected a political motive behind Joseph's assassination.⁶³ Chief among them was campaign manager, apostle, and wounded victim of the Carthage mob John Taylor. On 27 June 1854, exactly ten years after the martyrdom, Taylor spoke at the packed Tabernacle in Salt Lake City as the last survivor of that fateful day. He chronicled the enemies inside the church in 1844 and their machinations, including how a conspiring "political party" angry over "Mormon political power" induced local rabble to "destroy the Mormons" because of their religion. The influence of Joseph's political foes was "the great cause of this animosity and trouble," Taylor testified. "Strong political feeling existed against Joseph Smith, and [Taylor had] reason to believe that [Joseph's] letters to Henry Clay were made use of by political parties opposed to Mr. Clay and were the means of that statesman's defeat."⁶⁴

Nathan T. Porter remembered that Joseph's enemies "began to be jealous of his success in a political as well as religious [point] of view." They "began with renewed diligence to stir up more violent persecutions against him." Latter-day Saint dissenters were used in the conspiracy to offer "false accusations and vindictive charges issuing out writs of indictment." They, "like Judas, betrayed him into the hands of his enemies."⁶⁵ Joseph L. Robinson recalled that "wicked rulers . . . became mad, also saying if we let this fellow (Joseph) alone he will surely take away our place and nation. We must dispose of him in some way. So they got up persecutions and sent officers to Nauvoo that the prophet might be stopped."⁶⁶

Lyman O. Littlefield published *The Martyrs* in 1888 to tell the story of the assassination to a new generation of Saints. He was privy to information from eyewitnesses as well as from the testimonies of the accused murderers at trial. His research revealed a politically motivated conspiracy.

There existed "powerful influences and jealousies in the circle of some of the leading men at the capital of the nation" because of the "presidential canvass that was in progress," Littlefield asserted. "There were good grounds for the belief that an understanding was had between them [national political figures] and the Governors of Missouri and Illinois, and from them down through some of the State and County officers, that Joseph was getting too much power and influence, and his career must come to a close before the end of the campaign."[67]

Few electioneers would disagree with the conclusions of Lorenzo Snow, the first electioneer to leave Nauvoo to advocate for Joseph's presidency, president of the campaign in Ohio, and future president of the church. After hearing of the assassination, Snow observed, "The details of that horrid transaction are sufficient to show that no protection can be expected by [Latter-day] Saints from the government." To twist the knife, the residents of western Illinois were now demanding that the Saints leave the state. Snow indignantly penned:

> Are we to be forever mobbed and murdered because we have a religion different from other people? . . . Does not the blood of liberty flow through my veins and the spirit of freedom burn in my bosom? Yes! Yes! . . . Then I ask this mobocratic government if it expects [that] my hand, my heart, and my tongue are going to be hushed in silence by their damnable and worse-than-savage deeds. I say no, no! For I have sworn before the Almighty God, the Maker of Heaven and Earth, that so long as the life pulses in this heart of mine, every power and faculty of my soul shall be employed in defending the cause of the oppressed the people of God, the Latter-day Saints.[68]

* * *

Though stunned, hurt, and dismayed, most of the electioneers remained faithful to their belief that Joseph Smith was the prophet of God. While opponents of the church were successful in killing Joseph and terminating his candidacy, they did not deter his cadre of electioneers. Many continued preaching, some until late 1845. Others strengthened and reassured outlying branches of the church, giving hope to shocked and beleaguered congregants. Returning to Nauvoo, they reunited with family and friends to mourn the loss of their beloved leaders. But there was work to do. "Joseph's measures" of building Zion and establishing a theodemocracy remained unrealized. The temple required completion. Latter-day Saints needed to be gathered from distant nations. With expulsion from Nauvoo imminent, refuge had to be found outside the United States. Who would lead the Latter-day Saint faithful into the West to create Zion under theodemocratic protection?

Joseph's electioneers were uniquely positioned and qualified for this unprecedented leadership challenge. They had begun their missions with high hopes of converting a nation, religiously and politically. Sacrificing much, they overcame privation, abuse, loneliness, and persecution to preach the restored gospel and advocate Joseph Smith for president. As they did, their hearts and minds became fixed on creating Joseph's Zion—a commitment that not even his death diminished. The work of Zion had to continue. How that would occur and who would lead them was still unknown, but the former electioneers—now field-tested and galvanized by loss of their prophet and continuing threats—would surely do their part. As William I. Appleby wrote, "The blood of the Saints [has] flowed to test [Zion], and [the work of building up Zion] must continue to roll on until the kingdom of this world becomes the kingdom of our Lord and his Christ."[69]

NOTES

1. Appleby, Autobiography and Journal, 122–33; and Stratton, Diary, 6–8.

2. U. Clark is a mystery. He's first mentioned in journals on 10 June 1844 as being near Philadelphia. Appleby is the only one who hints at a first name, simply writing "U." By the end of June, Clark vanishes from the journals as abruptly as he appeared. I searched everywhere in church records and national and state censuses looking for a Clark(e) with a first name starting with "U." I found no one in or out of the church. An intriguing possibility is that U. Clark is none other than "Hugh" Clark, a Catholic alderman in Philadelphia and central figure in the May and July 1844 Philadelphia Bible Riots. After news of the riots reached Nauvoo, Willard Richards, in his role on the campaign's Central Correspondence Committee, wrote to Clark. The letter,

dated 24 May 1844, said in part, "The Mormons and the Catholics . . . [are] the only two who have suffered from the cruel hand of mobocracy for their religion under the name of foreigners—and to stay this growing evil and establish Jeffersonian Democracy! . . . Help us to elect this man [Joseph] and we will help you to secure those privileges which belong to you, and break every yoke." Richards offered Clark a position on the Central Correspondence Committee, presumably as the Catholic liaison between the faiths. No record exists that Clark responded to this offer of political cooperation. However, the letter would have arrived in Philadelphia during the first week of June. The mysterious U. Clark appears a few days later in the journals of several electioneers as a campaign companion outside Philadelphia. He then disappears about the time that news of Joseph's death reaches Philadelphia and the Bible Riots recommenced. The possibility is alluring but requires more corroboration.

3. Stratton, Diary, 7.

4. See Appleby, Autobiography and Journal, 125–33.

5. "Preamble," *Nauvoo Expositor*, 7 June 1844, 2.

6. "Further Particulars from Nauvoo," *Warsaw Signal*, 12 June 1844.

7. *Warsaw Signal*, 29 May 1844.

8. "Resolutions," *Nauvoo Expositor*, 7 June 1844, 2. Joseph's being made a "king" was so widely known that Governor Thomas Ford later labeled it as one of the reasons the mob killed Joseph. See Ford, *Message of the Governor of the State of Illinois, in Relation to the Disturbances in Hancock County* (Springfield, IL: Walter and Weber, 21 December 1844), 5.

9. Sylvester Emmons, "The Expositor," *Nauvoo Expositor*, 7 June 1844, 2. This was undoubtedly a caricature of the apostles' February "moot congress" (see chapter 2).

10. "Prospectus of the *Nauvoo Expositor*," *Nauvoo Expositor*, 7 June 1844, 5; and Francis M. Higbee, "Citizens of Hancock County," *Nauvoo Expositor*, 7 June 1844, 3.

11. See, generally, *Nauvoo Expositor*, 7 June 1844; and *Nauvoo Neighbor*, 12 June 1844, 2.

12. Thomas Sharp, "Extra. The Time Is Come!," *Warsaw Signal*, 12 June 1844; original capitalization retained.

13. Taylor, *Witness to the Martyrdom*, 29.

14. Joseph Smith to Thomas Ford, 22 June 1844.

15. Alvin Kinsley, "From over the Border," *Saints' Herald*, 13 January 1904, 41.

16. John S. Fullmer to Wilford Woodruff, 18 October 1881.

17. This meeting is best explained in Wicks and Foister, *Junius and Joseph*, 164–66.

18. George T. M. Davis to John Bailhache, 26 June 1844, printed in *Alton Telegraph*, 6 July 1844.

19. Stephen Markham to Wilford Woodruff, 20 June 1856.

20. JSH, F-1:173 (26 June 1844).

21. JSH, F-1:174.

22. See "John Taylor Martyrdom Account," p. 46, The Joseph Smith Papers, https://www.josephsmithpapers.org/paper-summary/john-taylor-martyrdom -account/46. See also *History of the Church*, 7:100; and JSH, F-1:176.

23. JSH, F1:176–77.

24. Markham to Wilford Woodruff, 20 June 1856.

25. Sources and historians differ over whether Joseph fell or leaped out the window. Historians Wicks and Foister (*Junius and Joseph*, 178), Leonard (*Nauvoo*, 394–96), and Bushman (*Rough Stone Rolling*, 550), along with Willard Richards ("Two Minutes in Jail," *Nauvoo Neighbor*, 24 July 1844), argue that he fell. Eyewitnesses William Daniels (*JSP*, CFM:202n641) and William Clayton (ibid.) contend that Joseph leaped or sprang through the window.

26. See *JSP*, CFM:201, 202n641.

27. William Daniels, 4 July 1844 affidavit, as quoted in Wicks and Foister, *Junius and Joseph*, 178n75.

28. The number of musket balls that hit Joseph while he was on the window ledge is unclear, but he was still alive when he struck the ground. The evidence that Joseph was dead before hitting the ground comes from Willard Richards, "Two Minutes in Jail" (see n. 26 above), wherein he writes, "He fell on his left side a dead man." Most other sources and historians argue Joseph was still alive when he struck the ground. See note 27 above; Wicks and Foister, *Junius and Joseph*, 178n76; Bushman, *Rough Stone Rolling*, 550; and Leonard, *Nauvoo*, 397. For more on the evidence and debate surrounding Joseph's death, see *JSP*, CFM:190–204; Wicks and Foister, *Junius and Joseph*, 176–80, 230–45; and Oaks and Hill, *Carthage Conspiracy*.

29. "Bishop Edward Hunter," *Our Pioneer Heritage*, 6:319–26.

30. Littlefield, *Reminiscences of Latter-day Saints*, 162–63.

31. Mosiah L. Hancock, Autobiography, 30.

32. Riser, Reminiscences and Diary, 11.

33. "Bishop Edward Hunter," *Our Pioneer Heritage*, 6:319–26.

34. Loveless, "Autobiographical Sketch," 2.

35. Andrus, Autobiography, 6.

36. See Curtis, Reminiscences and Diary, 63.

37. Rich, Journal, 1.

38. Jacob, Reminiscence and Journal, 7.

39. Stratton, Diary, 5–8.

40. Smoot, "Day Book," 7–9.

41. See Burgess, Journal, 10–26 July 1844 (quotations are from 26 July, p. 64).

42. George Miller, "Correspondence," *Northern Islander*, 6 September 1855, 4.

43. Lee, Journal, 30.

44. Little, "Biography of William Rufus Rogers Stowell," 23–26.

45. Appleby, Autobiography and Journal, 149.

46. Holt, Autobiographical Sketch, 5–6.

47. George A. Smith, "History," 14–15 July 1844, 18.

48. Crandell, "History and Travels," 49.

49. Boyle, Autobiography and Diary, 8–9.

50. Tracy, Reminiscences and Diary, 29.

51. Flanigan, Diaries, 17.

52. Hamblin, Record of the Life of Jacob Hamblin, 103.

53. Joel Hills Johnson, "Voice from the Mountains," 3–4, 12–16.

54. Appleby, Autobiography and Journal, 244. This poem may also be proof that Council of Fifty members shared Joseph's coronation with some of the electioneers.

55. Post-1919 hymnals changed "stain Illinois" to "plead unto heaven."

56. *A Collection of Sacred Hymns, for the Church of the Latter Day Saints*, sel. Charles A. Adams (Bellows Falls, VT: S. M. Blake, 1845), 148, 149. The poem by W. W. Phelps originally appeared in *Times and Seasons*, 1 August 1844, 607, under the title "Joseph Smith."

57. Lee, Journal, 29.

58. Little, "Biography of William Rufus Rogers Stowell," 23.

59. Loveless, "Autobiographical Sketch," 2.

60. Lyman, Journal, 4 July 1844, 13.

61. Franklin D. Richards, Journal No. 2, 11–12 July 1844.

62. Hyde, Journal, 59–60.

63. Joseph's assassination has traditionally been interpreted as frontier extralegal action fueled by hatred of Joseph's religion, particularly plural marriage. This is partly correct but severely understates the role of politics, particularly Joseph's presidential campaign. Joseph was killed for his religion precisely because it included brazen politics in public and in private, the Council of Fifty, *and* plural marriage. But rumors of plural marriage had haunted Joseph for years and did not incite mobs. Most contemporary local and national criticisms of Joseph were about politics—particularly the theocratic nature of Nauvoo. Critics saw Joseph's election campaign as an attempt to nationalize such a system. Saints of Joseph's generation overwhelmingly believed the killings were political. His enemies, particularly those never affiliated with the church, had been talking politics all along and had organized against it—before the *Nauvoo Expositor* incident. Works such as Oaks and Hill's *Carthage Conspiracy*, Baker's *Murder of the Mormon Prophet*, and Wicks and Foister's *Junius and Joseph* all catalog in extensive detail the conspiracy's ties to politics. Both William Law and Governor Ford believed the beginning of Joseph's demise to be his personal involvement in the August 1843 Congressional elections and his political policies—particularly the campaign—that followed.

64. Carruth, "John Taylor's June 27, 1854, Account of the Martyrdom," 47–49; and Roberts, *Rise and Fall of Nauvoo*, 454. After Joseph's letter to Clay was published in the Nauvoo newspapers in mid-May 1844, it was republished with delight by Democratic newspapers across the nation. In 1850, when electioneer John Bernhisel, acting as Deseret's representative in Washington, DC, was introduced to Clay, the greeting was cold. Bernhisel wrote to Brigham that Clay was "still writhing under the infliction of a certain letter addressed to him by Pres. Joseph Smith in 1844." See John Bernhisel to Brigham Young, 21 March 1850.

65. Porter, Reminiscences, 125.

66. Robinson, "History," 47–48.

67. Littlefield, *Martyrs*, 50–52.

68. Lorenzo Snow, letter, 19 July 1844, in Snow, Journal, 185–87.

69. Appleby, Autobiography and Journal, 92.

CHAPTER 7

CONTRIBUTIONS TO THE SUCCESSION AND EXODUS, 1844–1847

I prophesied that the Saints would . . . be driven to the
Rocky Mountains, many would apostatize, others would . . . lose their
lives in consequence of exposure or disease, and some of you will live to
go and assist in making settlements and build cities and see the Saints
become a mighty people in the midst of the Rocky Mountains.

—Joseph Smith, 6 August 1842

Electioneer Experience: Abraham O. Smoot. When on 8 July 1844 newspapers alerted Abraham O. Smoot to the prophet's murder, he and the electioneers he led in Tennessee resolved to depart for Nauvoo. Along the way they informed and comforted their colleagues and other Saints about Joseph's death. They spent several days canoeing up the Mississippi, reaching St. Louis in time to catch the riverboat *Osprey*. After four days they arrived at Nauvoo's wharf on 28 July, where Smoot was greeted by his wife and a number of other Saints. He thanked the riverboat captain for transporting them without charge.

"I found the Saints in the city in fine spirits as to the general prosperity and progress of the great cause of Zion," Smoot observed, though he also perceived that "a melancholy gloom seemed to prevail [in] the city."

Indeed, "in every countenance there was pictured sadness and sorrow, and every breast seemed to feel the fatal blow that had been struck . . . [by] the assassination and martyrdom of our prophet and patriarch, . . . who [were] beloved by all the Saints as dear as life."

"These are days long to be remembered by me," Smoot continued, "for there seemed to be temptations present themselves on every hand by aspiring spirits and otherwise. . . . As it was after the days of crucifixion of the Savior that many of the Saints [were] returning to their former occupations in life, supposing that . . . all their works had been in vain. So it seemed to be with some of the Saints in Nauvoo. . . . They [were] returning some to their merchandise, others to their former homes, while some [were] actuated by an aspiring spirit wishing to feed the Church of Christ in the absence of Joseph and Hyrum, when God had not called them to that office. . . . [T]he great body of Saints did not want them to rule over them." Smoot was directly referencing Sidney Rigdon's failed attempt to become "guardian" of the church.[1]

Electioneer Experience: Lorenzo H. Hatch. Eighteen-year-old Lorenzo H. Hatch left Nauvoo on 15 April 1844 to preach and politick. His favorite uncle, Jeremiah Hatch, had given him his last "twelve and a half cents and regretted that he had no more to give." It was the first mission for Hatch and his companion, Thomas E. Fuller. After a difficult journey filled with many nights of sleeping "on the hard, cold ground, sometimes in the rain," they reached Fuller's family home in Saratoga Springs, New York, on 28 May. Extremely ill from exposure, Hatch convalesced there and fell in love with his nurse, Fuller's younger sister Hannah. Upon recovery, Hatch departed on 17 June for his assignment in Vermont, where he preached his first sermons at some of his relatives' homes. Receiving positive responses, his confidence grew.[2]

On 27 June, the day Joseph was assassinated, Hatch traveled to Northfield with fellow electioneers John D. Chase and Alvin M. Harding. There they planned to attend the Vermont conference directed by Erastus Snow. Snow never showed, so his companion William Hyde presided. Snow had felt a "dreadful pressure of sorrow and grief and sense of mourning than I had ever before felt, but knew not why."[3] He left to rendezvous with members of the Twelve in Salem, Massachusetts. Hyde conducted the conference, recording, "We had a very interesting time." Throughout the two-day meeting, "the course to be pursued [in] the ensuing presidential election by all the Saints throughout the Union was laid before the people." The electioneering of Hyde, Hatch, and the other missionaries was "met with a hearty response" from Saints and gentiles alike.[4]

However, the next week they learned that Joseph had been killed. "At first I could not believe it," Hatch wrote, "but at last was convinced that it was a fact." He "mourned and wept as the children of Israel did when Moses was taken from them. I

At age eighteen in Vermont, Lorenzo H. Hatch learned of Joseph's death. He heard a voice say, "Brigham Young is the man God has chosen to fill the vacancy." Courtesy of Church History Library.

was alone, a young man being but eighteen years old, 1,500 miles from home. The question in my mind was, Who would lead the church now that the Prophet Joseph was gone?" A possible answer arrived in the mail in August. The letter from Hatch's uncle Jeremiah stated plainly that "the Lord had called Sidney Rigdon to lead the church." Hatch recalled, "It was about noon. I stood in the middle of the sitting room reading the letter to my cousin when a voice plain and distinct said, 'Brigham Young is the man God has chosen to fill the vacancy.'" Hatch turned to his cousin and shared the truth with joy. He stayed in the East until the next spring, preaching the apostles as the legitimate leaders of the church. He returned to Nauvoo with Hannah, who had eloped with him.[5]

*   *   *

In the aftermath of Joseph's death, most commentators predicted the end of the church. They believed that deceived followers would flounder while looking for a new prophet and scatter. While some church members wandered and others made claims of prophetic succession, The Church of Jesus Christ of Latter-day Saints did not die. Most of the Saints followed Brigham Young, president of the Quorum of the Twelve Apostles. Church leaders finished building the temple, administered its sacred ordinances, and organized a mass migration to the West. Despite difficulty, tragedy, and even death, the church not only survived but strengthened. Brigham and the Council of Fifty established the State of Deseret, an independent, theodemocratic government to protect the new Zion. From the first weeks following Joseph's assassination to the creation of Deseret, church leaders made electioneers leaders in organizing, moving, and establishing Zion. Indeed, the electioneers were well suited to leadership callings. Their demanding missions had concretized Zion and theodemocracy in their hearts; and the assassination, while shocking and traumatizing, fortified their desires to finish "Joseph's measures."[6]

Shared trauma turned to united action. The apostles had labored throughout the country alongside these men, sharing missionary trials and triumphs and the agony of Joseph's death. It was natural for church leaders to look to the cadre of electioneers—whose desires were aligned with those of church leaders, whose loyalty had been tried, and whose names, abilities, and characters were known—to help lead the movement. They understood theodemocracy well, having advocated and suffered for it, and their minds were one with church leaders. No one could discount their unique preparation, as a body and to the man, to push the Lord's work forward. It is no surprise, then, that many electioneers emerged in the aristarchy as those on whom Brigham, the Quorum of the Twelve, and the Council of Fifty placed responsibility to assist in leading the Saints to the Great Basin and advancing the cause of Zion thereafter.

SUCCESSION

BRIGHAM YOUNG

The electioneers who returned in July and early August 1844 found Nauvoo in mourning and confusion. Rival factions coalesced around potential heirs to Joseph's role as church president. On 8 August Joseph's former counselor Sidney Rigdon and chief apostle Brigham Young addressed the Nauvoo Saints. Rigdon, a gifted orator but unstable leader, spoke for several hours until his voice gave out. He declared himself the church's "guardian" by angelic revelation and through his decade-long role as the prophet's counselor. Brigham spoke briefly, asserting that the keys of the kingdom were with the Twelve and that no one could come between the apostles and Joseph.

While Brigham spoke, some electioneers were among those who heard Joseph's voice or saw Joseph's face in place of Brigham's. Their miraculous experiences helped convince them to accept Brigham as Joseph's divinely approved successor. William Hyde recalled, "The voice of the same spirit by which Joseph spake was this day sounded in our ears, so much so that I once, unth[inking]ly, raised my head to see if it was not actually Joseph addressing the assembly."[7] Jacob Hamblin wrote, "The voice and gestures of the man [Brigham] were those of the Prophet Joseph. The people, with few exceptions, visibly saw that the mantle of the Prophet Joseph had fallen upon Brigham." Rising to his feet, Hamblin declared to the man beside him, "That is the voice of the true shepherd—the chief of the apostles."[8] For Nathan T. Porter, as Brigham arose "to speak to the people he was transfigured into Joseph's likeness in looks, appearance, and the sounding of his voice so that a low whisper ran through the vast assembly—'that's Joseph'—'that's Joseph.'"[9] Robert S. Duke, the young son of Jonathan O. Duke, sensed the speaker was Joseph, a frequent visitor in their home. He turned to his father and said, "Look, Papa, the Prophet is not dead." His father responded, "Hush, son, and remember this."[10]

The gathered congregation voted to follow the Twelve. Brigham soon declared, "You are now without a prophet, . . . but you are not without apostles who hold the keys of power . . . to preside over all the affairs of the church in all the world; being under direction of the same God." Regarding

Joseph's presidential campaign, he announced, "As rulers and people have taken counsel together against . . . [Joseph], and have murdered him who would have reformed and saved the nation, it is not wisdom for the Saints to have anything to do with politics, voting, or president-making, at present."[11] The campaign was officially over. Most Latter-day Saints, in Illinois and in the East, returned to their roots and voted for Democrat James K. Polk, who narrowly defeated Henry Clay.

Members of the electioneer cadre overwhelmingly transferred their fealty to Brigham and the Twelve. A staggering 83 percent stayed loyal through the 1846 evacuation of Nauvoo. Three-quarters tarried through Winter Quarters. Seventy-one percent remained loyal to Brigham as they traveled into the Great Basin, and 64 percent were loyal until their death. Besides the miraculous manifestation that some experienced, other factors led to their decision to follow Brigham. First, because they regarded the apostles as fellow electioneers firmly committed to Zion, they wanted to assist their comrades in finishing "Joseph's measures." Brigham and the other apostles moved quickly to consolidate control of the church in order to prevent further schism. In the October 1844 general conference, they added dozens of seventies quorums with more than four hundred new members, half of whom had been electioneers. This placed them under the Twelve, instead of under local, sometimes wavering leadership. Heber C. Kimball boasted that the apostles had "fourteen or fifteen hundred seventies to carry out our measures."[12]

Brigham then acted on Joseph's pronouncement that Zion was to encompass all of America. Under his direction the apostles chose eighty-five trusted high priests to relocate, each to a key congressional district where they were to build up church congregations and then return to Nauvoo with their converts so they could receive their endowments. These high priests then would move back with their initiates to their assigned areas and seek to establish stakes of Zion. Forty-four of the eighty-five high priests (52 percent) were chosen from the electioneer cadre, recently returned from months of electioneering.[13] The electioneer cadre was represented disproportionately well in this group, given the fact that when they left on their missions, they accounted for only about 15 percent of potential priesthood holders. Yet using so many of the electioneers as leaders in building up Zion made sense—they were experienced missionaries who had worked earnestly to organize political and religious work throughout the nation. That field experience would surely stand them in good stead in the related work of building up stakes. However, persecution drove the Saints from the nation before most of the cohort of high priests could begin their missions.[14]

OTHER SUCCESSORS

Although Brigham and the apostles were firmly in control of the church organizationally, only half of the Latter-day Saints followed them west. Shocked at the sudden loss of their prophet, many simply left the church or chose to let the church leave them. This attrition involved the electioneers as well, though at a much lower relative percentage. For various reasons, some electioneers looked not to Brigham but to other aspirants to Joseph's mantle, such as Sidney Rigdon, James J. Strang, William Smith, Lyman Wight, James Emmett, James Brewster, and Charles B. Thompson (see table 7.1).[15] In all, more than half of the electioneers (55 percent) who did not follow Brigham simply quit the Latter-day Saint movement altogether.

Table 7.1. Electioneer Apostates by Affiliation, 1844–1850*

James J. Strang (41)	26%
Sidney Rigdon (16)	10%
Others (15)	9%
No affiliation (88)	55%

* Data is available for 160 of the 195 missionaries who did not follow Brigham Young and the Twelve after Joseph Smith's death.

Defeated in Nauvoo, Sidney Rigdon decided to organize his own church. Rigdon and some followers scoured the eastern branches for adherents. On 6 April 1845 in Pittsburgh, Rigdon organized the Church of Christ. His church mirrored Joseph's Zion ideal except for plural marriage, an omission that no doubt attracted some members. Disaffected electioneers were prominent in Rigdon's movement, as they were in the other

Despite having been Joseph's running mate, Sidney Rigdon was unable to persuade many electioneers to follow him. C. R. Savage photo of earlier engraving courtesy of Church History Library.

splinter groups. Rigdon's first presidency included his son-in-law and former electioneer Ebenezer Robinson. Rigdon called twelve apostles, four of whom had been electioneers: Hugh Herringshaw, Benjamin Winchester, Elijah W. Swackhammer, and Joseph M. Cole. Among the seven presidents of Rigdon's seventy were electioneers Frederick Merryweather, George T. Leach, and James M. Greig. However, in less than two years, the movement collapsed owing to Rigdon's erratic behavior and leadership.[16]

In contrast, James J. Strang was the strongest rival to Brigham from 1845 to 1855. In the spring of 1844 Strang visited Joseph in Nauvoo and was baptized by him. Strang then returned to Wisconsin to spread the faith. After Joseph's murder, Strang produced a letter that he claimed was from the prophet. The correspondence, dated nine days before Joseph's death, appointed Strang the president of the church and instructed him to gather the Saints to Voree, Wisconsin. Additionally, Strang claimed an angel appeared to him to announce his succession. He soon declared he had translated metal plates from ancient prophets, just as Joseph had. Strang was intelligent, confident, and charismatic, and his claim to succession impressed those that missed the revelatory nature of Joseph's leadership. He eventually gathered his followers to Beaver Island, Michigan, where he attempted to establish a Zion kingdom.

A small clique of electioneers advocated Strang as Joseph's successor. Their experience and status promoted them immediately to positions of responsibility among Strang's following. Although he had been excommunicated in February 1844 by Joseph and Hyrum for publicly teaching plural marriage, Hiram P. Brown nonetheless served faithfully as an electioneer. Even so, in 1846 he became one of Strang's converts and leaders, and he eventually rose to the rank of apostle.[17] James Greig, one of Rigdon's seventy, switched allegiances and directed the Strangites in Pittsburgh. Strangite apostle Samuel P. Bacon declared, "With regard to Voree, . . . the saints are in the 'unity of spirit, in the bond of peace,' of one heart and one mind in the purposes of God, to work with all their might in the great work of the last days."[18]

Strang's missionary force almost rivaled Brigham's. They canvassed the Midwest and the East and even penetrated Brigham's strongholds in Nauvoo, Winter Quarters, and England. Not surprisingly, the most effective Strangite missionaries had electioneered for Joseph. Stephen Post joined Strang in 1846 after reading a news article about him.

The strongest rival to Brigham Young, James Jesse Strang filled his leadership ranks with disaffected electioneers. Undated photo by Sainsbury and Johnson courtesy of Church History Library.

Post labored in Pennsylvania as a missionary before moving his family to Beaver Island. Samuel Shaw, Chicago branch president and son-in-law of campaign leader William W. Phelps, also threw in his lot with Strang. Seizing on this prized convert, Strang ordained Shaw a high priest and sent him to proselytize in Nauvoo. Shaw later served on Voree's high council and became Strang's "agent of temporal affairs." Increase Van Deuzen labored effectively in Illinois, Michigan, and Canada. He and his wife published a pamphlet exposing the endowment ceremony they had participated in at Nauvoo. Zenos H. Gurley labored extensively in Wisconsin and Illinois, baptizing fifty-two converts in two months alone. He also created the branch at Yellowstone, Wisconsin, that would eventually become the nucleus of the Reorganized Church. David Rogers, after delivering the

1844 Latter-day Saint vote in New York to the Democrats, became Strang's leader in New York City.[19]

Strang brazenly sent former electioneers to Nauvoo, where they had some success in gaining adherents. Hiram S. Stratton's quorum president Jehiel Savage excommunicated him for Strangite apostasy. Ironically, three weeks later the quorum had to excommunicate Savage for following Stratton. Savage later became a Strangite apostle. To settle the matter, Brigham invited Moses Smith to present "Strangism" in the temple. Smith was a relative of Strang, a Strangite apostle, and the leader of the Strangite missionaries in Nauvoo. Joined by former electioneers Hiram S. Stratton, William Savage, and Samuel Shaw, Smith declared "the doctrine and claims of James J. Strang" to those assembled. Brigham then arose and said, "I but simply ask the people if they had heard the voice of the Good Shepherd in what had been advanced." After a resounding "No!" church leaders publicly excommunicated the Strangite missionaries and Strang himself (his second dismissal). However, the Strangite missionaries did not leave Nauvoo empty-handed; they gathered around one hundred converts.[20]

The Strangite missionaries sent to Winter Quarters also had some success. In 1847 Uriel Nickerson received news that his father and fellow electioneer, Freeman Nickerson, had died at Winter Quarters. Uriel arrived to retrieve his widowed and destitute mother. He testified to all who would listen that he knew Strang was the "Lord's anointed" and that their afflictions were God's curse for following Brigham. He implored everyone to leave with him for Voree. Only a handful followed him. Nickerson preached the same message at encampments throughout Iowa, gaining a few more converts. Ironically, Nickerson's mother eventually split with him and chose to go to Utah. The decision to send Strangite missionaries in force to Winter Quarters began after Brigham and the apostles reached Salt Lake City. The effort was led by former electioneer John W. Grierson, who had abandoned Brigham at Winter Quarters. From 1847 to 1851, Strangite emissaries claimed more than one hundred converts from the area.[21]

Strangite missionaries, from the beginning, battled with rival former electioneers loyal to Brigham. Strang first publicly declared his revelation at a conference in Michigan on 5 August 1844—just days before the confrontation between Brigham and Rigdon. Strang's strategy was to proselytize at church conferences in the Midwest, away from the apostles. However, the Michigan conference did not go as Strang had hoped. Led by Crandell Dunn, Norton Jacob, Harvey Green, Moses Smith, and several other electioneers, the conference denied Strang's claim, saying the letter "carried upon its face the marks of a base forgery . . . and [was] dishonorable to the name of Joseph Smith, whose signature it bore in a hand he never wrote." They directed Strang not to talk of the letter and to go to the Twelve for verification. Strang and his associate Aaron Smith "absolutely refused, and so they passed on East seeking proselytes."[22] The conference excommunicated them and assigned electioneers Norton Jacob and Moses Smith (the latter a relative of both Aaron Smith and Strang) to take a copy of Strang's letter to Nauvoo.[23] The apostles likewise denounced Strang's letter and warned Moses Smith to follow the Twelve on the matter. Paying no heed, he soon left Nauvoo, taking up with electioneer colleague James Emmett and later with his brother Aaron and nephew-in-law Strang.[24]

Similar confrontations occurred in the eastern United States and overseas in England as well. As president of the Eastern States Mission, William I. Appleby almost single-handedly battled a growing Strangite influence in the area. He warned and then had to excommunicate local leaders David Rogers and David S. Hollister (both electioneers), along with fifty others. When Strang sent three of his best missionaries to England—electioneers Lester Brooks and Moses Smith and Book of Mormon witness Martin Harris—they met with stiff resistance from their electioneer colleagues on missions for Brigham. Cyrus H. Wheelock recorded their public debate, which he and his companions won so decisively that Martin Harris switched sides by the end. Unable to gain a Strangite foothold in England, Brooks and Smith returned to the United States defeated.[25]

Embarrassment in England was only the beginning of Strang's unraveling. Electioneer Samuel P. Bacon, president of the Strangite apostles, stumbled upon "fragments of those plates which Strang made the Book of the Law from." Having exposed Strang's fraud, Bacon secretly fled Beaver Island with his family. When William Savage and others discovered financial mismanagement by Strang, they too vanished with their families. Acting in his role of sheriff, George Miller attempted to return Savage and the others to "jury duty," leading to a shootout on Lake Michigan between former electioneers. The escapees so savagely shot up Sheriff Miller, his men, and his boat that they had to be rescued while Savage and the others escaped.[26]

Former electioneers George Miller and Lucien Foster moved Strang organizationally and doctrinally toward the church as it was in Nauvoo, especially its political arrangements and the practice of plural marriage. They shared confidential information about the activities of the Council of Fifty, including Joseph's coronation. Thus Strang was elected to the Michigan State House, created his own kingdom on Beaver Island, and was publicly crowned king. Moreover, he secretly entered plural marriage with Elvira Field, the nineteen-year-old daughter of Reuben Field, an electioneer in Ohio who converted to Strangism. Elvira clandestinely accompanied Strang on a tour of the eastern states. At a conference in New York, electioneer Increase Van Deuzen and Lorenzo D. Hickey accused Strang of polygamy, claiming to have incriminating letters. Shoving Strang in the chest, Van Deuzen yelled, "You are guilty! You are guilty!" Consequently, the conference disfellowshipped Hickey and excommunicated Van Deuzen. Throughout the proceedings, Elvira, disguised as cousin "Charley Douglass," silently watched.[27]

Strang's decision to embrace Nauvoo politics and plural marriage alienated most of his followers, including some electioneers. Stephen Post confided to his brother, "I have not as strong confidence in Br. Strang as I had in his predecessor Joseph." Post left the Strangites to become the successor to Sidney Rigdon's faltering movement. Support for Strang ebbed until disgruntled followers shot and killed him in 1856. His church all but disappeared. Loyal to the end, George Miller stayed by Strang's bedside until he passed. Now an orphan of three different Latter-day Saint movements, Miller—the former Nauvoo bishop, electioneer, and Council of Fifty member—somberly chose to go to California. He died before arriving.[28]

A few others claimed leadership of the church. William Smith, Joseph's younger brother, quickly became disaffected from his fellow apostles, joined the Strangites, and later formed a short-lived sect. His small band of followers included electioneers Joseph Younger, Selah Lane, and Omar Olney. Before the prophet Joseph died, Lyman Wight and fellow

Council of Fifty member George Miller had permission from the council to establish a colony in Texas. Wight, refusing to follow Brigham, left for Texas and settled there. Miller initially accepted Brigham's leadership, but after the two had a confrontation, Miller followed Wight to Texas. Electioneers Jeremiah Curtis, Samuel Heath, Lorenzo Moore, and Ira T. Miles also followed Wight, who ineptly led his small colony until his death in 1858. Other brief contenders for Joseph's legacy included electioneers James Emmett and Charles B. Thompson, both of whom tried unsuccessfully to create Zion communities in Iowa. Notably, the key leaders in each schismatic group were former electioneers.

A slight majority of the electioneer cadre who did not follow Brigham and the apostles after Joseph's death chose to have nothing to do with any of the splinter groups. Darwin J. Chase apostatized while on the church's official gold mission in California in 1849. He joined the US Army and was killed by American Indians at the Bear River Massacre in 1863. Ironically, the army buried him in Farmington, Utah, among his former friends.[29] Shaken by the death of his wife while he was away electioneering, Sylvester B. Stoddard left Nauvoo and briefly flirted with the Rigdonites. After returning to Kirtland, Ohio, he and several others armed themselves and took possession of the former temple and church farm.[30] Excommunicated for preaching false doctrine in Cincinnati following the campaign, Henry Elliot never returned to the church. Despite being a high priest and working on the Nauvoo Temple, Stephen Litz ultimately moved to Missouri, severing his affiliation with the church. After his electioneering mission, Peter Van Every stayed in Michigan, becoming an important

George Miller electioneered in Kentucky and, after Joseph's death, followed Brigham Young, then Lyman Wight, and finally James J. Strang until Strang's death. Portrait by unknown artist. © IRI.

figure in financial and political circles there. As rumors of plural marriage grew in Nauvoo, Joseph J. Woodbury and his brother William H. decided to leave the church. Joseph returned to his native Massachusetts and lived out his life as a Methodist preacher while William moved to southern Illinois and became a wealthy businessman and physician.[31]

EXODUS

NAUVOO TEMPLE ENDOWMENT

The electioneer veterans following Brigham made completion of the Nauvoo Temple their highest priority. In 1845 church leaders sent forty-six men throughout the nation for the purpose of "collect[ing] donations and tithings for the temple in the city of Nauvoo."[32] Thirty-one were drawn from the body of electioneers, a staggering 67 percent considering they constituted just 15 percent of available priesthood holders at the time. Brigham and other leaders knew they could trust these men, committed as they were to "Joseph's measures" and having recently been working among the Latter-day Saint congregations around the nation.

Between 11 December 1845 and 6 February 1846, more than five thousand Saints received their temple endowments in Nauvoo. Working day and night, church leaders and their associates diligently performed as many ordinances as possible before the spring exodus. Brigham relied on many electioneers to assist in this mammoth project. Not counting apostles, half of the men who dispensed the initiatory rites of washing and anointing were electioneers; and 79 percent of those who performed the endowment ceremony came from that same group. Given the electioneers' much smaller representation among priesthood members (13 percent of total male endowment participants), such numbers once again demonstrate the immense trust the electioneers had earned.

This strong representation in the church's most sacred ordinances foreshadowed the electioneers' rise in the aristarchy of the future Great Basin kingdom. Of the 509 electioneers who were loyal to Brigham, 343 received their endowments and held higher priesthood office than that of their peers In fact, the percentage of electioneers who were high priests almost doubled that of the endowed priesthood population in Nauvoo (see table 7.2). Moreover, most of the electioneers had received a higher priesthood office than that of their peers in preparation for, during, or (especially) after their electioneering service. Their decision to serve in Joseph's campaign demonstrated their strong faith and brought them into the orbit of the apostles. Generally, an appointment to a higher priesthood office followed.

Table 7.2. **Priesthood Offices of Endowed Males in Nauvoo***

	Total Males (2,609)	*Electioneers (343)*
Apostle	.5% (12)	0%
High Priest	19% (504)	35% (121)
Seventy	65% (1,677)	59% (203)
Elder	6% (155)	2% (6)
Not Recorded	10% (261)	4% (13)

* Raw data from Brown, *Nauvoo Sealings, Adoptions, and Anointings.*

Another way to measure the influence of the electioneers is to note in which month they received their endowments. When they began performing temple ordinances in December 1844, church leaders recommended those whom they considered worthy and otherwise ready to receive the ordinance. Since the ceremony lasted more than three hours and thousands of eligible Saints wished to participate, the process needed to be efficient as well as orderly. Consequently, priority was given to trusted associates, many of whom either were leaders or would likely soon become such. In fact, many early recipients of the endowment in turn assisted in presenting the ordinance to others and performing related duties, thereby lightening the workload for church leaders and expediting the around-the-clock work. In this way the order in which the Saints received their endowments indicates something of their status in the church at that time (see table 7.3). Significantly, during December only 20 percent of males received the endowment, and yet 43 percent of electioneers did. Certainly church leaders did not elevate these men solely because of their electioneering service. However, the numbers demonstrate that their labor and loyalty in the shared experiences of the campaign with the Twelve made them *more likely* to be chosen. They had become visible, or more visible, as steadfast allies.

Table 7.3. Month Endowment Received*

	Total Males (2,597)	Electioneers (343)
December 1845	20% (529)	43% (147)
January 1846	54% (1,401)	45% (156)
February 1846	26% (667)	12% (40)

* Raw data from Brown, *Nauvoo Sealings, Adoptions, and Anointings*.

MARRIAGE SEALINGS, PLURAL MARRIAGE, AND SECOND ANOINTINGS

Brigham and the Twelve also exercised their sealing keys, uniting couples eternally. They sealed 740 couples in the Nauvoo Temple period (December 1845 to early February 1846), and 175 of the husbands were former electioneers—again a number larger than their statistical footprint. Plural marriages among the same group would increase dramatically as well. By 1850, 103 electioneers (almost a quarter of the surviving total) had married additional wives. Because plural marriage required the invitation of church authorities, the electioneers' disproportionate participation in that practice is also indicative of their increasing influence.

Second anointings were another such indicator of the electioneers' faithfulness. Reserved for a select few, this ordinance, in addition to its religious significance, confirmed one as a "king and priest" capable of ruling in the kingdom of God. Only 6.6 percent of endowed males during the temple period received this honor, yet 19 percent of endowed electioneers did—a percentage nearly threefold that of the first group. In fact, 38 percent of all second anointings were given to electioneers despite the fact that the group represented only 13 percent of endowed males.

The long-awaited temple ordinances prepared the electioneers spiritually for the hardships before them. Franklin D. Richards recorded, "For the privilege of assisting in this part of the endowment, I know not how to be so thankful as I desire, and I pray that the knowledge which I have here obtained of the laws of the kingdom of God may prove an eternal blessing unto me and redound to my salvation."[33] Norton Jacob wrote, "It was the most interesting scene of all my life and one that afforded the most peace and joy that [I] had ever experienced."[34] The high level of participation in giving and receiving the temple ordinances marked the electioneers as trusted, loyal, and dedicated— true believers in Zion's earthly mission. Church leadership now turned to them to help evacuate the Saints from the United States and build Zion in the West.[35]

Electioneers received and assisted others in receiving sacred ordinances in the Nauvoo Temple before the Saints' exodus west. Daguerreotype of the Nauvoo Temple courtesy of Harold B. Lee Library Digital Collections, BYU.

EXPULSION

"To carry out Joseph's measures is sweeter to me than . . . honey," Brigham declared on 1 March 1845 when he reconvened the Council of Fifty—a covert body of priesthood leaders tasked with establishing the government of the kingdom of God. He announced that Joseph had "laid out work for this church which would last them twenty years."[36] They needed to get busy. The council sustained Brigham as the standing chairman. Later, like Joseph, they ordained him king, priest, and ruler over Israel on earth. Brigham dropped unfaithful council members and admitted new ones. Of the twenty-eight men who joined the Council of Fifty between 1845 and 1850, half were former electioneers.[37] The "living constitution"[38] met regularly "to find a place where [they could] dwell in peace and lift up the standard of liberty." Brigham further instructed that it was time to turn from the "gentiles" and begin "uniting the Lamanites [American Indians] and sowing the seeds of the gospel among them."[39] While the consolidation of the tribes ultimately did not occur, the Saints certainly turned from the gentiles.

The decision to continue Joseph's Zion ideals led to renewed friction with Nauvoo's neighbors. Electioneer Henry Bigler remembered, "It appeared that because 'Mormonism' did not die out with the death of the prophet and patriarch as was anticipated and seeing too that our people were one in political matters all voting one way that hatred grew in the breasts of people against us to such a pitch that every kind of falsehood that was calculated to prejudice the mind of the public was resorted to."[40] William W. Phelps added that "the greatest fears manifested by our enemies is the union of church and state."[41] Mobs burned outlying settlements while the Illinois legislature rescinded Nauvoo's charter and legion. The writing was on the wall; the Saints faced violent expulsion again. Responses by those in the Council of Fifty were furious, apocalyptic, and vindictive. Phelps insinuated that the legislators of the nation had conspired to "destroy the prophets." It was time to leave and be among and convert the American Indians, who in time would be the instruments of God as they "come out of their hiding places and go forth to waste and destroy with fire, pestilence, &c."[42]

The Council of Fifty believed they were justified in declaring independence from the United States. While such talk could be construed as treason, council members were adamant that God had established them as a sovereign kingdom. The nation had repeatedly rejected them, ultimately assassinating Joseph while he was a presidential candidate. "What is the patriotism of these United States?" Phelps questioned since no redress had been made for the Saints' expulsion and loss of life and property in Missouri and Illinois.[43] With confidence Phelps declared that the council was "the center of gravity" with "plans which will ultimately free the world. . . . We are the hammer of the whole earth, and we will break it in pieces."[44] Brigham agreed. On 11 March 1845, the one-year anniversary of the Council of Fifty, members decided to send a letter to each governor of the Union in a final attempt at reconciliation. "This is the last call we will make to them, and if they don't listen to it we will sweep them out of existence," Brigham announced. "Let the damned scoundrels be killed, let them be swept off from the earth, and then we can go and be baptized for them, easier than we can convert them. . . . The gentiles have rejected the gospel; they have killed the prophets."[45] While such violent hyperbole is shocking to modern ears, it accurately describes how most Saints felt in the wake of Joseph's assassination.

Using maps acquired in Washington, DC, during the campaign, the Council of Fifty planned to settle in the Great Basin. The first refugees crossed the frozen Mississippi in early February 1846. Electioneers suffered alongside fellow Saints. Benjamin Brown sold his house and six-thousand-tree nursery, valued at $3,000, for only $250. Others, like Jonathan Browning, locked their homes and shops and simply left. Joseph Holbrook penned: "The city of Nauvoo now presented a scene of desolation. . . . Every man [made] every effort in his power to leave his home, and a great many of the Saints were obliged to go without realizing one cent for their dwellings. Thus the hand of persecution had prevailed."[46]

Henry Bigler later recorded, "To tell the truth, I knew not where we were going, neither did I care much, only that it might be where I and my people could have the liberty to worship Almighty God according to the dictates of our own conscience without being mobbed for it."[47] Throughout 1846 the Saints lay scattered across Iowa Territory, struggling through adverse weather and near-impossible road conditions and hunted by disease and hunger. The camp's slow pace forced a decision to winter along the east and west banks of the Missouri River—Council Bluffs and Winter Quarters, respectively. The Saints built towns of log cabins surrounded by hundreds of wagons—what Young named "the Camp of Israel."

Death stalked the electioneers even before they headed into the wilderness. From the presidential campaign until the end of 1850, fifty-eight of that group died. The first, Jesse Berry, perished on 6 August 1844 in Nauvoo, just after returning from electioneering. Peter Melling died in September while still on his mission in Indiana. Cholera claimed John Jones Sr. and John Jones Jr. in the same month. Amos Hodges was murdered in 1845 in Nauvoo, and Amos Condit was murdered two years later in Winter Quarters. Dozens of electioneers perished in Iowa and Nebraska from 1846 to 1850. Samuel Bent worked himself to death as he suffered from malnutrition and disease while presiding at Garden Grove, a way station in Iowa. Perhaps the saddest tale was the death of Clark Hallet, his wife, and all their children, all from exposure-related sickness, at Mount Pisgah, another temporary community. Four electioneers died in the Great Basin: William Coray, John Tanner, Joseph Stratton, and George W. Langley.[48] Langley was the first person buried in the Salt Lake cemetery.

WINTER QUARTERS

In and around Winter Quarters, electioneers helped build a temporary Zion in the wilderness. Church leadership created a "municipal high council" to "preside in all matters spiritual and temporal." This council, containing electioneers Andrew H. Perkins, Johnathan H. Hale, and Daniel Spencer, reflected the Zion ideal. Religiously and politically, the council was to "oversee and guard the conduct of the Saints and counsel them, that the laws of God and good order are not infringed upon." Economically, they were to "use all means in [their] power to have all the poor Saints brought from Nauvoo" and "assist and counsel the bishops, who [were] appointed to take charge" of the Mormon Battalion families.[49] Electioneers filled other important leadership positions as well. Fifteen were bishops, and Samuel Bent (mentioned above) and Lorenzo Snow (who presided at Mount Pisgah) were presiding authorities. William Cutler was chief scout and given charge of the camp's cattle. The council commissioned Howard Egan and Nathan Tanner to trade and buy corn. Levi Stewart supervised mail within Iowa.[50]

THE MORMON BATTALION

In May 1846 Mexico and the United States went to war. Colonel James Allen of the US Army carried orders from President James K. Polk to enlist a battalion of five hundred "Mormons." As Allen moved west to Winter Quarters, he met with resentment and resistance at each encampment. For these refugees the request was particularly galling coming around Independence Day. Electioneer Henry Bigler recalled that "[Senator Thomas Hart] Benton of Missouri argued at Washington that the Mormons were disloyal and urged that the government make a demand on us, in order to prove our loyalty, and if we failed to comply there was a plan to call out the military . . . to cut us off and put a stop to our people going into the wilderness."[51] The Saints were disgusted. Electioneer William Hyde penned: "The government of the United States . . . not being satisfied with . . . driving and plundering thousands of defenseless men, women, and children . . . must now . . . call upon us for five hundred . . . men, the strength of our camp, to go and assist them in fighting their battles. When this news came I looked upon my family and then upon my aged parents and upon the situation of the camps in the midst of an uncultivated, wild Indian country and my soul revolted."[52]

What Hyde and most Saints did not know was that Brigham had sent electioneer Jesse C. Little to Washington, DC, to ask for just such an opportunity. He hoped it would raise the cash needed for the exodus. Little collaborated with Latter-day Saint sympathizer Thomas L. Kane to negotiate with President Polk, who agreed to enlist five hundred "Mormons . . . with a view to conciliate them, attach them to our country, and prevent them from taking part against us."[53] Kane and Little hurriedly traveled west to inform church leaders of the deal, and Brigham and others went camp to camp encouraging men to enlist.

Some electioneers accepted Brigham's appeal to enlist despite the hardships it created. William Hyde, whose soul days before "revolted" at the government's request, reversed course and displayed the intense loyalty to the church that often characterized the electioneers. "When our beloved president came to call upon the Saints to know who among all the people were ready to be offered for the cause, I said, 'Here am I, take me.'" Hyde recalled, "The thoughts of leaving my family at this critical time are indescribable." The Saints remaining at Winter Quarters would be "far from . . . civilization with no dwelling save a wagon with the scorching midsummer sun to beat upon them, with the prospect of the cold December blasts finding them in the same place."[54] Given the electioneers' proven loyalty and steadfastness, it is surprising that of the 540 battalion members, only forty-one, or 7 percent, were drawn from the cadre of electioneers, less than half of their statistical representation in the Camp of Israel. This is the *only* post-campaign circumstance of these veterans being utilized less than their peers were.

Why so few? Perhaps it was intentional on the part of church leaders. For example, when Jonathan Browning tried to enlist, Brigham hurriedly pulled him away to say, "Brother Jonathan, we need you here."[55] Brigham and other church leaders may have desired the same for many of the electioneers so they could support the suffering Saints and plan for the spring migration to the Great Basin. Furthermore, many of them were already serving in leadership roles that may have been critical to maintain. Regardless, the recruits needed shepherds, and under the muster agreement Brigham had the authority to choose the officers. Out of seventy-five such officers, sixteen were electioneers, some of whom served at the invitation of church leadership. For example, on 6 July 1846 Brigham made James Pace one of only five first lieutenants alongside electioneer colleagues Elam Luddington and George P. Dykes.[56] Another example is David Pettegrew, who later recalled, "[I] received word from President Young wishing me to join the battalion." Pettegrew informed Young that his son, James Phineas, had enlisted and that it was "impossible for both of us to go." Young responded, "If you both can't go, I wish you to go by all means, as a kind of helmsman." Pettegrew immediately enlisted.[57] Thus while constituting only 7 percent of the battalion, electioneers represented 21 percent of the leadership.[58]

After the battalion was formed, Lt. Colonel James Allen died. Electioneer Jefferson Hunt became acting commander until new leadership arrived. Hunt and electioneer comrades Daniel Tyler and Levi W. Hancock preached daily to the men the need for faith and solidarity in their journey to southern California, where they arrived in January 1847. The nineteen-hundred-mile march, the longest in United States military history, tested the resolve of the men and was key to acquiring the territory that became Utah, Arizona, New Mexico, Nevada, and California. It was also a time for introspection. While on guard duty one evening, young electioneer Henry G. Boyle heard wolves and watched a grizzly bear walk past the camp. He recorded that his "mind wandered back over the years gone by and . . . the strange events that had brought [him] to the present time and place." He had given up his life and family in Virginia for the gospel and was now serving the government that had exiled him. Yet, he noted, "I love the people I am associated with and the principles of the gospel better than all else."[59]

CALIFORNIA GOLD

Upon discharge, several members of the Mormon Battalion found work at Sutter's Fort and discovered gold in the American River. Electioneer Henry Bigler made this historic entry in his diary: "This day some kind of metal was found in the tail race that looks like gold." Within a week Bigler and electioneer companions Samuel Rogers and Guy Keyser harvested "more than a hundred dollars" of gold.[60] They eventually brought $17,000 in bullion to Salt Lake City. As word spread throughout the nation and world, Brigham sent several electioneers on church-sanctioned "gold missions" to procure gold and receive tithing receipts from the California Saints. Electioneer comrades Howard Egan and Jefferson Hunt made careers of guiding gold-seeking "forty-niners" and others to California.

In general, however, church leaders strongly counseled against prospecting. Yet, as electioneer Joseph Holbrook wrote, "Many of our brethren left the valley to dig gold, contrary to the counsel of the servants of God."[61] At least four electioneers departed for California: Joseph Mount, George W. Hickerson, Seabert Shelton, and George G. Snyder. Mount divorced his wife, a decision he lamented the rest of his life, when she and their children would not go with him to California. Hickerson also left for California in search of fortune. He later returned to his family barely alive and penniless from a debilitating illness. Shelton and Snyder became wealthy by operating hotels for prospectors. Shelton remained in California, never rejoining the church. Snyder returned after four years and became a noted economic, religious, and political leader.[62]

PIONEER COMPANIES

At Winter Quarters Brigham and the Council of Fifty selected those who would lead emigration parties in 1847. Brigham himself led the vanguard company of 143 that contained twenty-two electioneers. Some felt a sense of excitement and long-denied freedom. On 4 July Norton Jacob recorded, "This is Uncle Sam's day of Independence. Well, we are independent of all the powers of the gentiles, and that's enough for us."[63] On 21 July electioneers Erastus Snow and Orson Pratt became the first Latter-day Saints to enter the Great Salt Lake Valley. Snow recorded, "When we arrived . . . near the mouth of Emigration Canyon, which gave us the first glimpse of the blue waters of the Great Salt Lake, we simultaneously swung our hats and shouted 'Hosanna,' for the Spirit witnessed that here the Saints should find rest."[64] Howard Egan noted, "My heart felt truly glad, and I rejoiced at having the privilege of beholding this extensive and beautiful valley that may yet become a home for the Saints."[65] Impressively, electioneers captained six of the seven additional companies of 1847. Between then and 1850, forty-six wagon companies journeyed to the Salt Lake Valley, and electioneers led twenty-four of them, or 52 percent. During the years that followed, electioneers continued to be integral to the gathering of the Saints to the Great Basin. Ezra T. Benson alone captained six companies over a decade.[66]

More than two hundred Saints bound for California set sail from New York City aboard the clipper *Brooklyn* on 4 February 1846—the very day that the exodus from Nauvoo began. The company was led by electioneer Samuel Brannan. Electioneers John M. Horner, Elijah W. Pell, and Quartus S. Sparks joined him. These voyaging emigrants were following apostolic counsel to the Saints living outside Nauvoo: "We do not want one Saint to be left in the United States. . . . Let every branch . . . flee out of 'Babylon,' either by land or sea."[67] The *Brooklyn* reached San Francisco on 31 July 1846, just days after a US armada subdued the small Mexican contingent there. Ironically, the *Brooklyn* Saints found the very nation they were escaping stationed at their destination. However, under Brannan's direction, the group quickly purchased land and began farming. Brannan brought the printing press that he had used to print *The Prophet* in New York during the presidential campaign. He printed the first newspaper in California—the *California Star*, which would launch the gold rush.

*   *   *

Following Joseph's martyrdom, the church hierarchy continued to call on a high percentage of electioneers for responsible service not only because they had faithfully campaigned for Joseph at great personal sacrifice, but also because of what that service had decisively made them to be. To be sure, they certainly showed loyalty and faith before the campaign, but these qualities and related ones appear to have deepened and matured during their electioneering service as a result of their unstinting labors on behalf of their prophet. They emerged from their missions as men of tested ability and character. Most had the fortitude to endure the disappointment and confusion surrounding the prophet's death and the succession crisis. That they would bear leadership roles following the campaign suggests that church leaders knew these men had developed the requisite qualities to succeed in those roles and would be prepared to assume future theodemo-cratic roles as well. Their loyalty and faith stood them in good stead. In fact, it is apparent that no other pre-campaign variables could predict the high number of electioneers in postmartyrdom leadership. Not income, previous church position, age, occupation, family connection, priesthood office, or missionary service were predictors of those who would help lead Zion that autumn and forward.

The electioneers had been no different from their Latter-day Saint peers except for a loyalty and faith that prompted them to storm the nation in advocacy of Joseph's election. This mission was a watershed moment: it enabled them to internalize the campaign's theodemocratic themes, to develop familiarity with the Twelve and earn their trust, and to weather the trauma of Joseph's death. For one to be a leader in the Great Basin theodemocracy, loyalty to Joseph and a commitment to carry out his mea-sures had to transfer to loyalty to Brigham, the Twelve, and the Council of Fifty. In this the electioneers had a distinct advantage over their fellow Saints who had not served in trusted, challenging, and prolonged capac-ities. Although not all of the electioneer cadre followed Brigham west or received leadership positions, many did so, creating a corps of valiant men on whom church leaders could rely.

In the challenging geography of the Great Basin, Brigham began re-building Joseph's Zion. "This is a good place to make Saints," he once observed.[68] Having endured the devastation of Joseph's death, the tumult of the succession crisis, the humiliation of expulsion, and the harsh exodus to the valley of the Great Salt Lake, those who followed Brigham now confronted the privations of a new wilderness home a thousand miles from civilization. The faith and fortitude to come this far emanated from tested testimonies, none more so than those of the electioneers. They were now poised to form the core of the initial aristarchy of the kingdom of God.

NOTES

1. JSH, D-1:1362. The entry for 6 August 1842 was written in July 1845, when the historians entered it into the record. The quotation above was penciled in sometime after that and attributed to a memory of Anson Call. Several other sources from 1840 and 1842 clearly show that Joseph was not just talking about the Rocky Mountains but was making plans to settle there and assigning missions. See Esplin, "'Place Prepared,'" 75–78.
2. Smoot, Day Book, 28 July 1844, 56–59.
3. Hatch, Autobiography, 2–7.
4. Erastus Snow, Autobiography, 9.
5. William Hyde, Journal, 59.
6. Hatch, Autobiography, 8. Uncle Jeremiah Hatch is not to be confused with the Jeremiah that is his nephew and the older brother of Lorenzo Hatch. Nephew Jeremiah was assigned to Vermont but for unknown reasons electioneered in Michigan. After Joseph's death, Uncle Jeremiah followed Sidney Rigdon and married his daughter Lucy.
7. "Conference Minutes," Times and Seasons, 1 November 1844, 694.
8. William Hyde, Journal, 66.
9. Quoted in Little, Jacob Hamblin, 21.
10. Nathan Porter, Reminiscences, 132.
11. Duke Family Organization, Journal of Jonathan Oldham Duke, addendum 5, 53.
12. "An Epistle of the Twelve," Times and Seasons, 15 August 1844, 618–19.
13. Council of Fifty, Minutes, 1 March 1845, in JSP, CFM:2.
14. See "Conference Minutes," Times and Seasons, 1 November 1844, 696.
15. Church leaders ordained 203 of Joseph's electioneers to be seventies.
16. Of this group, Emmett and Thompson were former electioneers.

17. See Van Wagoner, *Sidney Rigdon*, 270–75.

18. Black, "Hiram Brown," Latter-day Saint Vital Records II Database (hereafter "LDSVR"). See Robin Scott Jensen, "Strangite Missionary Work, 1846–1850," 78.

19. *Voree Gospel Herald*, 29 November 1849, as quoted in Speek, *James Strang and the Midwest Mormons*, 95.

20. See Post, Journal, 19 June 1846; Samuel Shaw to Brigham Young, 1 October 1844; Speek, *James Strang and the Midwest Mormons*, 82; Black, "Zenos Hurley," LDSVR (database); Woodruff, *Wilford Woodruff, Fourth President of the Church*, 3:151–52; *Voree Gospel Herald*, 29 November 1849, as quoted in Speek, *James Strang and the Midwest Mormons*, 148; and David Rogers to Brigham Young, 17 August 1844. Rogers's convincing of local Saints to vote Democratic rather than sit out the election may have helped James K. Polk in his razor-thin upset of Henry Clay in New York and, thus, in the general election.

21. Samuel Hollister Rogers, Reminiscenses and Diary, CHL, 67.

22. See *Zion's Reveille*, 25 February 1847, which mentions the death of Nickerson's father and his mother's destitute condition; *Gospel Herald*, 29 November 1849, 197; Fitzpatrick, *King Strang Story*, 191; and Strang, "Brethren and Sisters," *Chronicles of Voree*, 14 August 1846, 102.

23. Jacob, Reminiscence and Journal, 8.

24. See Dunn, "History and Travels," 1:53–54.

25. See Jacob, Reminiscence and Journal, 14.

26. See Appleby, Autobiography and Journal, 165–66; and Wheelock, Journal, 25 October 1846.

27. Speek, James Strang and the Midwest Mormons, 175–77.

28. Launius and Thatcher, *Dissenters in Mormon History*, 184; and Speek, *James Strang and the Midwest* Mormons, 54, 56, 63–85, 150, 175–77.

29. Speek, *James Strang and the Midwest* Mormons, 68, 73–75, 171, 222–25.

30. See "The Fight with the Indians," *Deseret News*, 4 February 1863, 253; and Black, "Darwin J. Chase," LDSVR (database).

31. See Black, "Josiah Butterfield," LDSVR (database); Black, "Amos Davis," LDSVR (database); and Anderson and Bergera, *Joseph Smith's Quorum of the Anointed*, 158.

32. The Woodburys appear in censuses but not on membership rolls of any Latter-day Saint sect. For more on Elliot, see *Times and Seasons*, 15 August 1844, 623. On Van Every, see Bingham, *Early History of Michigan*, 654. On plural marriage, see Woodbury, *History of the Jeremiah Woodbury Family*, 11.

33. *Times and Seasons*, 15 January 1845, 780.

34. Franklin D. Richards, Diary, as quoted in Anderson and Bergera, *Nauvoo Endowment Companies*, 412.

35. Jacob, Reminiscence and Journal, 24.

36. The foregoing information on ordinations is from Brown, *Nauvoo Sealings, Adoptions, and Anointings*.

37. *JSP*, CFM:382–83 (1 March 1845).

38. See Quinn, "Council of Fifty," 193–97; Ezra T. Benson, Horace S. Eldredge, Lucien R. Foster, David Fullmer, John S. Fullmer, Joseph L. Heywood, John Pack, Franklin D. Richards, Lorenzo Snow, Willard Snow, Daniel Spencer, Joseph Young, and Phineas Young.

39. Lyman, Journal, 18 February 1845, 12.

40. *JSP*, CFM:377 (1 March 1845).

41. Bigler, Diary of a Mormon in California, 4–5.

42. *JSP*, CFM:285 (4 March 1845).

43. *JSP*, CFM:286 (4 March 1845).

44. *JSP*, CFM:288 (4 March 1845).

45. *JSP*, CFM:272, 273 (1 March 1845).

46. *JSP*, CFM:300 (11 March 1845).

47. Holbrook, Life of Joseph Holbrook, 76.

48. Bigler, Diary of a Mormon in California, 5.

49. William Coray died at age twenty-six from tuberculosis that he acquired in California as part of the Mormon Battalion. John Tanner died of natural causes at age seventy-two. Joseph Stratton died from exposure-related illness at only twenty-nine years of age while scouting faster routes through the mountains for emigration to Salt Lake Valley. George W. Langley died at age thirty-one from exposure-related illness while on guard duty in Salt Lake Valley.

50. Journal History of the Church, 21 July 1846.

51. The bishops were Jonathan H. Hale, Ellis M. Sanders, Levi W. Hancock, Edson Whipple, Jacob Myers, William G. Perkins, Andrew H. Perkins, Thomas Guyman, John Tanner, Daniel Spencer, Jonathan C. Wright, Abraham O. Smoot, Isaac Houston, Jesse C. Little, and John Vance. See Clayton, Journal, 120.

52. Gudde, *Bigler's Chronicle of the West*, 17.

53. William Hyde, Journal, 73.

54. Polk, *Diary of a President*, 109.

55. William Hyde, Journal, 73–74.

56. Browning and Gentry, *John M. Browning, American Gunmaker*, 4–5.

57. See Pace, "Biographical Sketch," 5.

58. Pettegrew, "History of David Pettegrew," 185–232.

59. Electioneer officers were Jefferson Hunt, James H. Glines, Elam Luddington, William Coray (who also brought his newlywed wife), William Hyde, David P. Rainey, Thomas Dunn, John D. Chase (and his wife), Daniel Tyler, Richard D. Sprague, George P. Dykes, Nathaniel V. Jones, James Pace, Samuel Gully, and Levi W. Hancock.

60. Boyle, Reminiscences and Diaries, 26–28. See William Coray, Journal, 7.

61. Bigler, Diary of a Mormon in California, 30 January 1848.

62. Holbrook, Life of Joseph Holbrook, 128.

63. Official cadre "gold missionaries" included Howard Egan, Jefferson Hunt, Bradford W. Elliott, Darwin J. Chase, Peter M. Fife, Charles C. Rich, and Amasa Lyman. See Hickerson, "Autobiographical Sketch," p. 5; and Gregory, *History of Sonoma County, California*, 794.

64. Jacob, Reminiscence and Journal, 4 July 1847.

65. Erastus Snow, Autobiography, 11–12.

66. Egan, *Pioneering the West*, 103.

67. Electioneer company leaders in 1847 were Edward Hunter, Abraham O. Smoot, Daniel Spencer, Jedediah M. Grant, Charles C. Rich, Levi W. Hancock, Jefferson Hunt, James Pace, and Samuel Gully. Gully died while leading his company.

68. Quoted in Roberts, *Comprehensive History of the Church*, 3:25.

69. *Deseret News*, 10 September 1856, 213.

CHAPTER 8

DESERET: EMERGING ARISTARCHY OF THE KINGDOM, 1848–1851

High on the mountain top, / A banner is unfurled. /
Ye nations, now look up; / It waves to all the world. / . . .
Then hail to Deseret! / A refuge for the good, / And safety for
the great. / . . . God with plagues will shake the world /
Till all its thrones shall down be hurled.

—Joel H. Johnson, "Deseret"[1]

RAISING A STANDARD TO THE NATIONS

Two days after arriving in the valley of the Great Salt Lake, Brigham Young and others climbed a domed precipice north of their encampment. It was the same peak that Brigham declared the deceased Joseph Smith had shown him in vision. The gathered men, which included electioneers Lorenzo D. Young and Erastus Snow, viewed the valley below. Brigham explained they were fulfilling Isaiah's prophecy that in the last days God would "lift up an ensign [banner or standard] to the nations" (Isaiah 5:26). Here Zion would be built and righteous people of the world would gather to prepare for the return of Jesus Christ. In their poverty, the only banner the weary emigrants could wave was a dirty yellow handkerchief tied to the end of a walking stick. Yet they had lifted God's standard to the nations—symbolizing the literal Zion of the scriptures.

Two days later Brigham declared, "We shall erect the Standard of Freedom."[2] An actual flag would yet fly. In fact, church leaders had planned such an event since the first day of the Council of Fifty in March 1844. The minutes record, "All seemed agreed to look to some place where we can go and establish a theocracy." The council determined to create the earthly kingdom of God "according to the mind of God." It would be complete with a "standard to the people, an ensign to the nations," and the council was confident that "all nations would flow unto it."[3] In a later meeting Hyrum Smith expressed his belief that "if we will set up the standard and raise the ensign the honest in heart of all nations will immediately begin to flock to the standard of our God."[4] The council saw this standard as being a symbolic *and* literal flag.

A cryptic reference in the Council of Fifty's minutes notes under the date of 22 June 1844—the night Joseph fled across the Mississippi River to escape apprehension—that he "gave orders that a standard be prepared for the nations."[5] He expected to take the sixteen-foot banner with him. The Saints began crafting the flag the day before Joseph's death, and his murder did not extinguish but only delayed the quest to plant the standard. In January 1846 Brigham declared to the Fifty that "the saying of the prophets would never be verified unless . . . the proud banner of liberty [is made to] wave over the valleys that are within the mountains." He then said, "I know where the spot is, and I know how to make the flag."[6]

Some of the electioneers were directly involved in creating and displaying the banner. On 27 February 1847, Jedediah M. Grant, Ezra T. Benson, Erastus Snow, and others of the Council of Fifty huddled with Brigham at Winter Quarters. The council determined that "the time had come to prepare the flag that Joseph Smith had first talked about." They wanted the "best stuff in the eastern markets," and they increased the size from Joseph's sixteen-foot flag to a ninety-by-thirty-foot "mammoth flag" that could be seen from afar. A hundred-foot flagpole would ensure the standard's visibility. The council chose Grant to visit "various seaports" to find the appropriate material. Grant's letter of authorization asked eastern Saints to contribute "means to accomplish [this] great work," which would be "an ornament to the cause" of Zion. While Grant was gone, the vanguard company embarked on its journey west. Grant succeeded in his peculiar assignment, returned to Winter Quarters, and departed west— but not in time to raise a proper ensign with Brigham's company on Ensign Peak. In fact, the flag created from Grant's material would not debut until 24 July 1849, the second anniversary of the pioneers' arrival in the Salt Lake Valley.[7]

The Saints planned a big day of celebration that year, which became a tradition—Pioneer Day—repeated every July up to the present day. This first festivity, at the base of Ensign Peak, included "parades, banners, decorations, music, and dinner—each done on a scale meant to convey saga."[8] Brigham entrusted cadre comrades Lorenzo Snow, Jedediah M. Grant, and Franklin D. Richards to plan the theodemocratic celebration. The evening before, two hundred men erected a 104-foot flagpole. In the morning, an honor guard raised the 65-foot "mammoth flag." Gun salutes, band music, and the ringing of the Nauvoo temple bell greeted the banner. Gentiles passing through the valley described the flag—the flag of Deseret, as locals called it—as blue and white, fashioned after the United States flag. In contrast to the US flag, the field had twelve stars circling a large star and twelve alternating white and blue stripes. The blue symbolized heaven; the white, purity; the twelve stars and large star, the apostles and Christ; and the stripes, the twelve tribes of Israel. A mix of theocratic and American symbols, this flag confused the gentiles at the celebration.

Furthermore, a smaller copy of the flag led the parade that day. This "kingdom flag" was carried on horseback by the parade's marshal, electioneer veteran Horace S. Eldredge. Next came a brass band and the city's twelve bishops, seven of them electioneers.[9] Twenty-four young men and twenty-four young women followed. The men were dressed in "white pants, black coats, white scarfs on the right shoulder, and coronets on their heads, each carrying in his right hand a copy of the Declaration of Independence and the Constitution of the United States, and each wearing a sheathed sword by his side." The women were "dressed in white, with blue scarfs on the right shoulder and wreaths of white roses on their heads, each carrying a Bible and a Book of Mormon."[10] The number twenty-four coupled with the crowns signified the "kings [and queens] and priests [and priestesses]" surrounding God's throne, as portrayed in the book of Revelation (1:6; 5:10). The message of the crowned men holding America's founding documents and the crowned women holding the scriptures was clear to all. This was the marriage of democracy and religion—theodemocracy.

Next came the apostles (including electioneers Lorenzo Snow, Franklin D. Richards, Charles C. Rich, and Erastus Snow), followed by the stake presidency of Daniel Spencer, David Fullmer, and Willard Snow (all electioneers). Last in line were twenty-four "Silver Greys" (men over sixty years old). One held the US "Stars and Stripes" with an inscription that read "LIBERTY OR DEATH." The parade marched to Brigham's house, where Brigham and Heber C. Kimball joined in. As the procession returned to the Bowery, the young people sang a new song called "The Mountain Standard," whose words praised "Freedom's banner," "Zion's standard wide unfurled," waving "for all the world."[11]

Under the shadow of the Deseret flag, the amassed Saints clamored, "Hosanna to God and the Lamb!"—a sacred shout based on Jesus Christ's triumphal entry into Jerusalem. Next they cheered, "Hail to the governor of Deseret!" as Brigham passed by. After an invocation from Erastus Snow, Brigham stood and led the crowd in three cheers of "May they live forever!" Phineas Richards, a recently selected member of the Council of Fifty and father of electioneers Franklin D. and Samuel W. Richards, then gave a "loyal and patriotic address" on behalf of the "aged sires."[12]

Phineas focused on the Saints' expulsion from Nauvoo and their status as true inheritors of American republican ideals. Joseph had been "inspired by the Spirit of the Almighty . . . and, with the pencil of heaven" (alluding to *Views*), declared the nation's "impending desolation and ruin." The prophet, "prompted by an unction from the upper world, essayed to put forth his hand to preserve the tottering fabric [of the Constitution] from destruction." Instead, his enemies have assassinated him and "have driven the Saints from their midst, . . . and now the vengeance of insulted heaven awaits them!" Phineas offered the solution—the establishment of Latter-day Saint theodemocracy: "It devolves upon us, as a people instructed by the revelations of God, with hearts glowing with love for our fallen country, to revive, support, and carry into effect the original, uncorrupted principles of the Revolution and the constitutional government of our patriotic forefathers."

"To you, President Young, as the successor of President Smith, do we now look, as to a second Washington, so far as political freedom is concerned," continued Phineas. It was the duty of Brigham—president of the church; standing chairman and prophet, priest, and king of the Council of Fifty; and governor of the State of Deseret—to "replant the standard of liberty, to unfurl the banner of protection." Brigham's "godlike integrity . . . [in] support of our murdered prophet" gave the Saints the "utmost confidence" to support him in finishing Joseph's measures. "Let us prove to the United States that when they drove the Saints from them . . . they . . . drove [out] . . . the firmest supporters of American Independence." With his cadence now in crescendo, Phineas proclaimed that, starting with Deseret, "let a standard of liberty be erected that shall reach to heaven and be a rallying point for all the nations of the earth." As revolutions and upheaval destroy kingdoms and nations, "*here* let the ensign of peace, like a heavenly beacon, invite to a haven of rest, an oasis of civil, political, and religious liberty. From here let the paeans [ancient songs of victory] of theodemocracy or republicanism reverberate from valley to valley, from mountain to mountain, from territory to territory, from state to state, from nation to nation, from empire to empire, from continent to continent." The assembly assented, arising to shout three times, "Hosanna! Hosanna! Hosanna to God and the Lamb, for ever and ever, amen and amen!"[13]

For two years church leaders continued to raise the flag of their theodemocratic state—Deseret. Electioneer Joel H. Johnson penned a poem about the flag raising titled "Deseret." Later set to music, it became a popular Latter-day Saint hymn, one still sung today—"High on the Mountain Top."

High on the mountain top a banner is unfurled.
Ye nations, now look up; it waves to all the world.
In Deseret's sweet, peaceful land,
On Zion's mount behold it stand!

For God remembers still his promise made of old
That he on Zion's hill Truth's standard would unfold!
Her light should there attract the gaze
Of all the world in latter days.[14]

Indeed, the flag of Deseret *did* attract the gaze of Saints and gentiles that day in 1849. Latter-day Saints viewed the banner as biblical prophecy fulfilled—a sign that they were God's people and about his work. In their State of Deseret, they not only satisfied prophecy but also redeemed the Declaration of Independence and Constitution. They looked forward to people gathering in the valley from all over the world to build up the earthly kingdom. But what that kingdom's relationship would be with the rest of the United States was still tenuous. Several hundred forty-niners on their way to California were guests that day. The mix of patriotic, religious, and even theocratic symbols and rhetoric was confusing, if not jarring. One visitor penned that the day's events, particularly the flag of Deseret, demonstrated that the "Mormons" were "upstart traitors" and their leaders "desperadoes." He gleefully recorded that in the evening a strong wind toppled the liberty pole, the flag plummeting into the dirt. He thought it a fitting omen. Historically it would be.[15]

A replica of the flag of Deseret, first used in 1849, flies today at Ensign Peak alongside the US and state of Utah flags. Photo courtesy of the author.

The events behind the creation and unfurling of the flag of Deseret witness that church leaders and the electioneers remained loyal to the theodemocracy of Joseph's political campaign. Just as the 1849 commemoration was planned and executed largely by electioneers, their work for the kingdom was the reality behind the rhetoric and symbolism of the day. Veterans of the electioneer cadre, under the direction of church leaders, formed the foundation of the emerging aristarchy of the Great Basin kingdom. Their previous faithfulness and work for the campaign and in other "measures" of Joseph ensured that. Ultimately, Deseret would only last a few years, but its replacement, the Territory of Utah, would function as a form of theodemocracy for several decades. Yet in the end the winds of change blown by the federal government would bring the flag, and the kingdom it represented, crashing down.[16]

THE STATE OF DESERET

BEGINNINGS

Brigham Young and his vanguard company arrived in the Salt Lake Valley as exiles. Before evacuating Nauvoo, Brigham declared that the Saints "owed the United States nothing, not a farthing, not one sermon. . . . They have rejected our testimony, killed our prophets; our skirts are clear from their blood. We will go out from them."[17] And so they did. Electioneers still on preaching missions in the United States shared similar sentiments. Norton Jacob mocked the "republican Spirit of the People" who had driven them out. "God deliver me from such a government!!"[18] In 1847 electioneer William I. Appleby wrote, "The American nation is yet at war with Mexico, . . . the American arms thus far proving victorious. [Yet] the race is not always to the swift, nor the battle to the strong," he added, perhaps expressing hope for an outcome that would leave the nascent Zion safely beyond US borders. "But may our Heavenly Father's will be done," he concluded.[19]

In 1848 the United States defeated Mexico in short order. The following year, Appleby now saw in the American victory, coupled with the revolutions in Europe, God's hand in "rending to pieces" the "kingdoms of the

Gentiles." Now American "Republicanism" could spread and "prepare the way . . . that the gospel may be proclaimed . . . by the servants of God" so that the "honest in heart" could receive it and gather to Zion and "not perish with the wicked and ungodly of the gentile kingdoms."[20] This collective feeling of fundamental respect for American institutions, but disdain for those in power and their treatment of the Saints, strongly influenced how Brigham conducted political affairs in the Great Basin.

The vanguard company of 1847 quickly went to work building the new Zion. Former electioneers were heavily involved. Surveyor Henry G. Sherwood helped Orson Pratt lay out the new city in the grid design of Joseph's original Zion plat. The soil was so rocky in areas that Levi N. Kendall's plow broke. They built a dam on a creek to provide irrigation. Lorenzo D. Young planted the first flowers and vegetables in the valley. Levi W. Hancock harvested the first crop of wheat. Expeditions went north, south, and west to scout the surrounding geography. Joseph Mount and Jedediah M. Grant and a few others explored the Great Salt Lake and its environs. The company's leaders gave Isaac and John D. Chase permission to build mills on area creeks. Osmon Duel constructed the first log home in the valley, while George W. Langley built the area's first adobe abode. Brigham sent electioneers Henry G. Sherwood, Jesse C. Little, and Daniel Spencer to buy out Miles Goodyear, the only other American in the area, with gold from electioneers discharged from the Mormon Battalion.[21]

On 26 August 1847 Brigham and several others departed for Iowa. Before leaving, they organized a high council with municipal duties, mirroring the one in Winter Quarters. The apostles, as presiding members of the Council of Fifty, were purposely planting theodemocracy in the valley. Brigham instructed, "It is the right of the Twelve to nominate the officers, and the people to receive them."[22] They chose John Smith, Joseph's uncle, who was coming in a subsequent pioneer company, to preside. They nominated electioneers Charles C. Rich and John Young as his counselors. Seven of the twelve members of the high council were also electioneers. Like the Winter Quarters Municipal High Council, Brigham gave the Salt Lake High Council religious, political, and economic authority to "observe those principles which have been instituted in the stakes of Zion for the government of the church, and to pass such laws and ordinances as shall be necessary for the peace and prosperity of the city for the time being."[23]

The municipal high council, acting under its mandate to protect the "peace, welfare and good order of [the] community," enacted laws "for the government and regulation of the inhabitants of this . . . valley."[24] The first ordinances targeted idleness, disorder, sexual misconduct, stealing, drunkenness, and cursing. Zion's prerequisite of righteousness remained. The council acted as a unified legislative, judicial, and executive entity like the Winter Quarters Municipal High Council—an echo of Joseph's combined government in Nauvoo. It adjudicated all issues, including a quarrel between electioneers Isaac Chase and Ira S. Miles over flour. Meanwhile, in Winter Quarters the gathered Quorum of the Twelve reorganized the First Presidency on 27 December 1847, naming Brigham Young, Heber C. Kimball, and Willard Richards as its members. When church leaders returned to the Salt Lake Valley the following summer, they found the valley Saints barely alive. With fresh supplies, the settlement survived.[25]

THEODEMOCRACY FIRMLY PLANTED

The US victory over Mexico made the Great Basin US territory. The Saints were now back in the nation they had fled—the nation that had exiled them. Throughout 1848 church leaders debated how to obtain political autonomy for their new Zion. Options included a petition to become a federal territory, become a new state in the Union, or have total independence. For information helpful in their deliberations, they relied on apostles George A. Smith and Ezra T. Benson (the latter a former electioneer), who were in the East on a fundraising mission. In a June dispatch they explained that since a treaty had not yet been approved, it was impossible to determine which nation will "have jurisdiction over the basin, . . . but as we are in the possession of the soil, our destiny would be independence should Mexico maintain her old lines." While a decision to join the United States "would give us facilities for doing business by agents in the US and thus save great expense and loss, . . . we go in, for once in all our life, if possible, to enjoy a breath of sweet liberty and independence."[26] Smith and

Benson would soon learn that the Mexican and American congresses had ratified a treaty—the Great Basin was already American.

Smith and Benson sent a second letter in October. Now they discouraged seeking territorial status because the Saints might fall victim to "starved office seekers . . . to be governor, judges and big men, irrespective of the feelings and rights of the hardy emigrants who had opened the country," as had happened in Oregon. Their counsel echoed that of the Saints' advocate Thomas L. Kane. Meeting the next year with apostle Wilford Woodruff and John M. Bernhisel (a former electioneer), Kane advised, "You are better without any government from the hands of Congress than with a territorial government, [because] the political intrigues of government officers will be against you. You can govern yourselves better than they can govern you; . . . you do not want corrupt political men from Washington strutting around you." Kane believed that the Saints were in a position of strength to negotiate statehood. "You have a government now, which is firm and powerful," Kane wrote, "and you are under no obligation to the United States."[27]

Kane referred to the government that Brigham and the Council of Fifty had created and were administrating. After establishing a quorum on 9 December 1848, the Council of Fifty prepared paperwork to follow California and New Mexico in applying for statehood. They discussed boundaries and a name for the new state. Choosing the Book of Mormon word *Deseret*, meaning "honeybee," they highlighted their collective effort to build Zion. In the petition, Deseret ambitiously claimed all modern-day Utah and Nevada, as well as western Colorado and New Mexico, most of Arizona, and southern California. Since the Saints were the only organized Americans in the region, such an expanse of territory seemed possible. The Council of Fifty nominated Brigham Young for governor and other members to fill other executive positions. On 6 January 1849, the council delegated John M. Bernhisel to deliver the statehood petition to Washington. Then it was resolved that "the [Salt Lake] high council be relieved from municipal duties."[28] So it was that the electioneer-laden Council of Fifty officially assumed the functions of government from the electioneer-laden municipal high council.

Throughout the winter and spring, the Council of Fifty governed temporal affairs through regular meetings and committees. It made decisions about all aspects of the growing colony: cattle storage, bridge construction, specie circulation, food scarcity, price inflation, taxation, crime, destruction of predatory animals, cemetery location, and reconstitution of the Nauvoo Legion. Some believe that Brigham and his associates made these decisions simply to fill the vacuum of governance. Yet in reality, their underlying intent coincided precisely with the mission of the Council of Fifty—to create a government as a shield for Zion based on Joseph's theodemocratic principles. On 1 February 1849 the Council of Fifty gave notice of a convention scheduled for 5 March in Salt Lake City "for the purpose of taking into consideration the propriety of organizing a territorial or state government."[29]

Church leaders then switched hats and turned to reorganizing the priesthood, after which they would align theodemocracy to that ecclesiastical framework. In early February 1849, they restructured the high council into a formal stake of Zion. Daniel Spencer was president of the Great Salt Lake Valley Stake with David Fullmer and Willard Snow as counselors. Church leaders then named Spencer mayor of Great Salt Lake City. The entire stake presidency and a third of the high council consisted of electioneers.[30] The high councilors doubled as city councilors. This fledgling theodemocracy governed Saints and gentiles alike. As gold seekers stopped in Salt Lake City in 1849, they had no choice but to have their grievances heard before Daniel Spencer and his high council. Some felt justly dealt with. Others did not, spreading their misgivings far and wide. In the coming years, as the number of outsiders in Salt Lake Valley increased, Latter-day Saint political dominance would lead to conflict as it had in Nauvoo.[31]

On 12 February 1849, in the home of electioneer George Wallace, Brigham called four new apostles. They filled the vacancies created by the reconstitution of the First Presidency and the excommunication of Lyman Wight. All four were electioneers—Charles C. Rich, Franklin D. Richards, Erastus Snow, and Lorenzo Snow. They joined fellow electioneer Ezra T. Benson, called to the apostleship in 1846. Not coincidently, since Joseph's murder, all five men who became apostles were veterans of Joseph's election campaign.

Two days later, Brigham divided the city/stake into nineteen wards. Seven of the bishops were electioneers.[32] Brigham appointed each bishop as the justice of the peace for his ward, thus creating theodemocratic ward units presided over by theocratic bishops. On 4 March, just a day before the planned constitutional convention, the Council of Fifty announced an election on 12 March "for the purpose of electing and appointing officers for the government of the people in the valley."[33] Later that day "the subject of nominating officers for election for a provisional government was presented" before the council, and it was "voted that the names already approved [on 9 December 1848] be brought before the people for ratification."[34] The council chose Daniel Spencer, David Fuller, and Willard Snow, the newly called Salt Lake Stake presidency, to be election judges. Finally, the council created a committee consisting of John Taylor, Parley P. Pratt, and electioneers William W. Phelps, Amasa M. Lyman, and Jedediah M. Grant to "fill out the ticket for the ensuing election." The next day the convention opened with Daniel Spencer presiding. A committee of ten was created to draft a constitution "under which the inhabitants of said territory may organize and govern themselves."[35] All on the committee were original members of the Council of Fifty. Of the ten selected, seven were electioneers.

That the constitution was prepared in less than two days strongly suggests that the Council of Fifty had crafted it previously. The final product was loosely based on the Constitution of Iowa, ratified in 1846. In Nauvoo the Council of Fifty had operated as a "living constitution," freely exercising the liberal powers of the Nauvoo Charter in pursuance of theodemocracy. Now in the position of needing federal approval for statehood, the council presented a proposed constitution that was palatable to Americans. The "living constitution" of the Council of Fifty would continue to pull the levers of theodemocratic power, but behind a governmental framework the rest of the nation could accept. On Saturday, 10 March 1849, the convention debated and then adopted the Constitution of the State of Deseret.

The Council of Fifty also met that day, and the council's committee on elections "presented the election ticket."[36] On Monday, 12 March, electioneer Hosea Stout recorded, "Today was our first political election.

CONSTITUTION

OF THE

STATE OF DESERET,

WITH THE

JOURNAL

OF THE CONVENTION WHICH FORMED IT,

AND THE

PROCEEDINGS OF THE LEGISLATURE CONSEQUENT

THEREON.

KANESVILLE,

PUBLISHED BY ORSON HYDE,

1849.

The Constitution of the State of Deseret gave formal structure to the "living constitution" of the Council of Fifty's theodemocracy, protecting the new Zion in the West. Image courtesy of Harold B. Lee Library Digital Collections, BYU.

... A large assemblage of men convened when many subjects were discussed.... There [were] 655 votes polled for the following offices: Brigham Young for governor; Willard Richards for secretary; H. C. Kimball, chief justice; N. K. Whitney and John Taylor, associate judges; H. S. Eldredge [electioneer], marshal; D. H. Wells, attorney-general; N. K. Whitney, treasurer; A. Carrington, assessor and collector; Jos. L. Heywood [electioneer], supervisor roads."[37] Additionally, the male populace elected all nineteen bishops as justices of the peace for their wards. In early May, with the trail reopened, electioneer veteran John M. Bernhisel headed for Washington with copies of the petition and the constitution and a list of the officers of Deseret.

The process of religious leaders writing a state constitution, nominating candidates based on aristarchy, and ratifying elections in unanimous voting was and is foreign to the American political experience. Joseph's ideal of aristarchic theodemocracy was radical and outside accepted notions of American governance. It is no coincidence that the Council of Fifty held the election on 12 March, the fifth anniversary, almost to the day, of Joseph's organization of the body. If the United States accepted Deseret, Brigham and the Council of Fifty would have what they wanted. The theodemocratic kingdom of God would be an official government entity, one that was independently created but protected under the wing of the American eagle. It appeared that Zion had a chance of finally being secure.

The creation of Deseret was exclusively the domain of the Council of Fifty. It called the convention, assigned its members to the drafting committee, and approved the document before ratification. That the convention adopted the constitution verbatim demonstrates the broad and uncontested authority of the Council of Fifty in the Deseret theodemocracy. Latter-day Saints looked to their leaders as prophets inspired by heaven and, by common consent, routinely voted to sustain them as their ecclesiastical leaders. The same was true on the political side of the coin. The Council of Fifty was tasked to operate political Zion, and its ranks contained all the leaders of the church. It made the decisions that the rest of the population voted to accept. The result was unity, which was what the Saints valued above all else—even freedom.

Yet while the electioneers and other Latter-day Saints celebrated their theodemocracy, most citizens of the United States viewed the developments with suspicion. For many, Deseret seemed a despotic, theocratic kingdom of religious zealots led by conspiring, unpatriotic men duping uneducated commoners and foreigners. What Latter-day Saints believed was humble obedience to prophets called to build up God's kingdom, other Americans saw as an autocratic, dangerous, and expanding empire amid their nation, which now spanned the continent. Deseret represented a potential outpost of treason in a nation committed to the separation of church and state. Adding polygamy to the equation, Latter-day Saints appeared not only undemocratic but also immoral. When federal authorities reacted, the Saints huddled closer to their leaders. They viewed every government decision as oppression, reinforcing the strong feelings of persecution that had forced them into the wilderness. This created forty years of conflict between Latter-day Saint theodemocracy and the United States government for political control of the Intermountain West—the "Mormon Question."[38]

One searches antebellum American history in vain to find similarities to Latter-day Saint theodemocracy. The two-party system dominated politics, and Democrats and Whigs gathered adherents from diverse religions. Catholics were the exception. Like Latter-day Saints, many Catholics were recent immigrants. Numerous Americans accused Catholics of following the pope instead of political authority. The Catholic response was to assimilate into the Democratic Party, where they found political power and protection. This was much different from the Latter-day Saints forming their own government as a kingdom on earth preparing for the return of Jesus Christ. Ironically, the mechanics of Latter-day Saint theodemocracy mirrored party politics in one important aspect—those who governed the political process were elites. But that's as far as the comparison goes. The Latter-day Saint elites nominated one candidate for each office, whom the faithful then voted to approve, there being only one choice. In contrast, with the political parties, the electorate could choose between two different candidates, two different platforms.

For two years the provisional State of Deseret governed the Great Basin. It was no coincidence that most of its "elected" officers were Council of Fifty members, electioneers, or both. The General Assembly convened on 2 July 1849 for its first session despite no elections having taken place for the House and Senate. Ostensibly, the Council of Fifty's committee of elections chose and elected the candidates between the March constitutional convention and July. That arrangement begs the question, Where did sovereignty lie? In Deseret it rested with God and was interpreted and exercised by church leaders. The Saints willingly acquiesced to those decisions. Not surprisingly, electioneers filled Deseret's House of Representatives and Senate.

The General Assembly passed no legislation in its first session. There was no need to. The Council of Fifty had run the temporal affairs of the Great Basin kingdom since January, and as the living constitution, the council continued to direct proceedings without legislation. In fact, "the formal establishment of the State of Deseret . . . was little more than a *de jure* confirmation of a *de facto* situation."[39] The council's purpose was more to secure statehood than to govern. The machinery of state fronted the religious elite to placate American public opinion. However, the State of Deseret did give the Council of Fifty the means and personnel to extend its mission to even the most remote Latter-day Saint colony.

Perhaps the most important piece of legislation passed concerned the creation of unique probate courts. The governor and legislature appointed these judges. Because Council of Fifty members filled the executive and legislative branches of Deseret, their chosen jurists became projections of the council to plant and protect local theodemocracy throughout the Great Basin. Naturally, probate judges were disproportionally electioneers. These judges exercised extensive influence in the county governments of Deseret and later in Utah Territory. They chose the first county officers and exercised authority comparable to that of county commissioners. Because many of their decisions were judicial and autonomous, the "living constitution" nature of governance continued. In 1852 the probate courts would be given jurisdiction of all civil and criminal cases and, three years later, original jurisdiction equal to that of federal district courts.

In Washington, DC, in 1849, federal representative of Deseret John M. Bernhisel had orders to obtain for Deseret "admission as a sovereign and independent state in the Union upon an equal footing with the original states."[40] However, negative feelings in Congress and contemporary events defeated this effort. In the aftermath of the Mexican-American War (1846–48), the territory of the United States nearly doubled. Friction over the slavery question in this new territory was overheating dangerously. The famous Compromise of 1850 settled the differences for a decade. One part of the pact created Utah Territory, significantly stripped in size from Deseret. The territories of Utah and New Mexico would also operate under popular sovereignty—where the populace in the territory would decide whether or not to permit slavery. Bernhisel lobbied US president Millard Fillmore to fill the Utah territorial offices with Latter-day Saints. However, fearing that the Senate would not accept an "all-Mormon slate," Fillmore split the offices between Latter-day Saints and gentiles.

In February 1851 Brigham learned that Fillmore had appointed him governor and that he was responsible for taking a census and creating legislative districts. Church leaders acted promptly to adopt and expand the idea of popular sovereignty into a bulwark for defending Zion through self-rule. In March the General Assembly of Deseret voted to dissolve itself. In his role as governor, Brigham administered a census and held new elections, all before the gentile officers arrived. Questionable in its legality, the preemptive strike showed Brigham's desire to create the territory as much in the image of Deseret as possible before outsiders interfered. The new legislature reelected Bernhisel as the territory's delegate to Congress and reenacted most laws of Deseret as territorial law. Though Brigham and the Council of Fifty governed Deseret for only two years, they had created institutions that would allow abundant autonomy for decades to come.[41]

THE ELECTIONEERS' RELIGIOUS CONTRIBUTIONS

ORDINATIONS

In 1850 the call of five new apostles—all electioneers—was only the beginning of electioneer advancement in priesthood responsibilities. Between 1844 and 1850, Church leaders called many electioneers to priesthood offices of significant responsibility. Electioneers saw sizable increases in the offices of seventy (248 percent), high priest (143 percent), bishop (530 percent), and apostle (667 percent). The increase in seventies is logical because most elders under thirty-five became seventies at the October 1844 Nauvoo conference. However, the increases in the other offices reflect the continuing and even growing confidence of church leaders in the leadership capabilities of the electioneer cadre. Perhaps the percentage of those who held high priesthood office is not as good an indicator of electioneer loyalty, faithfulness, and leadership ability as the number of available leadership positions they held. Again, in 1850 *all* five new apostles were electioneers. Recall as well that Daniel Spencer presided over the church's *only* stake of Zion and also that of the thirty-one wards or branches in the Great Basin, electioneers led eleven. The electioneers were fast becoming a dominant influence in the aristarchy that Brigham was fashioning as the religious superstructure of Zion.

MISSIONARY WORK

During this time of crisis and relocation, Brigham never lost focus on spreading the restored gospel. Of course, the electioneers were a well-qualified pool of prospective preachers. The missionaries who served in the United States concentrated on gathering scattered branches of the church to the Great Basin and raising money for their exodus. Libbeus T. Coons spent 1848 touring the eastern states and fundraising, which included writing letters to each state's governor. Again in 1849, church leaders appealed to the citizens of the nation for financial aid, sending electioneers Ezra T. Benson, Amasa M. Lyman, Erastus Snow, and William I. Appleby to raise funds. Chapman Duncan proselytized in his native Virginia, finding his wife along the way. Edson Whipple labored with apostle Wilford Woodruff in the eastern states, urging members to emigrate to the West.

During the late 1840s, many former electioneer missionaries participated in the fruitful harvest of converts in the British Isles. Tragically, missionaries James H. Flanigan and William Burton died during their service. In addition to the work in England, apostle Erastus Snow and George P. Dykes labored in Scandinavia and then Germany, publishing the Book of Mormon and gospel tracts. Another electioneer, apostle Lorenzo Snow, journeyed to Italy, where he converted a small group of Protestants.

Electioneers serving as missionaries in Europe had a threefold purpose. First, they comforted the Saints regarding Joseph's death. Elijah F. Sheets was the first post-martyrdom missionary in Europe. Of a conference in September 1844, he wrote, "I told them concerning the murder of Bro[ther] Joseph and Hyrum, and the bigger part of the congregation was [bathed] in tears, both saints and sinners."[42] Crandell Dunn recorded, "I spoke at some length on the history of the church and the persecutions that the prophet Joseph Smith had met with and the death of him and his brother Hyrum."[43] Second, they also proselytized. Between 1845 and 1850, more than thirty thousand converts joined the church in Great Britain alone. Third, the missionaries encouraged new Saints to gather to the Great Basin. Many of these missionaries had seen the new Zion and urged the converts onward. Before leaving England, Lorenzo Snow spoke to a large conference. "Upon the journeyings of the Saints in the wilderness, their settling in the valley of the Great Salt Lake, to their present and future prospects, both spiritual and temporal, the audience was very attentive to all [and] appeared to partake of the spirit of the speakers and he spoke by the Spirit of the living God."[44] The message was clear. Zion was still alive—come help build it.

THE ELECTIONEERS' RISE IN
RESPONSIBILITY, MEANS, AND INFLUENCE

From 1847 to 1850, the initial work of building a desert kingdom required capable leadership in many areas and at many levels. As the main governing body in Deseret, the Council of Fifty led out in this regard and, as was true for the work of managing the exodus, often turned to the loyal and capable electioneer veterans for those leadership needs. As opportunities to work and lead in greater capacities came their way, the electioneers were enabled to rise in prominence and stature in the Great Basin theo-democracy. Their enlarged scope of influence grew out of their increasing involvement in political, social, and economic affairs stemming from their religious offices and stations.

From 1845 until 1850, the Council of Fifty added twenty-seven men to its ranks to fill vacancies caused by deaths and excommunications. Of those newcomers to the council, twelve (44 percent) were electioneers, well above their 10–13 percent representation among priesthood holders. In 1850 the Council of Fifty had fifty-six members, twelve of whom had been general authorities in 1844 and twenty-two of whom were veteran electioneers. Thus electioneers constituted 39 percent of the council (50 percent if not counting pre-1844 general authority members).[45] Because the Council of Fifty appointed the first officers of the government of Deseret, it is not surprising that electioneers were among those selected. In 1849 the Deseret House of Representatives had twenty-six members, twelve (46 percent) of whom were electioneers. Notably, electioneer Willard Snow was elected Speaker of the House. In the Senate, seven of the fourteen members were electioneers. Thus in 1850, electioneers made up fully half the members of the Council of Fifty *and* of the General Assembly of Deseret.[46] This high level of involvement in political affairs and the attendant perquisites positioned the electioneers to take on added responsibilities and contribute to the prosperity of Deseret in other spheres as well.

For example, though plural marriage was not publicly announced until 1852, many electioneers entered the practice in the 1847–1850 period. Twenty-seven percent had multiple wives—a percentage three times the norm. While most plural marriages involved two wives, electioneers averaged 2.7, with a median of three wives. Why the difference? Leaders were expected to set the example with plural marriage. As electioneers were elevated to positions of religious and political influence, they were able to enter into more plural marriages. In fact, the five electioneers who became apostles and political leaders had between three and six wives. Electioneer John D. Lee, Council of Fifty member and adopted son of Brigham, led his electioneer colleagues in this regard with eleven wives.[47]

For Saints loyal to Brigham, this period brought great poverty and suffering. They endured poor weather, crop failure, and legions of locusts. However, through strong leadership and cooperation, the colony in Salt Lake Valley grew and new ones were begun. Brigham's vision was to colonize every habitable region in the Great Basin. He and other church leaders believed that ongoing missionary work and the establishment of the Perpetual Emigrating Fund would bring tens, perhaps hundreds, of thousands to the Great Basin. New colonies would provide homes for them. Also, if every desirable location held a Latter-day Saint colony, gentile settlement in the Great Basin would be minimal.

In all, Latter-day Saints settled fifty-two separate towns during these four years. Electioneers settled twenty-two of them. However, since the electioneers represented only about 10 percent of available priesthood men (owing to death and disaffection), their relative contribution was impressive. The average electioneer helped settle 1.2 colonies in the 1847–1850 period. This still left most of them in Salt Lake City, and the Council of Fifty used them to build up a strong capital. Even so, some electioneers had become colonizing experts by 1850. For example, Aaron F. Farr helped settle Salt Lake City, Big Cottonwood, and Irontown; and Joseph L. Robinson did the same for Bountiful, Farmington, and Irontown. Council of Fifty member and recently called apostle Charles C. Rich was similarly instrumental in the growth of Salt Lake City, Big Cottonwood, and Provo.[48]

Beginning with the colonization of what was called Great Salt Lake City in 1847, church leaders incorporated Zion principles of stewardship and inheritances into the distribution of land. They endeavored to avoid the real estate speculation of Kirtland and the competition of Nauvoo, both of which had fractured the church. Consequently, individual lots were given as "inheritances" and distributed by lottery. "No man can ever buy land here," Brigham told immigrants in 1848, "for no one has any land to sell, . . . but every man shall have his land measured unto him, which he must cultivate in order to keep it."[49] Speculation and division of inheritances were prohibited, "for the Lord [had] given it to [them] without price."[50] Bishops distributed land equally "according to circumstances wants and needs," in conformity with the law of consecration. People received their own land after paying a small fee to the recorder and surveyor. Two caveats in the process had great significance for the economic mobility of the electioneer cadre: single men could not receive an inheritance, while men with plural wives received separate lots for each family.[51]

Electioneers in Utah had roughly twice as much wealth as their neighbors had, and those with plural wives had more than three times the wealth of their fellow Saints (see table 8.1). Entering into plural marriage guaranteed additional land. The wealthiest electioneer in Utah in 1850 was John D. Lee, whose estate was valued at $5,500. The second wealthiest was Ezra T. Benson, who became an apostle and member of the Council of Fifty in 1846, married five women, and was a councilor of the State of

Deseret. His estate was worth $3,500. Alfred D. Young's $250 estate was the median. An accomplished missionary in Tennessee, he immigrated to Utah in 1848. By 1850, he was a president of a quorum of seventy though monogamous and was renowned for his spiritual gifts.[52]

Table 8.1. Electioneers' Wealth in 1850 Utah*

	Median Wealth	Average Wealth
Electioneers (176 total)	$250	$417
Electioneers w/ Plural Wives (59)	$400	$641
Salt Lake City Residents	$150	$252
Utah Territory Residents	n/a	$201

* Non-electioneer figures are from Travis, "Social Stratification and the Dissolution of the City of Zion in Salt Lake City," 74.

By 1850 most of the electioneers who had come to Utah were among the economic elite. As mentioned, their increased ecclesiastical and political responsibilities meant greater access to plural marriage and, concomitantly, land ownership. These advantages in large measure enabled them to become landed farmers and businessmen at almost twice the rate of their contemporaries at a time when Salt Lake City mirrored most other US towns and cities insofar as land ownership was generally lower than 40 percent (see table 8.2). Indeed, the electioneer veterans in Utah were already evolving into a landed economic elite.[53]

Table 8.2. Occupational Comparison, 1850*

Occupation	Electioneers (176 total)	Electioneers with Plural Wives (59)	Salt Lake City Residents
Business-Professional**	59% (104)	73% (43)	40%
Skilled	26% (46)	22% (13)	29%
Unskilled	15% (26)	5% (3)	31%

* Figures are from Travis, "Dissolution of the City of Zion," 74.
** Includes landed farmers.

＊　　＊　　＊

The electioneers' role as church and political leaders and their willingness to enter into plural marriage translated into growing wealth and influence in the State of Deseret. Their zeal and proven ability in working to establish Zion as a unified religious, political, social, and economic kingdom brought the dream of a theodemocratic kingdom that much closer to reality. From the ashes of Joseph's presidential campaign arose a leadership cadre uniquely equipped to help Zion bloom in the primitive territory of the Great Basin. In the three years after leading the Saints to the valley of the Great Salt Lake, church leaders bestowed abundant responsibility for building and administering Zion on the shoulders of Joseph's electioneers. These men were prominent in administering temple ordinances, leading pioneer companies to the valley, colonizing new towns, and guiding the Saints as bishops and legislators. Their growing influence in the kingdom's aristarchy would continue over the next two decades.

NOTES

1. Johnson, "Deseret," *Zion's Songster, or the Songs of Joel, Book Third*, Joel Hills Johnson Papers, CHL, 19 February 1853, 376; punctuation per *Hymns of The Church of Jesus Christ of Latter-day Saints* (Salt Lake City: The Church of Jesus Christ of Latter-day Saints, 1985), no. 5.

2. Quoted in Jacob, Reminiscence and Journal, 28 July 1847.

3. *JSP*, CFM:42 (11 March 1844).

4. *JSP*, CFM:52 (19 March 1844).

5. JSH, F-1:137.

6. Lee, Journal, 13 January 1846, 79.

7. See Bullock, Council Meeting Minutes, 26 February 1847, as quoted in Walker, "'Banner Is Unfurled,'" 75–76.

8. Bullock, Council Meeting Minutes, 26 February 1847, as quoted in Walker, "'Banner Is Unfurled,'" 84.

9. The electioneer bishops were John Lowry, Benjamin Brown, William G. Perkins, David Pettegrew, Edward Hunter, Abraham O. Smoot, and Joseph L. Heywood.

10. Eliza Snow, *Record of Lorenzo Snow*, 97.

11. Eliza Snow, *Record of Lorenzo Snow*, 97, 98.

12. Eliza Snow, *Record of Lorenzo Snow*, 99, 100.

13. Eliza Snow, *Record of Lorenzo Snow*, 103–105. For a full account of the celebration, see pp. 96–107.

14. Johnson, "Deseret."

15. Walker, "'Banner Is Unfurled,'" 86.

16. After Deseret became Utah Territory, the flag of Deseret was rarely seen. It was displayed on the day of Brigham's funeral and then placed in his casket.

17. Jesse Wentworth Crosby, Autobiography, 6 October 1845.

18. Jacob, Reminiscence and Journal, 16.

19. Appleby, Autobiography and Journal, 166.

20. Appleby, Autobiography and Journal, 220–21.

21. See "Salt Lake's Original Nineteen LDS Wards." See also Kate Carter, *Heart Throbs of the West*, 12:208.

22. Quoted in Egan, *Pioneering the West*, 127.

23. Journal History of the Church, 9 September 1847. The high council was composed of electioneers Henry G. Sherwood, Levi Jackman, Daniel Spencer, Edson Whipple, John Vance, Willard Snow, and Abraham O. Smoot. The other members were Thomas Grover, Stephen Abbott, John Murdock, Ira Eldredge, and Shadrach Roundy.

24. Journal History of the Church, 27 December 1847.

25. "Pioneer Forts of the West: High Council Meetings," Utah, Our Pioneer Heritage (database). The incident occurred on 11 October 1847.

26. Journal History of the Church, 28 June 1848.

27. Quoted in Morgan, *State of Deseret*, 69–70.

28. Journal History of the Church, 6 January 1849.

29. Constitution of the State of Deseret, 1.

30. The high council members were Isaac Morley, Phineas Richards, Shadrach Roundy, Titus Billings, Eleazer Miller, Ira Eldredge, William Major, Edwin D. Woolley, and former electioneers Henry G. Sherwood, John Vance, Levi Jackman, and Elisha H. Groves.

31. See Journal History of the Church, 6 and 14 February 1849; Jenson, "Daniel Spencer," in *Latter-day Saint Biographical Encyclopedia*; and Unruh, *Overland Emigrants and the Trans-Mississippi West*, 262.

32. The bishops were John Lowry, Benjamin Brown, William G. Perkins, David Pettigrew, Edward Hunter, Abraham O. Smoot, and Joseph L. Heywood.

33. Journal History of the Church, 4 March 1849.

34. Lee, *Diaries of John D. Lee*, 98–110. The council replaced electioneer John M. Bernhisel with electioneer Horace S. Eldredge as marshal because Bernhisel would be leaving for Washington.

35. Journal History of the Church, 5 March 1849. The committee consisted of Albert Carrington, Parley P. Pratt, John Taylor, and electioneers William W. Phelps, Charles C. Rich, David Fullmer, Joseph L. Heywood, John S. Fullmer, Erastus Snow, John Taylor, and John M. Bernhisel.

36. Journal History of the Church, 10 March 1849.

37. Stout, *Diary of Hosea Stout*, 2:348.

38. Fred Rogers, *Unpopular Sovereignty*, 3.

39. Klaus Hansen, *Quest for Empire*, 157.

40. Brigham Young to Orson Hyde, in Journal History of the Church, 19 July 1849.

41. See Rogers, *Unpopular Sovereignty*, 63–64.

42. Sheets, Journal, 22 September 1844.

43. Dunn, "History and Travels," 1:165.

44. Cutler, Diary, 9 May 1850.

45. See Quinn, "Council of Fifty," 22–26. I use the term *general authority* to refer to those of the church's three presiding quorums—the First Presidency, the Quorum of the Twelve Apostles, and the seven Presidents of the Seventy. Use of the term here is not anachronistic. It was first used in print by the church in the 1835 edition of the Doctrine and Covenants and has since been used to describe the highest officers of the church.

46. See Morgan, *State of Deseret*, 35–36. Electioneer representatives were Willard Snow, David Fullmer, John S. Fullmer, John Pack, Joel H. Johnson, Lorenzo Snow, Joseph A. Stratton, George B. Wallace, Jedediah M. Grant, Jefferson Hunt, Franklin D. Richards, and Hosea Stout. Electioneer state counselors were Reynolds Cahoon, William W. Phelps, John Young, Daniel Spencer, David Pettigrew, Abraham O. Smoot, and Charles C. Rich.

47. See Danel W. Bachman and Ronald K. Esplin, "Plural Marriage," in *Encyclopedia of Mormonism*, 1091.

48. See Beecher, "Colonizer of the West," in *Lion of the Lord*, 173–207.

49. Quoted in Beecher, "Colonizer of the West," 173.

50. William Clayton's Journal, 28 July 1847, 326.

51. For an example, see electioneer Elisha Groves, who served as bishop and legislative representative for Parowan, established in 1851. Journal History of the Church, 16 May 1851.

52. Some electioneers who did not follow Brigham west held considerable wealth. John Duncan, a follower of Sidney Rigdon, owned thirty thousand dollars of land in Pennsylvania. Amos Davis, a merchant just outside Nauvoo had assets amounting to three thousand dollars. George Pew, a plantation overseer in Louisiana, and John Swackhammer, a carpenter in New York City, each had recorded wealth of twenty-five hundred dollars.

53. See Travis, "Dissolution of the City of Zion," 153–54.

CHAPTER 9

RELIGIOUS ARISTARCHY OF THE KINGDOM, 1851–1869

First get the families united, then get the wards, the towns, the cities, and the
counties regulated, and you will have every part of the territory right. . . . I would
like to see the work of reformation commence and continue until every man had
to walk to the line; then we should have something like union.

—Jedediah M. Grant, 13 July 1855

Electioneer Experience: Franklin D. Richards. Franklin D. Richards became president of the British Mission—the largest of The Church of Jesus Christ of Latter-day Saints—on 1 January 1851. Although he was only thirty years old, this was already his second time as a leader in Europe. It would not be his last. From the moment of his call as an electioneer at age twenty-three, Richards catapulted into church leadership. While electioneering in the East, he learned of Joseph's death and obediently returned to Nauvoo. In 1845 church leaders sent him to Michigan to gather funds for the temple. Traveling a thousand miles in frigid weather, he collected an impressive five hundred dollars. After receiving his temple ordinances in early 1846, Richards responded to a call to join his brother and fellow electioneer Samuel W. Richards on a mission to England. After helping his pregnant wife and infant daughter cross the Mississippi River, he and Samuel headed for

England. The last letter he read before embarking overseas explained that his wife lay at death's door and his newborn son had already crossed that threshold.

Upon arrival in Liverpool, leaders appointed Richards to preside in Scotland, with Samuel assisting. Soon Richards was a counselor to Orson Spencer, president of the British Mission. In February 1848 Richards took leadership of a company of European Saints heading for Salt Lake City. The last letter from home that he read before departing again broke his heart. After contracting an illness in the Mormon Battalion, his brother Joseph had died. Compounding that tragedy, his own infant daughter had succumbed at Winter Quarters.

In October 1848 he and his wife arrived in Salt Lake City. Richards sold everything to construct a crude adobe home. Freezing in that rudimentary abode was not the only shock of the winter. On 12 February 1849, Brigham called twenty-eight-year-old Richards to the apostleship. Then, as was typical in theodemocratic governance, the following month he joined the Council of Fifty and the Assembly of Deseret. October saw him headed to England again, this time as president of the British Mission. He established the European infrastructure of the Perpetual Emigrating Fund (PEF), oversaw multiple publications, and presided over a spike in converts—more than sixteen thousand. In 1852 he personally led a PEF company to Salt Lake, where he reentered what was now the territorial legislature and traveled south to help bolster the floundering Iron Mission.

His work done in southern Utah, he returned to Salt Lake City only to be sent again to England. This time, however, all of Europe was one mission, with Richards at its head. European missionary work flourished under his touch, including the opening of several new countries to proselytizing. In 1856 he and fellow electioneer Cyrus H. Wheelock led another PEF company to Utah. Richards was also partly responsible for two handcart companies that encountered disaster that season. They had started the trek to Utah late and were caught on the high plains in subzero snowstorms. Despite the heroics of rescue parties, 210 of the nearly 1,000 emigrants perished. The blame fell at the feet of Richards and electioneer colleague Daniel Spencer, who was in Nebraska supervising emigration. Brigham rebuked them publicly, saying that they should "have known better than to rush men, women, and children on the prairie in the autumn months . . . to travel over a thousand miles."[1]

Yet whatever blemish Brigham's words gave Richards, the prophet still trusted him as a leader. In the following three months Richards was re-elected to the legislature, renamed regent of the University of Deseret, and made a brigadier general in the Nauvoo Legion. Brigham sent Richards to southern Utah in 1859 to reorganize all the settlements politically. For the next seven years, Richards was a religious, political, social, and economic leader in the territory. In 1860 he had thirteen wives and seven thousand dollars in wealth. His fourth mission to England began in 1866, once again as president of the European Mission. Converts and emigrants continued to increase under his watch, which ended in late 1868.

The career of Franklin D. Richards is the epitome of the electioneers' stunning postcampaign success. Courtesy of Church History Library.

Arriving back in Utah, Richards was immediately assigned to Ogden. The intercontinental railroad was nearing completion, bringing with it a flood of gentile influence that concerned church leadership. Ogden was ground zero for this coming clash, and Brigham wanted Richards in charge. He became not only president of the Weber Stake but also a member of the territorial legislature and Weber County probate judge. In these positions he effectively defended theodemocratic Zion in Weber County from the infringements of gentile culture and the federal government for two decades.

Franklin D. Richards was the epitome of the electioneer cadre's stunning postcampaign success in becoming a crucial component of the aristarchy in the Great Basin kingdom. In 1844, as a poor, inconsequential young man, he had volunteered to campaign for his prophet. By 1869 he was a territorial elite and Brigham's right hand in defending the theodemocracy they both had advocated for as electioneer missionaries and later had helped establish in the West. Priesthood office and positions came his way *during* the election campaign and continued throughout his life. As he wrote presciently during the campaign, "[I am] on my way to perform this important mission [to campaign for Joseph Smith], the faithful and acceptable performance of which involves my future prosperity in church life."[2]

One might credit all this to nepotism—he was the nephew of apostle Willard Richards. However, Willard Richards and other Nauvoo-era apostles had hundreds of nephews, sons, brothers, and other male relatives. None rose as Franklin did, so quickly and so high. Those that came close were, like Franklin's younger brother Samuel, also electioneers. It was apparent to church leaders from the early days of electioneering that Franklin and others like him had the right attributes to be entrusted with leadership responsibilities. Early postcampaign assignments fulfilled well led to more and more responsibilities until the electioneer cadre for the kingdom became the critical core of the aristarchic cadre of the kingdom—the workhorses of Zion.

* * *

The electioneers' contributions to the Great Basin Kingdom from 1851 to 1869 occurred against the background of significant religious, political, social, and economic events and trends. Shaping these events while being shaped by them, the electioneers endured as a critical corps in building and strengthening Zion despite looming threats to its existence such as the Utah War, the Civil War, and the Transcontinental Railroad. With thousands of Latter-day Saint immigrants arriving in the valley each summer, established towns in Deseret grew in population even as church leaders created new settlements. This intensified the need to create municipal governments and to fill important roles in the theodemocracy in order to better direct this expansion. As before, it often fell to the capable electioneers to help lead settlements, counties, and even the nascent Utah Territory in all aspects of life.

In 1860, the midpoint of the time period under discussion, the average Latter-day Saint male in the Great Basin was nineteen years old and had British parents and several siblings. He labored in construction or agriculture and was a priest or elder.[3] By comparison, the average electioneer was fifty years old, with American-born parents and multiple wives. He was a prosperous landed farmer and a high priest with local or even territorial religious, political, and economic responsibilities. By calling on the electioneers' experience along those lines, church leaders could continue creating theodemocracy in the Great Basin.

Church leaders orchestrated the building up of Zion at a rapid pace throughout the 1850s and 1860s. In 1851, with Salt Lake City as the new headquarters of Zion now secure under the wings of a church-dominated territorial government, Brigham increased the urgency of the gathering effort. He made four decisions that enabled many Saints to flock to Deseret and receive temple ordinances that would set them apart from the world and cement their commitment to the cause of Zion. Electioneer veterans factored in each decision. First, he ordered the evacuation of the faithful but destitute Saints still camped along the Missouri River. Second, he increased the number of missionaries and expanded their fields of labor. Third, these same missionaries were to strongly encourage their converts to gather to Zion, and even provide financial assistance for doing so. Fourth, Brigham expanded the number of colonizing missions in the Great Basin to create space for new arrivals and to protect Zion from outside settlement. To see that these measures were carried out, Brigham and other leaders regularly turned to the electioneers.

EVACUATION OF WESTERN IOWA

In 1849 church leadership created the Perpetual Emigrating Fund, whereby Latter-day Saints donated money to "promote, facilitate, and accomplish the emigration of the poor." Emigrants were expected to repay the costs so the program could continue in perpetuity. Brigham charged fund officers Ezra T. Benson and Jedediah M. Grant (both electioneer veterans) to evacuate the Saints stranded in western Iowa. In a general epistle to the church, Brigham declared that Benson and Grant were "sent expressly to push Saints to this valley."[4] And push they did. Benson and Grant told the Saints in Iowa "not to be afraid of the plains, but to encounter them with any kind of conveyance that they can procure, with their handcarts, their wheelbarrows, and come on foot, pack and animal, if they have one, and no other way to come."[5] In 1851 twenty-five hundred Saints reached the Salt Lake Valley. The following year more than six thousand pioneers made the trek—the largest flow of the two-decade emigration. When Benson and Grant returned to Salt Lake in August 1852, they left Iowa "almost entirely vacated by the Saints."[6]

With most Saints in North America gathered, Brigham commenced construction of the Salt Lake Temple. On 6 April 1853, Saints throughout the region gathered to witness priesthood leaders dedicate the cornerstones. Four of the eight officiators were electioneers. Presiding bishop of the church Edward Hunter laid the southwest stone, declaring, "I have acted in the priesthood and the part allotted me, with the love and fear of God before my eyes, by the aid of His Spirit to the best of my ability, and I hope acceptably in the sight of God and those who preside over me in this latter-day work."[7] His counselor and electioneer comrade Alfred Cordon offered the stone's dedicatory prayer. John Young gave the oration at the placing of the northwest cornerstone, followed by a dedicatory prayer from fellow electioneer George B. Wallace. Electioneer Joseph Curtis, who had made the fifty-mile trip from Payson, captured the solemnity of the moment, recording, "O Lord, may I never forget."[8]

EXPANDED MISSIONARY WORK

Although the church was now headquartered in the West, some former electioneers continued to labor as missionaries throughout the United States. However, the church's public pronouncement of plural marriage in 1852 made Latter-day Saints pariahs and limited their missionary success. The Utah War and Civil War further disrupted proselytizing efforts. George W. Hickerson, serving in Mississippi in 1854, wrote to his wife, "My labours [are] . . . all traveling and no preaching. It is very seldom I get the opportunity to preach. [A]s a general thing the people that have heard don't want to hear anymore, and those that have not heard do not wish to hear, for the name of a Mormon is enough for them."[9]

In August 1852, at a special conference of the elders in Salt Lake City, church leaders called 110 missionaries to proselytize around the world. This extraordinary meeting was an echo of the April 1844 meeting that selected the electioneers. In fact, this new missionary force was the largest since Joseph's campaign. Naturally, electioneers figured predominantly—twenty-four in all.[10] Throughout the 1850s and 1860s, electioneers served as missionaries, most often as presiding officers. Amasa Lyman, Charles C. Rich, Lorenzo Snow, Franklin D. Richards, and Chauncey W. West took turns presiding over the European Mission. In France, Andrew Lamoreaux presided, fulfilling a prophecy Joseph made in 1839. In tears, Joseph had told Lamoreaux that when he completed this future mission he would die and not return to his family. While accompanying converts immigrating to Utah, Lamoreaux died of cholera in St. Louis.[11] George C. Riser worked with such zeal and success as the German Mission president that the authorities imprisoned him.[12] Daniel Tyler presided over the Swiss, Italian, French, and German missions with few conversions despite continual travel and labor.[13]

The largest segment of missionaries, including electioneers, served in Europe. European Saints felt "more highly favored" to hear from a former electioneer missionary "of the old stock" because they "had a knowledge of Joseph, the prophet, and an acquaintance with him."[14] Great Britain continued to be fertile ground for converts. For two decades, electioneers serving as missionaries found proselytes there.[15] Dan Jones, one of the last electioneers to have seen Joseph alive, continued to fulfill the prophecy that he would preach with great success in Wales. Under his leadership, thousands converted and emigrated to Utah.[16]

Fifty-two of the 110 missionaries left for California to find passage to their missions in Asia, Australia, and the islands of the Pacific. A dozen were electioneers. The combined one-way total for all their voyages was more than six thousand dollars. They dispersed to find work and soon raised the money. Between January and April of 1853, they began sailing to their destinations. Curiously, wealthy but disaffected California electioneers John S. Horner and Samuel Brannan financed several of the

electioneer missionaries. While not devoted to Brigham, disaffected electioneers often remained loyal to their electioneer colleagues.

Brigham assigned electioneer veterans to lead the Asia Mission. Nathaniel V. Jones opened India and served as mission president for three
years.[17] Elam Luddington and Chauncey W. West, assigned to Siam,
worked with two other missionaries in Calcutta, India, and then Bangkok.
Luddington later wrote that the group traveled thirty thousand miles on
three different ships, baptizing sixteen converts.[18] Chapman Duncan and
Hosea Stout landed in Hong Kong in April 1853. Upon arrival the men
found "the situation and conditions in that country entirely the reverse
from what [they] expected."[19] Unable to speak Chinese, the missionaries
approached the small European population, all of whom rejected them,
even disseminating lies about the missionaries' intentions. With money
and welcome running out, the missionaries returned to California.

Twenty-one missionaries traveled to the Society Islands to continue
the work begun in the mid-1840s. The conditions were so difficult that
all but three returned home. Not coincidentally, the three who remained
were dedicated former electioneers: Sidney A. Hanks, Jonathan Crosby,
and Simeon A. Dunn.[20] They converted hundreds until 1853, when after
a change in government they were banished.[21] Hanks managed to remain
for eight years until he was accidentally rediscovered by other missionaries. They communicated his situation to Brigham, who promptly released
him to come home.[22] Nathan Tanner, William McBride, Lorenzo Snow,
and Ezra T. Benson all served in the Sandwich Islands (Hawai'i), converting sizable congregations.[23] Charles W. Wandell introduced the church to
Australians in 1851. When he returned home in 1853, Augustus A. Farnham presided and, along with Josiah W. Fleming, continued the church's
growth in Australia.[24]

Prolonged and extensive missionary work in faraway lands took its
toll on electioneer missionaries and their families. A few even died during
their exertions. Levi Nickerson, called to Great Britain, became sick during
extreme weather in Iowa. Severely ill, he lingered for a year before being
found dead in his tent, orphaning six children in Utah. In tragic irony, he
died only miles from where his father perished seven years earlier.[25] Stephen Taylor passed away in the eastern United States, and William Burton

died in England.[26] Willard T. Snow, a territorial legislator and member of the First Quorum of the Seventy, became violently ill in Denmark.[27] He died en route to convalesce in England. Thomas Atkinson and his companion died when their steamer, *Ada Hancock*, exploded in San Pedro Harbor.[28]

Upon arriving home from Australia, Augustus A. Farnham met a small boy playing near his house. He called, "Hello, sonny, what's your name?"

The child answered, "Gussy Farnham."

"Is that so—that's my name, too," Augustus responded. When he entered the house, he found his wife packed and ready to leave for the East. No amount of persuasion could prevail on her to stay. The child was his own son—born after he had departed for his assignment. His wife also took their daughter, a tragic end to his five-year mission.[29]

Upon Israel Barlow's call to Great Britain, his wife asked that he stop in Nauvoo to rebury their infant son James, who had been hastily interred at their former farm. Barlow struggled to find the grave because the farm's layout had changed. He eventually found the coffin and the remains scattered and all but destroyed. He quickly and brokenheartedly reburied them. As he turned to leave, he heard a voice plead, "Daddy, do not leave me here." Obedient, Barlow carefully moved the remains to Nauvoo's public cemetery. He wrote to his wife that the decision brought "a very peculiar calm and peace of mind which before I did not feel." Barlow placed the

Israel and Elizabeth Barlow courageously sacrificed throughout their lives to build up Zion's theodemocracy. Courtesy of Israel Barlow Family Association.

remains in a new coffin and buried it in the cemetery with a "rude stone" to mark the grave.[30]

Pondering over the new resting place of his firstborn son, Barlow "felt a desire to dedicate [him]self" to the work of Zion so that he might have his son again in the Resurrection. Melancholy, he wrote to his wife that he had fulfilled her request, adding grape and apple seeds from their former farm in the envelope. He concluded, "If I have desire to glory in anything, it is in aiding to build up that kingdom, and I do most candidly confess that I do feel to glory in the cause I am engaged in, for it seems all glorious to me at times."[31] While Barlow was in England, his family suffered. Two sons died and another came perilously close. Local priesthood leaders, including Barlow's electioneer companion David Candland, did what they could to minister to the family.[32]

EMIGRATION

Brigham sent electioneer veterans Abraham O. Smoot, Willard Snow, and Samuel W. Richards to coordinate the PEF in England. Leaders there chose Smoot to captain the first PEF company. The relative smoothness of the operation opened the floodgates for European Saints to emigrate. Over the next decade and a half, several electioneers led companies of converts to Zion.[33] Richards, while presiding over the work in England, testified before the British House of Commons to allay concerns regarding the Latter-day Saint emigration. While he and his brother Franklin (also a former electioneer) presided in England, more than fourteen thousand Saints traveled to Utah.[34] Electioneer missionaries helped converts emigrate from other nations as well, most notably Australia. In 1856 Augustus A. Farnham and Joseph Fleming sailed from Sydney with a company of Saints bound for Zion. Joseph A. Kelting led another group the following year.[35]

Church leaders in St. Louis were the linchpins in this intercontinental mass migration. St. Louis became the major way station for European Saints to rest while PEF agents provided wagons, oxen, and supplies for the trip across the plains. Throughout the 1850s, Brigham placed trusted electioneers in St. Louis to preside over the Saints and to supervise the PEF. Starting in 1852, Horace S. Eldredge served there for two years. It was not an easy assignment. Cholera plagued emigrants, and Eldredge himself became sick. Yet he worked tirelessly to comfort and arrange the affairs of thousands of converts. Hundreds of Saints contributed to purchase a gold ring for him, a token of their gratitude.[36] Brigham chose Aaron F. Farr to replace Eldredge, followed by Milo Andrus. Erastus Snow next oversaw a two-year period, expanding and strengthening St. Louis as a Latter-day Saint outpost. He organized a stake of Zion, published the *St. Louis Luminary*, and constructed a new outfitting post.[37]

COLONIZING MISSIONS

In 1850 church leaders sent a colonizing mission south in search of iron ore. This decision was part of Brigham's goal to be free from the gentiles through economic self-sufficiency. Apostles George A. Smith and Ezra T. Benson (electioneer) led the group, dubbed the Iron Mission.[38] Church leaders selected several electioneers for the expedition.[39] By summer a town existed with school, mills, stores, and surrounding farms.[40] Edson Whipple's journal details the roles he played. Called by Brigham to join the colony, Whipple was appointed by local leaders as associate justice of the nascent county. They also selected him as a militia captain. Of the plans presented to lay out the settlement, Whipple proudly wrote, "Mine was accepted and adopted, and Parowan was built up according to my plan." Local church leaders nominated Whipple, and he was subsequently elected to the Parowan City Council.[41]

Latter-day Saints also colonized San Bernardino, California. Brigham wanted the colony to become the primary way station for emigrating converts coming from San Diego and up the "Mormon Corridor" of settlements to Salt Lake City. Again, electioneers were in the lead. In 1851 Brigham selected electioneer apostles and California veterans Amasa Lyman and Charles C. Rich to lead a company of more than four hundred Saints to San Bernardino. Lyman and Rich recruited families for the mission, including men from the electioneer cadre.[42]

The experiences of two electioneers illustrate the successes, the difficulties, and ultimately the failure of the venture. Jefferson Hunt, former commanding officer of the Mormon Battalion and veteran of the

California trails, was an obvious choice for the company's scout. Using his contacts in California, Hunt negotiated the massive purchase of land, personally guarding the twenty-five thousand dollars in gold coins. His impeccable reputation among Californians won important concessions for the Saints. He was so highly regarded that the governor appointed him commander in chief of the California Militia. Hunt represented the Saints in the California legislature and served as an assemblyman in San Bernardino County. Concurrently, church leaders placed him on the colony's high council. Hunt bought half interest in the colony's sawmill and held the mail contract between San Bernardino and Salt Lake City. Unfortunately, he and the others abandoned San Bernardino in 1857 because of the Utah War. He sold his interest in the sawmill for one-tenth its value and moved back to Parowan.[43]

Henry G. Boyle reluctantly moved his young family to San Bernardino when electioneer colleagues Amasa Lyman and Charles C. Rich recruited him. A Mormon Battalion veteran, Boyle did not wish to return to the land of his earlier suffering. Little did he know that his grief was just begin-

ning. A year after arriving, Boyle's young wife died. "She has been a faithful good Mormon," he wrote, "and I feel the loss to be very great." A widower with young children, Boyle served several missions, including a "gold mission." Continued time away from his small family destroyed his peace. So too did seeing former friends excommunicated for dissent. "It is a painful thing to be a witness of," he penned; "it makes my blood chill in its veins. God grant that I may never depart from the truth."[44] He too fled San Bernardino in 1857 owing to the Mormon War. "I think I shall feel like I have been released from hell when I shall have got away from here," Boyle wrote. He never returned to San Bernardino.[45]

Jefferson Hunt served in the Mormon Battalion and in the Deseret and California legislatures and helped settle San Bernardino, California. Courtesy of Myron Taylor.

When the Civil War stopped cotton ship-ments, church leaders decided to create a colony in southern Utah to produce cotton and other amenities. The "Cot-ton Mission" settled present-day St. George in 1862 with several hundred families. Electioneer apostle Erastus Snow directed the effort, declaring, "I feel to go body and spirit, with my heart and soul, and I sincerely hope that my brethren will endeavor to do the same."[46] In the first company, and over the years, numerous electioneers participated in colonizing St. George. For example, Lysander Dayton built the first home there and served on the high council, and Lewis Robbins served as Washington County's repre-

Henry G. Boyle experienced the difficulties of creating theodemoc-racy in San Bernardino, California. Courtesy of Church History Library.

sentative to the territorial legislature until he tragically died in an accident at the temple site.[47]

Difficulties sometimes outweighed success in these and other colonies in the Great Basin kingdom. As it turned out, the Iron Mission yielded very little iron, and for decades Utah's "Dixie" failed to produce enough cotton for the effort to be viable. The church's hope for a stronghold in California evaporated with the abandonment of San Bernardino. Even smaller colonies were not immune to the troubles of planting theodem-ocratic Zion. The experiences of James Pace and other electioneers who settled Payson, Utah, illustrate the difficulties. Pace led several Saints to southern Utah Valley in 1850. Brigham ordained him branch president and named the settlement in his honor—Payson. Pace recorded, "During the remainder of the season nothing of importance transpired excepting the ordinary routine of trials, confusions, and difficulties at tending the building up of a new settlement with all classes of men to do it with, in-cluding all their peculiarities and notions of right and wrong."[48]

The aforementioned difficulties came to a head in late 1851. Pace excommunicated James McClellan but refused to go to the high council in Provo to explain his action. The council promptly removed Pace as branch president and placed McClellan in his stead. Electioneer and Paysonite Joseph Curtis recorded that the series of events created "quite a sensation throughout the branch." "Unpleasant feelings" persisted among the members there, threatening unity and progress.[49] Brigham intervened by sending Pace on a three-year mission to England with fellow electioneer Calvin Reed. Curtis looked after Pace's family by threshing wheat, administering priesthood blessings, and otherwise shepherding them. Peace prevailed for a year in the settlement now presided over by Bishop Blackburn. However, in June 1853 Charles Shumway was disfellowshipped for "unchristian conduct." The next day, a penitent Shumway pleaded for forgiveness and Blackburn restored him to fellowship. Less than a month later, a letter from Pace accused Blackburn of trying to steal his wife while he was away on his mission. Blackburn denied the charge. When two weeks later an American Indian shot and killed a settler, the outside threat dampened the internal dissension and the settlement literally closed ranks. In December 1855, the First Presidency stopped in Payson while traveling to central Utah. They held a conference at the home of Pace, who had just returned from England, to settle the issues dividing the community. The next day, the residents, including Pace, submitted to rebaptism to demonstrate their commitment to obey the gospel and their appointed leaders.[50]

Yet colonizing itself also further cemented electioneers to the cause of Zion. During these years they overcame obstacles and accomplished remarkable feats in settling hundreds of towns in the Great Basin. As ecclesiastical and political leaders, they directed many of the fledgling colonies. Because church leadership carefully selected those who led each new outpost of Zion, it is no coincidence that they so often turned to the familiar, faithful, and capable electioneer veterans. Many electioneers assisted in building multiple settlements. Daniel Allen settled seven towns while plying his trade as a shoemaker. Nine settlements benefited from talented carpenter David Savage. John D. Chase served as mayor of Moroni, as bishop in Manti, and as a member of the Juab (Utah) and Carson Valley (Nevada) high councils, with a mission to England squeezed in.

Chapman Duncan colonized Big Cottonwood and Parowan before leaving on a mission to China in 1852. Upon his return, he settled Carson Valley and then became the county recorder and probate judge in St. George. He later struck out on his own, founding Duncan's Retreat. George G. Snyder aided in settling eleven settlements in California, in Nevada, and throughout Utah. During that time he also served a mission in England and was a bishop and probate judge. These and many other electioneers responded to calls from church leadership to build, community by community, the Zion they longed for. Their experience and leadership were invaluable to church authorities.

REFORMATION

However, a decade of living in the wilderness took a spiritual toll on the Saints. To counter what he saw as backsliding, in late 1855 Brigham instigated a "home missionary program." It was the beginning of what is often called the "Mormon Reformation"—a concerted effort to stem apostasy, increase devotion, and build unity among the Saints.[51] "Many are stupid, careless, and unconcerned," Brigham declared. "They . . . are off their watch, neglect their prayers, forget their covenants and forsake their God, and the devil has power over them."[52] One reason for Brigham's harsh correction was three straight years of grasshoppers, canyon fires, and harsh winters destroying crops and livestock. He saw these events as the chastening hand of God because the Saints were backsliding. It was the biggest crisis yet of the Great Basin kingdom. Zion seemed to be collapsing.

Brigham turned to the rod of repentance. Later reminiscing, he said, "One day, I told a number of the brethren how I felt, as well as I could; and Brother Jedediah M. Grant [former electioneer] partook of the Spirit that was in me and walked out like a man, like a giant, and like an angel, and he scattered the fire of the Almighty among the people."[53] Grant, a counselor in the First Presidency, attended a four-day conference in Kaysville in which he delivered a thunderous message of repentance that was powerful and unforgiving. "The church needs trimming up, and . . . you will find in your wards certain branches which had better be cut off." The solution was simple: "First get the families united, then get the wards, the towns,

Jedediah M. Grant, a former electioneer and later a member of the First Presidency and mayor of Salt Lake City, led the Reformation, a constant effort that eventually cost him his life. Courtesy of Church History Library.

the cities, and the counties regulated, and you will have every part of the territory right. . . . I would like to see the work of reformation commence and continue until every man had to walk to the line; then we should have something like union."[54] Grant created a catechism that included spiritual and temporal questions. It became the model for similar versions used by home missionaries throughout the church charged with watching over their fellow Saints.

Electioneer leaders stepped into line. In December 1856, Provo Stake president Jonathan O. Duke and his counselors reported, "Catechizing the Saints . . . by the catechisms got up by the First Presidency of the Church, which the Lord has graciously been pleased to pour out his Spirit on the Saints in these valleys, and a great reformation is tak[ing] place in settlements."[55] Joseph Holbrook remembered Grant visiting his ward for a two-day conference. After the members had been rebaptized, Grant emphasized that "every brother and sister be careful to sin no more for fear a more terrible scourge should wait them, as they could not commit iniquity with the same degree of allowance as they could before they received their covenants in the waters of baptism." Holbrook stated that after rebaptism they were all "catechized as [to] what we had been guilty of in our every act so that we might now begin anew to possess eternal life."[56] Like so many others, Holbrook promptly married a plural wife to show his devotion.

The Reformation's reach extended even to England. In February 1857 apostle Ezra T. Benson, Phineas Young (both electioneers), and other leaders in England met together. "We then took into consideration the president's [Brigham] letter on reformation," Phineas wrote, "and unitedly agreed to reform our lives, repent of our sins and do better than we had ever done, and fast the next day."[57] That evening they renewed their covenants through rebaptism, an act repeated in branches throughout the church. Meanwhile, Brigham, Kimball, and Grant kept up the pressure, rebuking the Saints for "lying, stealing, swearing, committing adultery, quarreling with husbands, wives, and children, and many other evils."[58] Grant continued thundering his message of reformation from settlement to settlement until he suddenly died from rheumatic fever.

Grant's untimely passing was not the only result of the Reformation of 1855–57. There was a spike in religious devotion, seen in dramatically increased church attendance, tithing receipts, communal unity, and especially plural marriage.[59] Electioneer David Fullmer recorded that the Reformation had "turned away the anger of the Lord" and that he had never seen such a time of unity and blessings since he had come into the church.[60] Unfortunately, the excessive and hyperbolic rhetoric of the Reformation, intended to instigate commitment, gave enemies of Zion ammunition to accuse the Saints of provoking violence and was a precursor to the Utah War. Furthermore, rushed marriages led to a later rash of divorces, including among electioneers.[61] Overzealous leaders and home missionaries also created hard feelings among some of their charges. For the electioneers, perhaps their reactions were much like that of James Pace: "I participated in the Reformation, then prevalent among our people," he wrote, "though not to the extent of wild enthusiasm that some manifested."[62]

DISSIDENTS

During the years of 1851–68, some electioneers chose to break with Brigham and the cause of theodemocratic Zion. Others who had previously dissented continued their lives outside the faith. Many people in both categories ultimately found a religious home in the Reorganized Church of Jesus Christ of Latter Day Saints (now known as the Community of Christ), organized in 1853. Disaffected electioneers were at the center of its genesis. After Joseph's assassination, Zenos H. Gurley Sr. chose to follow James J. Strang, serving as an effective missionary for that spin-off movement. In 1851 Gurley denounced Strang when the latter began

Former electioneer Zenos H. Gurley declared a revelation to "reorganize" the church and later ordained Joseph Smith III as president of the Reorganized Church of Jesus Christ of Latter Day Saints. 1868 photo by R. Thompson courtesy of the Community of Christ.

practicing plural marriage. Gurley and Jason Briggs, brother of electioneer Silas H. Briggs, claimed to have received a revelation authorizing them to reorganize the faithful under the leadership of Joseph Smith III. Briggs took temporary leadership of the movement on 8 April 1853, calling Gurley to join him as an apostle. The "New Organization," as it was called, numbered fewer than three hundred but boldly announced its claim and called on Joseph's son to lead. On 6 April 1860, exactly thirty years since the organization of The Church of Jesus Christ of Latter-day Saints, Joseph Smith III assumed leadership of the now retitled Reorganized Church of Jesus Christ of Latter Day Saints. He was ordained as president by none other than Zenos Gurley.[63]

The Reorganized Church outlasted all other alternative sects of the Latter-day Saint movement. It dismissed plural marriage, temple ordinances, and "political Mormonism" as products of Brigham. Many midwestern and eastern Saints who chose not to follow Brigham, or who were remnants of failed offshoot movements, joined the Reorganized Church. Over time they also claimed some converts from Brigham's fold, including a few electioneers. Generally, such men were weary of Young's heavy hand and the demands of colonization, or they rejected plural marriage.[64]

Perhaps the RLDS Church's most significant electioneer conversion was prolific proselytizer George P. Dykes in 1863. Dykes, a longtime Utah resident, used his contacts to create inroads for the RLDS Church in Utah and soon led a congregation of three hundred. In a letter to a friend who "expressed surprise" at his conversion, Dykes laid out his case. He declared that only the "posterity" of Joseph could lead and "[the fact] that young Joseph is the lawful head of the church . . . is positively evident from many scriptures." Dykes was grateful that with "divine assistance [he was] turning scores from darkness to light and from the power of Satan to God, who are once more rejoicing in the fulness of the everlasting gospel."[65] Yet only two years later Dykes left the RLDS Church as suddenly as he had joined.

Other electioneers found more solitary routes to fill the void of their former faith. Increase Van Deuzen rejected Strangism when Strang began teaching polygamy. In 1860 he returned to Kirtland, Ohio. That same year, he interrupted a meeting in the temple, walking across the tops of the pews and then leaping up on the pulpit. He

George P. Dykes presided over Indiana during Joseph's campaign, became a prolific missionary in Europe, and for a time headed the RLDS Church in Utah. Photo by Olson and Kearney courtesy of the Community of Christ.

turned and faced the alarmed audience and stripped off his coat, tearing it to shreds. He commenced stamping and hissing and swinging what remained of his coat while shouting repeatedly, "Now is come the time of your trial!" Frightened women fled the temple, and all experienced a very memorable meeting.[66] Stephen Post continued to support Sidney Rigdon, serving as his spokesman and single-handedly keeping the struggling movement alive.[67] David Judah became an apostle in the small "Hedrickite" movement centered in Independence, Missouri. The group purchased, and owns to the present day, the famed temple site there. Judah led the movement's only known proselytizing effort, an unsuccessful mission to American Indian tribes.[68]

A small number of electioneers simply left the faith all together. Phillip H. Buzzard originally followed Strang but became disaffected and left for California before settling down in Iowa and creating a freight company between Iowa and Utah. He remained nominally a Latter-day Saint until one visit to Utah. Ordered to pay tithing because of his wealth, Buzzard vehemently objected and eschewed the church permanently. He later moved to Spokane, Washington.[69] Joseph M. Cole remained in the Midwest and in 1856 fought alongside his nephew in the "Bleeding Kansas" skirmishes sparked by attempts to make the proposed state of Kansas a slave state.[70] Daniel Gardner left Utah and the church for the Washington Territory in 1854, becoming a justice of the peace, schoolteacher, and minister for the United Brethren Church.[71] Omar Olney returned to his native New York, becoming a very successful lawyer and author. Perhaps seeking to explain his past, he wrote a scorching exposé of the church.[72] Lester Brooks followed Strang after Joseph's death but by 1854 had become a leader of the national movement of the Spiritualists.[73] Elijah Swackhammer, after following Rigdon, left the Latter-day Saint tradition altogether. The most radical and eccentric of the dissenters, he joined a group centered in Utica, New York, called "the Reformers." They advocated free love and social communities, and they believed evil did not exist. Swackhammer continued to lecture on the Reformers' philosophy for more than a decade and became an associate of abolitionist William Lloyd Garrison. A later census shows him listed as a "reverend" in New York.[74]

Some Great Basin electioneers, like Bushrod Wilson, felt persecuted within Brigham's theodemocratic Zion. Wilson chafed under the leadership of the small village of Palmyra in Utah County: "I left Palmyra getting nothing for my farm and houses. I have been mobbed by the gentiles for being a Mormon, and at last I have been mobbed by the Mormons because I was not willing to do all that they told me to do, so I left for California."[75] Arriving in San Bernardino, Wilson saw firsthand the struggle for political leadership in the colony. In April 1854 he wrote that "Br. J. Grouard and Frederick Van Leuven and Ruben Herron [were] disfellowshipped or cut off from the church for opposing the council of the church in politics. My faith in such doings is weak. I hate usurpation and tyranny."[76] Wilson stayed in San Bernardino after the Saints evacuated three years later.

At least two dissident electioneers rejoined the flock during these decades. John Duncan, a veteran of the famous Zion's Camp, initially joined Rigdon's church after Joseph's death. He moved to Pittsburgh, where he lived even after Rigdon's movement collapsed. Following the Civil War, Duncan's son Homer, who had gone west with the Saints, went to Pittsburgh to search for his father. Finding him, Homer Duncan brought John back into fellowship with the Saints.[77] In 1868 John attended his first Zion's Camp reunion. Only twenty-nine veterans remained, and at eighty-nine years of age, he was the oldest. He enjoyed reuniting with former colleagues, who amicably called him "Father Duncan."[78]

James Burgess was the other returning prodigal. As a recent English convert, he electioneered in Vermont. When Joseph was killed, Burgess continued his mission for another year. After marrying Lydia Stiles, he returned to Nauvoo, where he worked on the Nauvoo Temple, received his endowment, and was sealed to Lydia. Upon the evacuation of Nauvoo, Burgess and his campaign companion and fellow Englishman Alfred Cordon returned to Burlington, Vermont, in search of work. Cordon eventually went west with the Saints, but Burgess stayed in Vermont working as a carpenter. In 1863, now living in Iowa, Burgess joined the RLDS Church, becoming an effective missionary for almost a decade. In 1872 he moved to Utah and reunited with the Saints, living until 1904. Fitting capstones of his religious life were the two sons he named Joseph—the first born in 1847 in Vermont and the second born to his third wife fifty-three years later in Utah.

ECCLESIASTICAL LEADERSHIP

Surviving electioneers experienced changes in priesthood office from 1851 to 1869 (see table 9.1). Continued movement from the office of elder and seventy to high priest was natural with increasing age and wide opportunities to act in those offices. What is remarkable, though, is the increase in electioneers holding the office of bishop, patriarch, or Seventy in the First Council of Seventy, particularly the office of bishop. While the growth of Zion required more bishops, their numbers remained small until the large increase in electioneers called as bishops—further evidence of how their belief and experience in preaching and living the ideals of Zion and theodemocracy were qualifying attributes that church leaders valued. In Latter-day Saint settlements, the bishop presided over all the religious, social, political, and economic activities of his ward. Bishops were the major workhorses for Zion and theodemocracy—and a very disproportionate number of them were electioneers. The number of electioneers chosen as local, regional, and general authorities increased as well (see table 9.2). Most impressive was the rise in leadership positions at the regional level and bishops at the local level: stake president (340 percent of electioneers), conference/mission president (1,300 percent), and bishop (82 percent). These positions were central to religious governance, supervising the basic ecclesiastical units of Zion. Furthermore, these assignments most often carried political office in the Great Basin theodemocracy.

Table 9.1. Percentage of Electioneers Holding Specific Priesthood Offices, 1850–1869

Priesthood Level	Priesthood Office	1850*	Highest Office 1851–1869**	Change
Elite	Apostle	2.3% (5)	2.6% (7)	13%
High	First Council of Seventy	1.4% (3)	1.5% (4)	7%
	Patriarch	0.0%	0.7% (2)	n/a
	Bishop	11.1% (24)	17.0% (46)	53%
Middle	High Priest	24.9% (54)	31.5% (85)	27%
Low	Seventy	57.3% (125)	44.3% (121)	-29%
	Elder	3.2% (7)	3.0% (8)	-7%

* Total electioneers in 1850 = 218.
** Total electioneers in 1851–1869 = 273.

In fact, despite their small numbers among total priesthood holders, the electioneers represented a significant percentage of the regional and local leadership of the church (see table 9.3). In 1850, despite accounting for less than 10 percent of the priesthood population, they accounted for 35 percent of all bishops and 100 percent of all stake president positions.

Table 9.2. Percentage of Electioneers Holding Specific Priesthood Leadership Positions, 1851–1869

Leadership Level	Position	1850*	1851–1869**	Change
General Authority	First Presidency	0%	0.4% (1)	n/a
	Quorum of Twelve	2.3% (5)	2.2% (6)	-5%
	First Council of Seventy	1.4% (3)	1.5% (4)	7%
	Presiding Bishopric	0%	0.4% (1)	n/a
Total		**3.7% (8)**	**4.5% (12)**	**22%**
Regional Authority	Stake President	0.5% (1)	2.2% (6)	340%
	Conf./Mission Pres.	0.5% (1)	7.0% (19)	1300%
	High Council	3.2% (7)	3.7% (10)	16%
Total		**4.2% (9)**	**12.9% (35)**	**207%**
Local Authority	Bishop	8.7% (19)	15.8% (43)	82%
	Branch President	0.5% (1)	0.7% (2)	40%
	Seventy Qrm. Pres.	9.6% (21)	7.3% (20)	-32%
Total		**18.8% (41)**	**23.8% (65)**	**27%**
None		73.4% (160)	59% (161)	-24%
Total		**73.4% (160)**	**59% (161)**	**-24%**

* Total electioneers in 1850 = 218.
** Total electioneers in 1851–1869 = 273.

Such numbers reveal the electioneers as the backbone of the aristarchy. Over time, as the electioneers died and church growth produced more leaders and leadership positions, their influence slowly diminished. Yet even in 1865, when they represented only 2 percent of the priesthood population, they still accounted for six times that many bishops and fifteen times that many stake presidents.

Table 9.3. Percentage of Electioneers as Bishops or Stake Presidents, 1851–1865

Year	Electioneers as Percentage of Total Priesthood*	Percentage of Total Bishops	Percentage of Total Stake Presidents
1850	8.5%	35.5% (11/31)	100% (1/1)
1855	4.9%	28.1% (18/64)	40% (2/5)
1860	3.3%	20.0% (19/95)	50% (2/4)
1865	2.1%	12.8% (19/149)	33% (1/3)

* There are no definitive numbers of total priesthood holders during these years. I have used a formula to derive an approximate number of priesthood-age men in the Utah Territory using census and church almanac numbers.

* * *

Whether in missionary work, gathering, colonizing, or leading the Great Basin kingdom, throughout the 1850s and 1860s church leaders made the electioneers the preeminent part of the aristarchy tasked with building and guiding Zion. Because the fusing of religious and political governance was inherent to theodemocracy, the creation of the Utah Territory was a boon to the church's kingdom-building enterprise, giving the church hierarchy legally sanctioned governance to protect and guide the growth of Zion. To ensure optimal success, Brigham and his associates determined they would nominate and elect to political offices their general, regional, and local ecclesiastical leaders. In their combined roles, electioneer veterans such as Chauncey W. West became the workhorses of theodemocratic Zion, striving to bring the power of unity to their people. Although their apex of influence was in the late 1840s through the 1850s, the aging yet ever-capable cadre of electioneers continued to significantly build, shape, and lead the church through the 1860s.

NOTES

1. Brigham Young, "Remarks," *Deseret News*, 12 November 1856, 283, as quoted in Christy, "Weather, Disaster, and Responsibility," 23.

2. Franklin D. Richards, Journal No. 2, 27 May 1844, 3.

3. See Wahlquist, "Population Growth in the Mormon Core Area," 132–33.

4. First Presidency, "Sixth General Epistle [22 September 1851]," *Deseret News*, 15 November 1851, 2.

5. Brigham Young to Ezra T. Benson, Journal History of the Church, 31 January 1852. The letter itself directed Benson and Grant to say similar words to the Saints in Iowa.

6. First Presidency, "Eighth General Epistle [13 October 1852]," *Deseret News*, 16 October 1852, 2.

7. Jenson, "Hunter, Edward," *Latter-day Saint Biographical Encyclopedia*, 1:231–32.

8. Curtis, Reminiscences and Diary, 96.

9. "Letters of a Missionary, George Hickerson," Utah, Our Pioneer Heritage (database).

10. Some of those called were already on their missions. Electioneers sent to Europe—England: Daniel Spencer, Millen Atwood, Benjamin Brown, Osmon M. Duel, James Pace, Levi Nickerson, John S. Fullmer, and Duncan McArthur; Wales: Dan Jones; France: Andrew L. Lamoreaux; Germany: George C. Riser; Gibraltar: Nathan T. Porter. Electioneers sent to Asia—Hindustan: Nathaniel V. Jones; Siam: Chauncey W. West; China: Hosea Stout and Chapman Duncan; West Indies: Alfred B. Lambson and Aaron Farr. Electioneers sent elsewhere—St. Louis: Horace S. Eldredge; Australia: Augustus Farnham, Josiah W. Fleming, and William Hyde; Sandwich Isles (Hawai'i): William McBride and Nathan Tanner.

11. See "Andrew Lamoreaux," Utah, Our Pioneer Heritage (database).

12. See Susan Easton Black, "George C. Riser," Latter-day Saint Vital Records II Database (hereafter "LDSVR").

13. See Black, "Daniel Tyler," LDSVR (database).

14. Paxton, "History of John S. Fullmer," 6.

15. Electioneers who served in Europe between 1851 and 1868 but were not called in 1852 included Nathaniel H. Felt, Samuel W. Richards, Jonathan Crosby, Jacob Gates, Henry J. Doremus, Abraham O. Smoot, George Snyder, Franklin D. Richards, and Chauncey W. West.

16. See Black, "Dan Jones," LDSVR (database).

17. See Black, "Nathaniel V. Jones," LDSVR (database).

18. Luddington, "Luddington Family," folio 4.

19. Hosea Stout to Brigham Young, 27 August 1853.

20. See "Society Islands Mission," Utah, Our Pioneer Heritage (database).

21. See "Society Islands Mission," *Enduring Legacy* (database).

22. See "Society Islands Mission," *Enduring Legacy* (database).

23. See Jenson, "Benson, Ezra T.," *Latter-day Saint Biographical Encyclopedia*, 1:101.

24. See Black, "Augustus A. Farnham," LDSVR (database); and "Augustus A. Farnham," Utah, Our Pioneer Heritage (database).

25. See Black, "Levi Nickerson," LDSVR (database).

26. See Black, "Stephen Taylor," LDSVR (database); and Black, "Appleton Milo Harmon," LDSVR (database). Harmon wrote a poem about Burton's death.

27. See Anderson and Bergera, *Joseph Smith's Quorum of the Anointed*, 144.

28. See Black, "Thomas Atkinson," LDSVR (database).

29. "Augustus A. Farnham," Utah, Our Pioneer Heritage (database).

30. Israel Barlow to Elizabeth Barlow, 12 September 1853.

31. Israel Barlow to Elizabeth Barlow, October 1853.

32. See Israel Barlow to Elizabeth Barlow, 30 November 1854.

33. See Jenson, "Richards, Samuel Whitney," *Latter-day Saint Biographical Encyclopedia*, 1:718–19. Company leaders who were electioneers included Milo Andrus, John S. Fullmer, Israel Barlow, Lorenzo Hatch, Joseph France, Cyrus Wheelock, John O. Angus, and Samuel and Franklin Richards. Other electioneers helped in different ways—for example, Howard Egan donated one hundred gold coins from his California trips.

34. See Larson, *Prelude to the Kingdom*, 133.

35. See "Ships Sailing from the Islands," Utah, Our Pioneer Heritage (database).

36. See Black, "Horace S. Eldredge," LDSVR (database). See also "Ships Sailing from the Islands," Utah, Our Pioneer Heritage (database).

37. See Farr, Journal, 41; Milo Andrus, Autobiography; and Erastus Snow, Autobiography, 17–18.

38. See Larson, *Prelude to the Kingdom*, 172.

39. These electioneers included Ezra T. Benson, Chapman Duncan, Aaron F. Farr, Nathaniel Felt, Elisha Groves, John D. Lee, Elijah Newman, Elijah F. Sheets, William P. Vance, Edson Whipple, James Harmison, Joseph L. Robinson, and Jefferson Hunt. Others joined the colony later.

40. See May, *Utah: A People's History*, 72; and Duncan, "Biography," 12.

41. Jenson, "Whipple, Edson," *Latter-day Saint Biographical Encyclopedia*, 561–62.

42. The electioneers in this company were Henry G. Boyle, Ellis Eames, Jefferson Hunt, Harley Mowrey, Justus Morse, Calvin Reed, Henry Sherwood, Nathan Tanner, and William Hyde.

43. See Elliott, *Biographical Sketch of Jefferson Hunt*, 12–14.

44. Boyle, Reminiscences and Diaries, 1:14.

45. Boyle, Reminiscences and Diaries, 1:146.

46. Quoted in Larson, *Prelude to the Kingdom*, 185–86.

47. See Wilkerson, *Lewis Robbins: A Biography*, 2–3.

48. Pace, "Biographical Sketch," 10.

49. Curtis, Reminiscences and Diary, 92.

50. See Curtis, Reminiscences and Diary, 91–109 (quotation on p. 98).

51. Peterson, "Mormon Reformation of 1856–1857," 61.

52. Brigham Young, "Necessity of Home Missions—Purification of the Saints—Chastisement—Honesty in Business," in *JD*, 3:115 (8 October 1855).

53. Brigham Young, in *JD*, 5:168 (30 August 1857).

54. Jedediah Grant, in *JD*, 3:60 (13 July 1855).

55. Jonathan O. Duke, Reminiscences and Diary, 13 December 1856.

56. Holbrook, Life of Joseph Holbrook, 134–36.

57. Phineas Young, Diary, 4 February 1857.

58. Woodruff, *Wilford Woodruff's Journal*, 4:448.

59. See Daynes, *More Wives than One*, 101–10, 118, on the spike in plural marriages.

60. Salt Lake Fifth Ward Fellowship Meeting Minutes, 28 June 1857, as found in Peterson, "Mormon Reformation of 1856–1857," 76.

61. At least twelve Reformation marriages of electioneers ended in divorce.

62. Pace, "Biographical Sketch," 11.

63. See Speek, *James Strang and the Midwest Mormons*, 282, 320.

64. Thirty-three cadre members joined the RLDS Church. Almost all had previously left The Church of Jesus Christ of Latter-day Saints.

65. George P. Dykes to Mrs. King, 8 August 1864.

66. The incident was recorded many years later in Van Deuzen's obituary in the *Painesville Telegraph*, 10 August 1882, 3.

67. See M. Guy Bishop, "Stephen Post: From Believer to Dissenter," in *Dissenters in Mormon History*, ed. Launius and Thatcher, 190–92.

68. See Jenson, *Historical Record*, 5:14.

69. See "Buzzard, P. H.," Polk County 1880 Saylor Township Biographies.

70. See Reader, "The First Day's Battle at Hickory Point," Samuel James Reader Papers.

71. See Gardner, "Daniel and Lorena Gardner."

72. See Hand, ed., *History of the Town of Nunda*, 167.

73. See N. P. Tallmadge, *Spiritualists Memorial to Congress*, as found in Hardinge, *Modern American Spiritualism*, 128–33; and Tuttle and Peebles, *Year-Book of Spiritualism for 1871*, 226.

74. "The Cause and Cure of Evil," *New York Times*, 2 September 1858, 4; and Religious Society of Progressive Friends, *Thirteenth Yearly Meeting of the Religious Society of Progressive Friends held at Longwood Chester, PA., 5–8th of June 1865* (Hamorton, Chester Co., PA: Isaac Mendenhall, 1865), 6.

75. Wilson, Journal, 3.

76. Wilson, Journal, 3.

77. See Morrell and Deeben, "History and Genealogy of John Chapman Duncan," 8.

78. "From Monday's Daily," *Deseret News*, 14 October 1868, 285.

CHAPTER 10

POLITICAL, SOCIAL, AND ECONOMIC ARISTARCHY OF THE KINGDOM, 1851–1869

*If the people of the United States will let us
alone for ten years, we will ask no odds of them.*

—Brigham Young, 24 July 1847[1]

Electioneer Experience: Chauncey W. West. When his family joined the church in upstate New York in 1842, Chauncey W. West was only fifteen years old. His father and future electioneer colleague, Alva West, was a poor tenant farmer. Chauncey seemed destined for the same life's work until, in a rare move, the missionaries ordained him a priest. The ordination surely opened the way for Charles Wandell, president of Joseph's election campaign in New York, to call him in 1844 to be a traveling electioneer in the region near his home.[2] At seventeen, West was the second youngest electioneer in Joseph's campaign. The diligence, energy, and loyalty that he showed in that assignment would in time lead to priesthood advancement with its attendant religious and political responsibilities.

Following Joseph's death, West moved to Nauvoo with his parents. A church leader there described him as "a [young] man of untiring energy and industry," whose "boundless hope doubtless led him into enterprises from which other men would shrink."[3] Within a few months, church

Chauncey W. West's call at age seventeen to electioneer for Joseph led to an array of leadership opportunities in the Great Basin. His career encapsulates the electioneer cadre's experience. 1867 photo by Savage and Ottinger courtesy of Church History Library.

leaders ordained him a seventy, again one of the youngest ever appointed. He also married seventeen-year-old Mary Hoagland. After the expulsion from Nauvoo, the West family settled in Winter Quarters, where West's father, mother, and brother perished that winter. Undaunted, West led the rest of his father's family to the Salt Lake Valley in 1847. Brigham called West and thirty-six other men in 1852 to serve missions in East Asia. West worked tirelessly in Bombay and Ceylon preaching and trying to raise money to go to Siam, his original assignment. His mission was a series of persecutions, privations, and frustrations. Never able to reach Siam, West and a few others sailed back to San Francisco and arrived in Utah in July 1855. Despite these hardships, West remained positive. He wrote, "I now report myself on hand for duty whenever the servants of God call, for the priesthood is my law."[4]

Like that of his fellow electioneers, West's fealty to theodemocratic Zion motivated him to accept church leadership as binding as law and to submit to any duty in any location. In the Great Basin community, the duties of such religiously successful electioneers often included service in political positions, which led to enhanced socioeconomic status. This was true for West and other uneducated eastern farm boys who had exhibited fervor, loyalty, and skill. As a result, they were becoming powerful political, social, and economic elites in Deseret's aristarchic theodemocracy.

* * *

THE ELECTIONEERS' POLITICAL CONTRIBUTIONS

GOVERNING THE GREAT BASIN THEODEMOCRATIC KINGDOM

The first territorial election of 1851 showed continuing electioneer domi-nance in the aristarchy of the Great Basin kingdom (see table 10.1). The Territorial House of Representatives had twenty-five members, twelve of whom were electioneers. The House continued to have a high percentage of electioneer veterans throughout this period, particularly when com-pared to their percentage in the overall population. The Territorial Coun-cil (which became the Utah Senate in 1896) consisted of thirteen men, four of whom were electioneers. Electioneers held 30 percent of Territorial Council seats, above their numbers in the male population by more than three to one. The year 1855 saw a precipitous drop to just under 8 percent and a ratio of less than two to one. After rebounding in 1860 to 15 percent and a ratio of five to one, the numbers in 1865 would reach an astounding 46 percent and a ratio of twenty-three to one.

Table 10.1. Percentage of Electioneers Elected as Utah Territorial Legislators, 1851–1865

Year	Electioneers as Percentage of Total Priesthood*	Council Members	Members of House of Representatives
1851	8.5%	30.8% (4/13)	48.0% (12/25)
1855	4.9%	7.7% (1/13)	57.7% (15/26)
1860	3.3%	15.4% (2/13)	20.0% (5/25)
1865	2.1%	46.2% (6/13)	23.1% (6/26)

* There are no definitive numbers of total priesthood holders during these years. I have used a formula to derive an approximate number of priesthood-age men in the Utah Territory using census and church almanac numbers.

Why the volatility? The 1855 decline can be explained by men having been "reassigned" to election in the House or called to lead proselyting or colonizing missions. As to the incredible rebounds in 1860 and 1865, the answer may be the Civil War. Brigham and other church leaders saw the conflict as a likely fulfillment of Joseph's prophecy in 1832.[5] Considering the possibility that the United States would soon collapse, Brigham wanted the kingdom ready to independently govern the Great Basin. It is likely that electioneer church leaders were reassigned from other roles into the Council. By the end of the war, they constituted almost half of the Council's number. In fact, of the thirteen Council positions, ten were held by apostles—five of whom were electioneers. Of the three non-apostolic members, two were electioneers. One was Daniel Spencer, president of the 1844 mission in Massachusetts, mayor of both Nauvoo and Salt Lake, and Salt Lake Stake president. The other, Aaron Johnson, was a former Territorial Speaker of the House with significant political and governing experience. Preparing for a government that might begin to expand beyond the Great Basin, Brigham assigned his best men to the council.

Local elections in two Latter-day Saint towns further illustrate the depth of theodemocracy and the involvement of the electioneers. Parowan was the center of the Iron County Mission. On 16 January 1851 the mission's leaders called for an election the next day to organize the county. Apostle, chief justice of Deseret, and Iron County Mission president George A. Smith led the nomination process. Electioneers claimed six of fifteen positions, including the five most powerful: representative to the State of Deseret, Jefferson Hunt; associate judges, Edson Whipple and Elisha H. Groves; magistrates, Aaron Farr and John D. Lee.[6] The next day, the men of the Iron County Mission, in theodemocratic fashion, unanimously elected all of the nominees.

The next month, news reached the Great Basin that Congress had created the Territory of Utah, requiring new elections. Brigham toured the Basin, supervising the nomination process for territorial, county, and even locally elected officers. On 16 May 1851 Brigham met with the men of Parowan and counseled on nominations, reversing most results of an election held a mere four months ago. They nominated John M. Bernhisel (electioneer) as delegate to Congress, George A. Smith to the Territorial Council, and Elisha Groves (electioneer) to the Territorial House for the upcoming August elections.

While the electioneer-filled county offices stood, the council turned to nominating and electing local officials. A mayor, aldermen, and councilors were chosen, including electioneers John D. Lee (alderman) and Joel H.

Johnson and Elijah Newman (councilors). With selection and election completed, Brigham addressed the men regarding government. He entitled his remarks "Union Is Power"—a phrase from Joseph Smith's 1844 pamphlet *Views*. When the territorial elections took place on 4 August 1851, all nominees were unanimously elected, as expected under theodemocratic rule. The pattern of general, regional, and local church leaders counseling together to nominate men for government office and the people voting unanimously to elect them continued without significant interruption in Latter-day Saint settlements through the 1860s.

Before 1869, only in San Bernardino did theodemocracy struggle. Initially the colony accepted theodemocratic governance under electioneer apostles Amasa Lyman and Charles C. Rich. After nearly three years, the first election of city officers occurred in 1854. Lyman was nominated and then elected as mayor, and Rich and fellow electioneer Quartus S. Sparks won office on the five-man city council.[7] Political unity, however, lasted only a year. Trouble began with elderly electioneer Henry G. Sherwood. He had embraced the restored gospel in 1832 and played an instrumental role in strengthening the church during the next twenty years. Joseph had placed him on high councils in Kirtland and Nauvoo. He had been elected as city marshal in Nauvoo and had labored at Joseph's Nauvoo campaign headquarters during the 1844 election. Arriving in the first pioneer company to Salt Lake Valley, Sherwood spent the next six years surveying settlements in the Basin.

Called to help settle and survey San Bernardino in 1853, Sherwood irritated Lyman and Rich with his words and actions. They wrote to Brigham asking if there was anywhere in the "wide range of Zion's domains" where the seventy-year-old Sherwood could be "rendered useful." The two leaders, forty-one and forty-three respectively, described Sherwood as "too conceited to be taught [and] too old to be managed by men so much his junior."[8] Sherwood left for Salt Lake City in 1854, only to return to San Bernardino the following year with another group of settlers. Together they refused to buy land from the church's ranch, knowing that government land was available at far lower prices. Contention and dissension followed.

By 1855 San Bernardino had become an outpost for those who wished to stay nominally Latter-day Saints but chafed under the realities of theodemocracy. California gave them physical and, they hoped, political distance. Several even opposed the apostles in subsequent elections but were dealt with sternly. As noted previously, three men were excommunicated for not submitting politically to their leaders' direction.[9]

Rich reported to Brigham in May 1856 that Sherwood "now stands at the head of the 'anti-Mormon' movement in this place; he makes speeches and uses his influence against the church."[10] Sherwood called Rich and Lyman sycophants of Brigham and threatened to disclose alleged secrets about the three leaders.

While opposition to Rich and Lyman grew, it never gained enough power to change San Bernardino's theodemocracy. Yet conflict continued to occur, leading to church discipline, legal action, and even violence. Before evacuating San Bernardino in 1857, some of the apostates reconciled, including Sherwood.[11] Ultimately, Brigham's vision of theodemocracy continued to thrive in every Latter-day Saint settlement except San Bernardino. After the Utah War, Brigham chose not to reestablish the community.[12]

UTAH WAR

Brigham's theodemocracy and the federal government had been inching toward a confrontation for a decade. The Compromise of 1850 created Utah and other territories under popular sovereignty. Brigham and church leaders, of course, were thrilled with the idea, seeing popular sovereignty as an instrument to maintain self-rule. Yet after the church publicly proclaimed the practice of plural marriage, the nation with its Protestant and Victorian sensibilities painted the Latter-day Saints as immoral and enslaved by despotic rule—and therefore subject to forfeiture of any claim of popular sovereignty.

Popular sovereignty, however, was already bleeding. National angst over ruffian settlers in Kansas violently imposing their viewpoints spotlighted the weaknesses of the doctrine. Utah became increasingly cited in public arguments about Kansas because popular sovereignty was allowing "un-American Mormons" self-rule. In part, the fallout of the Kansas and Utah debates gave rise to the Republican Party in 1856. Its motto to extinguish the "twin relics of barbarism"—slavery and polygamy—put Demo-crats on the defensive, including newly elected president James Buchanan. With exaggerated rumors of Latter-day Saint despotism, public uproar over polygamy, and the chance to intimidate the secession-contemplating South, he acted.[13]

Buchanan replaced Brigham with Alfred Cumming as governor. An army of twenty-five hundred men accompanied Cumming to suppress the Saints. Brigham was purposely not informed. On 1 July 1857 Salt Lake City mayor and electioneer Abraham O. Smoot learned in Independence, Missouri, that a large contingent of soldiers was heading for Utah to forc-ibly replace Brigham. Smoot and his companions raced west at full speed, reaching Salt Lake on 23 July. Brigham and many of the valley Saints were in Big Cottonwood Canyon preparing for the next day's celebration—the tenth anniversary of the pioneers' arrival in the Salt Lake Valley. Smoot found Brigham on the twenty-fourth and relayed the news. Church lead-ers had heard rumors of an army for two months, but now it was con-firmed. At nightfall Brigham stunned the revelers when he announced the government's intentions. He instructed everyone to return to their homes the following day.[14]

Brigham readied the territory for what he deemed an invasion. He activated the territorial militia, including its senior electioneer officers.[15] Placing the territory under martial law, he prohibited the selling of grain or other foodstuffs to passing emigrants. Messages were sent to mission-aries around the world and to distant colonies to return and help defend Zion. Brigham sent electioneer Samuel W. Richards to England to call home all missionaries and deliver two letters. The first was to President James Buchanan informing him that the army should not enter Utah until a peace commission met. The second was for Latter-day Saint sympathizer Thomas L. Kane, pleading for him to aid the Saints once again. The *New York Times* interviewed Richards. His story, eloquently denying the Saints were in rebellion, put their perspective in the national eye.

For the electioneers it felt like mid-1840s Nauvoo had come back from the dead. Although Latter-day Saint self-rule employed the outward mechanics and doctrines of American politics, it was viewed as despotic. Branding the Saints as "un-American," as in Illinois and later across the nation, made moving against them palatable. Once again the Saints' strong political influence was seen as an obstacle to national expansion warranting coercive action. Would this be a repeat of Nauvoo, with leaders murdered and the people forced to find another home? Or would it be Missouri—a war of extermination, rape, theft, and expulsion? With Kansas already bleeding, it seemed Utah was next.

Church leaders avoided direct confrontation with the approaching army, hoping for negotiations. Several electioneers led or took part in raids to burn the US Army's supplies and scatter its livestock.[16] William R. R. Stowell's experience proved particularly important. US soldiers captured Stowell, who tried to dispose of his journal and orders because they revealed the Saints' strategies. While trying to do so, he twice remembered hearing a voice: "Keep them, for they will do more good than bad." Army personnel found and read his papers. Stowell boldly declared that the plans were not only true but would succeed. With supplies running low, winter setting in, and Stowell's intimidating intelligence, the army chose to halt for the winter. They charged Stowell with treason. He escaped, was recaptured, and eventually received immunity.[17]

With past persecutions in mind, Brigham ordered the Saints to preemptively evacuate northern Utah. David Evans, Dominicus Carter, and other Utah Valley electioneer leaders prepared for the influx from the exodus. The experience of electioneer Simeon A. Dunn was typical of other Saints forced to flee. Recently widowed, Dunn loaded a few provisions and his children into his wagon and left Brigham City early in April 1858. At Kay's Creek (Kaysville), his three-month-old son Henry fell ill and died. Leaving his family as comfortable as possible, Dunn returned the little body to the Brigham City cemetery. He considered spending the night in his home, but it was so quiet and lonely that he could not bear it. Instead he slept beside his oxen in the stable. Returning to his family, they continued to Payson. The Dunns bivouacked there for several months until told to return home.[18] Thirty thousand Saints made the journey south.

Thomas L. Kane persuaded Alfred Cumming to come to Salt Lake City for negotiations. The parties agreed that Brigham would make way for Cumming in exchange for immunity for the Saints and the stationing of the army forty miles distant from Salt Lake City. Electioneer veteran

Howard Egan escorted Kane back to Washington, DC, with details of the settlement. After the army built Camp Floyd in Cedar Valley, the Saints returned to their towns and homes.

Electioneer leader Joseph Curtis once heard Brigham state that "all hell could not drive us from these mountains."[19] Curtis noted the irony of the army coming to suppress a rebellion only to find the people at peace. Had they figured it out sooner, he wrote sarcastically, "a vast expense might have been saved."[20] In fact, "Buchanan's Blunder," as the incident came to be called nationally, became an economic windfall for the Saints: when after three years the army abandoned Utah for the Civil War, four million dollars of surplus equipment went to the Saints. However, economic "victory" in the Utah War was Pyrrhic. The federal government had proved it was ultimately in charge. Utah would not have a Latter-day Saint governor after Brigham until statehood, forty-two years later. Theodemocratic Zion would now always be contested. The Saints would not to be left alone as a people and kingdom apart ever again.

While direct battle with the US Army was avoided, the Mountain Meadows Massacre ensured that the Utah War was not bloodless. On 11 September 1857 in southern Utah, Latter-day Saints and Paiute Indians butchered 120 Arkansas emigrants en route to California. The company, unable to resupply because of Brigham's martial law edict, had grown increasingly irritated while traveling south. Minor disputes in settlements boiled over in Cedar City. Both sides gave insults and made threats. After the wagons left town, stake president and militia commander Isaac Haight sent word to his military superior asking for permission to go after the emigrants. The reply was to leave them alone. Haight and others would not let it go, and they concocted a plan to have Paiute Indians ambush the wagon train. Haight recruited electioneer standout John D. Lee to assemble and direct the Paiutes. However, Lee and the Indians attacked at an earlier time and place than agreed. The botched raid led to a five-day siege of the emigrants, who knew that their attackers included Latter-day Saints. Fearful that news of the Saints' involvement amid a fluid war environment could bring federal retaliation, Haight, with implied consent from his superior, changed the plan—all the emigrants must die. He sent a contingent of the militia to Lee with the order.

John D. Lee directed the Mountain Meadows Massacre and was the only conspirator tried and convicted. Photo courtesy of Sherratt Library Special Collections, Southern Utah University.

On 11 September, Lee entered the camp under a false flag of truce and brokered a cease-fire. He promised the company safe passage from the "Indian threat" back to Cedar City if they would surrender their firearms. Seeing no other choice, the emigrants agreed. One cannot miss the painful irony of Latter-day Saints, in official militia assignments, confiscating their adversaries' weapons—exactly what their Missouri and Illinois enemies had done to them before killing and expelling them. At a predetermined signal, the militiamen murdered the men while the Paiutes and other militiamen killed the women and older children. Seventeen young surviving children were given to local families. Immediately, Lee and Haight covered up their involvement, misinforming others that the Paiutes alone were responsible. Over time, however, information leaked out that pointed to militia involvement. In later years, Brigham released Haight and others from their leadership positions. Some were also excommunicated.[21]

Electioneer leader John D. Lee directed the massacre. He lived in nearby Fort Harmony, where he served as an alderman, militia commander, and representative from Iron County to the Territorial House. He was no stranger to violence. Continually beaten as a child and later abandoned, Lee had a vicious temper. After accepting the church in 1837, he moved to Missouri just in time for the Mormon War. In fact, he had been part of the voting scuffle that initiated the conflict. As a member of the official Caldwell County militia and the Latter-day Saint vigilante "Danite" group, he had fought at the Battle of Crooked River. Intense loyalty toward Joseph gave Lee unprecedented status. Before Joseph's campaign, Lee entered plural marriage and was placed in the Council of Fifty. He directed the 1844 election campaign efforts in Kentucky.

After Joseph's murder, Lee returned to Nauvoo, named his newborn son Joseph Hyrum Lee, and passed his unflinching fealty to Brigham, becoming the new prophet's "lifeguard" by "sword and pistol."[22] Lee continued to serve Brigham and the church as a member of the Council of Fifty during the exodus west and in the council's governing years of Deseret. In 1850 Lee had the most wives and the most land wealth of any electioneer veterans. The 1860 census reported Lee's assets as an astounding forty thousand dollars in land and ten thousand dollars in personal wealth. However, after years of investigations, Lee was indicted for his role in the massacre. In 1876 he was convicted, taken to Mountain Meadows, and executed.

Electioneer Jacob Hamblin was a primary figure in the massacre's aftermath. Baptized in 1842, Hamblin campaigned for Joseph in the mid-Atlantic states. He was endowed with his wife in the Nauvoo Temple only to have her abandon him and their four children in Winter Quarters. Hamblin remarried and came west in 1850, settling in Tooele. While there he exhibited extraordinary talent in communicating and negotiating with local Indian tribes. Four years later Brigham sent him to southern Utah as an "apostle to the Lamanites." Hamblin quickly gained the respect of the tribes of central and southern Utah.

In 1856 Hamblin built a ranch in the Mountain Meadows valley. In compliance with church leaders' Reformation emphasis on plural marriage, he rode to Salt Lake City in August 1857 to marry a second wife and

The Mountain Meadows Massacre occurred near Jacob Hamblin's ranch. Not one of the conspirators, he buried the more than one hundred victims. Photo of Hamblin courtesy of Church History Library.

to escort Indian chiefs to a war council there. En route he met the Arkansas emigrant company in central Utah. When they asked where a good site would be to recuperate and feed their animals before crossing the desert to California, Hamblin suggested Mountain Meadows. Ironically, on 11 September, while Hamblin was being sealed to his plural wife, John D. Lee was leading the massacre at Mountain Meadows. On the trail back home, Hamblin heard about the bloodshed. He encountered Lee, and the two former electioneers talked. Hamblin later reported that as an emotional Lee rambled on, he disclosed some Latter-day Saint involvement, including himself.[23] Upon returning to his homestead, Hamblin visited the site of the carnage and later recalled, "Oh! Horrible indeed was the sight."[24] He counted and buried 120 corpses. He accounted for all seventeen surviving children and turned them over to a federal agent who returned them to kin in Arkansas.

CIVIL WAR

When telegrams in April 1861 declared the fall of Fort Sumter, Brigham assured President Lincoln that Utah stood with the Union. To be sure, Brigham and other Saints remembered Joseph's revelation prophesying the rebellion of South Carolina and an all-consuming war. The church straddled support of the Union with a measured anticipation of apocalyptic destruction paving the way for an independent Zion. Indeed, many Saints believed that soon God would take vengeance on the United States, in large part because of Joseph's assassination.

The war engulfed some electioneers directly. William H. Miles was serving as the Eastern States Mission president when hostilities began. He received a letter from twenty Saints in the Grand Army of the Potomac asking him to come and minister to them—a request he was unable to fulfill, having been recalled to Salt Lake City. Miles returned after the war to resume his role as mission president.[25] Lucius Scovil was a missionary in New York when the war erupted. He immediately mailed copies of Joseph's prophecy to several of his relatives. He advised eastern Saints "to wind up their business and leave Babylon" that spring.[26]

In a war often described as fratricidal, the electioneer brotherhood included those who fought and died on both sides. While most of these men had long separated from the church, it is nonetheless ironic that they found themselves fighting one another in a war that together they had campaigned to prevent. After Joseph's death, Martin H. Tanner alienated himself from his Latter-day Saint family. He moved to New York City and fought for the Union in the war.[27] William D. Lyman, after his mission to South Carolina, watched his parents and most of his siblings die at Winter Quarters. Grief-stricken and disenchanted with the church, he left, taking his remaining brother and sister with him to Tennessee, presumably to be close to the family of his wife Maria. "In April 1862 he was incarcerated in the rebel prison at Madison, Ga., because of his outspoken Northern sentiments." He got out by enlisting in the Tennessee cavalry and subsequently fought in several battles. Later he moved to Missouri, living out his life as a Methodist.[28]

Lorenzo Moore of Illinois served his electioneer mission in Louisiana. In the wake of Joseph's murder, he returned to Nauvoo and participated in temple rites. However, he soon left the main body of Saints to follow Lyman Wight to Texas, where he became a prosperous farmer and county commissioner. During the Civil War he fought in the cavalry of General John Hood's famous Texas Brigade. Following the war, he returned to his life in Texas.[29] John W. Grierson, originally from Maryland, campaigned for Joseph in Tennessee but did not return to Nauvoo after the prophet's death. In 1849 he converted to James J. Strang's movement and traveled to Iowa as a successful missionary for that cause. He later left Strangism and moved to South Carolina. A letter to his daughter in 1864 shows him fighting for the Confederacy in Mississippi. A decade after the war, while residing in Mississippi, Grierson encountered RLDS missionaries. He accepted their message and became the presiding elder in Mississippi.[30]

Perhaps the most intriguing story of Civil War electioneer Saints was the family of William E. Higginbotham. Converts in 1842 of fellow electioneer Jedediah M. Grant, William and his wife Louisa sold their extensive possessions (including a slave) and moved to Nauvoo. William labored in his native Virginia for Joseph's campaign. After Joseph's murder, William and his wife participated in temple ceremonies. At Winter

Quarters they learned that Louisa's father had died, leaving her a considerable inheritance in Virginia. They decided to go there to settle the estate. When their daughter Nancy married local merchant David Perry, who bitterly opposed the church and refused to let her gather to Utah, William and Louisa chose to stay. By 1860 William was again a very wealthy farmer with two slaves. When the war began, their son Simon and son-in-law David Perry enlisted in the Confederate army.

In 1862 Simon and David returned from battle wounded and stricken with typhoid fever. Though they would live, in a twist of fate the disease killed William, Nancy and all but one of her siblings, and Perry's parents. Now a widower, Perry took the counsel of his mother-in-law to investigate the church. Clinging to the doctrine of eternal marriage, he converted. A local elder baptized him in the winter of 1863 with a foot of snow on the ground. Later that year, Louisa and her daughter Eliza fled Virginia with two thousand dollars in gold coins, crossing federal lines with the help of a Confederate officer. They rendezvoused in Union-occupied Kentucky with Simon and David, who had deserted the Confederate army. The family emigrated to Utah, where Perry then married Eliza, the remaining sibling of his deceased wife. He later became a prominent business leader.[31]

Church leadership, believing that the Civil War might destroy all nations and governments, prepared the kingdom of God to fill the void. In 1862 a constitutional convention re-created the State of Deseret and applied to Congress for admission. Denied, the legislature of Deseret instead met after each territorial session—a kind of government in exile—and enacted identical legislation. However, the war ended and the United States, though bloodied and bruised, still stood. It was not yet time for the political kingdom of God to ascend.

THE ELECTIONEERS' SOCIAL CONTRIBUTIONS

In 1852 Orson Pratt publicly pronounced the doctrine of plural marriage. The Saints were required to accept the doctrine, though not all were required to live it.[32] Plural marriage quickly became the preferred and most honored institution of marriage.[33] Church leaders practiced plural marriage more than their congregants and strongly counseled regional and local leaders to model the practice. Since those of higher church rank were viewed as more likely to attain exaltation, they became attractive marriage candidates for women seeking the same blessing. In fact, studies show that church office was more important than wealth in predicting plural marriage. A man was much more likely to enter plural marriage in the five years following a rise in ecclesiastical rank than in the five years previous. Practicing plural marriage was not a prerequisite to higher priesthood office or its attendant duties, but it did become a responsibility for those who received such positions.[34]

The first wife of electioneer Franklin D. Richards, Jane Snyder was humble and courageous in undertaking plural marriage. Photo ca. 1873 by J. Hoffman courtesy of Church History Library. © IRI. Used by permission.

Two-thirds of the electioneers in good standing practiced plural marriage between 1851 and 1869.[35] With fourteen wives, apostle Franklin D. Richards topped the list. His first wife, Jane Snyder, was humble and courageous in living plural marriage. Jane cared for Richard's first plural wife, Elizabeth McFate, in 1846–47 while he was away on a mission. However, McFate succumbed in Winter Quarters, as did Franklin and Jane's firstborn daughter, four-year-old Wealthy. Now completely alone and ill herself, she later penned, "I only lived because I could not die."[36] Even with such an inauspicious beginning to their family's plural marriages, Jane continued to accept the practice. During the Reformation, Richards added seven plural wives to the four he already had, while marrying three more in later years. Some electioneers needed prodding from their leaders to enter plural marriage. Prominent leader Samuel W. Richards, brother of Franklin, abstained until Brigham ordered him to enter the practice.[37] At first Charles W. Hubbard did not marry plurally even when advised to do so. However, with the consent of his wife, he eventually married again.[38] The median number of plural wives among electioneers in this time period was three, with the average mean closer to four (see table 10.2). Electioneers generally married more wives than others who practiced plural marriage because the former's higher religious and political rank encouraged it.

Table 10.2. **Percentage of Polygamous Men in Relation to Number of Wives, 1851–1869***

Number of Wives	Electioneers (200 total)	Manti	Great Basin
2	32% (63)	66%	66%
3	32% (63)	21%	21%
4	12% (24)	8%	7%
5+	25% (50)	5%	6%

* Daynes, *More Wives Than One*, 129. Daynes draws on Stanley Ivins's 1956 study to provide the Great Basin statistics.

The Reformation of 1856–57 created a spike in plural marriages as men and women clamored to prove their loyalty to the church. The resulting wave of marriages led apostle Wilford Woodruff to write, partly in jest, that "nearly all are trying to get wives, until there is hardly a girl 14 years old in Utah but what is married, or just going to be."[39] A comprehensive study of plural marriage in Utah noted that in 1856–57, 65 percent more plural marriages took place than in any other two-year period in Latter-day Saint history.[40] The same was true for the electioneers. In 1856 forty-six of them married sixty-four wives, and in 1857 fifty-five married eighty-seven wives. Ten married plurally in both years. The increase in demand for plural wives continued into the 1880s, even among surviving electioneers.

Many electioneers and their wives found plural marriage difficult, adding friction to relationships already stretched by Zion's demands. Israel Barlow's third wife doubted the principle until receiving a definitive sign during prayer.[41] Dominicus Carter, a church and political leader in Provo, struggled at times with two of his six wives. One neighbor remembered being asked to give a priesthood blessing to one of Carter's wives: "I found hardness existing between her and her husband and some others of his wives. I refused to lay on hands until all difficulty was settled. I laid hands on her the same evening; all difficulties being settled, she got well."[42] Later, Carter's second wife, Sylvia, took her two small children and left him, deciding she could not live in polygamy.[43] Norton Jacob's first wife objected to his taking a second wife. His journal shows that although she finally relented, it produced a domestic life of constant discord.[44]

The second of the twin evils denounced in the Republican Party platform, polygamy took a back seat only to slavery. As the Civil War raged, however, the federal government did not lift a finger to enforce new antibigamy laws. Regardless, enforcement would have proved difficult. Local probate judges were all Latter-day Saints, including several electioneer members. Because the courts of first jurisdiction were subject to territorial law, convictions were next to impossible.

THE ELECTIONEERS' ECONOMIC CONTRIBUTIONS

WEALTH

The wealth of electioneers, polygamous and monogamous, relative to heads of household in Salt Lake City in 1860 yields insightful comparisons (see table 10.3). Monogamous electioneers were more likely to have below-average wealth, probably because they lived in settlements across the Great Basin where economic opportunity was significantly less than in Salt Lake City. In smaller towns, land was the measure of wealth; and because land allotment was assigned by family size, monogamous men were at a disadvantage. An astounding 44 percent of polygamous electioneers, however, held wealth two and half times greater than that of other Latter-day Saint men. Yet there was more to their wealth than the land-distribution model. Because many electioneers were local or regional political and religious leaders, they often were assigned (or assigned themselves) to water, logging, and other resource rights. Furthermore, they were better connected to local, regional, and Basin-wide leaders and thus more aware of economic opportunities. With two-thirds of them practicing financially advantageous plural marriage, the electioneers were as much an economic aristarchy as a religious and political one.

Table 10.3. Electioneers' Wealth in 1860

Wealth	Polygamous Electioneers (181 total)	Monogamous Electioneers (52)	Salt Lake City*
Elite ($2,000+)	44% (80)	17% (9)	18%
Average ($200–$1,999)	51% (93)	58% (30)	68%
Below Average (< $200)	4% (8)	25% (13)	14%

* The Salt Lake City numbers come from Travis, "Social Stratification and the Dissolution of the City of Zion in Salt Lake City," 138.

Levi Stewart's post-electioneer career included positions of trust for decades throughout Utah. Unknown date and photographer. Courtesy of Church History Library.

The wealthiest electioneer in 1860 was John D. Lee. He had almost double the wealth of his next wealthiest peer, Levi Stewart. Ironically, Lee and Stewart were childhood friends in Illinois. Their stories illustrate the electioneers' rise to economic prominence owing to previous service and loyalty to Joseph's vision for Zion. As adults with families in 1837, Lee and Stewart separately entertained missionaries, joined the church, and moved to Missouri. After being involved in the Mormon War, they moved to Nauvoo. The following year they labored together as missionaries in Illinois, Ohio, Kentucky, and Tennessee. In 1844 Lee headed campaign efforts in Kentucky while Stewart electioneered in Illinois.

Levi Stewart's economic success in Utah also began with his election-eering mission.[45] Shortly after his return from that assignment, he was unexpectedly made a high priest. In the Nauvoo Temple, Stewart and his wife were part of the less than 1 percent of Latter-day Saints who received the second anointing. Like many other electioneers, he was instructed to enter plural marriage before 1850. When Stewart arrived in Utah in 1848, his proven loyalty along with his priesthood, political, and plural marriage status qualified him for the extensive plots of land given to him. Stew-art leveraged these assets to become one of the leading merchants in Salt Lake City and an officer of the Brigham Young Express Company. In 1865 Brigham instructed Stewart to sell everything and move to Big Cotton-wood to set up a paper mill. Stewart obediently did so.

Two years later, comfortable and wealthy, Stewart again heard from Brigham, who had decided to restart the recently abandoned remote set-tlement of Kanab. Brigham chose Stewart to lead this second attempt. Fifty-eight-year-old Stewart sold his possessions and moved with his wives yet again. Called as bishop of Kanab, he supervised the planting of crops, the assignment of land, and the building of a sawmill. Although his wealth mea-sured in dollars dropped significantly since his earlier time in Salt Lake City, he was by far the wealthiest man in the area throughout the early 1870s, with owner-ship of land, cattle, the sawmill, and the regional Zion's Cooperative Mercantile Institution. In 1874 he divested himself of his wealth and holdings and presided over the town's attempt at consecration in the United Order. When the order collapsed three years later, he had to be-gin financially anew—again. Deciding to open a mercantile store, Stewart and his son left for Salt Lake City to procure supplies. Stewart died of a stroke before arriving.[46]

Electioneer Jonathan O. Duke, who became a religious and political leader in Provo, Utah, named his twins after Joseph and Hyrum Smith. Photo ca. 1865 courtesy of Darby Smith.

Jonathan O. Duke held the median slot in terms of electioneer wealth in 1860. At that time he was a stonemason in Provo with three wives and thirteen hundred dollars in assets. Born in England, he was raised as a Methodist and became a mason's apprentice. He emigrated to the United States in 1829. In 1837 his wife converted to the church while visiting Latter-day Saint relatives in Brooklyn. Despite reservations, Jonathan followed suit in 1839 and even served a mission to Massachusetts. By 1840 he had moved his family to Nauvoo, where he continued to work as a mason. Church leaders assigned him in 1844 to campaign in Delaware. So significant were the deaths of Joseph and Hyrum to him that exactly twenty years later he named his twin boys Joseph and Hyrum.

Duke and his family arrived in Utah in 1850 and immediately moved to Utah Valley. However, Duke chose to work in Salt Lake City on the church's public works. He longed to hear the preaching of Brigham and Heber C. Kimball (he first met the latter during his electioneering mission). When church leaders organized the town of Provo, they selected Duke as bishop and, in theodemocratic fashion, nominated and elected him as town councilman. Duke remained central to Provo politics and religion until his death in 1868.[47]

OCCUPATIONS

By 1860, 78 percent of electioneers (85 percent if polygamous) were landed farmers or professionals (see table 10.4), a 30 percent increase from 1850. In contrast, the percentage of all Salt Lake City men in the same occupational category declined slightly. Even electioneers who were monogamous continued to rank higher in upward occupational mobility than their non-electioneer counterparts.

This pattern is illustrated in previously mentioned electioneer Chauncey W. West. After eleven years of dedicated missionary service from New York to Bombay, he returned to Salt Lake City in 1855 and was called to move to Ogden and enter plural marriage. Obedient, he immediately married a second wife and then seven more over the next twelve years. Church leaders ordained him bishop of the Ogden First Ward and presiding bishop of Weber County. They also nominated and elected him

Table 10.4. Electioneers' Occupations in 1860

Occupation	Electioneers (236 total)	Monogamous Electioneers (56)	Electioneers with Plural Wives (180)	Salt Lake City Residents*
Business-Professional**	78% (183)	54% (30)	85% (153)	34%
Skilled	15% (35)	30% (17)	10% (18)	36%
Unskilled	8% (18)	16% (9)	5% (9)	30%

* The Salt Lake City numbers come from Travis, "Social Stratification and the Dissolution of the City of Zion in Salt Lake City," 138.
** Includes landed farmers.

to the Territorial House and the Ogden City Council. These positions and the land allotments he received to support his multiple wives expanded his local and regional business connections and yielded real estate opportunities. With his tireless work ethic and business acumen, he built and maintained a cattle ranch and several timber mills as well as a tannery, stable, blacksmith shop, meat market, mercantile shop, flour mill, hotel, and freight company. He became the largest employer in Ogden.

During the Civil War, church leaders called West to preside over the European Mission. In the course of constant travel from Ireland to Italy to oversee missionary work, he contracted a severe respiratory infection (from which he never fully recovered) and was released to return to Utah.

After a brief respite, West returned to his religious, political, and economic duties with renewed vigor. In 1868 Brigham decided to have the church contract the local work on the transcontinental railroad. Young asked Weber County leaders Ezra T. Benson, Lorin Farr, and Chauncey W. West (all electioneers) to carry the Central Pacific contract. As the youngest of the three, West assumed much of the work and was rewarded as one of the honored dignitaries at the "Golden Spike" ceremony the following year. West's rise to prosperity had been dramatic since his inauspicious beginnings as the son of a poor tenant farmer in upstate New York.

But West's incredible religious, political, and economic success was doomed. Central Pacific paid him less than half of the more than two million dollars contracted. West divested himself of all properties and businesses to pay as many subcontractors as possible. He made several trips to California to obtain the rest of the promised monies, but to no avail. Just eight months after the railroad's completion, while on one of these trips, West collapsed and died three days later at the age of forty-three. His family soon had more to mourn: his nine widows and dozens of children were not only penniless but subjected to vexing lawsuits for unpaid bills.

Chauncey West's life and death are a fitting microcosm of the success of the electioneer veterans in theodemocractic Zion and its ultimate demise. His life's trajectory illustrates what the electioneers could achieve because of their faith-inspired commitment to join the sacred with the secular. West's death, however, foreshadowed the passing of theodemocracy itself. It is ironic that the "martyr of the transcontinental railroad" died at the hands of greedy railroad barons who epitomized the American capitalist industry.[48] Although their railroads connected the Great Basin to the people, ideas, goods, and markets of the rest of the United States, within two decades these influences destroyed the electioneers' Zion dream. By 1890 in Utah there was no more unity in elections, no more publicly authorized plural marriages, and no more cooperative, stewardship-based economics. Disunity had destroyed power. Theodemocracy had lived for forty-six years, just three more than West. Gone was the political framework that had protected Joseph's Zion. Just like West's large family, the church was saddled with debt and left to pick up the pieces. Fatefully, conditions were ripe for the electioneer cadre's biggest success story—Lorenzo Snow—to salvage a changing Zion.

*   *   *

Most electioneers came from humble beginnings but accomplished much in devotion to their prophet's Zion. They made theodemocracy a reality. As one historian noted:

> The spirit within the Church . . . turned the commonplace into greatness. . . . The Church did not attract great men. It produced great men. . . . It gave them an opportunity for growth. It heaped upon them responsibilities which forced them to grow or die.[49]

With ecclesiastical responsibility came aristarchic political power, the two seamlessly united by the glue of theodemocratic values. Thus the election-eers held multiple commissions that fueled their rise to prominence. The grand experiment worked. As the *Deseret News* declared in 1868: "We have enjoyed such an exemption of strife and contention at elections since our settlement of these valleys. . . . Our citizens being united upon religion and other questions, have thought that, to be consistent, they should be united in political matters."[50]

Leadership in the Great Basin community also meant practicing plural marriage. Leaders at every level were expected to set an example by marry-ing multiple wives. A large majority of electioneers accepted the principle, and all in leadership positions did. With increased allotments of land as a result, polygamous men, as most of the electioneer veterans were, held a distinct economic advantage. As theodemocratic leaders, their outsized in-fluence held sway over local as well as regional economic policies. As able professionals, businessmen, and landed farmers, they oversaw the blossom-ing of economic activity and opportunity within their geographical spheres.

From 1851 to 1869, many of the men who campaigned for Joseph in 1844 continued to be part of the religious, political, social, and economic aristarchy of the Latter-day Saint Great Basin kingdom. As part of the gov-erning elite, they implemented Joseph's Zion as orchestrated by Brigham, thereby fashioning a Zion people "of one heart and one mind . . . [who] dwelt in righteousness . . . [with] no poor among them" (Moses 7:18). Into this hard-won theodemocracy came the transcontinental railroad, perma-nently connecting the Great Basin kingdom to the rest of America. The result would be tumultuous for Zion and her aristarchy, including elec-tioneers whose influence was already waning in the face of age and death.

NOTES

1. Young, "The United States' Administration and Utah Army," in *JD*, 5:226. In this discourse of 13 September 1857, Brigham recalls what he said at an anniversary celebration on 24 July 1847.

2. "A Conference," *The Prophet*, 3 August 1844, 2. The conference was in Por-tage, Allegheny County, New York.

3. Letter from George Q. Cannon to Joseph Alma, in Jenson, "West, Chauncey Walker," *Latter-day Saint Biographical Encyclopedia*, 1:753.

4. Chauncey W. West, "The India Mission," *Deseret News*, 14 November 1855, 286. This article is one of six written by West for the newspaper.

5. See Doctrine and Covenants 87.

6. See "Iron County," *Treasures of Pioneer History*, 3:341–42.

7. See "The Mormons in San Bernardino," *Utah, Our Pioneer Heritage* (database), 4:403.

8. Lyman, *San Bernardino*, 122.

9. Boyle, Autobiography and Diary, 14.

10. Lyman, *San Bernardino*, 316.

11. See Lyman, *San Bernardino*, 335.

12. Sherwood's intransigence started in the pioneer company of 1847 when Brigham labeled him the "chief grumbler"; see Elliott, *Biographical Sketch of Jefferson Hunt*, 12–14.

13. See Rogers, *Unpopular Sovereignty*, 137.

14. See Walker, Turley, and Leonard, *Massacre at Mountain Meadows*, 30, 37. See also David L. Bigler, *Forgotten Kingdom*, 145; and Cooley and Young, *Diary of Brigham Young*, 49–53.

15. Electioneer officers were Horace S. Eldredge, Joseph Holbrook, Jesse C. Little, Robert Burton, Willard Snow, David Evans, Howard Egan, Jonathan O. Duke, and Chauncey W. West.

16. Electioneers who participated in the raids were Enoch Burns, Lindsey A. Brady, Jonathan O. Duke, Howard Egan, Robert T. Thomas, Robert T. Burton, Chauncey W. West, Hosea Stout, and William R. R. Stowell.

17. Little, "Biography of William Rufus Rogers Stowell," 42–57.

18. See Carter, "The Move South: Box Elder County," *Heart Throbs of the West*, 10:259–60.

19. Curtis, Reminiscences and Diary, 126.

20. Curtis, Reminiscences and Diary, 127.

21. See Walker, Turley, and Leonard, *Massacre at Mountain Meadows*, 129–210.

22. Lee, Journal, 56.

23. Little, *Jacob Hamblin*, 43. Hamblin subsequently informed Brigham Young and George A. Smith what Lee had told him. He would later testify against Lee in Lee's federal trial. See "Testimony in the Trials of John D. Lee," http://

law2.umkc.edu/faculty/projects/ftrials/mountainmeadows/leetestimony
.html.

24. As quoted in Black, "Jacob Hamblin," Latter-day Saint Vital Records II Database (hereafter "LDSVR").

25. See "Mormon Participation in the Civil War."

26. Scovil, Journal, 28 April 1861.

27. See Rev. George C. Tanner, *William Tanner, Sr.*, 309.

28. See R. I. Holcombe, "Campbell Township," chap. 33 in *History of Greene County, Missouri* (St. Louis, MO: Western Historical Co., 1883), s.v. "William D. Lyman," https://thelibrary.org/lochist/history/holcombe/grch33.html.

29. All the documents for the pension application of Lorenzo Moore's wife Mary are available in the online database *Alabama, Texas and Virginia, Confederate Pension Applications, 1884–1958*, https://www.ancestry.com/search/collections/texasconfederatepensions/. Her pension file number is 11476.

30. See "John W. Grierson," https://www.genealogy.com/forum/surnames/topics/cudaback/1/; and Heman Smith, *History of the Reorganized Church*, 4:22.

31. See Tullidge, *Tullidge's Histories*, 2:210–14; and Orson F. Whitney, *History of Utah*, 4:270–71.

32. See Daynes, *More Wives than One*, 73.

33. See Daynes, *More Wives than One*, 71.

34. See Daynes, *More Wives than One*, 128.

35. That is, 201 of 305 electioneers who remained loyal to Brigham and came west to settle what became the State of Deseret practiced plural marriage.

36. Black, "Jane Snyder Richards," LDSVR (database).

37. See Black, "Samuel W. Richards," LDSVR (database).

38. See Hubbard family, "Biography of Charles Wesley Hubbard," 9.

39. Journal History of the Church, 1 April 1857.

40. See Van Wagoner, *Mormon Polygamy*, 92.

41. See Mecham, Family Book of Remembrance, 306.

42. Carter, "Journal and Diary of William Marsden," *Heart Throbs of the West*, 12:152.

43. See Black, "Dominicus Carter," LDSVR (database).

44. See Black, "Norton Jacob," LDSVR (database).

45. Lee's rise to wealth is discussed earlier in this chapter.

46. Black, "Levi Stewart," LDSVR (database).

47. See Duke, Reminiscences and Diary, 9–11.
48. McDonough, "Chauncey Walker West," 14–15.
49. Berrett, *Restored Church*, 146.
50. "General Election," *Deseret Evening News*, 18 July 1868, 2.

CHAPTER 11

THEODEMOCRACY'S TWILIGHT, 1869–1896

We are told to be united, for in union is strength. Are we united?
. . . Now where is Zion? . . . What does it all mean?

—Former electioneer Nancy Naomi Tracy in 1896

"Now where is Zion?" penned Nancy Naomi Tracy, the only female to number among Joseph's devoted cadre of electioneer missionaries who had stormed the nation in 1844. Sadly, when she raised that lament-tinged question in 1896, theodemocracy in Utah had already descended below the horizon of time. Two decades of relentless pressure from the federal government had backed the Saints into a corner. Polygamy was the bogeyman for Protestant, Victorian America, and "Mormon Theocracy" would no longer be tolerated in the United States. The former would be used to destroy the latter. When church president Wilford Woodruff sought heaven's counsel in 1890, the answer was to end plural marriage. Moreover, the following year the church disbanded its political party (the People's Party) and the Saints separated into Republicans and Democrats "like everyone else," as President Grover Cleveland demanded. Compliance brought statehood in 1896, but theodemocractic Zion was the sacrifice—the ram caught in the thicket.

The aging electioneers lamented the loss of their dream. For decades following Joseph's assassination, they had engineered theodemocratic Zion. They had worked wonders, serving as a critical component of the aristarchy of the Great Basin kingdom. Now that kingdom was all but gone. They had prepared to gather Israel out of the nations to a literal divine standard. And while many converts had indeed come from diverse countries, the nations and kingdoms of the world themselves had not crumbled as many had expected. Instead the United States had grown into a continental-sized world power, with only one small pocket of political and moral nonconformity—Utah.

Even as Zion's hope faded, the dwindling number of electioneers remained true believers. John M. Bernhisel, who had been Joseph's personal physician and confidant, became Deseret's and Utah's delegate to Congress from 1848 through the Civil War. All that time he had managed the difficult relationship between Brigham Young's theodemocracy and the federal government. Historian Orson F. Whitney interviewed Bernhisel near the end of his life. Despite all the change occurring around him, Bernhisel looked forward to the day when every Saint "[would] work, not for his individual aggrandizement, but purely with an earnest desire to promote the interests of the Kingdom of God on the earth." He then testified of Joseph, the Restoration, and Zion.

When Whitney asked Bernhisel if "he really believed such a Utopia would ever be realized," the elderly electioneer got a gleam in his eye and responded with emotion, "As surely as the sun now shines in heaven." That "enthusiastic fervor" so impressed Whitney that he could "vividly" recall that moment the rest of his life.[1] Nancy Naomi Tracy expressed her certainty of Zion's triumph with the same celestial metaphor: Zion and its mission "are part of my makeup. . . . I am a firm believer of the prophecies," she wrote. "I believe they will be fulfilled as sure as the sun shines by day and gives light."[2] However, theodemocractic Zion had been diminishing for some time. The sun set gradually. After the arrival of the transcontinental railroad in 1869, Brigham Young, John Taylor, and Wilford Woodruff each in turn fought desperately to keep gentile influences at bay. Toward that end, they often appointed aged and experienced electioneers in vital religious, political, and economic positions throughout the territory. For a time, these efforts were somewhat successful. However, when the Supreme Court validated rigid anti-polygamy laws, dusk was at hand. The dream of Zion protected by a theodemocratic government that would rule not just the Great Basin but also eventually all the world passed into darkness. It would have to await the dawn of another day.

THE SETTING SUN

The completion of the transcontinental railroad on 10 May 1869 was a portent of difficult times ahead. Brigham understood that the railroad would bring to Zion a massive influx of "gentiles" whose different values and beliefs would create tensions with the Latter-day Saints. Seeing the coming storm, Brigham reconvened and reconstituted the Council of Fifty in 1867, a move that included the addition of electioneers Robert T. Burton, Edward Hunter, Abraham O. Smoot, and Hosea Stout.[3] The council created Schools of the Prophets throughout the territory. Composed of the leading high priests in each settlement, these mini-Councils of Fifty discussed "theology, church government, [and] problems of the church and community . . . and [had] appropriate action taken."[4] Up until the mid-1870s, when these schools were dissolved, electioneers had a governing role in them. They acted to secure their communities economically. Following the example of electioneer apostle Lorenzo Snow's work in Brigham City, they created economic cooperatives in order to limit financial interaction with outsiders. They controlled the flow of merchandise into Utah by creating Zion's Cooperative Mercantile Institutions (ZCMI). For nearly a decade, the schools functioned successfully as a new level of theodemocracy.

After the national financial panic of 1873, Brigham created radical communal economic efforts called "united orders." Within a year, 150 existed throughout the territory. After Brigham's death in 1877, John Taylor replaced the failing orders with "Zion's Boards of Trade." Like the Schools of the Prophets, the boards were governed by the religious, political, and economic leaders of each stake in the Great Basin. At each semiannual conference, Taylor and other leaders instructed the boards on how to improve the economic situation of the Saints. By 1884 these boards had succeeded in increasing production and employment with regulated competition. Integrating industry, crafts, and agriculture, the church was closer to its goal of economic independence than at any time in its fifty-year history.[5] In all of these cooperative economic initiatives, electioneer veterans filled many of the leadership roles.

Within a decade, however, all this success would end in ruin as the United States government launched an offensive against the church. The intense prosecution of polygamy, what the Saints called "the Raid," was the culmination of decades-long political pressures within and without the church. More than a thousand Latter-day Saint men were convicted and jailed in these raids. Many leaders, including electioneers, went into hiding to escape prosecution. At the same time, communal economic progress faded with the resultant loss of leadership in towns and cities across the Great Basin.

In 1870 disaffected Latter-day Saint merchants and intellectuals joined a growing number of gentiles to create the Liberal Party. In response church leaders created the People's Party. The Liberals' first triumph was recruiting electioneer apostle Amasa M. Lyman. The Quorum of the Twelve had already dropped him in 1867 for teaching "spiritualist" doctrines and denying Jesus Christ's atonement. But hearing of Lyman's commitment to the Liberals, the Twelve and First Presidency excommunicated him. To ensure that ruling majorities of Latter-day Saint men continued in the governments of Utah, the legislature followed Wyoming's recent example of enfranchising women, doubling the Saints' advantage. In elections for seventeen years, the Liberals had only one victory—Tooele County from 1874 to 1878—because gentile miners outnumbered Latter-day Saints there at that time.

However, Liberal eyes were always on Ogden and Salt Lake City, Utah's biggest cities and railroad centers with large gentile populations. As mentioned earlier, to ensure that Ogden did not fall, Brigham sent electioneer apostle Franklin D. Richards to Weber County,[6] where he served in church and political offices of influence. He installed electioneer colleague Lorin Farr as leader of the Ogden School of the Prophets. Richards and his counselors became the Weber County Central Committee of the People's Party. For nineteen years they successively foiled Liberal aspirations.

Municipal Officers of Ogden, Utah, 1889. At the height of anti-polygamy persecution in 1889, the people of Ogden elected Liberal Party officers for the first time. The same would happen in Salt Lake City the following year. 1889 photo by the Adams Bros. courtesy of Church History Library.

However, in 1889 the Liberals took Ogden, and then Salt Lake the following year. This was possible because intense prosecution of polygamists disenfranchised tens of thousands of Latter-day Saint voters. The Poland Act of 1874 transferred all civil and criminal cases to federal judges and away from Latter-day Saint probate judges (many of whom were electioneer veterans). Church leaders appealed to their First Amendment right to exercise freedom of religion, but the Supreme Court ruled against them. Yet proving bigamy in court was problematic because polygamous women refused to testify against themselves. Then came the Edmunds Act of 1882 that defined bigamy as cohabitation, making conviction easier. Anyone found guilty paid stiff fines and was disenfranchised and imprisoned. A new federal commission oversaw all elections and interpreted polygamous belief alone as bigamy. The first year saw twelve thousand Latter-day Saint men and women disenfranchised. After another test case in 1885 went against the church, full-scale prosecution began, netting more than a thousand convictions. Many surviving electioneers were convicted and imprisoned.[7] Church leaders, including electioneers, went into hiding. An underground network of Saints concealed their leaders, safely moving them from location to location.[8]

President John Taylor remained undaunted. Still carrying a musket ball in his leg from Joseph's assassination, he did not wilt in the face of the church's enemies. In 1880 he recalled the Council of Fifty and replaced twenty-two deceased men (seven of them electioneers) and released five others (four of them electioneers) owing to age—actions showing that time had diminished the electioneers' four-decade influence. Thirty-three new men entered the council. Only one, Lorin Farr, was an electioneer. However, sons of electioneer veterans Franklin D. Richards, Amasa Lyman, Jeremiah Hatch, Jedediah Grant, and David Cluff became members, signaling a new generation of electioneer influence.

Despite the efforts of the reconstituted Council of Fifty, anti-polygamy legislation was too powerful to counter. With leaders on the underground, administration of the church was severely disrupted. With electioneers and other church leaders not able to hold public office, the Zion trade boards they chaired collapsed. Yet, defiant like their prophet, they chose to continue in plural marriage. The exception was Franklin D. Richards. With the First Presidency in hiding and fellow apostles in prison or on the underground, Richards, by assignment, became the public face of the church by conforming to the law. He resided with only one wife while financially supporting his others. This arrangement allowed him to publicly transact church business and to project to church members that the leadership was still in control.[9]

Taylor remained resistant and in hiding until his death in 1887. He spoke and wrote of the confrontation in apocalyptic tones. He and many Saints believed that the second coming of Jesus Christ might occur in 1890.[10] They saw the persecution over plural marriage as but the final test of their faith. More than four months before Taylor died on 25 July 1887, the Edmunds-Tucker Act took effect. It dissolved the church as a corporate body, divested it of property, disbanded the Perpetual Emigrating Fund, abolished women's suffrage, and created an anti-polygamy test oath to vote, hold elected office, or serve on juries. The federal government had taken off the gloves to destroy the political and economic power of the church. Disenfranchised, the People's Party lost the Ogden elections in 1889 and the Salt Lake City elections in 1890. Additionally, in May 1890 the Supreme Court upheld the Edmunds-Tucker Act. Federal officials publicly stated they would go after the church's temples.

In this context, the new president of the church, Wilford Woodruff, released what became known as the Manifesto. Fearing the loss of the temples and the cessation of saving ordinances, he prayerfully received a revelation for the church to cease the practice of plural marriage. In the October conference, church members sustained the action. The church lay decimated, no longer protected by theodemocratic governance. Woodruff looked for political deliverance from federal oppression through obtaining statehood. The cost was political unity.

In 1891 church leaders agreed to disband the People's Party and encourage members to align with either the Republican or Democratic parties. To ensure compliance, some local leaders even split their congregations in half in order to assign equal numbers to each party. Certainly the transition was rocky. While most of the hierarchy aligned with the Republicans, President B. H. Roberts of the Seventy and Moses Thatcher of the Twelve ran as the Democratic nominees for the US House of Representatives and Senate, respectively, in 1895. Both lost. The First Presidency and the Quorum of the Twelve (which included electioneer apostles Lorenzo Snow and Franklin D. Richards) issued the Political Manifesto that same year. It required general authorities to receive permission from the First Presidency before running for office. Roberts grudgingly signed it, while Thatcher refused and was dropped from the Twelve. This was a dramatic change from the decades when apostles were automatically elected to high government positions.

By the time Utah gained statehood in 1896 with the backing of national Republicans, gone was unity in politics. Gone also was theodemocracy as a prelude to and bulwark for a Zionlike society. Socially, the practice of plural marriage was over. Economically, church businesses were in shambles. Plans of financial unity and self-sufficiency had vanished into a whirlpool of immense debt. The dream of Joseph's theodemocratic Zion had slipped away.

NANCY NAOMI TRACY AND THE LAMENT OF THEODEMOCRATIC ZION

Living electioneers like Nancy Naomi Tracy struggled with the lost Zion. In 1896 she wrote in her journal, "We are told to be united, for in union is strength. Are we united? . . . What does it all mean?"[11] Her questions reflected the reactions of many of her surviving comrades. Nancy was born and raised in Jefferson County, New York, becoming well educated by sixteen. She married Moses Tracy in 1832. Two years later the young couple converted to the church and moved to Kirtland to join the Saints. They experienced the persecutions of Ohio and Missouri. They knew Joseph intimately, once giving him all the money they possessed. In Nauvoo, Nancy became a leader in the newly formed Relief Society and taught school while Moses worked as a carpenter and merchant assistant.

When Moses was appointed to electioneer in New York, Nancy convinced him to ask Joseph if she too could go. Not only was the answer yes, but knowing of Nancy's education and oratorical gifts, Joseph told Moses that Nancy "would prove a blessing to him."[12] The small family of four made their way to Sackett's Harbor, New York, arriving in three weeks. They visited their families and former friends, teaching them the gospel and using *Views* to advocate Joseph for president. They then continued to Ellisburg, the location of Moses's assignment, where Naomi stood side by side with her husband in preaching and electioneering. It was there that they heard of Joseph's death.

When they returned to Nauvoo, their two-year-old passed away and was buried next to his brother who had died three years earlier. After receiving their temple ordinances, the Tracys fled Nauvoo and clung to life for three years in Winter Quarters. In 1850 they finally immigrated to Utah and settled in Ogden. In 1856 their eldest son, Mosiah, left the family and the faith, never to be seen again. Moses died the following year after a long bout of illness. A forty-two-year-old widow, Nancy worked her small farm to support her seven children. In 1860 she plurally married her deceased husband's brother Horace Tracy. She lived out her life in Weber County, proudly seeing her sons serve missions and sorrowfully abiding the time that some of them were imprisoned for plural marriage.

Viewing her dream of theodemocratic Zion slipping away, she questioned "the divisions and strife in the political field: some for one party and some for another." She lamented this lack of unity and its associated perils, believing the Saints "would be the only ones that would hold the constitution together after our enemies had torn it to shreds." Nancy declared that

Nancy Naomi Tracy, the lone female electioneer in 1844, lamented in 1896 the passing of the theodemocratic Zion that she and her peers had labored a half century to produce. Portrait ca. 1860s courtesy of Church History Library.

"the crisis is at our doors" and that "the time is not far distant when the Kings of Kings will come and set up his own government." Her undying loyalty to Joseph's vision of theodemocratic Zion did not square with the new politics of Republican-Democrat schism. She longed for a future day when the Saints again "all with one accord will vote the same ticket." While firmly believing that God was still directing events, she believed that he was not pleased with the partisanship all around her. Such a future, she believed, "certainly will try the Saints to the heart's core and is altogether of a different nature from the persecutions in the early days of the Church."[13]

She, her husband, their family, and the wider community of electioneers had sacrificed everything to build up the political kingdom of God. What would be harder, she pondered—the persecutions of the past or watching Zion wane and disappear? She vented her frustration at the "gentile world," whose laws have not "allowed [the Saints] the liberty of conscience which other people have enjoyed and which the Constitution guarantees for us to worship as we please." However, she declared, "This kingdom will roll on and eventually triumph over all others." Such thoughts gave her "consolation and satisfaction to know that we shall eventually become the head and not the tail." Envisioning the theodemocratic Zion she had spent half a century trying to achieve, she penned for posterity, "This is worth living for, and, if needs be, to die for."[14]

Nancy Naomi Tracy died on 11 March 1902, the fifty-eighth anniversary of the organization of the Council of Fifty. Her words express the shock and disbelief that surviving electioneers felt upon seeing all they had built begin to crumble and vanish. Gathering to Zion, theodemocracy, plural marriage, and economic unity had all ceased. Although millennial fervor still burned in the hearts of Nancy and others, the second- and third-generation Latter-day Saints were adjusting to a new reality. What prominently remained of Zion were living prophets and temple ordinances sealing families eternally. Tellingly, in Nancy's words, those themes shared equal time with her discontent over losing Zion. The church's unique experience in American history was dropping below the horizon. Soon the term *kingdom of God* would come to mean only the ecclesiastical structure of The Church of Jesus Christ of Latter-day Saints and not the theodemocratic Zion of the faith's first generation of earnest believers.

THE 1893 WORLD'S FAIR AND THE VANISHING FRONTIER

Amid this transition, church leaders attended the World's Columbian Exposition of 1893 in Chicago, Illinois. It provided an opportunity for Latter-day Saints to interact with the rest of America. The Utah Territory display was given a prime location, and tens of thousands of visitors walked past it each day. In every detail, church leaders orchestrated a softening of the controversial past of the church. While in some respects it worked, the results were mixed. The ecumenical Parliament of Religions refused to include the church or even a Latter-day Saint delegate because the church and its people were considered "un-Christian." Conversely, the Mormon Tabernacle Choir took second prize, marking the beginning of America's love affair with it. The church, stripped of its political, social, and economi-

In 1893 the Parliament of World Religions refused to allow a Latter-day Saint delegate, highlighting the struggle of the church to gain acceptance. Photo of the convened parliament at the 1893 World's Columbian Exposition courtesy of the Council for a Parliament of the World's Religions.

cal interests, retained its core mission of proselytizing and administering priesthood ordinances. Church leaders understood that continuing caricatures of the Saints would impede that mission. Such prejudice had to be overcome, and that could happen only through interaction with wider America. The exposition was a perfect place to begin and foreshadowed two decades of mixed reception from fellow Americans.

At the exposition, the soon-to-be famous historian Frederick Jackson Turner presented his landmark paper, "The Significance of the Frontier in American History," at a meeting of the American Historical Association there. Turner's ideas became the starting point for a century of portraying the American West, the American experience, and American exceptionalism. He used the 1890 census's declaration that a discernible American frontier no longer existed to create an epic narrative of the frontier as the defining feature of American history. For Turner, the West was where eastern Americans and emigrants left civilization for cheap land and freedom. The ascent back to civilization created a unique American people—doggedly independent, pragmatic, and democratic. As the frontier receded, in its wake society was reborn as distinctly American in thousands of towns. For Turner this distinct American process created endless opportunities for social mobility.

LORENZO SNOW, FIRST AND
EXEMPLARY ELECTIONEER

Among the church's delegation at the 1893 exposition was Lorenzo Snow—the first electioneer missionary, then-current president of the Twelve, and future church president. While there is no record of any Latter-day Saint in Turner's audience that day, let alone an electioneer, what might Snow have thought of Turner's thesis? In many ways Snow would have disagreed. Turner's assertions were certainly not the electioneers' experience on the frontier. They had not moved from the East to Missouri in search of inexpensive land, but rather according to a sacred geography. Their motive was neither land ownership nor financial independence, but a faith-driven determination to unitedly build a Zion society in the Missouri, Illinois, and Utah frontiers. They arrived in the western frontier actually expecting *less* independence financially, spatially, and even politically than what their fellow Americans enjoyed. This was because Zion meant a commitment to sharing economic resources rather than competing to accumulate them. It also required a united people deferential to ecclesiastical leadership rather than beholden to governance resulting from contested elections. What's more, the frontier for them was a sacred locus for the gathering of the house of Israel, the building of Zion and a refuge from God's impending vengeance, and the welcoming of Jesus Christ.

Snow would likely have challenged Turner's argument that taming the frontier created a unique American people who were fiercely independent, wary of hierarchy, and democratically participative. What Snow experienced on the frontier was entirely different. The success of Zion lay in its *cooperative* nature. Instead of a loose concentration of family farms that developed into a village, the Saints erected towns and cities with temples at their cores. Whereas Turner's frontier encouraged individuals to jostle for economic security and political position, the Saints cooperated economically and chose to be politically subservient to religious authority. Recalling Hawn's Mill, the gang rape of his sister, Carthage, and the Raid, Snow would have vehemently disagreed with Turner's assertion of pluralistic frontier democracy because Latter-day Saints so often experienced persecution and violence from their neighbors on the frontier. Thus they were a counterculture movement in America taking "flight from American pluralism."[15]

The frontier in Utah represented something more. For a time it was a protected, isolated space in which to fully implement Joseph's Zion with its thoroughly un-American traits. These counterculture characteristics of the church—namely, combining of church and state, collectivist economic policy, and plural marriage—were not created by interaction with the frontier. Rather, church leaders brought those values and institutions with them from Nauvoo. Their genesis was Joseph and his vision of Zion, not the frontier experience. Indeed, the fact that the Great Basin lay far *beyond* the fringe of the American frontier gave church leaders and their electioneer associates the chance to fully implement "Joseph's measures."[16]

Yet, ironically, Turner's quixotic and oft-criticized vision of social mobility on the frontier perhaps found its most concrete expression in the electioneers' experience. Overall, it was the electioneers who experienced significant social mobility in the Great Basin. As the very first electioneer, and one who reached the highest echelon of leadership in the church, Lorenzo Snow furnishes an illuminating case study. He was born in Ohio to a common farm family. He studied books and valued education. His older sister Eliza joined the Saints and often wrote to Lorenzo about her faith. His visceral reaction was to trust in education and say "good-bye to all religions." However, the church intrigued him, and after some investigation he joined in 1836. He longed for a spiritual experience to confirm his intellectual choice, and upon receiving it he immediately set out on proselytizing missions to Ohio and later to Kentucky. Snow continued to teach school during the winters until he was ordained a high priest and called on a mission to England. There he honed his organizational skills, presided over the several hundred Saints in London, and even presented a leather-bound copy of the Book of Mormon to Queen Victoria. He returned to Nauvoo in the spring of 1843, at the head of several hundred British converts.

In the April 1844 church conference, Snow "received an appointment by the Twelve to form a political organization throughout the state of Ohio for the promotion of Joseph for the Presidency." Snow left for Ohio on the steamboat *Osprey*—the first electioneer to embark. He recorded, "[I] delivered . . . the first political lecture that was ever delivered to the world in favor of Joseph for the Presidency."[17] As mentioned earlier, he organized an effective electioneering corps in Ohio that was in full swing when he heard rumors of Joseph's assassination. Snow providentially found fellow electioneer Amasa Lyman, who confirmed the news. "Struck . . . with profound astonishment and grief, which no language can portray," Snow closed the campaign in Ohio and headed to Nauvoo.[18] He returned to teaching school and married his first wife. Church leaders were impressed by what he had done in Ohio. In 1845 they re-sent him to canvass the Ohioan branches for money to finish the temple. Snow wrote that the money "credited on my book [was] about 300 dollars."[19] That December, he married a second wife and received all the temple ordinances, including the second anointing.

In the westward trek, Brigham Young appointed Snow to manage the Mount Pisgah way station in Iowa, an immense responsibility for a young former schoolteacher. He excelled. Snow later traveled to Salt Lake City, and in February 1849 Brigham called him to the apostleship along with fellow electioneers Franklin D. Richards, distant cousin Erastus Snow, and Charles C. Rich. Within six months, he was in Italy opening that nation to missionary work. When he returned to Utah in 1852, Brigham assigned him to preside in Box Elder County. As the stake president, Snow built and led Brigham City in complete theodemocratic style. He created a successful economic cooperative that by 1875 was the pride of Utah, being an incredible 95 percent efficient. Financially unfazed by the Panic of 1873, the Brigham City cooperative instantly became famous, and journalists from throughout the country visited to report on it. Snow also profited from his community's success. The 1870 census recorded six wives, four thousand dollars in real estate, and ten thousand dollars in personal wealth.

Brigham used Snow's model to create cooperatives and later united orders throughout the territory.

In 1885 during the Raid, Snow was arrested, fined, and sentenced to prison, serving eleven months. In 1889, with theodemocracy in its death throes, Snow became president of the Quorum of the Twelve. After the completion of the Salt Lake Temple in 1893, he became its president. The temple became the new "gathering," the new locus of Zion as generational sealings began to replace the focus on a now-fading temporal Zion. Becoming president of the church in 1898, the first missionary of theodemocracy ironically inherited the church stripped of its political, social, and economic power. The church itself was in financial ruin from the anti-polygamy crusade that had escheated property and disrupted church businesses and finances. Snow preached throughout the Basin's settlements, renewing the Saints' commitment to tithing. It paid off. The church was out of debt in less than a decade, never to return. Zion's identity changed from theodemocracy, a collectivist economy, and plural marriage to tithing, adherence to the Word of Wisdom, and generational temple work attendance.

Snow in many ways personifies the electioneer cadre, of which he is the most famous. He began as a young farmer with better-than-average education and no desire for organized religion. He had already begun a career in education when he accepted the restored gospel.

The first and later the most recognizable electioneer, Lorenzo Snow personified the electioneers' amazing post-1844 campaign success in becoming a key part of theodemocratic Zion. Photo of Snow circa 1893 by Sainsbury and Johnson courtesy of Church History Library.

Because Snow embraced Zion and demonstrated competence and unstinting loyalty and sacrifice, including in Joseph's 1844 campaign, he did not remain a common teacher in Ohio. Instead he traveled all of Europe in the Lord's service, met Queen Victoria, and—most significantly—received religious, political, and economic positions of authority over thousands and, ultimately, hundreds of thousands of fellow believers.

In sum, Snow excelled in all four spheres of influence in which the electioneers operated. In the religious sphere, he rose in trusted responsibilities and became an apostle within five years of his electioneering mission. Later he became president of the Quorum of the Twelve, and in 1898 he was elevated to president of the church. In the political sphere, the organizational skills and hard work Snow exhibited in directing Joseph's campaign in Ohio soon found application in Utah. He served in the influential Council of Fifty and was a Territorial Councilor from 1852 to 1884 (an astonishing thirty-two consecutive years) and president of the Council for many of those years. In the social sphere, his religious and political positions required participation in plural marriage. True to the principle, he married nine wives and had forty-three children. In the economic sphere, he created opportunities that lifted his community and led to shared prosperity. Snow's successful cooperative inspired economic revitalization throughout the territory and even garnered national attention. His wealth included large tracts of farmland, stock shares, and other personal assets in the tens of thousands of dollars. In short, Snow was not only the first but also the premier electioneer—one who reached pinnacles of religious, political, and economic power and influence still remembered today. Most of the other faithful electioneers accomplished much good in those same four areas and attained prominence in their own communities as well, though in varying degrees.

Through the lens of his experience, Snow, unlike his contemporary Frederick Jackson Turner, would have seen more than the closing of the frontier in 1890. It was also the end of the church's Zion-driven, counter-American uniqueness that had been sheltered by that very frontier. The church's escape from secular time and space was over. When a staunchly pious resistance failed to keep an encroaching American secularism at bay, or bring about hoped-for apocalyptic judgments attending Christ's return, church leaders, including Snow, worked on accommodation with a society that had rejected them. With Snow and other church leaders at the Chicago World's Fair in 1893, the new mandate to deemphasize certain aspects of the church's uniqueness was just the beginning. Sadly, the curtain had closed for the time being on carrying out Joseph's vision of theodemocracy.

NOTES

1. Orson F. Whitney, "John Milton Bernhisel," *History of Utah*, 4:664.

2. Tracy, Reminiscences and Diary, 53.

3. See Quinn, "Council of Fifty," 22–26; and Jedediah Rogers, *Council of Fifty*, 247–55. Seventeen new members were admitted. Eleven of the six were sons of pre-1844 apostles. Of the six others, four were electioneers.

4. Arrington, *Great Basin Kingdom*, 245.

5. See Arrington, *Great Basin Kingdom*, 349; and Ridge, "Closing of the Frontier," 142.

6. See *Tullidge's Histories*, 2:315–16, 335.

7. Electioneers who served prison sentences included, at least, Henry G. Boyle, David Candland, Edmund Ellsworth, Elijah F. Sheets, William R. R. Stowell, and Lorenzo Snow.

8. In 1886 electioneer James H. Glines hid church president Wilford Woodruff in Vernal, 172 miles west of Salt Lake City. Then, after a short period, Glines drove Woodruff 400 miles to St. George. See Glines, Reminiscences and Diary, 61.

9. See Talbot, *Acts of the Modern Apostles*, 157–69.

10. See Doctrine and Covenants 130:14–17. Taylor and others interpreted these verses to mean that Christ could return in the eighty-fifth year of Joseph's life, 1890.

11. Tracy, Reminiscences and Diary, 53, 60.

12. Tracy, Reminiscences and Diary, 27.

13. Tracy, Reminiscences and Diary, 60–61.

14. Tracy, Reminiscences and Diary, 60–62.

15. See generally Hill, *Mormon Flight from American Pluralism*.

16. See Davis Bitton, "Re-evaluation of the 'Turner Thesis,'" 326–33.

17. Lorenzo Snow, Journal, 48–49.

18. Eliza R. Snow, *Record of Lorenzo Snow*, 80.
19. Lorenzo Snow, Journal, 53.

A LOST BUT LASTING LEGACY

ABRAHAM O. SMOOT

The church's appearance at the World's Columbian Exposition in 1893 signaled the beginning of American acceptance of the Latter-day Saints and the Americanization of the church. However, the rejection of B. H. Roberts as a delegate to the World Parliament of Religions proved that the nascent reconciliation had its boundaries and portended a rocky relationship still ahead. Roberts was a general authority, an intellectual and historian, and a polygamist. For the Protestant-led parliament, it was the last trait that was abhorrent. Five years later when Roberts won a seat in Congress, the lingering prejudice against the church was clear. Despite Roberts's pardon by US president Grover Cleveland, Republicans, urged on by Protestant ministers, blocked Roberts from being seated. The incident presaged the contested seating eight years later of apostle, electioneer son, and Republican senator-elect Reed Smoot. Abraham O. Smoot's fatherly relationship to his son Reed encapsulates the rise of the electioneer missionaries, their leading role in the Great Basin kingdom, that kingdom's eventual capitulation to American cultural forces, and the consequent loss of memory about the electioneers' influence in Latter-day Saint history. It also exemplifies the enduring legacy of the electioneer cadre through their descendants.

Born in 1815 in Kentucky, Abraham O. Smoot was the son of a poor Tennessee farmer. He received only a very rudimentary education and was just thirteen when his father died. His mother joined the church in 1833, and he followed her example two years later. The missionaries ordained Smoot a deacon and left him to preside over a small branch. He soon became an elder and later a seventy. He served four short missions in Kentucky and Tennessee and one in South Carolina. In 1838, while still in prison for his role in the Mormon War, Smoot married. He then settled in Iowa across the Mississippi River from Nauvoo.

Despite his meager schooling, indigent upbringing, and young age of twenty-nine, Smoot was "called and sent by the conference of the church . . . and Quorum of Twelve" to preside over the electioneer missionaries in Tennessee.[1] Campaigning in the South with a platform advocating the end of slavery proved challenging. Tennesseans shot at, threw brickbats at, and vandalized the property of Smoot and his companions. They sued him under Tennessee's statutes to prevent him from printing copies of Joseph Smith's *Views*. Others directed death threats at him and his electioneers. Yet Smoot and his men persevered. He preached and politicked throughout Tennessee, holding conferences with fellow Saints and electioneers. He debated with ministers of religion and political foes alike. On 8 July 1844 he received the first rumors of Joseph's murder, which were confirmed four days later. As "awful forebodings seared [his] mind," Smoot slowly returned to Nauvoo.[2] Finding Nauvoo in a "melancholy gloom" mirroring his own feelings, Smoot recorded, "These are days long to be remembered by me."[3]

The apostles remembered Smoot's courageous campaigning and loyalty. Just months later, they ordained him a high priest and selected him and forty-three other electioneers as part of a cohort of eighty-five high priests. Their assignment was to preside over the church in one of eighty-five key congressional districts. Although most did not undertake this assignment, Smoot did. He traveled to Alabama with his family, arriving in December 1844 on what would have been Joseph's thirty-ninth birthday. Smoot held a conference and began his work. He traversed Alabama, just as he had Tennessee, confidently preaching and setting in order all the branches through April 1845, when the Twelve recalled him. In Nauvoo,

Smoot was endowed, introduced to the principle of plural marriage, and sealed to two additional wives.

During the Saints' exodus, Smoot led companies in the years 1847, 1852, and 1856. Brigham placed him on the Municipal High Council in Salt Lake in 1847. He was the first justice of the peace in the Great Basin and, for a time, the only one west of the Missouri River. He was called as bishop of the Salt Lake City Fifteenth Ward in 1849. The following year he and fellow electioneer Jedediah M. Grant used their resources and connections to form a business importing eastern merchandise. In 1852 Smoot served another mission, this time in England. His companions were fellow electioneers Willard Snow and Samuel W. Richards. Church leaders in England selected Smoot to lead the first Perpetual Emigrating Fund company to Salt Lake City. The smoothness of the operation set the tone for the decades-long program and "did credit to Bishop Smoot, as a wise and skillful manager."[4] Upon Smoot's return, Brigham reassigned him as bishop of South Cottonwood.

After the death of Jedediah M. Grant, Smoot's business partner and mayor of Salt Lake City, Brigham nominated Smoot to fill his place. Unanimously elected the city's second mayor, he served for a decade. Like Lorenzo Snow, he personified the electioneers' social mobility. In 1860 he was a mayor and bishop with five wives, and he had amassed nine thousand dollars of real estate and ten thousand dollars in personal wealth—a far cry from his humble beginnings as an uneducated Tennessee farmer. In 1867 he was admitted to the Council of Fifty. The next year Brigham sent him to Utah County ahead of the railroad's arrival to be the county's theodemocratic leader charged with protecting the Saints from inevitable gentile influences. Smoot took charge of the Utah (Valley) Stake and was elected mayor of Provo, an office he held until 1881. In 1872, when the Liberal Party began challenging the territory's firm theodemocratic governance, Smoot exerted an even stronger countervailing influence: chairing the Utah County People's Party nominating committee and accepting election to the Territorial Council, all the while continuing as stake president over the county and mayor of Provo.

Smoot also excelled in managing the business operations of the county. At his death in 1895, he owned half of the stock in the Provo Cooperative

Institution that he began in 1868. He was the president of two banks and the Provo Woolen Mills, the largest of its kind west of the Mississippi. He also served as president of Brigham Young Academy, the precursor to Brigham Young University.

In Abraham O. Smoot are concentrated all the best characteristics of the aristarchy of the theodemocratic Zion kingdom. His electioneer service in Joseph's campaign helped catapult his meteoric rise in leadership responsibility and influence. Before the campaign, he was like many others who had joined the church and spread the restored gospel as a missionary—sharing in its joys and persecutions. But his life course took a new direction when he first stepped forward to respond to the call for electioneers. The trying experience of campaigning and preaching in the face of persecution and then mightily persevering in the mission field under the pall of Joseph's assassination was the crucible that created in the young man an unswerving loyalty to the cause of theodemocratic Zion. The cycle of rising to formidable challenges and succeeding continued throughout his life, leading to increasing positions of trust and responsibility.

REED SMOOT

Abraham O. Smoot's third wife, Anne Mauritzen, gave birth to son Reed in January 1862. Reed began school at a young age and was numbered with the first graduating class of Brigham Young Academy (in 1879), where his father was president. Reed studied business and during academic breaks worked at the Provo Woolen Mills, founded and directed by his father. Upon graduation, Reed took a job in the Provo Cooperative, which, again, his father oversaw. Eighteen months later he became manager of his father's woolen mills.

In 1884 Reed married the daughter of electioneer Horace S. Eldredge, one of the seven presidents of the Seventy. By that time, marriage between electioneer children was very common since these families, by nature of their friendships and status, moved in the same social circles. In 1890 Reed, like his father, served a mission to England. Although some people had viewed Reed as more concerned about business than religion, his mission apparently helped equalize the two interests. In clerking for European

The career arcs of electioneer Abraham O. Smoot (left) and his son Reed (right) illustrate the rise, success, demise, and ultimate continuation of the electioneer cadre. Photo of Abraham Smoot by Edward Martin courtesy of Church History Library. Photo of Reed Smoot courtesy of National Archives, George Gantham Bain Collection.

Mission president Brigham Young Jr., Reed gained valuable experience that would serve him well in later assignments in both the church and government. Fittingly, the electioneer son was assisting the apostle son of Brigham Young—the next generation of leadership mirroring the previous one.

Returning to Utah in 1891, Reed resumed his duties as manager of the Provo Woolen Mills and branched out, founding and directing a bank and an investment company. He became vice president of two mining companies, director of the Clark-Eldredge Company and of ZCMI, and a director of the Los Angeles and Salt Lake Railroad. After his father's death in 1895, Reed was ordained a high priest and called as a counselor in the stake presidency that succeeded his father. In 1900 church president Lorenzo Snow called thirty-eight-year-old Reed to be an apostle, replacing former electioneer Franklin D. Richards.

Reed came to adulthood during the Raid and chose monogamy. His business acumen and focus, coupled with church leaders' outreach to the Grand Old Party in hopes of attaining Utah statehood, made Reed a natural Republican. In the same year he became an apostle, he considered running for the Republican nomination for the US Senate. Because of the church's Political Manifesto, he first needed permission from the First Presidency. After deliberation, President Lorenzo Snow, whose earlier accomplishments in both ecclesiastical and political arenas had made him the epitome of theodemocratic success, decided against Reed's request. However, when Snow died in 1901, Reed approached new president Joseph F. Smith, who gave his approval. Reed went on to win the Republican nomination and the Senate election in 1903. Thus the nephew of assassinated presidential candidate Joseph Smith Jr. gave approval for an electioneer son and apostle to seek high government office—a different shade of theodemocracy for a new generation.

Reed's victory turned into a national debate over whether the church had definitively abandoned plural marriage, was loyal to the country, and had desisted from combining church and state. After Reed was seated, hearings began to unseat him. Over four years, the hearings filled thirty-five hundred pages, examined more than a hundred witnesses (including Joseph F. Smith), and solicited enough letters to senators to make it the largest such collection in the National Archives to this day.[5] Church leaders and practices were lampooned in political cartoons nationwide. The uproar over stories of continued polygamy caused President Smith in 1904 to issue the Second Manifesto. It reiterated the church's prohibition of plural marriage and threatened excommunication for any future incidents. To counter charges of theocratic politics in Utah, Smith and the First Presidency issued a statement in 1903 proclaiming political neutrality and encouraging Latter-day Saints to vote their conscience. After a deal between the church and Republican leaders, the Senate finally voted in 1907 and Reed was able to retain his Senate seat. He continued to serve as a senator until defeated in the 1932 election, and he remained an apostle until his death in 1941.

RESTORING A LOST BUT LASTING LEGACY

We have seen how the career arcs of Abraham O. Smoot and his son Reed capture the electioneers' influence on the rise and fall of Latter-day Saint theodemocracy and the church's unsteady transition to Americanization. The senior Smoot exemplifies the electioneers' rise to power following the failed 1844 presidential campaign. In the wake of Joseph's assassination, the more than six hundred political missionaries became a pool of proven leaders that Brigham relied on to move the faith safely beyond the American frontier and the persecution that had so often followed them. Under theodemocracy in the Great Basin, they became an integral part of the aristarchy that Brigham needed to build and guide Joseph's Zion in hundreds of settlements. Often holding key business and political positions in their communities, they emphasized unity in politics and cooperation in economic affairs. As local, regional, or general church authorities, they obediently practiced plural marriage as a commandment and as an example to other Saints. With multiple wives came the advantage of additional farmland and town plots. This increased wealth could be successfully leveraged using connections to other electioneer leaders throughout Utah or multiplied as a result of appointments to leadership positions that promoted industry and cooperative commercial enterprises. As discussed, a vast majority of the electioneer veterans experienced upward mobility religiously, politically, socially, and economically.

As the frontier encircled Utah, American values of Protestantism, partisan politics, Victorian morality, and economic capitalism—backed, as became clear in many instances, by the full force of the federal government—choked the church's unique, un-American characteristics. This drama played out while the electioneers' influence was waning because of age, death, and persecution. With capitulation followed by statehood, home rule returned to Utah, but under a new set of rules. It would take twenty-five tenuous years before the church became acceptably harmonious with Americanism. During this transition emerged the next generation of Latter-day Saint religious, political, social, and economic leaders. Like Reed Smoot, these new leaders were often the sons of electioneers, but with generational differences reflective of changing times. In religious practice, they were monogamous and focused on keeping the Word of

Wisdom and the law of tithing and doing temple work. As Americanized citizens, they politicked as Republicans and Democrats and championed individual capitalism and self-sufficiency.

Interestingly, while church priorities changed over a generation, the families of its high-ranking leaders did not change as quickly or as much. The Grant, Tanner, Smoot, Benson, Rich, Lee, Snow, and Smoot families are only a few of many families that can trace their lineage from election-eers through subsequent and current church leaders. In fact, electioneer surnames (often hidden in matriarchal lines) remain until today a virtual who's who of Utah's religious, political, social, and economic leaders a century after Americanization. Although federal suppression and the passage of time disrupted and weakened aristarchal authority in Utah, a new echelon rose to take its place. Sons replaced fathers in a world contoured to match, in innovative ways, the one that had just passed. The electioneers left a legacy through family connection that would prove advantageous for their descendants who would ascend the rungs of church leadership.

One last example may suffice. Electioneer John Tanner was a wealthy businessman who spent his fortune assisting Joseph in building Zion in Kirtland and Nauvoo. His sons Nathan and Martin joined him in election-eering in New York. While Martin never came west, Nathan, eight other sons, and John's only living daughter joined him in the Great Basin. Nathan alone "was the ancestor of Hugh B. Brown, apostle and counselor to President David O. McKay; of Fern Tanner Lee, wife of President Harold B. Lee; of President Nathan Eldon Tanner, counselor in four First Presidencies; and of Victor L. Brown, Presiding Bishop of the Church."[6] John's daughter Louisa Maria married electioneer apostle Amasa Lyman, and their son Francis M. Lyman and grandson Richard R. Lyman became apostles. Former member of the Presidency of the Seventy Marion D. Hanks is also a descendant. John's son Myron served for twenty years on the Provo City Council and twenty-three years as bishop of the Provo Third Ward. He donated his thriving businesses to Abraham O. Smoot to support the Provo Cooperative. Myron's son Joseph was the first Latter-day Saint graduate of Harvard University, the second commissioner of church education, and the president of Utah State College. Joseph's son Obert became a successful businessman, professor of philosophy, and noted philanthropist.

John Tanner's son Joseph Smith was mayor of Payson, Utah, and its bishop for twenty years. And these are just *some* of John Tanner's descendants (the examples from other electioneers are too numerous for the scope of this book). It is noteworthy that while capitulation to American culture ensured the church's survival, Americanization left power mostly in the hands of those who had always held it—namely, the faithful electioneers and many of their equally faithful descendants.

*   *   *

Lamentably, the passage of time, assisted by biased intergenerational memory, relegated Joseph Smith's 1844 presidential campaign to a mere historical footnote. As much as Frederick Jackson Turner's "frontier thesis" is the narrative beginning of the history of the American West, B. H. Roberts's writings became the interpretive foundation from which Latter-day Saints have written their history for more than a century.[7] When Roberts wrote, edited, and provided commentary in his works, the church was in the middle of its difficult transition to national acceptance and often a source of ridicule. Church leaders were attempting to minimize the controversial aspects of the faith's past. Roberts himself was not far removed from Congress's refusal to seat him over plural marriage and issues of church and state. In this political context, it is not surprising that while the daily documentary evidence shows the unfolding centrality of Joseph's presidential campaign in 1844 Nauvoo, Roberts's editorializing minimized its importance. He downplayed statements of Joseph's determination to win and opined that the campaign was not serious, attributing it to other motives.

In the years that followed, historians in and out of the church who commented on Joseph's campaign tended to follow Roberts's dismissive interpretation. The exceptions did not produce the historical narrative that reached most Saints. However, one cannot read the primary-source documents about Joseph and his colleagues from November 1843 until his death in June of 1844 without seeing that the campaign and its wider political context were a major focus (if not an exclusive one at that time) of the prophet and other church leaders. The Council of Fifty minutes have

now concretized the fact. Joseph's actions and his enemies' reactions, especially his assassination, do not completely fit together without factoring in
the centrality of the election campaign at that time. That there would not be
another Latter-day Saint missionary force as large as the 1844 electioneer
missionaries (and never one as proportionally large vis-à-vis total church
membership) until 1902, the year Roberts published *History of the Church*,
further attests the campaign's importance. Thus as Zion slipped below the
horizon, so did memory of Joseph's campaign with its nation-storming
electioneers and their kingdom-building contributions.

To be sure, as demonstrated in this book, Joseph Smith Jr. ran a serious campaign for president of the United States—one that directly led to
his death. More importantly, this work has uncovered the stories of many
electioneer missionaries as well as their contributions not only to the campaign but also to the church's post-martyrdom trajectory—particularly
theodemocratic Zion. Ironically, hundreds of thousands or more of Latter-
day Saints and others alive today are direct descendants of the forgotten
electioneers. The hundreds of men and one woman who campaigned for
Joseph have been underappreciated, overlooked, or forgotten, as have their
outsized contributions to The Church of Jesus Christ of Latter-day Saints.

The story of Joseph Smith's cadre of electioneers *is* the church's early
story. Enduring the tempests of persecution in Ohio, Missouri, and Illinois, they longed for, and became perfect foot soldiers of, a theodemocracy
to protect their Zion dream. This courageous volunteer cadre knowingly
and defiantly strode into a political hurricane. Resolute faith in Joseph and
Zion drove them. When assassins murdered their prophet-candidate, the
electioneers picked up the pieces of their shattered campaign and, with
their fellow Saints, fled the nation that had rejected them. In the Great Basin, finally, they were able to build their dream: theodemocratic Zion. As
religious, political, social, and economic leaders, they worked with and as
church leaders to shelter Zion from further storms for decades. In the end,
as their influence dwindled with age and death, they watched helplessly as
the whirlwinds of the federal enforcement of American culture destroyed
the heaven-directed endeavor of their lifetimes. Even then, those still living did not give up the dream of Zion. They still believed with "enthusiastic fervor" that one day "Zion in her beauty" would rise *and remain*—"as

surely as the sun now shines in heaven." They have much to teach their descendants, all Latter-day Saints, and Americans generally—not the least of which is "Unity is power."[8]

NOTES

1. Smoot, Day Book, 1.
2. Smoot, Day Book, 8 July 1844.
3. Smoot, Day Book, 28 July 1844.
4. Larson, *Prelude to the Kingdom*, 159–60.
5. See Flake, *Politics of American Religious Identity*, 9–10.
6. Leonard J. Arrington, "The John Tanner Family," *Ensign*, March 1979.
7. Particularly, B. H. Roberts published *The Rise and Fall of Nauvoo* (1900), edited the seven-volume *History of the Church* (1902), and authored the six-volume *Comprehensive History of the Church* (1930).
8. The quotes are from electioneer John M. Bernhisel (see chapter 11, note 3); Partridge, "Let Zion in Her Beauty Rise," *Sacred Hymns* (1835), 86; and Joseph's *Views*, 4.

LIST OF ELECTIONEERS

Note: Members of the Quorum of the Twelve do not appear in the following list of electioneers because the primary focus of this study is those who accepted the Twelve's call to preach and electioneer for Joseph.

* Designates electioneers discovered in my research.

Adams, Charles Augstus
*Adams, "Elder" D.
*Akes, Harmon Jackson
*Alexander, Randolph
Allen, Daniel
*Allen, John
Allen, Orville Morgan
*Amy, Dustin
Anderson, Miles
*Andrews, Benjamin
Andrus, Milo
Angus, John Orson
*Appleby, William Ivins
*Arnold, "Elder"
Ashby, Nathaniel
*Atkinson, Thomas

*Atwood, Millen
Babbitt, Lorin Whiting
Bacon, Samuel P.
*Badlam, Alexander
*Ball, Joseph T.
Barlow, Israel
Barnes, H. W.
Barney, Edson
Barrows (Barrus), Ethan
Bartlett, Milton F.
Barton, Isaac (Burton)
*Bassett, Charles Henry
Bates, Archibald
Bates, Marcellus L.
Bathrick, Almon
Batson (Badson), William

*Beach, Orson Gillett
*Beckwith, John D.
Beebe, Isaac
*Beebe, William A.
Bell, Alfred
Bennett, Hiram Bell
*Bennett, James Arlington
Benson, Ezra T.
*Benson, Martin Luther
*Bent, Samuel
Bentley, Gregory
*Bernhisel, John Milton
*Berry (Burry), Jesse
*Berry, Wilson
*Bevan, James
*Bigler, Henry William
*Bills, Samuel
Blanchard, John Reed, Sr.
*Bois, "Elder"
Bosworth, Joseph Buckley
*Bottoms, John
*Bowen, Peter C.
*Boyle, Henry Green
Boynton, Abraham Dodge
*Brady, Lindsey Anderson
Brandon, George Washington
Brandon, Thomas Jefferson
*Brannan, Samuel
Briggs, Silas Hugh
*Brinton, David
*Brooks, Charles
Brooks, Lester
Brothers, William
Brown, Alfred
*Brown, Benjamin
*Brown, Francis A.
*Brown, Hiram J. or P.
*Brown, Samuel
*Brown, Uriah
*Browning, Jonathan
Burgess, James

Burnham, James (Jacob) L.
*Burns, Enoch
Burton, Isaac
*Burton, Robert Taylor
*Burton, William
Butler, Lorenzo Dow
Butterfield, Josiah
Buys, Hyrum DeBaun
Buzzard, Phillip Hammond
*Cahoon, Reynolds
*Calkins, Edwin Ruthuen (Ruthvin)
*Camp, Williams
Candland, David
*Card, David
Carlin, Edward
Carpenter, Samuel E.
Carroll, James
Carter, Dominicus
Carter, Simeon Dagget
Casper, John Austin
Casteel (Castell), Jacob Israel
Chamberlain, George
Chase, Darwin J.
Chase, Isaac
Chase, John Darwin
Childs, Nathaniel
*Church, Hayden Wells, Sr.
*Clair, Mr.
Clapp, Benjamin Lynn
*Clark, Calvin R.
*Clark, Israel Justus
*Clark, U.
Clark, William Ogelby
Cluff, David, Sr.
*Coates, Ralph J.
*Cobb, Roland
Cole, Joseph Mortimer
Coltrin, Graham
*Coltrin, M. J.
Coltrin, Zebedee
Condit, Amos W.

Cook, Henry Lyman
Cooley, Alvin
Coons, Libbeus T.
Cooper, John Andrew
Coray, Howard
Coray, William
Cordon, Alfred
Cornish, Denman (Demmon)
*Cowan, David B.
*Cram, John
*Crosby, Jesse Wentworth
*Crosby, Jonathan
Crouse, George W.
Curtis, Jeremiah
Curtis, Joseph
*Curtis, Theodore
*Cutler, Alpheus
*Cutler, William Lathrop
Davis, Amos
Davis, Edward Horace
*Davis, Elisha
Dayton, Hiram
Dayton, Lysander
Dean (Deam), Henry H.
*Divoo (Devoo), L.
Dobson, Thomas
*Doremus, Henry J.
*Dorland, William
*Dougherty, Edward S.
Downing, James
Dryer, William Wakely
Duel, Osmon M.
Duke, Jonathan Oldham
Duncan, Chapman
Duncan, John
Duncan, William A. H.
*Dunn, Crandell
Dunn, Simeon Adams
Dunn, Thomas James
*Dyer, John W.
Dykes, George Parker

Eames, Ellis
Edwards, Francis M.
Edwards, Thomas S.
Egan, Howard
Eldredge, Horace Sunderlin
Elliott, Bradford White
Elliott, Henry G.
Ellsworth, Benjamin C.
*Ellsworth, Cyrus
Ellsworth, Edmund
Emmett, James
*Ensign, L. L.
Evans, David
Ewell, John Martin
Ewell, Pleasant
Farlin, Orrin Day
Farnham, Augustus Alvin
Farr, Aaron Freeman
*Farr, Lorin
Felshaw, William
*Felt, Nathaniel Henry
*Field, Reuben
*Fielding, Amos
Fife, Peter Muir
Fisher, Daniel
*Flanigan, James Henry
*Fleming, Josiah Wolcott
Folsom, William Harrison
Foote, Timothy Bradley
Foster, Joseph Hollis
*Foster, Lucian Rose
Foster, Solon
Fowler, George Washington
*France, Joseph
Frost, Samuel Buchanan
Fuller, Thomas Eldridge
*Fullmer, David
Fullmer, John Solomon
Gardner, Daniel White
Gardner, Morgan Lewis
*Gates, Jacob

*Geer, Aretus
Gillett, Truman
*Gillibrand, Robert
Glaeske, Andrew Jackson
*Glines, James Harvey
*Godfrey, Riley
*Goforth, "Mr."
*Goforth, William Gano
Goldsmith, Gilbert Davis
*Goodale, Jackson
Gould, John
Graham, James
*Grant, Jedediah Morgan
Green, Harvey
*Green, William, Jr.
*Greig, James M.
Gribble, William
*Grierson, John William
*Griffith, Richard
Groves, Elisha Hurd
*Guard, David
*Guinard, Julius Joseph
*Gully, Samuel L.
Gurley, Zenos Hovey
Guyman, Thomas
Haight, William
Hale, Jonathan Harriman
*Hall, Alfred
*Hall, Allen
Hall, Lyman
*Hallet, Clark Thatcher, Sr.
Hamblin, Jacob Vernon
Hamilton, Robert
Hammond, John
Hampton, Jonathan Victor
Hancock, Levi Ward
*Hanks, Sidney Alvarus
Harding, Alvin Milton
*Hardy, John G.
Hardy, Zachariah
*Harman (Harmon), J.

*Harrison (Harmison), James
*Haskins, Nathan
Hatch, Jeremiah
*Hatch, Lorenzo H.
*Hathaway, "Captain"
*Haws, J.
*Haws, Peter
*Heath, Samuel
*Henderson, William
Herriman, Henry
*Herringshaw, Hugh
Hess, Thomas
*Heywood, Joseph Leland
Hickerson, George Washington
Higginbotham, William Elliot
Hodges, Amos
*Hodges, Curtis, Jr.
Holbrook, Chandler
Holbrook, Joseph
*Hollister, David Sprague
*Holman, Joshua Sawyer
*Holmes, Milton
Holt, James
Holt, John
Hopkins, Charles A.
*Horner, John Meirs
Houston, Isaac
Houston, John
Hovey, Orlando Dana
*Howe, Frederick Wakefield
Hoyt, Homer Collins
Hoyt, Samuel Pierce
Hoyt (Hoit), Timothy Sabin
Hubbard, Charles Wesley
Hunt, Daniel Durham
Hunt, Jefferson
*Hunt, "Mr."
*Hunter, Edward
*Hurd, W.
Hutchings, Shepherd Pierce
Hyde, William L.

*Idle, W. B.
*Ivie, Richard Anderson
Jackman, Levi
Jacob, Norton
Jacobs, Henry Bailey
*James, Nathaniel B.
*Jennings, Henry
*Johnson, Aaron
*Johnson, Hunting
*Johnson, Joel Hills
Johnstun, Jesse Walker
*Jones, "Captain" Dan
Jones, David
Jones, John, Jr.
Jones, John, Sr.
*Jones, Nathaniel V.
*Jones, P.
Jordan, William Harrison
Judah, David
Kelly, John
Kelting, Joseph Andrew
Kendall, Levi Newell
*Kerr, Archibald
Kershner, David J.
*Keyser, Guy Messias
King, Joseph
*King, Thomas Jefferson
*Kinnamon, Richard H.
Lamb, Abel
Lambson, Alfred Boaz
Lamoreaux, Andrew Losey
*Lane, Leeler
*Lane, Selah
Langley, George Washington
Laurence (Lawrence), George
*Leach (Leech), George T.
*Leach, John
*Leaver, Samuel
Leavitt, Nathaniel, Jr.
LeBaron, Alonzo Harrington
*Lee, Ezekiel

Lee, John Doyle
Lemmon, Washington
Lewis, Clark
Lewis, David
*Lewis, Lemuel
*Little, James (Jesse) C.
Littlefield, Lyman Omer
*Litz, Stephen
*Livingston, Jonas
Lloyd, George
*Long, T.
*Losee, Isaac H.
Loveland, Daniel
Loveless (Lovelace), John
Lowry, John
*Luddington, Elam
Lyman, Amasa
Lyman, William Davis
Mack, Chilion
Mackley (Mackey), John
*Mallory, Lemuel
*Manchester, Asa
Markham, Stephen
*Martin, Thomas
Martindale, William Addington
*Mason, Lincoln
*McAllister, Ananias
McArthur, Duncan
*McBride, William
*McCauslin, Younger
*McGinn, Eli
McIntire, William Patterson
McIntosh, John A.
McKeown, Marcellus
McRae, Alexander
McTaggart, Thomas
*Melling, Peter
*Merrill, Valentine
*Merryweather, Frederick
*Meynell, J. B.
Mikesell, Garrett Wells

Mikesell, Hyram Washington
*Mikesell, John Aylor
*Miles, Ira Simonds
*Miles, William Hart
*Milford, Norman
Miller, Bethuel
*Miller, George
*Miller, William
*Mitchell, "Brother"
Moffett, Armstead
Moon, John
Moore, Lorenzo
*Moore, William A.
Morris, Jacob
Morse, Justus
*Moss, David
Mott, Hiram
Mower (Mouer), Henry
Mowrey (Morey), Harley
Mount, Joseph
Mulliner, Samuel
*Munroe (Monroe), James M.
*Myers, Jacob
*Myers, John
*Myers, William H.
*Neal, George Augustus
*Nelson, "Elder"
Nelson, James
Nelson, William
Newberry, James
*Newell, Garret T.
Newland, William
Newman, Elijah
*Newton, Joseph H.
Neyman, Hiram
Nichols, John
Nickerson, Freeman
Nickerson, Levi Stillman
Nickerson, Uriel C.
*Nixon, Theophilus W.
Noble, Joseph Bates, Sr.

Norris, Patrick
Olmstead, Harvey, Sr.
*Olney, Omar
Ott, Frederick
*Outhouse, John
Owens, Horace Burr
*Pace, James
Pack, John
Palmer, Abraham
Park, James Pollock
*Parker, Joshua
Parker, Samuel
Parshall, William Knapp
*Patten, John M.
*Peirson (Pierson), Edwin D.
*Pell, Elijah Ward
Penn, George
Perkins, Andrew Huston
*Perkins, William Gant
Perry, Josiah Henry
*Perry, Stephen Henry
Pettigrew (Pettegrew), David
Petts, John F.
Pew (Pugh), George
Phelps, Joshua R. G.
Phelps, Morris
*Phelps, William J.
*Phelps, William Wines
Phippin, James Worthington
Porter, Jared
Porter, Nathan Tanner
Post, Stephen
Powers, John Milton
Pratt, William Dickson
Rainey, David Pickney
*Ray, John E.
Razor, Aaron
*Reader, George
Redfield, David Harvey
Reed, Calvin
Reed, Elijah

Reed (Reid), John Henderson
*Reese, Enoch
*Reheey, Robert
*Reid, John S.
Rich, Charles Coulson
Richards, Franklin Dewey
*Richards, Levi
Richards, Samuel Whitney
*Richardson, William A.
Riley, William Wommack
Riser, George Christian
Riser, John Jacob
*Robbins, Lewis
Roberts, John Wesley
*Robinson, Ebenezer
*Robinson, Jesse
*Robinson, Joseph Lee
*Robinson, Lloyd
*Rogers, Amos Philemon
*Rogers, David
 Rogers, David Daniel H.
*Rogers, David W.
*Rogers, Samuel Hollister
Rose, Joseph
Rule, William Griffin
*Sanders, Ellis Mendenhall
Sanderson, James
Sasnett, John Gosney
Savage, David Leonard
*Savage, Jehiel
Savage, William
*Scott, Andrew Hunter
*Scovil, Lucius Nelson
Seabury, William
*Searle, Breed B.
*Shamp, Joseph
*Shaw, Samuel
Shearer, Daniel
*Sheets, Elijah Funk
*Sheffield, Anson
Shelton, Seabert

*Shenask, "Dr."
*Sherwood, Henry Garlie
Shoemaker, Jacob
*Sirrine, Mephibosheth
*Sly, James Calvin
Smith, Jackson Osborne
Smith, John Glover
*Smith, Moses
*Smith, P. R. (K?)
Smith, Warren
Smith, William
Smoot, Abraham Owen
Snow, Charles
Snow, Erastus Fairbanks
Snow, James Chauncey
Snow, Lorenzo
Snow, Warren
Snow, Warren Stone
Snow, Willard Trowbridge
Snow, William
*Snyder, George Gideon
*Sohn, Joseph
Sparks, Quartus Strong
*Spaulding, Ira N.
*Spavei, L.
Spencer, Daniel, Jr.
*Spicer, John
Sprague, Richard Demont
Spry, Charles
*Steele, "Elder"
Stewart, Levi
Stewart, Urban Van
Stoddard, Lyman
Stoddard, Sylvester B.
*Stout, Hosea
Stow, Nahum Milton
Stowell, William Rufus Rogers
*Stratton, Hiram
*Stratton, Joseph Albert
Strong, Ezra, Jr.
Strong, Reuben William

Swackhammer, Elijah
*Swackhammer, John
*Swanner, Samuel
*Tadlock, Alexander
*Taney, William
Tanner, John
Tanner, Martin Henry
Tanner, Nathan
*Taylor, Stephen
*Terry, Jacob Err
*Thayer (Thayre), Ezra
*Thayer (Thayre), (son of Ezra)
*Thomas, John H.
*Thomas, Robert T.
Thompson, Charles Blanchard
*Thompson, Ezra
*Thompson, George Vaughn
*Thompson, Hiram
*Thompson, Jared
Timmons, Andrew A.
Titus, Martin
*Tracy, Moses M.
*Tracy, Nancy Naomi
Truly, Ekells
Tufts, Elbridge
Tulley (Talley), Allen
*Turner, Ephraim
Twiss, John Saunderson
Tyler, Daniel
*Van Ausdall, William
*Van Deuzen, Increase
*Van Every, Peter
Van Natta, James Henry
*Van Nostrand, James Madison
Vance, John
Vance, William Perkins
Vincent, Ezra
Wait, Allen
*Wait, James W.
*Wakefield, John Fleming
Walker, John Beauchamp

*Wallace, George B.
Wandell, Charles Wesley
*Ware, William G.
Warner, Charles
Warner, Salmon
*Wasson, Lorenzo D.
*Watkins, G.
Watkins, William Lampard
Watt, George
Watt, George Darling
*Weaver, Peter
*Webb, Edward Milo
*Webb, Pardon Knapp
*Wells, "Elder"
Welton, Michael (Micah) B.
*West, Aaron
*West, Alva
*West, Chauncey Walker
*West, Joseph
West, Nathan Ayres
Wheelock, Cyrus Hubbard
Whipple, Edson
*White, Charles
White, Samuel Dennis
Whitney, Alonzo Wells
*Wight, Lewis
Wilbur, Melvin
*Willard, Edward
*Willard, Lemuel
Willard, Stephen D. (C.)
*Williams, Abraham
*Wilkes, Ira
Wilson, Bushrod Washington
Wilson, Henry Hardy
Winchester, Benjamin
Winchester, Stephen
*Winters, Hiram
Woodbury, Joseph Jeremiah
Woodbury, Thomas Hobart
Woodbury, William Hamilton
Woodworth, Lucien

*Woolley, Edwin Dilworth
*Wright, Abraham Reister
*Wright, Jonathan Caulkin
*Wright, "Mr."
*Wyckoff, "Mr."
Yearsley, David Dutton
Young, Alfred Douglas
Young, Alphonso
Young, John M. Jr.
Young, Joseph
Young, Lorenzo Dow
Young, Phineas Howe
Younger, Joseph W.
*Zeigler, Lewis
Zundel, Jacob

BIBLIOGRAPHY

ABBREVIATIONS

BYUSC   L. Tom Perry Special Collections. Harold B. Lee Library. Brigham Young University. The Church of Jesus Christ of Latter-day Saints. Provo, UT.

CHL   Church History Library. The Church of Jesus Christ of Latter-day Saints. Salt Lake City, UT.

JD   *Journal of Discourses.* 26 vols. London: Latter-day Saints' Book Depot, 1854–86.

JS   Joseph Smith.

JSH, A-1   Joseph Smith, History, 1838–1856. Volume A-1 (23 December 1805–30 August 1834). The Joseph Smith Papers. https://www.josephsmithpapers.org/paper-summary/history-1838-1856-volume-a-1-23-december-1805-30-august-1834/1.

JSH, C-1   Joseph Smith, History, 1838–1856. Volume C-1 (2 November 1838–31 July 1842). The Joseph Smith Papers. https://www.josephsmithpapers.org/paper-summary/history-1838-1856-volume-c-1-2-november-1838-31-july-1842/1.

JSH, D-1   Joseph Smith, History, 1838–1856. Volume D-1 (1 August 1842–
           1 July 1843). The Joseph Smith Papers. https://www.josephsmith
           papers.org/paper-summary/history-1838-1856-volume-d-1-1
           -august-1842-1-july-1843/1.

JSH, E-1   Joseph Smith, History, 1838–1856. Volume E-1 (1 July 1843–30
           April 1844). The Joseph Smith Papers. https://www.josephsmith
           papers.org/paper-summary/history-1838-1856-volume-e-1-1-july
           -1843-30-april-1844/1.

JSH, F-1   Joseph Smith, History, 1838–1856. Volume F-1 (1 May 1844–8 Au-
           gust 1844). The Joseph Smith Papers. https://www.josephsmith
           papers.org/paper-summary/history-1838-1856-volume-f-1-1-may
           -1844-8-august-1844/1.

JSJ   Joseph Smith, Journal, September–October 1838, December 1841–
           22 June 1844. The Joseph Smith Papers. https://www.josephsmith
           papers.org/the-papers/journals/jsppj1.

JSJ 3   Joseph Smith, Journal, December 1842–June 1844; Book 3, 15 July
           1843–29 February 1844. The Joseph Smith Papers. https://www
           .josephsmithpapers.org/paper-summary/journal-december-1842
           -june-1844-book-3-15-july-1843-29-february-1844/1.

JSJ 4   Joseph Smith, Journal, December 1842–June 1844; Book 4,
           1 March–22 June 1844. The Joseph Smith Papers. https://www
           .josephsmithpapers.org/paper-summary/journal-december-1842
           -june-1844-book-4-1-march-22-june-1844/1.

JSP   *Joseph Smith Papers.* Church Historian's Press. The Church of Jesus
           Christ of Latter-day Saints. Salt Lake City, UT.

JSP, CFM   Matthew J. Grow, Ronald K. Esplin, Mark Ashurst-McGee, Gerrit J.
           Dirkmaat, and Jeffrey D. Mahas, eds. *Administrative Records:
           Council of Fifty, Minutes, March 1844–January 1846.* Vol. 1 of the
           Administrative Records series of *The Joseph Smith Papers,* edited by
           Ronald K. Esplin, Matthew J. Grow, and Matthew C. Godfrey. Salt
           Lake City, UT: Church Historian's Press, 2016.

JSP, D7   Godfrey, Matthew C., Spencer W. McBride, Alex D. Smith, and Christopher James Blythe, eds. *Documents, Volume 7: September 1839-January 1841.* Vol. 7 of the Documents series of *The Joseph Smith Papers,* edited by Ronald K. Esplin, Matthew J. Grow, and Matthew C. Godfrey. Salt Lake City, UT: Church Historian's Press, 2018.

ARCHIVAL MATERIALS

Adams, George J. Letter to Brigham Young, August 1844. General Correspondence, Incoming, 1840–1877. Brigham Young Office Files, 1832–1878. CHL.

Allen, Orval Morgan. Diary of Orval Morgan Allen, September–October 1846. CHL.

Amy, Dustin. Autobiography. Seventies Record, 11th Quorum, 1845. Seventies' Autobiographies Compiled by Nauvoo Restoration. CHL.

Andrus, Milo. Milo Andrus Autobiography, 1875. CHL.

Appleby, William I. William I. Appleby Autobiography and Journal, 1848–1856. CHL.

Barlow, Israel. Israel Barlow Diary, March–August 1854. CHL.

———. Letter to Elizabeth Barlow, 12 September 1853. Israel and Elizabeth Haven Barlow Correspondence, 1853–1855. Barlow Family Collection, 1816–1969. CHL.

———. Letter to Elizabeth Barlow, October 1853. Israel and Elizabeth Haven Barlow Correspondence, 1853–1855. Barlow Family Collection, 1816–1969. CHL.

———. Letter to Elizabeth Barlow, 30 November 1854. Israel and Elizabeth Haven Barlow Correspondence, 1853–1855. Barlow Family Collection, 1816–1969. CHL.

Barney, Edson. Edson Barney Autobiography. Biographical Information Relating to Mormon Pioneer Overland Travel Database, 2003–2017. CHL.

Bernhisel, John M. Letter to Brigham Young, 21 March 1850. Brigham Young Office Files, 1832–1878. CHL.

Bigler, Henry. Diary of a Mormon in California; Discovery of Gold, 1848. Utah and the Mormons Collection. CHL.

Blockhouse (Iowa) Branch Record, 1846–49. CHL.

Boyle, Henry G. Henry G. Boyle Reminiscences and Diaries, 1846–1888. 2 vols. CHL.

Browning, Jonathan. "Biographical Sketch" (typescript). Manuscript Collection. BYUSC.

Bullock, Thomas. Thomas Bullock Journals, 1843–1849. CHL.

Burgess, James. James Burgess Journal, 1841–1848. CHL.

Cannon, Abraham H. Abraham H. Cannon Diaries, 1879–1895. CHL.

Carter, Simeon. Letter to Brigham Young, 1 October 1844. General Letters, 1840–1877. General Correspondence, Incoming, 1840–1877. Brigham Young Office Files, 1832–1878. CHL.

Cass, Lewis. "Letter from Lewis Cass, 9 December 1843," p. [1]. The Joseph Smith Papers. https://www.josephsmithpapers.org/paper-summary/letter-from-lewis-cass-9-december-1843/1.

Clayton, William. William Clayton, Journal, 1 April 1843. The Joseph Smith Papers. http://josephsmithpapers.org/paper-summary/appendix-william-clayton-journal-excerpt-1-4-april-1843.

———. The Nauvoo Diaries of William Clayton, 1842–1846: Abridged. CHL.

Cleveland, Sarah. "A Record of the Organization and Proceedings of the Female Relief Society of Nauvoo," and other articles (1842–1844). "Women of Covenant" Drafts 1960, 1965, 1984, 1987–1994, 2000. CHL.

Cluff, Harvey Harris. Autobiography of Harvey Harris Cluff (1836–1846). Microfilm Collection. BYUSC.

Cole, Joseph M. Letter, Council Bluffs, Iowa, to Adelia B. Cole, 19 May 1852. CHL.

Coonville Branch (Iowa). Coonville Branch Record, 1848–1851. CHL.

Coray, Howard. Autobiographical Sketches. Howard Coray Papers, circa 1840–1941. CHL.

———. Letter, Sanford, Colorado, to Martha Jane Lewis, 2 August 1889. CHL.

Coray, William. Journal, August 1846–August 1847. CHL.

Cordon, Alfred. Alfred Cordon's Journal and Travels in the Ministry of the Gospel. Alfred Cordon Reminiscences and Journals, 1839–1849, 5 vols. CHL.

Crosby, Jesse Wentworth. Autobiography (1820–1869). BYUSC.

———. The History and Journal of Jesse W. Crosby, 1820–1869. Americana Collection. BYUSC.

Crosby, Jonathan. Autobiography, 1850–1852. Jonathan Crosby, Papers, 1807–1882. Utah State Historical Society, Salt Lake City.

Curtis, Joseph. Joseph Curtis Reminiscences and Diary, October 1839–March 1881. CHL.

Cutler, William L. William L. Cutler Diary, January 1849–December 1850. CHL.

Davis, Amos. Amos Davis Account Book, 1839–1842. CHL.

Dunn, Crandell. "History and Travels of Elder Crandell Dunn." Vol. 1. Crandell Dunn Papers, 1842–1895. CHL.

Dykes, George P. Letter to Brigham Young, 29 October 1844. General Correspondence, Incoming, 1840–1877. Brigham Young Office Files, 1832–1878. CHL.

———. Letter to Mrs. King, 8 August 1864. CHL.

Eldredge, Horace Sunderlin. Horace S. Eldredge Journal, September 1852–April 1854. Daughters of Utah Pioneers Collection, 1828–1963. CHL.

Elliot, Bradford. Autobiography, 1842–1845. Seventies Record, 2nd Quorum. Seventies' Autobiographies Compiled by Nauvoo Restoration, 53. CHL.

Ellsworth, Edmund. Edmund Ellsworth Reminiscence, undated. CHL.

Far West (Missouri) Stake. The Conference Minutes and Record Book of Christ's Church of Latter Day Saints, 1838–1839, 1844. CHL.

Flanigan, James Henry. James H. Flanigan Diaries, 1842–1851. CHL.

Fullmer, John S. Letter, Springville, Utah, to Wilford Woodruff, 18 October 1881. Historian's Office Correspondence Files, 1856–1926. CHL.

Gates, Jacob. Jacob Gates Journals, 1836–1861. CHL.

Glines, James H. James H. Glines Reminiscences and Diary, March 1845–December 1899. CHL.

———. Statement, 9 August 1899. CHL.

Groves, Elisha Hurd. Autobiography (1797–ca. 1866). Seventies' Autobiographies Compiled by Nauvoo Restoration, 67. CHL.

Guinand, Julius J. Autobiography (1846). Seventies Record, 2nd Quorum. Seventies' Autobiographies Compiled by Nauvoo Restoration, 69. CHL.

Harding, Ralph. Letter to Dwight Harding, 22 August 1844. Ralph Harding Correspondence, 1844–1846. CHL.

———. Letter to Dwight Harding, 3 March 1846. Ralph Harding Correspondence, 1844–1846. CHL.

Harriman, Henry. Henry Harriman Autobiography, circa 1847. CHL.

Hamblin, Jacob. Record of the Life of Jacob Hamblin: As Recorded by Himself, circa 1854. CHL.

Hancock, Levi W. Levi W. Hancock Autobiography, circa 1854. CHL.

———. Levi W. Hancock "Autobiographical Sketch," 1878. CHL.

Hancock, Mosiah Lyman. Mosiah L. Hancock Autobiography, undated. CHL.

Hatch, Lorenzo Hill. Autobiography, 1826–1846. Lorenzo Hill Hatch Journals. BYUSC.

Heywood, Joseph Leland. Joseph L. Heywood Diary, May 1855–January 1857. CHL.

———. "Letter from Joseph L. Heywood, 23 October 1843." The Joseph Smith Papers. https://www.josephsmithpapers.org/paper-summary/letter-from-joseph-l-heywood-23-october-1843/1.

———. Letter to Nephew, 28 July 1841. Joseph L. Heywood Letters, 1841–1847. Joseph L. Heywood Collection, 1839–1912. CHL.

Hickerson, George Washington. George W. Hickerson Autobiographical Sketch, 1866. CHL.

Historian's Office. Nauvoo, Illinois, 6–9 April 1844. Historian's Office General Church Minutes, 1839–1877. CHL.

Holbrook, Joseph. The Life of Joseph Holbrook, 1806–1871. Americana Collection. BYUSC.

Hollister, David Sprague. "Letter from David S. Hollister, 9 May 1844." The Joseph Smith Papers. https://www.josephsmithpapers.org/paper-summary/letter-from -david-s-hollister-9-may-1844/1.

———. Letter to JS, 26 June 1844. CHL.

Holt, James. James Holt Autobiographical Sketch, 1881. CHL.

Hunt, Daniel Durham. Daniel D. Hunt Diary, May–September 1844; January 1845. CHL.

Hyde, William. William Hyde Journal, circa 1868–1873. CHL.

Hyde, Orson. Letter to David Fullmer, 19 July 1847. Garden Grove Branch Papers Relating to Reinstatement of Branch. CHL.

———. "Letter from Orson Hyde, 30 April 1844." The Joseph Smith Papers. https://www.josephsmithpapers.org/paper-summary/letter-from-orson-hyde -30-april-1844/8.

———. Letter to JS, 9 June 1844. Joseph Smith's Office Papers. CHL.

———. "Appendix 3: Orson Hyde, Statement about Quorum of the Twelve, circa Late March 1845." The Joseph Smith Papers. https://www.josephsmithpapers .org/paper-summary/appendix-3-orson-hyde-statement-about-quorum-of -the-twelve-circa-late-march-1845/1.

Jackman, Levi. Levi Jackman Journal and Autobiography, 1835–1847. CHL.

Jacob, Norton. Norton Jacob Reminiscence and Journal, May 1844–January 1852. CHL.

———. The Record of Norton Jacob. Edited by C. Edward Jacob and Ruth S. Jacob. N.p.: Norton Jacob Family Association, 1953. CHL.

Johnson, Benjamin Franklin. "An Interesting Letter from Patriarch Benjamin F. Johnson to George S. Gibbs (1911)." Delbert L. Stapley Files, 1951–1976. CHL.

Johnson, Joel Hill. Joel H. Johnson Autobiography, circa 1880. Nineteenth Century Western and Mormon Manuscripts. BYUSC.

Johnstun, Jesse Walker. Jesse W. Johnstun Reminiscences, 1849–1853. CHL.

King, Joseph. Letter to Brigham Young, 29 October 1844. General Correspondence, Incoming, 1840–1877. Brigham Young Office Files, 1832–1878. CHL.

Knapp, Edward K. Autobiography (n.d.). Seventies Record, 27th Quorum. Seventies' Autobiographies Compiled by Nauvoo Restoration, 91. CHL.

Lambson, Alfred Boaz. [Letter]. In Donnette Smith Kesler, *Reminiscences by Donnette Smith Kesler: The Wife of Alonzo Pratt Kesler* [1952], 102–5.

Langley, George W. Autobiography of George W. Langley (1845). Seventies Record, 25th Quorum. Seventies' Autobiographies Compiled by Nauvoo Restoration, 92. CHL.

Lee, John D. John D. Lee Journal, May 1844–November 1846. John D. Lee Journals, May 1844–November 1853. CHL.

Lewis, David. David Lewis Autobiography, 1854. CHL.

Littlefield, Lyman Omer. "Lyman Omer Littlefield Autobiography [1819–1848]." *Reminiscences of Latter-day Saints: Giving an Account of Much Individual Suffering Endured for Religious Conscience.* Logan, UT: Utah Journal Company Printers, 1888. CHL.

Loveless, John. John Loveless Autobiographical Sketch, 1859. CHL.

Luddington, Elam. "Luddington Family and All Existing Portions of an Autobiographical Sketch." Family History Library. The Church of Jesus Christ of Latter-day Saints. Salt Lake City.

Lyman, Amasa. Journal, 4 June 1844–16 March 1845, 24 January–18 April 1845. Amasa M. Lyman Collection, 1832–1877. CHL.

———. Journal, 4 June to 13 August 1844. BYUSC.

Markham, Stephen. Letter, Fort Supply, to Wilford Woodruff, 20 June 1856. Materials Used by Church Historians, 1854–1856. Joseph Smith History Documents, 1839–1860. CHL.

McArthur, Daniel Duncan. Daniel D. McArthur Autobiography, undated. CHL.

McIntire, William Patterson. William P. McIntire Notebook, 1840–1845. CHL.

Minutes of the Council of Fifty, Saturday April 10, 1880, Meeting 10 am at Council House and 2 pm at City Hall. Americana Collection. BX 8608 .A1a no. 1295. BYUSC.

Minutes of the Provo School of the Prophets, 1868–71. Utah State Historical Society Archives.

"Minutes of a Special Conference of the Elders and Members of the Church of Jesus Christ of Latter-day Saints, Held in Philadelphia, December 14th, 1840." *Gospel Reflector* (Philadelphia, PA), no. 1 (January 1841): 23–24.

Moore, William A. Letter to Brigham Young, 25 September 1844. General Correspondence, Incoming, 1840–1877. Brigham Young Office Files, 1832–1878. CHL.

Morris, Jacob. Letter to Charles Allen, Nauvoo, Illinois, circa November 1844. CHL.

Moss, David. Autobiography. Seventies Record, 9th Quorum (1858). Seventies' Autobiographies Compiled by Nauvoo Restoration, 115–16. CHL.

Nashville (Iowa) Branch Membership Roster, 1839–1843. CHL.

"Nauvoo Aaronic Priesthood Minutes and Biographical Sketches, 13 January 1844 to 15 June 1845." CHL.

Nauvoo Stake High Council Minutes. CHL.

Nichols, John. Diary. Manuscript Collection. BYUSC.

Nuttall, L. John. Notebook, 1880–1882. Council of Fifty, Papers, 1845–1883. CHL.

Ott, Frederick. Frederick Ott Autobiography, circa 1844. CHL.

Pace, James. A Biographical Sketch of the Life of James Pace, undated. CHL.

Perry, Josiah H. Autobiography. Seventies Record, 2nd Quorum (1845). Seventies' Autobiographies Compiled by Nauvoo Restoration, 125. CHL.

Pettegrew, David. David Pettigrew's Journal, 1840–1857, 1926–1930. David Pettegrew Family Collection, 1836–1883; 1926–1930. CHL.

Phelps, William Wines. Funeral Sermon of Joseph and Hyrum Smith, 1855. CHL.

Phippen, James W. Autobiography. Seventies Record, 12th Quorum (1858). Seventies' Autobiographies Compiled by Nauvoo Restoration, 127–28. CHL.

Porter, Nathan Tanner. Nathan T. Porter Reminiscences, circa 1879. CHL.

Post, Stephen. Journal, July 1839–December 1848. Stephen Post Papers, 1835–1921. CHL.

Pottawattamie County High Priests Record Minutes, 2 January 1848–7 September 1851. CHL.

Pratt, Parley P. "Letter from Parley P. Pratt, 19 April 1844." The Joseph Smith Papers. https://www.josephsmithpapers.org/paper-summary/letter-from-parley-p -pratt-19-april-1844/4.

Record of Seventies, 1835–1843. First Council of the Seventy Records, 1835–1885. CHL.

Record of the 30th Quorum of Seventies, Nauvoo, Ill. (1844). CHL.

Rich, Charles Coulson. Journal, 1 March–20 September 1845. Charles C. Rich Collection, 1832–1908. CHL.

———. Journal, 14 May–28 July 1844. Charles C. Rich Collection, 1832–1908. CHL.

Richards, Franklin D. Journal Typescript, May 1840–1844. Franklin D. Richards Journals, 1844–1899. Richards Family Collection, 1837–1961. CHL.

———. Journal No. 2. Volume 1, 21 May–22 July 1844. Richards Family Collection, 1837–1961. CHL.

Richards, Samuel Whitney. Diary. BYUSC.

Richards, Samuel Whitney. Samuel W. Richards Statement, circa 1900–1909. CHL.

Richards, Willard. Letter, Nauvoo, to Orson Hyde, 25 May 1844. Outgoing Correspondence. Willard Richards Journals and Papers, 1821–1854. CHL.

———. Journal (Volume 10), March–August 1844. Willard Richards Journals and Papers, 1821–1854. CHL.

———. Proposed Plan for a Moot Organization and Congress, 6 February 1844. Joseph Smith's Office Papers, 1835–1844. CHL.

Rigdon, Sidney. *Oration Delivered by Mr. S. Rigdon, on the 4th of July, 1838, at Far West, Caldwell County, Missouri.* Far West: Printed at the Journal Office, 1838. CHL.

Riley, William Wommack. William W. Riley Diary, circa 1844–1861. CHL.

Riser, George Christian. Reminiscences and Diary Entries, undated; 1864–1869. CHL.

———. "Unfinished Life Story." Special Collections. J. Willard Marriott Library. University of Utah.

Robbins, Lewis. Autobiography. Seventies Record, 2nd Quorum (1845). Seventies' Autobiographies Compiled by Nauvoo Restoration, 143–44. CHL.

Robinson, Joseph Lee. "History of Joseph Lee Robinson." Autobiography and Journals, 1883–1893. Joseph Lee Robinson Autobiography and Journals, 1883–1892. CHL.

Rogers, David. Letter to Brigham Young, August 1844. General Correspondence, Incoming, 1840–1877. Brigham Young Office Files, 1832–1878. CHL.

Rogers, Samuel Hollister. Samuel H. Rogers Reminiscences and Diary, 1841–1886. CHL.

———. Letter, Harford County, Maryland, to Daniel Page, Newport, New Jersey, 21 April 1844. CHL.

Savage, William. Letter, Flintville, Wisconsin, to J. M. Waite, Binghamton, Wisconsin, 23 October 1872. CHL.

Scott, Andrew Hunter. Autobiography. Seventies Record, 34th Quorum. Seventies' Autobiographies Compiled by Nauvoo Restoration, 150. CHL.

Scovil, Lucius. Lucius N. Scovil Journal, 1846–1847; 1860–1861. CHL.

Seventies' Autobiographies. Compiled by Nauvoo Restoration. CHL.

Sharp, Thomas C. Typed Transcript and Manuscript Copies of Unsigned Letter to the Editor of the *Warsaw Signal*, 15 February 1844. Beinecke Rare Book and Manuscript Library. Yale University Library. Yale University. Newhaven, CT.

Shaw, Samuel. Letter to Brigham Young, 1 October 1844. General Correspondence, Incoming, 1840–1877. Brigham Young Office Files, 1832–1878. CHL.

Sheets, Elijah Funk. Elijah F. Sheets Journal, August 1845–July 1904. Elijah F. and Margaret H. Sheets Journals, 1843–1904. CHL.

———. Elijah F. Sheets Journal, May 1844–August 1845. Elijah F. and Margaret H. Sheets Journals, 1843–1904. CHL.

Smith, Emma Hale. "Emma Smith Blessing," 1844. CHL.

Smith, George A. George A. Smith Autobiography and Journals, 1839–1875. CHL.

Smith, Joseph, Jr. *General Smith's Views of the Powers and Policy of the Government of the United States*. The Joseph Smith Papers. https://www.josephsmithpapers.org/transcript/general-smiths-views-of-the-powers-and-policy-of-the-government-of-the-united-states-7-february-1844?print=true#ft-source-note.

———. Letter to James Arlington Bennet, 13 November 1843. CHL.

———. "Letter to Presidential Candidates, 4 November 1843, Draft." The Joseph Smith Papers. https://www.josephsmithpapers.org/paper-summary/letter-to-presidential-candidates-4-november-1843-draft/1.

———. "Letter to Thomas Ford, 22 June 1844–B." The Joseph Smith Papers. https://www.josephsmithpapers.org/paper-summary/letter-to-thomas-ford-22-june-1844-b/1.

———. Letter, Liberty, MO, to Presendia Huntington Buell. Clay Co., MO, 15 March 1839. In Joseph Smith, History, 1838–1856, vol. C-1, 897–98. CHL.

Smoot, Abraham Owen. "A. O. Smoot's Day Book or Journal From the City of Nauvoo, Beginning Tuesday, the 7th of May, AD, 1844, Through the State of Tennessee." Journal, May 1844–April 1845. Abraham O. Smoot Diaries, 1837–1845. CHL.

———. "Early Experience of A. O. Smoot." In *Early Scenes in Church History: Eighth Book of the Faith-Promoting Series*. Salt Lake City: Juvenile Instructor Office, 1882. 21–24.

Snow, Erastus. Erastus Snow Autobiography, 1875. CHL.

———. Erastus Snow Journals, 1835–1851; 1856–1857. CHL.

Snow, James Chauncey. James C. Snow Reminiscences, circa 1836. CHL.

Snow, Lorenzo. Journal, 1836–1845. Lorenzo Snow Journals, 1836–1845; 1872. CHL.

Snow, Warren Stone. Warren S. Snow Reminiscences and Notebook, circa 1874. CHL.

Snow, William. William Snow Autobiography (ca. 1850). Vault Manuscript Collection. BYUSC.

Spaulding, Ira N. Autobiography. Seventies Record, 2nd Quorum (1846). Seventies' Autobiographies Compiled by Nauvoo Restoration, 167. CHL.

Spencer, Thomas Daniel. Biography of Daniel Spencer, 1953. CHL.

Stout, Hosea. Letter, San Francisco, to Brigham Young, 27 August 1853. Deseret News Editor's Files, 1850–1854. CHL.

Stowell, William R. R. Manuscript. BYUSC.

Stratton, Joseph Albert. Joseph A. Stratton Diary, May 1844–October 1846. CHL.

Strong, Ezra, Jr. Ezra Strong Notebook, circa 1882–1884. CHL.

Taylor, John. Revelations Dated June 25–26, 1882. BYUSC.

———. Revelation Dated June 27, 1882. BYUSC.

Terry, Jacob E. Jacob E. Terry Journal, May–July 1844. CHL.

Tracy, Moses. Moses Tracy Papers, 1836–1857. CHL.

Tracy, Nancy Naomi Alexander. Nancy A. Tracy Reminiscences and Diary, May 1896–July 1899. CHL.

Tyler, John. "Message of the President of the United States." Appendix to the *Congressional Globe*, 28th Congress, First Session, 1843.

Watkins, Joseph H. "William Lampard Watkins: Continuation of His Life's History after His Arrival in the Salt Lake Valley" (1946). CHL.

Watkins, William Lampard. "A Brief History of the Life of William Lampard Watkins from His Birth until His Arrival in Utah on 12 September 1852." CHL.

Webster, Noah. *An American Dictionary of the English Language.* 1st ed. New York: S. Converse, 1828. Available online at webstersdictionary1828.com.

West, Joseph. Autobiography. Seventies Record, 2nd Quorum (1846). Seventies' Autobiographies Compiled by Nauvoo Restoration, 184. CHL.

Wheelock, Cyrus H. Cyrus H. Wheelock Journal, June–October 1846; March–July 1849. CHL.

Whitney, Alonzo Wells. Autobiography. Whitney Family Genealogies. Manuscript Collection. BYUSC.

Whipple, Edson. Diary, December 1850–September 1851 and November 1871–February 1872. Edson Whipple Record Book and Diary, circa 1849–1873. CHL.

———. Edson Whipple Record Books, circa 1836–1936. CHL.

Wight, Lyman, George Miller, Phineas R. Bird, Pierce Hawley, and John Young. Lyman Wight Letter, Black River Falls, Wisconsin, to JS, 15 February 1844. Joseph Smith Collection (Supplement), 1833–1844. CHL.

Wight, Lyman, and Heber C. Kimball. "Letter from Lyman Wight and Heber C. Kimball, 19–24 June 1844." The Joseph Smith Papers. https://www.joseph

smithpapers.org/paper-summary/letter-from-lyman-wight-and-heber-c-kimball -19-24-june-1844/1.

Wilcox, Edward. "Death of Faithful Veteran: Sketch of the Life of Elder Daniel Allen." 19th Century Western and Mormon Manuscripts. BYUSC.

Wilson, Bushrod W. Bushrod W. Wilson Journal, circa 1856. Daughters of Utah Pioneers Collection, 1828–1963. CHL.

Woodward, William. Reminiscences, undated. William Woodward Collection, 1851–1919. CHL.

Woodruff, Wilford. Letter, Nauvoo, Illinois, to Solomon Copeland, Henry County, Tennessee, 9 March 1844. Joseph Smith's Office Papers, 1835–1844. CHL.

Yearsley, David Dutton. David D. Yearsley Account Book, circa 1843–1845. CHL.

———. Letter to Ziba C. Wolerton, 20 September 1844. General Correspondence, Incoming, 1840–1877. Brigham Young Office Files, 1832–1878. CHL.

Young, Alfonso. Letter to JS, 6 May 1842. Whitney Family Papers. BYUSC.

Young, Alfred Douglas. "Alfred D. Young Vision, circa 1888." CHL.

Young, Brigham. *Manuscript History of Brigham Young, 1801–1844*. Vol. 1. Compiled by Elden Jay Watson. CHL.

———. Journal, 28 September 1844–3 February 1846. Journals, 1832–1877. Brigham Young Office Files, 1832–1878. CHL.

———. Letter, Nauvoo, Illinois, to Lebbeus T. Coons, Camp Creek, Illinois, 16 September 1845. CHL.

———. Letter, St. George, Utah, to Samuel Mulliner, Lehi, Utah, 8 March 1877. CHL.

Young, Brigham, and Willard Richards. Letter to Reuben Hedlock, 3 May 1844. General Correspondence, Outgoing, 1843–1876. Brigham Young Office Files, 1832–1878. CHL.

Young, Joseph. Joseph Young Diaries, 1844–1881. CHL.

———. Joseph Young Hawn's Mill Massacre Account. BYUSC.

———. Letter, Clarksburgh, Ohio, to Jane A. Young, Nauvoo, Illinois, 14 June 1844. CHL.

———. Joseph Young Autobiographical Sketch, circa 1872. CHL.